SOBERING UP

SOBERING UP

From Temperance to Prohibition in Antebellum America, 1800-1860

IAN R. TYRRELL

Contributions in American History, Number 82

GREENWOOD PRESS

WESTPORT, CONNECTICUT • LONDON, ENGLAND

Library of Congress Cataloging in Publication Data

Tyrrell, Ian R.
    Sobering up.
    (Contributions in American history; no. 82 ISSN 0084-9219)
    Bibliography: p.
    Includes index.
    1. Temperance—History. 2. Prohibition—United States—History. 3. Alcoholism—United States—History.
I. Title.
HV5291.T97   322.4'4'0973   78-22132
ISBN 0-313-20822-0

Library of Congress Catalog Card Number: 78-22132
ISBN: 0-313-20822-0
ISSN: 0084-9219

First published in 1979

Greenwood Press, Inc.
51 Riverside Avenue, Westport, Connecticut 06880

Printed in the United States of America

10 9 8 7 6 5 4 3 2 1

To my mother

CONTENTS

Contents

ACKNOWLEDGMENTS

One of the pleasures of completing a manuscript is the opportunity provided the author to thank those individuals and institutions that have given assistance in the course of research and writing. My study of the temperance movement began in a seminar conducted by Sydney Nathans of Duke University, and I have subsequently benefited both from his advice and his close scrutiny of early drafts of this manuscript. Richard Watson, also of Duke University, provided much assistance and advice in the course of my graduate work. Others who read all or part of the manuscript and helped clarify either ideas or style include: Allan Johnston of Melbourne University (who produced a sustained and thoughtful critique); Marion Roydhouse, Stephen Ellis, Norma Landau, Keith Sipe, Peter Fish, and Richard Preston, all at present or formerly of Duke University; and Kathleen Woodroofe, Peter Shergold, and Alan Gilbert of the University of New South Wales. Conversations with a number of friends and colleagues have sharpened my understanding of the temperance movement and of larger issues of social history. I would like especially to thank Max Harcourt and Tony Mitchell among colleagues, and Kenneth Clow (Duke University) and Dennis McNamee (University of Connecticut) among the graduate students who have helped me.

Acknowledgments

This book could not have been written without the courteous and competent assistance of the staffs at a large number of archives and libraries in the United States: Massachusetts Historical Society; Massachusetts State Archives; the Widener and Houghton libraries of Harvard University; Radcliffe Women's Archives; Boston Public Library; Congregational Historical Society, Boston; Essex Institute, Salem, Massachusetts; Worcester Historical Society; Worcester Public Library; American Antiquarian Society, Worcester, Massachusetts; New York Public Library; New-York Historical Society; Syracuse University Library; Historical Society of Pennsylvania; University of Pennsylvania Libraries; Presbyterian Historical Society, Philadelphia; Ryan Memorial Library, St. Charles Seminary, Philadelphia; Maryland Historical Society, Baltimore; Library of Congress; Alderman Library, University of Virginia; Duke University Library; Southern Historical Collection, University of North Carolina, Chapel Hill; North Carolina Department of Archives and History, Raleigh; and Maine Historical Society.

Two institutions aided the completion of the manuscript. The original research was done with the support of grants from the Duke University Graduate School, and a subsequent visit to the United States for further research and completion of the manuscript was made possible by a study leave from the University of New South Wales.

Several friends have provided aid and assistance. In particular I wish to thank Patrick and Margaret Buckridge, Sydney and Elizabeth Nathans, Tony and Gail Mitchell, Gordon and Marie Kidd, and the Colford family, especially Eugenia Colford, for taking an interest in my work and providing a place to work at a crucial juncture. To my mother and family, I owe a large debt of gratitude.

Ian R. Tyrrell

ABBREVIATIONS

ATS   American Temperance Society (American Society for the Promotion of Temperance)
ATU   American Temperance Union
AAS   American Antiquarian Society, Worcester
DU   Duke University
JATU   *Journal of the American Temperance Union*
MHS   Massachusetts Historical Society, Boston
HSP   Historical Society of Pennsylvania, Philadelphia
LC   Library of Congress
MeHS   Maine Historical Society, Portland
MSA   Massachusetts State Archives, Boston
MSSI   Massachusetts Society for the Suppression of Intemperance (also known after 1834 as the Massachusetts Temperance Society)
MTS   Massachusetts Temperance Society
MTU   Massachusetts Temperance Union
NYAICP New-York Association for Improving the Condition of the Poor
NYCTS   New-York City Temperance Society
NYHS   New-York Historical Society
NYPL   New York Public Library

Abbreviations

SU   Syracuse University
UNC   University of North Carolina, Chapel Hill
UV   University of Virginia

SOBERING UP

INTRODUCTION

Temperance and antislavery were the central reform movements of the antebellum decades. But although opposition to slavery has been the subject of an extensive literature, the temperance movement has been neglected.[1] Temperance and prohibition were powerful issues in local and state politics in the 1840s and early 1850s. Free soil ultimately dominated the politics of the 1850s, but politicians in the northern states feared the temperance issue more until 1855. Temperance conventions, claiming the support of millions of voters, scrutinized the attitudes of every candidate for office and organized politically to defeat the opponents of prohibition at the polls.[2] Temperance societies ran their own candidates for state and local office, pushed through prohibition in thirteen states and territories, and came close to victory in five other states. At the grass-roots level, the temperance issue generated massive discontent with established parties and politicians. The defection of temperance men from the major parties undermined the existing party structures and contributed to the ultimate disintegration of the Whig party in the 1850s.[3] Not until the twentieth century would the temperance movement produce a political upheaval which rivaled the antebellum agitation in scope and intensity.

Even more than influencing the political destinies of Americans, the temperance movement helped to shape their cultural and moral standards. Drink had been socially acceptable in colonial America, but in the first half of the nineteenth century, a revolution in social attitudes took place: drinking ceased to be respectable. It was this shift in habits that most impressed the English observer Richard Cobden when he toured America in 1859. "I have been much struck," he wrote John Bright, "with an alteration in the drinking habits of the people." Upper- and middle-class Americans seemed to be drinking less, at least on social occasions, than they had during Cobden's first visit to America in 1835. [4] Figures for the consumption of alcohol, although an uncertain guide, suggest that Americans were becoming more temperate in their drinking habits. The census figures show that per-capita consumption of liquor declined from over five and one-half gallons in 1810 to four gallons by 1850. Consumption of distilled spirits, by far the most alcoholic of intoxicating beverages, declined precipitously from four and one-half to two and a quarter gallons per capita over the same period. Because of inaccuracies in the census returns, the actual decline in drinking was probably more dramatic than the census figures indicate. [5]

How much this shift in consumption reflected the impact of the temperance agitation is impossible to say, but most supporters of the temperance movement claimed success and took sustenance from the growing unpopularity of drinking in antebellum society. It seemed to reformers that drinking was an archaic custom which was bound to disappear from society. Temperance and total abstinence could easily be equated with moral progress in early and mid-nineteenth century America. [6]

Important as temperance was for antebellum social customs, its significance far exceeded the narrow question of the consumption of alcohol. Temperance reformers championed their cause not to eliminate liquor alone but to eradicate the central social problems of Jacksonian society: crime, immorality, poverty, and insanity. To be sure, other solutions to such problems competed for the allegiance of Americans. Most notable were the asylums which served to house, punish, and reform the social deviants troubling Americans in the first half of the nineteenth century. The proliferation of these institutions has led one recent historian to call the Jacksonian era the "age of the asylum." [7] However, the emergence of asylums was only a partial response to social chaos in the Jacksonian era. As prison and asylum reformers themselves perceived, only the elimination of the grogshop would provide a permanent remedy for vice and crime. Case histories of criminals and social misfits which asylum reformers compiled almost invariably noted the crucial role of drink in the making of deviants. As temperance reformers developed more effective and credible tactics to combat the drink problem, temperance attracted to its ranks reformers seeking the most comprehensive solution to social ills. Americans did not cease to support asylums as a means of controlling deviance, but by the 1830s, many came to view asylums as a remedial rather than the root reform of the era.[8]

Why did so many Americans identify drink as the root of all evil and prescribe temperance as the ideal solution? For the temperance reformer, there was a simple answer: the excessive consumption of alcohol demanded the vigorous efforts of all those who cared for the moral welfare of the people of the United States. Temperance reformers emphasized their case by pointing to the growing incidence of social problems which intemperance seemed to promote. Alarmed at the extent of poverty, crime, insanity, and immorality, reformers argued that only temperance could save the nation from widespread social disorder. Yet the connection between intemperance and pressing social problems was never as clear to contemporaries as the rhetoric of reformers might suggest. Temperance was a prosperous social movement, but by no means all Americans practiced abstinence, and prohibition created sharp political divisions in American communities. The reports of temperance reformers themselves claimed that about one in every ten Americans actually abstained in the 1830s.[9] Although the influence of temperance grew stronger in the following two decades, the message of reform remained both controversial and selective in its impact. In geographic spread, too, the success of the movement varied markedly. Temperance found its strongest support in the northeastern states and until after the Civil War lagged badly in the South. The temperance movement's own census, taken in 1831, showed that over one-third of the temperance pledges in the country came from New England, a region with less than one-sixth of the nation's population. In contrast, the southern states, with 44 percent of the population, supplied only 8.5 percent of pledges. Temperance did not flouish uniformly throughout the nation.[10] If the appeal of temperance is to be understood, the specific social groups which promoted the movement must be examined, the rhetoric of reformers must be penetrated, and the social functions of temperance laid bare.

Historians who have probed the social purposes of temperance agitation have typically labeled temperance as a conservative response to social change. In contrast, this study seeks to show that temperance was not a defensive ideology of groups seeking to reassert traditional values in a changing society. Temperance reform was not the provincial, reactionary movement of popular legend and historical interpretation.[11] A backward-looking impulse dominated only the very restricted and abortive campaign of the Massachusetts Society for the Suppression of Intemperance during and just after the War of 1812. The organized temperance movement which emerged in the 1820s, marked by the formation of the American Temperance Society in 1826, had its roots in the process of industrialization and the commercialization of agriculture; more important, the men and women who fashioned the temperance crusade sought to hasten the processes of social and economic change.

In the name of moral reform, temperance reformers embraced technological change, and employed modern organizational techniques to appeal to the people against the liquor interests. The tactics they used to further their cause also displayed a strong anti-traditional bias. Reformers quickly broke with colonial practices and attitudes toward the liquor problem by adopting the radical definition of temperance as total abstinence. In addition, the temperance movement sought to eliminate what they believed were archaic liquor laws sanctioning the liquor interest and promoting the traditional drinking culture. Reformers sought to solve social problems, not by restricting economic and social change, but by eradicating the traditional, irrational practices which they thought were obstructing the progress and the perfection of modern society. In the drinking problem, and in the social, legal, and political sanctions for drink which had persisted since colonial times, reformers believed that they had found the most harmful, irrational practices of them all. By instilling in individuals the ethic of self-improvement and by educating Americans to value sobriety and industry above all else, reformers hoped to create the conditions for permanent moral and material progress in America. But the progress they sought consisted in the removal of obstacles to the development of an acquisitive, industrial-commercial society.

In keeping with its ideology, temperance took its initial leadership and support from groups which promoted the material improvement of early nineteenth-century America. The temperance movement from its inception in the 1820s and 1830s received much of its support from economic entrepreneurs who stood to gain directly from a more disciplined, sober work force. Yet the support of entrepreneurs for temperance was not entirely self-serving. Those who joined the temperance movement attributed their prosperity to personal sobriety and believed that abstinence could promote national as well as individual progress. From their own careers, they acquired an almost obsessive concern with self-discipline, which they translated into a simple formula for the solution of complex social ills.

Allied with these upwardly mobile and acquisitive promoters of economic change were men who had no obvious stake in the material growth of Jacksonian society. Evangelical clergy, in particular, supported temperance as a means of promoting morality and saving souls. These churchmen hoped to build a temperate and Christian nation on the firm basis of the material improvement of society which they witnessed in the Jacksonian era.

Temperance received much of its leadership from urban-based reformers, but the movement also had strong rural support. Indeed the temperance reformers could not have been as successful as they were in the antebellum period without the support of rural groups, because American society was still predominantly rural in the 1830s. But in rural, as in urban, society, temperance reform received its strongest support in the 1820s and 1830s from people who were concerned with improvement, both economic and moral, and who saw temperance as a means of perpetuating social progress. Temperance was neither exclusively a rural nor predominantly an urban movement in this period. Rather it flourished in a society in transition from a rural to an urban-industrial order, and from small-scale farming to entrepreneurial forms of agriculture. Temperance received its strongest support from the very promoters who were working to bring those changes about. The dominance of these upwardly mobile promoters and their evangelical allies lasted until about 1840; this period, from about 1826 to 1840, might be called the first major phase of temperance reform.

What most disturbed these promoters of social change was the role of liquor within lower-class life. Though drinking was almost universal in colonial and early republican America, drunkenness was most conspicuous and most heavily concentrated in the lower classes. Liquor was not restricted to leisure time but was considered an important stimulant to labor. Throughout the early years of temperance agitation, one constant target was intemperance among the laboring classes. The Massachusetts Society for the Suppression of Intemperance had first identified this problem during the War of 1812 and proposed to solve it by enforcing old colonial laws against excessive drinking. After this strategy had failed, the American Temperance Society (ATS) emerged in the late 1820s to campaign for self-reform among moderate drinkers; but though it did not initially seek directly to reform drunkards, one aim was to mobilize the respectable elements in the population first, so that they would encourage temperance in the larger society, especially by denying liquor to laborers in their employ. Case studies of support for the temperance movement confirm that at the local level, popular support was strongest among manufacturers and farmers alarmed at high levels of intemperance among their workers and concerned to create a society of disciplined and predictable individuals appropriate to an industrializing society.

Yet there was much more to antebellum temperance than the agitation of these relatively well-to-do groups and their evangelical allies. In the 1840s, a new phase of temperance reform arose. Temperance societies emerged among artisans of the lower and lower-middle classes to promote self-help among people of humble and modest means.[12] These Washingtonian societies (named for the nation's first president) catered especially to largely working-class drunkards seeking to renounce the bottle. The relationship between the new and the old organizations was a complex combination of cooperation and hostility. At first, the Washingtonians won organizational and financial support from the temperance regulars; but when these older reformers began to denounce Washingtonian tactics and sought to take over control of the Washingtonian movement, the Washingtonian societies themselves fragmented. Though many issues provoked divisions within Washingtonian temperance, the most important was the character of the relationship between the Washingtonians and temperance regulars. Some Washingtonians (those most concerned with their respectability in the eyes of middle-class temperance reformers, those with evangelical connections, and those who were themselves members of the propertied middle class) chose to align with the older organizations and joined the campaign of the mainstream temperance movement for prohibition. Other Washingtonians (mainly wage earners and reformed drunkards) opposed the move toward legal coercion.

By the late 1840s, the temperance crusade had entered its final antebellum phase as evangelicals, entrepreneurs, and their allies among the middle and lower-middle classes tried to impose prohibition on American society. The Maine Law of the 1850s (the drastic form of prohibition so-called because it was adopted in Maine in 1851) had roots in the experience of these temperance reformers during the two previous decades, but its enormous popular appeal was new. Historians have explained this unprecedented if temporary popular appeal of the Maine Law in the early and mid-1850s as a reaction against the drinking of the masses of German and Irish immigrants who entered the United States between 1845 and 1855. Thus temperance in this period has been seen as a symbolic crusade to impose American cultural values on immigrant groups.[13]

While it is true that many of the enemies of the Maine Law in the 1850s were foreigners and that the Maine Law became closely tied up with political nativism, prohibition was never articulated as a purely antiforeign crusade, and the division in American society over the liquor question was never along purely ethnic lines. Had it been so, the Maine Law might have been more successful than it was, for foreigners were distinctly a minority of the American public. Prohibition was more a class than an ethnic phenomenon, for the Maine Law coalition represented an alliance of evangelicals, wealthy entrepreneurs, and respectable middle- and lower-middle-class people against the threat of pauperism and crime. American society underwent a long economic boom in the 1845-1855 period encompassed by the Maine Law agitation. As a consequence unprecedented numbers of transient, unskilled laborers and semiskilled workers and their families entered into small and medium-sized American communities which were undergoing rapid economic development. The attendant problems of crime and poverty could not be handled within the framework of liberal economic institutions; the Maine Law emerged as one means of controlling and reforming the laboring poor. The very forces of economic development which middle-class temperance reformers applauded created the social problems which prohibition claimed to be able to solve. Thus temperance reform in the antebellum period was closely interwoven with economic change; prohibition was not, as Richard Hofstadter argued in *The Age of Reform*, a historical detour from class conflict and the great economic issues of American life but was rather an intrinsic component part of the shaping of the modern American economic system. [14]

Although the main theme here is the social origins of temperance, there is a second and interrelated theme: the process of agitation. Changes in temperance tactics occurred within broad parameters set by social forces, but temperance reform also involved organization and agitation. Given the structure of American political and legal institutions and American conceptions of democratic values, there was a premium placed upon voluntary organizations to effect change. Under such a system, it was possible for articulate and well-organized minorities to achieve much more success and influence than their sheer numbers would indicate. So it was with temperance. In both its moral suasionist and prohibitionist varieties, the organizing and manipulative skills of temperance reformers promoted a substantial though unquantifiable degree of success. We cannot ignore the actual experience of agitation in considering the triumphs (and failures) of antebellum temperance.

Equally important, we cannot ignore the role of the agitational experience in promoting changes in temperance goals and tactics between 1830 and 1850—from temperance to teetotalism, and from moral suasion to prohibition. Temperance reformers devised tactics to solve the social problems which they perceived and then modified their approaches and priorities in response to changing social realities. The shift in temperance goals and tactics was a continuous process, resulting from the cumulative experience of temperance reformers in the battle against the liquor interests. The temperance

Introduction

movement was not a static, unchanging entity but a dynamic social movement which responded to social change and in turn sought to shape the larger society.

Any introduction to the study of nineteenth-century temperance must take note of the achievement of Brian Harrison in *Drink and the Victorians*. So sophisticated and convincing is Harrison's portrayal of mid-Victorian temperance that it is tempting to apply his conclusions to the American case. His interpretation of the strategies adopted by English temperance reformers revolves around his assessment of these reformers as members of an out-group. The mentality and social position of English dissent—its fundamental lack of authority and power in a society still dominated by a landed aristocracy—shaped the approach to reform among the dissenters who led the English temperance movement and made them unable or unwilling to consider moderate measures. Despite Harrison's sophisticated and subtle treatment of English temperance, his interpretation is drawn quite explicitly from Stanley Elkins's view of abolitionism as an anti-institutional impulse of frustrated and powerless intellectuals.[15]

Leaving aside the question of the value of this social theory for explaining the English temperance experience, Elkins's interpretation (and Harrison's reworking of it) runs into difficulties when applied to American temperance. It may be that American temperance reformers did constitute some sort of out-group. (In the 1820s and 1830s when temperance agitation began, the movement was supported by new and socially aggressive groups, which found their social and economic advancement opposed and to some extent blocked by established and powerful elites, though by the 1850s the mainstream temperance reformers had themselves become established and socially dominant.) It was not lack of power, however, that prompted the more extreme measures of prohibition and teetotalism. The evangelical equivalents of English dissent in America had no established church or hereditary aristocracy blocking the path to a dry republic. What is most striking about the mainstream evangelical and wealthy temperance reformers of the antebellum decades is not their rejection of institutional reform but rather the ease, relative to English temperance, with which these reformers were able to chan-

[11]

nel their views into socially dominant positions, and the extent to which institutions—legal and political, and voluntary associations—formed the route by which reformers were able to achieve a degree of social and political power. We must remember that in the antebellum United States prohibition became law in thirteen states and territories, a situation with no parallel in the English reform experience. Yet success—defined not as the eradication of intemperance but a degree of political power—did not encourage moderation; rather it was their success which encouraged temperance reformers to exploit institutional power to the full.

Any analysis of the origins of temperance agitation in America must begin with and concentrate on New England, and to a lesser extent the mid-Atlantic region. The first temperance societies emerged in Massachusetts in 1813, and the first national temperance society, the American Society for the Promotion of Temperance, was founded by New Englanders in Boston in 1826. As late as the mid-1830s, more than three-quarters of the temperance pledges were from the northeastern states. The cities and towns of the Northeast and border states, from Baltimore to Boston, proved most responsive to the Washingtonian revival of reformed alcoholics in the 1840s, and in the 1850s, New England was the center of the prohibitionist agitation of that decade. Prohibitory laws were called Maine Laws because the movement (and the laws) took shape in Maine. Indeed all six New England states passed prohibitory laws, and eight of the thirteen states and territories in the Maine Law column were in the East. If we discount the prohibitory laws passed by the territorial legislatures of Nebraska and Minnesota, only three midwestern states (Indiana, Michigan, and Iowa) passed the Maine Law, though Wisconsin came very close.

Not only was prohibition weaker in the Midwest than in the Northeast, but much of the prohibitory sentiment in Nebraska, Minnesota, Iowa, and (to a lesser extent) Wisconsin cannot be understood simply as an indigenous development of conditions and experiences in these states and territories. Prohibition was in fact imported to these regions by Yankee Protestant emigrants from northern New England, the "burned-over" district of western New York, and the western reserve of Ohio. Prohibition in those midwestern areas was thus derivative of experiences in the eastern states. Explaining this uneven geographic dispersal of the temperance and prohibitionist agitations is not difficult. The Northeast first felt the disruptive changes of industrialization, urbanization, and the increasing commercialization of agriculture, which called forth the organized temperance movement.

This is not to say that the Midwest will be entirely neglected in this study. Where the Midwest figured more prominently in antebellum temperance agitation, as it did during the Maine Law prohibition agitation of the 1850s, midwestern prohibition sentiment will be included. On the other hand, material on the South, where prohibition sentiment remained weak until after the Civil War, will be included only for comparative purposes and where pertinent to the larger analysis of northern temperance activity.

Notes

1. The only existing scholarly study of the antebellum temperance movement, John Allen Krout, *The Origins of Prohibition* (New York: Alfred A. Knopf, 1925), eschewed interpretation. Krout contented himself with describing the evolution of the temperance crusade. See also Joseph Gusfield, *Symbolic Crusade: Status Politics and the American Temperance Movement* (Urbana: University of Illinois Press, 1963), and Norman H. Clark, *Deliver Us from Evil: An Interpretation of American Prohibition* (New York: W. W. Norton, 1976), for brief, speculative essays on the entire course of temperance and prohibition history.

2. See below, chapter 10. There is a brief survey of prohibition politics of the 1850s in D. Leigh Colvin, *Prohibition in the United States: A History of the Prohibition Party and of the Prohibition Movement* (New York: George H. Doran, 1926), esp. pp. 44-47.

3. Cf. Michael Holt, "The Politics of Impatience: The Origins of Know Nothingism," *Journal of American History* 60 (September 1973): 309-31.

4. Elizabeth H. Cawley, ed., *The American Diaries of Richard Cobden* (Princeton, N.J.: Princeton University Press, 1952), p. 70.

5. Calculations in this paragraph have been drawn from Tench Coxe, *A Statement of the Arts and Manufactures of the United States for the Year 1810*, U.S. Census Office, 3d Census (Philadelphia: A. Cornman, 1814); *The Seventh Census: Report of the Superintendant of the Census, for De-*

cember 1, 1852; to *Which Is Appended the Report for December 1, 1851* (Washington, D.C.: Robert Armstrong, 1853); Daniel Dorchester, *The Liquor Problem in All Ages* (New York: Phillips and Hunt, 1884), p. 315. The 1810 census seems to have underestimated production of liquor by a greater margin than did the 1850 census. Carroll D. Wright, *History and Growth of the United States Census* (Washington, D.C.: Government Printing Office, 1900), p. 38, points out the gross inadequacies in the early censuses, especially up to 1850. The figures quoted are for production plus imports minus exports; in the case of distilled spirits, possibly 10 percent of production in 1860 was used for industrial and related purposes. See *The Cyclopedia of Temperance and Prohibition* (New York: Funk and Wagnalls, 1891), p. 130. The amounts used in industry in 1810 are not known, but there is no mention of industrial use in Coxe's *Statement of the Arts and Manufactures of the United States* or in other contemporary reports by temperance reformers.

6. P. T. Winskill, *The Comprehensive History of the Rise and Progress of the Temperance Reformation from the Earliest Period to September, 1881* (Crewe, England: Mackie, Brewtnall & Co., 1881), p. 335; N. Hewitt to editor, 29 December 1829 in *Journal of Humanity*, 13 January 1830; Dorchester, *Liquor Problem in All Ages*, p. 315; Daniel Drake, "Oration on the Causes, Evils, and Preventives of Intemperance" (1831), in Henry D. Shapiro and Zane L. Miller, eds., *Physician to the West: Selected Writings of Daniel Drake on Science and Society* (Lexington: University of Kentucky, 1970), p. 204.

7. David Rothman, *The Discovery of the Asylum: Social Order and Disorder in the New Republic* (Boston: Little, Brown, 1971).

8. Ibid., chap. 3, emphasizes the role of family instability in the case histories Rothman cites, but even this evidence, compiled by asylum reformers themselves, documents in almost every case the role of drink in leading the individual astray. For further evidence that asylum reformers placed temperance at the center of their analysis of social deviancy, see Benjamin J. Klebaner, "Poverty and Its Relief in American Thought, 1815-1861," *Social Service Review* 38 (December 1964): 382-84.

9. "Fifth Annual Report of the American Temperance Society," in *Permanent Temperance Documents of the American Temperance Society* (Boston: Seth Bliss, 1835), p. 161.

10. See Krout, *Origins of Prohibition*, p. 131.

11. The classic statement of this viewpoint is in Richard Hofstadter, *The Age of Reform: From Bryan to F.D.R.* (New York: Random House, 1955), p. 282. For a popular history, which embodies the common stereotypes of temperance and prohibition, see John Kobler, *Ardent Spirits: The Rise and Fall of Prohibition* (London: Michael Joseph, 1973).

12. Recent studies of Philadelphia and of Lynn, Massachusetts, emphasize the importance of artisan support for the temperance movement, a point developed below in chapter 7. See Paul Faler, "Cultural Aspects of the Industrial Revolution: Lynn, Massachusetts, Shoemakers and Industrial Morality, 1826-1860," *Labor History* 15 (Summer 1974): 367-94; Bruce Laurie, "'Nothing on Compulsion': Life Styles of Philadelphia Artisans, 1820-1850," *Labor History* 15 (Summer 1974): 337-66; Alan Dawley and Paul Faler, "Working-class Culture and Politics in the Industrial Revolution: Sources of Loyalism and Rebellion," *Journal of Social History* 9 (Summer 1976): 466-80; and David Montgomery, "The Shuttle and the Cross: Weavers and Artisans in the Kensington Riots of 1844," *Journal of Social History* 5 (Summer 1972): 416-46.

13. See Gusfield, *Symbolic Crusade*, p. 55, for example.

14. Hofstadter, *Age of Reform*, p. 289.

15. Brian Harrison, *Drink and the Victorians: The Temperance Question in England, 1815-1872* (London: Faber and Faber, 1971), pp. 380, 462-63; Stanley Elkins, *Slavery: A Problem in American Institutional and Intellectual Life*, 2d ed. (Chicago: University of Chicago Press, 1968), chap. 4.

1

LIQUOR IN COLONIAL AND
EARLY REPUBLICAN AMERICA

Until the nineteenth century, few Americans dreamed of excoriating liquor, which was widely accepted and deeply engrained in their social habits. Established elites employed drink, particularly through the use of liquor in elections, as a fundamental element in the system of social control—a means of preserving the existing social order. Thus an attack on liquor was an assault on some of the basic structures and values of colonial and early republican society.

The popular belief that Puritan America condemned the consumption of alcohol has no foundation in fact. New England did have a tradition of Puritan attacks on intemperance, and it was from this tradition that temperance reformers drew when they began their own temperance crusade, though nineteenth-century reformers changed a traditional ideal—temperance—into a new one: abstinence. The Puritans have been popularly stereotyped as fun-killers, but in drinking their ideal was moderation, not abstinence. Puritan divines warned against intemperance, as Increase Mather did in 1673, when he denounced the "sin of drunkenness" among his fellow Bostonians. Yet even Mather did not denounce drink itself; in fact, he conceded that "drink was in itself a good creature of God, and to be received with thankfulness." It was "the abuse of drink" which came "from Satan."[1]

By the middle of the eighteenth century, the Puritan ideal of moderation was very liberally interpreted in colonial America. Americans considered hard liquor a salubrious and innocent beverage. Its wide use in medicine—"to be Cordials to us under the Indispositions of our frail Bodies"—is well known. Doctors prescribed medicine not only for the relief of pain and as an anaesthetic, but also for the breaking of fevers, in the treatment of dyspepsia, and in various external applications for the treatment of inflammations.[2] Until Benjamin Rush produced his *Inquiry into the Effects of Ardent Spirits* in 1784, there was scarcely a ripple of medical dissent from the use and prescription of alcohol, and not until a broader community opposition to liquor emerged in the early nineteenth century did medical practice begin to undergo significant change.[3]

The social use of alcohol was equally pervasive. No bride could be given away without liquor to celebrate, nor was any funeral service complete without a liberal supply of alcohol to comfort the bereaved.[4] When one David Porter drowned in Hartford, Connecticut, in 1678, the winding sheet and coffin used at his funeral cost thirty shillings, but the liquor consumed exceeded twice that amount.[5] Ordination bills for the clergy were similarly replete with references to the cost of liquor; at an ordination which Lyman Beecher attended in Plymouth, Connecticut, in 1810, he found that "drinking was apparently universal" among the clergy. While none of the ministers attending was drunk, Beecher believed that "a considerable amount of exhilaration" was demonstrated.[6] The reminiscences of American clergymen of the period made clear that drinking was an occupational hazard, so much so that the General Assembly of Virginia in 1676 imposed a fine of "one half of one year's salary" for "such ministers as shall become notoriously scandalous by drunkenness."[7]

The dimensions of religious indifference to the alcohol problem can best be understood by examining the practice of groups which later led the temperance crusade. The Methodists in America inherited a distaste for intemperance from John Wesley, but in 1790 the Methodist church actually rescinded the Wesleyan rule forbidding the distilling or sale of liquor by church members. In addition, such Methodist circuit riders as James B. Finley and Peter Cartwright spent a good deal of their time reporting the high incidence of intemperance among Methodists.[8] Of the religious groups which later supported temperance, only the Quakers made any concerted effort to eradicate intemperance in the colonial and early republican eras, and Quaker concern was limited at first to the use of distilled spirits. Moreover the Friends did not begin to make the use or sale of spirits an offense subject to the discipline of their yearly meetings until the 1780s.[9]

Drinking also had an important place in politics. Elections were frequently won or lost with the free distribution of alcohol as voters went to the polls. In Frederick County, Virginia, Colonel George Washington stood for election to the House of Burgesses in 1758. The expense account for the election totaled thirty-seven pounds seven shillings, "of which over thirty-four pounds was for brandy, rum, cyder, strong beer, and wine."[10] The example of George Washington was by no means exceptional; Chilton Williamson's survey of voting practices mentions election treating in Connecticut, Maryland, New York, and Virginia, though the practice was probably more common in southern colonies than in the North. Nor should it be thought that the electoral use of liquor died out after the elitist and deferential politics of the colonial period gave way to mass political participation. As the Whigs' hard cider campaign of 1840 suggests, the use of liquor at the polls persisted well into the Jacksonian era and won the opprobrium of the organized temperance societies, which denounced it as "that most detestable species of bribery." The common practice in antebellum America of using taverns as polling places—as in Philadelphia in 1854—did not help stem the flow of liquor, and the result was not just to heighten electoral bribery but to stimulate electoral violence as well.[11]

Since each of these examples—politics, religion, medicine, social intercourse—suggests that liquor was an integral part of the colonial social fabric, it is hardly surprising to find that the use of liquor was intimately bound up with traditional concepts of work. The clear distinction between work and leisure in twentieth-century America did not apply in colonial times when Americans commonly incorporated aspects of recreation into their work routines, as farmers and farm laborers did with their cornhuskings. Like their European counterparts, colonials were able to mix work and play because the nature of work in a preindustrial society is spasmodic.[12] Great intensity of effort is required at certain times (for example, harvest-time), while at others regular labor or close attention to the job is not required. Because work in colonial America tended to be task rather than time oriented, the clock did not dominate the lives of preindustrial artisans or rural laborers. All these conditions meant that taking time off work to drink was not anathema to colonials. The workers at Hopewell furnace in late eighteenth-century Pennsylvania often took days off to go hunting or fishing, and account books showed that workers just as frequently lost their pay because they did not turn up for work but went instead to the local taverns. The Hopewell furnaces were situated in agrarian Pennsylvania, and rural attitudes to the use of time persisted among the artisans there. [13] Irregular work, the absence of intense pressures to produce, and the control of the conditions of the job by artisans themselves encouraged not only high degrees of absenteeism connected to the use of alcohol but also much drinking on the job.

In addition, there were positive incentives for eighteenth-century artisans to drink on the job. Americans believed that drink was a stimulus to labor and a means of reviving strength after heavy work. "Laboring men," wrote one observer of New England lumbermen, "thought rum absolutely necessary to do their work and preserve their health." [14] According to the conventional wisdom of the time, liquor was especially useful in jobs which involved exposure to the elements. Such jobs were legion in a largely rural society. As Cotton Mather conceded in his *Sober Considerations on a Growing Flood of Iniquity,* liquor "may not be amiss for many labouring men, especially when extreme *heat,* or extreme *cold,* endangers them in their labours." [15] This was not simply a sentiment of the writing classes, for laborers in early nineteenth-century New England sometimes demonstrated their own support for the rum ration by refusing to work without it. This attitude persisted throughout the antebellum period; farm laborers were still striking for their liquor issue in midwestern states in the 1850s. [16]

If one factor stimulating the widespread use of alcohol was the belief that liquor was an invigorating and healthful beverage, another was its cost. Distilled spirits were in abundant and cheap supply in this largely rural society. The vagaries of early transportation meant that grain could not always be taken to market. If not distilled, it would often rot in the fields. As late as 1818, the cost of wagoning corn 135 miles in Pennsylvania equaled its total market value in Philadelphia. [17] Thus farmers often distilled grain, especially corn and rye, on their farms or nearby. In addition to being more easily preserved than grain, whiskey was less bulky and thus more suitable for transportation in the isolated regions of western Pennsylvania, Tennessee, and Kentucky. [18] The liquor thus produced did not all reach distant markets, for whiskey was often used instead of money in frontier settlements where currency was scarce. For all these reasons, liquor was ubiquituous in colonial and early republican America, and because it was so readily available, whiskey tended to be very cheap—from twenty-five to fifty cents a gallon—and readily accessible even to common laborers. [19] Nor was whiskey the only cheap and readily available alcoholic beverage. Colonial New England's rum production is well known, but much more obscure yet important in rural areas was hard cider. An abundant supply of apples encouraged the production of cider, which became the most widely used beverage in rural New England. [20]

The cheap price and wide availability encouraged the excessive use of liquor, especially in frontier areas where these conditions were most pronounced; yet the factors shaping frontier drinking were social and cultural as well as economic. Recalling his life as a Methodist clergyman on the Kentucky frontier the Reverend Peter Cartwright emphasized that "if a man would not have [whiskey] in his family, his harvest, house-raising, log-rollings, weddings, and so on, he was considered parsimonious and unsociable." [21] The explanation clearly lay in the limited recreational opportunities of frontier people, who had to make their own entertainments; in consequence, they emphasized hospitality and simple celebrations, such as cornhuskings, which were frequently enlivened by a free supply of country liquor.

What was true of the frontier farmer held with still greater force for itinerants, miners, backwoodsmen and the like. Long periods of loneliness broken only by spasmodic social contact did not encourage moderation among these groups. Nor did the intermittent payment of wages, which encouraged rural and itinerant workers to splurge when they received their pay. An observer of frontiersmen in western North Carolina in the mid-eighteenth century wrote: "I have frequently seen them come to the Towns, and there remain drinking Rum, Punch, and other Liquors for Eight or Ten Days successively, and after they have committed this Excess, will not drink any Spirituous Liquors, 'till such time as they take *the next* Frolick as they call it." [22] These conditions would persist in the nineteenth century as the frontier moved west; as Allan Winkler points out, the temperance movement's center of strength was never the frontier but "established areas dominated by urban centers. Not until a territory was fairly well populated and stable communities had begun to develop could the reformers hope to make much progress." [23]

Where frontier drinking was spasmodic and disorganized, the drinking in settled communities was much more regular and, more to the point, had acquired legality and prominence in the social order. It is the place of alcohol in settled communities which must concern any student of the temperance movement, for it is this type of drinking which underwent drastic changes in the nineteenth century and which, clothed in all its legitimacy, temperance reformers were compelled to attack. The well-integrated place of drink in this social order is readily apparent in the role and functions of the tavern in colonial and early republican America.

The essence of the tavern's importance lay in its service as a utility institution in a society lacking a complex structure of more specialized institutions. Along with the church, the tavern was a central focus of community life. Its most obvious and central purpose was to house travelers; except in some of the larger cities, taverns were required by law to provide adequate sleeping accommodation for guests and stables and hay for horses. Yet the tavern also had important functions for local residents. Business was frequently transacted there over lunch, while the taverns of New England were also required to provide entertainment and refreshments on such public occasions as election days, town meetings, and militia musters. Here the purpose of legislators was as much to control as to dispense liquor, for colonial laws also forbad unlicensed sellers; Massachusetts law specifically forbad peddlers from selling liquor to the public on these occasions. [24] In addition, the tavern was a focus for the informal entertainments which enlivened community life. Such blood sports as boxing, bearbaiting, and cockfighting tended to occur in or around taverns where crowds gambled under the influence of intoxicating liquors. Though these sports were more widely practiced in the South, they were also part of the recreational traditions and the tavern culture of the northern colonies in the eighteenth century.[25] Taverns served, too, as centers of information in smaller communities, for their rooms would carry newspapers brought by the coaches from distant places and, on a more official level, town authorities in New England used taverns to post notices of town meetings, new laws, and other official communications.[26]

Because the taverns occupied so important a place in colonial life, legislators sought to put strict conditions on their operation. (The regulation of drinking contained in these provisions was not limited to New England, since similar restrictions applied in the southern colonies.)[27] Common prohibitions included gambling in taverns, drunken and rowdy behavior in the vicinity of taverns, drinking on the Sabbath, and the sale of liquor to slaves or Indians, or to servants or minors without "special permission of their respective parents, guardians or masters."[28]

A clear distinction was drawn in the colonial laws of eighteenth-century New England (and Virginia) between taverns and other retail outlets which did not provide accommodation for travelers. In theory, the latter were supposed to sell only by the jug or bottle for consumption off the premises. The assumption behind these restrictions was that a man was less likely to drink to excess or waste his time and money if he consumed his liquor within the confines of his family. In contrast, the liquor shop offered a stimulus to drink through the influence of drinking companions. Retail shops which violated the law and sold for consumption on the premises were known as dramshops. These provisions of the law against the sale of liquor in small quantities in retail shops did not apply, however, in the largest centers of population, such as Philadelphia and New York, where a complex array of coffee shops, restaurants, oyster houses, and the like met the demands of townspeople for liquor by the drink. After 1816 Boston entered this company with its victualing shops, which were specifically exempted from the requirement that there be lodgings for travelers.[29]

Most important among these restrictions enshrined in colonial law was the prohibition on the "idle tippling" of townspeople in taverns, for taverns were designed primarily to shelter and refresh travelers. This purpose did not preclude local townspeople from drinking in taverns, but it did entail restrictions on that drinking. Connecticut, for example, forbad residents of a town "to sit drinking or tippling" in a tavern "above the space of one hour." Under Massachusetts law, drunkards were to be named by town selectmen, and tavern keepers were forbidden to sell liquor to them. 30 In some of the colonies, as in New York and, after the Revolution, in the new state of Kentucky, the restrictions were much vaguer, yet still the law recognized the role of the tavern keeper himself as an agent in controlling unreasonable or excessive drinking among townspeople.

Until a great deal of statistical and legal research has been done on these colonial laws and their enforcement, it will be impossible to tell how effective they were. Douglas Greenberg, in his study of law enforcement in colonial New York, could find few cases of prosecution for drunkenness in over five thousand criminal court cases he studied, though whether the absence of records means an absence of enforcement, or merely the absence of records is, in Greenberg's opinion, uncertain. William Nelson suggests, on the basis of an examination of court records in colonial Massachusetts, that the restrictions on heavy drinking were taken seriously there; yet it remains true that tavern keepers, town officials, and ultimately court officials were left to interpret what constituted moderate drinking. The cultural evidence suggests that colonials were inclined to liberality in their interpretations of moderation. 31

The informal character of these restraints is their most impressive characteristic. All of the restrictive laws assumed cohesive and stable communities with few transients; they took for granted, too, a community of interest between liquor sellers and the magistracy. Tavern keepers would not only act as agents of social control for the town authorities but would be largely drawn from these local elites. The position of tavern keeper was, indeed, a highly respectable one in mid-eighteenth-century America. The office was frequently held by men who were also town selectmen, justices of the peace, representatives in the colonial legislatures, and even judges, all men of property and respectability. 32

If persons of status and influence were more likely to gain tavern keepers' licenses, it was also true that tavern keepers were likely to become men of standing and influence in their communities. As dispensers of liquor, they had a special advantage in election contests, provided they did not dispense the electoral cheer too indiscreetly. Moreover since they performed a number of important public functions, it is not surprising that such men should be considered worthy representatives in colonial legislatures and that their roles as tavern keepers should reinforce rather than undermine their status as community leaders.

John Krout suggested in his survey of colonial drinking practices that the standing of colonial tavern keepers declined during the eighteenth century as the number of licensees expanded.[33] Since Krout bases his conclusion solely on the social standing of the graduates of Harvard College and the occupations that their fathers held, his conclusions need to be qualified. The tavern keeper remained an important person, particularly in smaller communities. John Adams still found the social credentials and political influence of tavern keepers worthy of notice in 1771, and in the 1780s, a man like Ebenezer Webster, father of Daniel Webster, could attain enough social status as a tavern keeper to represent his town of Salisbury in the New Hampshire General Assembly and attend the ratification convention for for the state's constitution. It is likely that the decline in the social standing of the job occurred most noticeably in the larger seaport cities where the populations were more socially diverse than in the country and where the development of commerce encouraged the proliferation of taverns and a consequent decline in the standing and status of tavern keepers.[34]

In summary, the colonial regulatory system was designed to control what Americans believed to be a legitimate and useful trade that furthered their welfare and happiness. Only excess or abuse could pervert this legitimate purpose, and in this respect the rationale of eighteenth-century law and practice was the same as that offered in the late seventeenth century by Increase Mather. Yet though legislators framed these laws for the public good and the promotion of social order, the regulatory process at the same time restrained and legitimated the liquor industry. Eighteenth-century Americans would find nothing remarkable in this, but later generations of reformers would curse the sanction of law that colonial legislators had

cast over what nineteenth-century reformers thought was a despi-
cable and dangerous traffic.

This survey of eighteenth-century drinking culture demonstrates
that alcohol functioned as an integral part of that social order, that
drink served in fact to maintain and promote social cohesion. Drink
was a deeply entrenched economic and social interest, which had the
support and sanction of colonial and early republican laws. It would
have been unthinkable to suggest in the middle decades of the eighteenth century that drink was the primary source of evil, the root
cause of almost all conceivable social ills. Yet this was what many
Americans would come to believe by 1850. Clearly a great transformation in social attitudes had taken place by the mid-nineteenth century.

The most obvious explanation for this change suggests an increase
in drinking and drunkenness. Certainly the first generation of temperance reformers thought that such an increase had occurred. They
explained the change as a product of the Revolution. Soldiers had
been given rum rations during the war, and, without the sanction of
community restraints, consumption of liquor had become excessive.
Since the 1780s, the gradual erosion of established authority by
social and political changes set in motion by the Revolution had furthered the trend to increasing consumption of liquor.[35] Unfortunately reliable statistics on which to base such conclusions do not
exist. Since the first substantial body of statistical evidence on the
dimensions of the liquor industry is not available until 1810, it is not
possible even to measure the size of the problem, let alone its trend in
the decades between the Revolution and the War of 1812.

The best evidence for an increase in drinking is not statistical but a
logical inference from the economics of agriculture and distilling in
colonial and early republican times. The late eighteenth century saw
the opening up of new western lands in Pennsylvania, Tennessee,
and Kentucky. Transportation facilities were quickly outstripped by
the pattern and pace of westward movement; farmers could not get
their grain to market in its original form, and the most common solutions were to feed it to pigs or convert it to whiskey. From such conditions arose the profitable bourbon industry of Kentucky. Whiskey
shipments down the Mississippi increased markedly between the

1790s and the late 1820s and prompted one observer, Harrison Hall, to write in 1813 that "the vast quantities of grain which are produced by their fertile lands, beyond the necessary consumption, cannot be so well disposed of in any way as in pork and whiskey. Hence we already find Tennessee and Kentucky whiskey in our [eastern] sea ports, and it is generally preferred to that made nearer home."[36]

The chief reason whiskey was preferred was its much lower price compared to that of its chief competitor, rum. Rum had to be distilled from relatively expensive and scarce imported molasses, while whiskey was made from the abundant supplies of corn. In consequence, imported rum sold for more than twice the price of whiskey, and even locally produced rum was about 36 percent more expensive. This price differential increased during the first half of the nineteenth century; in 1844 New England rum was 50 percent more expensive than American whiskey. Rum was gradually being priced out of the market as a poor man's drink in favor of cheap and abundant supplies of American whiskey.[37]

The increased production of liquor resulted in increased consumption, since industrial uses for alcohol were few in the early nineteenth century and since the United States exported less than 2 percent of its total production of spirits. In fact, the United States imported ten times more spirits than it exported in the first decade of the nineteenth century.[38] All the evidence points to the conclusion that a new and cheap form of spirits had appeared in the Northeast in larger and larger quantities, and this beverage was most freely available because of its price to the lower classes, who were to become one of the chief objects of temperance reform.

The case for a new and dangerous threat from drink is still stronger considering the changing economics of the tavern industry. The development of the staging business in the 1780s and 1790s and the building of more and better turnpikes during the early national period made the years from about 1780 to 1830 a boom period for the tavern business. The expansion of travel necessitated more taverns and thus more licensees. In turn, these economic changes made the enforcement of restrictions on the sale of liquor more difficult and precipitated a gradual decline in the general standard of respectability of the tavern-keeping business.[39] An excellent example of this social process is provided by the town of Blandford in Hampshire County in Massachusetts. The development of staging in the 1780s and 1790s shifted the locus of economic activity away from the center of the old town toward the Albany Road; here speculators bought up property and opened taverns to cater to the growing through traffic. Sometimes these tavern keepers were older merchants relocating from the center of the town; sometimes they were new men like Timothy Hatch, who came to the town in 1781, saw the possibilities for trade on the Albany road, and quickly built a profitable business. Hatch found himself repeatedly in conflict with the local Congregational meetinghouse for his own drunken behavior and for having dispensed liquor too freely to others. The Hatch tavern was one of a number on the Albany Road which catered to the expanding through traffic as well as to local townspeople, and whose keepers dispensed liquor more freely than earlier licensees had done. [40]

Evidence from Worcester, Massachusetts, and Hartford, Connecticut, reinforces this picture of the changing social status of tavern keepers. None of the seventeen tavern keepers in Worcester in 1828 held an important representative or appointative office in the town. In fact, only two held any official position at all. In contrast, the Worcester of the 1730s had five taverns, and four of their keepers were selectmen or other town officials. As late as the Revolutionary period, the standard of tavern keeping in Worcester had reputedly been high, and the court of general sessions met in one of the town's inns. In Hartford, Connecticut, the situation by the 1820s was similar to that in Worcester, for none of the eight tavern keepers was a representative, justice of the peace, or city officer. Only one held a minor city post. [41]

If the evidence from Worcester, Hartford, and Blandford, together with the impressionistic comments of early temperance reformers, gives any indication, New England faced more than an increase in the supply of spirits in the 1780-1830 period; the character of the trade was undergoing rapid change, and the self-regulation process which colonial law assumed no longer functioned effectively. If temperance reformers were correct in believing that there was more public drunkenness in the 1810s than thirty years before, this decay in "publick morality" may have reflected not only the increased supply of cheap whiskey but also the freer dispensation of it by lower-status tavern keepers not bound by the restraints of colonial law.

The rise of the temperance movement cannot be correlated neatly with an increasing threat from drink, however. First, drinking seems to have been at what temperance reformers regarded as excessively high levels for several decades—at least since the 1780s. Yet no temperance movement had emerged, and few individuals had begun to denounce the heavy use of alcohol that they described in their accounts of colonial and early republican manners and customs. This fact suggests that we must look beyond the mere quantity of liquor consumed. More important for the argument to follow, the timing and strength of temperance agitation between the 1810s and the 1850s does not correlate with any clear pattern of rising consumption. The temperance movement grew stronger in the decades up to 1850, yet liquor consumption in that period seems to have fallen considerably. Despite the inaccuracies of the censuses, the trend was toward a more moderate use of liquor at precisely the time that the temperance movement waxed strongest. The temperance movement, through its earnest agitation, was able to help shape social attitudes in the direction of both moderation and abstinence; yet the rise and strength of the temperance movement itself seems to have reflected the changing social attitudes toward the use of liquor, which went much deeper and reflected profound changes in social relations, and in attitudes toward work and leisure.

We must give attention, therefore, not only to the reality of the drink problem but also to changing perceptions of that problem. It seems clear that the use of liquor—already heavy and widespread in the colonial era—was on the increase in the period between 1780 and 1810. Though there was ample justification for the emergence of a temperance movement during the Revolutionary and early republican periods, for the specific timing and the composition of that movement, we must look to other factors. The consumption of liquor did not seem a problem to everybody; in fact, the first temperance reformers came from a very select group in society. Something more than the existence of a problem must explain the emergence and, equally important, the content (ideas, organization, tactics, and strategies) of that reform agitation. We must inquire who was drinking and who was abstaining.

Notes

1. Increase Mather, *Wo to Drunkards: Two Sermons Testifying against the Sin of Drunkenness* (Cambridge: Marmaduke Johnson, 1673), p. 4.

2. Josiah Woodward, *A Dissuasive from the Sins of Drunkenness* (Lancaster, Pa.: W. Dunlap, 1755), p. 7; appendix to the Eighth Annual Report of the American Temperance Society, in *Permanent Temperance Documents of the American Temperance Society* (Boston: Seth Bliss, 1835), pp. 507-13. *The Permanent Temperance Documents*, vol. 1, comprise the fourth to ninth annual reports of the American Temperance Society and were written by Justin Edwards, the corresponding secretary of the society.

3. I have used a later edition of this pamphlet, *An Inquiry into the Effects of Ardent Spirits upon the Human Body and Mind, with an Account of the Means of Preventing, and of the Remedies for Curing Them*, 7th ed. (Boston: Manning and Loring, 1812).

4. Alice M. Earle, *Customs and Fashions in Old New England* (New York: Charles Scribner's Sons, 1898), pp. 164, 166, 172-74, 177.

5. Mary C. Crawford, *Social Life in Old New England* (Detroit: Tower Books, 1971), p. 454.

6. Barbara Cross, ed., *The Autobiography of Lyman Beecher* (Cambridge: Harvard University Press, 1961), 1:179.

7. Henry G. Crowgey, *Kentucky Bourbon: The Early Years of Whiskeymaking* (Lexington: University of Kentucky Press, 1971), p. 20.

8. Robert Emory, *History of the Discipline of the Methodist Episcopal Church* (New York: Carlton and Porter, 1857), p. 197; *Journal of the Rev. Francis Asbury, Bishop of the Methodist Episcopal Church* (New York: Easton and Mains, n.d.), 2:261, 481, 3:391; *Autobiography of Rev. James B. Finley, or Pioneer Life in the West* (Cincinnati: Jennings and Rye, n.d.), pp. 250-51; *Journals of the General Conference of the Methodist Episcopal Church* (New York: Carlton and Phillips, 1855), 1:112.

9. See Sydney V. James, *A People Among Peoples: Quaker Benevolence in Eighteenth Century America* (Cambridge: Harvard University Press, 1963), p. 271.

10. Crowgey, *Kentucky Bourbon*, pp. 16-17.

11. Chilton Williamson, *American Suffrage from Property to Democ-*

racy (Princeton, N.J.: Princeton University Press, 1960), pp. 40-61; *Permanent Temperance Documents*, p. 348; *Philadelphia Public Ledger*, 6 October 1854.

12. Herbert G. Gutman, "Work, Culture, and Society in Industrializing America, 1815-1919," *American Historical Review* 78 (June 1973): 531-88; E. P. Thompson, "Time, Work-Discipline, and Industrial Capitalism," *Past and Present*, no. 38 (1967): 56-97.

13. Joseph E. Walker, *Hopewell Village: A Social and Economic History of an Iron-making Community* (Philadelphia: University of Pennsylvania Press, 1966), pp. 94, 266, 381.

14. *Journal of Humanity*, 17 January 1831.

15. Cotton Mather, *Sober Considerations on a Growing Flood of Iniquity . . .* (Boston: John Allen, 1708), p. 5.

16. John Koren, *Economic Aspects of the Liquor Problem* (Boston: Houghton Mifflin, 1899), p. 35; "Original Communication," *New England Farmer*, 30 April 1830; David E. Schob, *Hired Hands and Plowboys: Farm Labor in the Midwest, 1815-60* (Urbana: University of Illinois Press, 1975), p. 100.

17. George R. Taylor, *The Transportation Revolution, 1815-1860* (New York: Holt, Rinehart and Winston, 1951), p. 133.

18. John H. Cocke to E. C. Delavan, July 1834, John Hartwell Cocke Papers, UV.

19. The most comprehensive price information is available in Arthur H. Cole, *Wholesale Commodity Prices in the United States, 1700-1861: Statistical Supplement. Actual Wholesale Prices of Various Commodities* (Cambridge: Harvard University Press, 1938).

20. Percy Bidwell, "Rural Economy in New England at the Beginning of the Nineteenth Century," *Transactions of the Connecticut Academy of Arts and Sciences* 20 (April 1916): 334.

21. Peter Cartwright, *The Backwoods Preacher: An Autobiography*, ed. W. P. Strickland (London: A. Heylin, 1858), p. 119.

22. Quoted Guion G. Johnson, *Ante-bellum North Carolina: A Social History* (Chapel Hill: University of North Carolina Press, 1937), p. 97.

23. Allan M. Winkler, "Drinking on the American Frontier," *Quarterly Journal of Studies on Alcohol* 29 (June 1968): 414.

24. *The Cyclopedia of Temperance and Prohibition* (New York: Funk and Wagnalls, 1891), p. 311.

25. John A. Krout, *Annals of American Sport* (New Haven: Yale University Press, 1929), p. 23.

26. Earle, *Customs and Fashions*, p. 196.

27. See C. C. Pearson and J. Edwin Hendricks, *Liquor and Anti-Liquor in*

Virginia, 1619-1919 (Durham, N.C.: Duke University Press, 1967), p. 21.

28. See "An Act for the Due Regulation of Licensed Houses," 28 February 1787, in *The Laws of the Commonwealth of Massachusetts, from November 28, 1780 . . . to February 28, 1807* (Boston: J. T. Buckingham, 1807), 1:380.

29. "An Act in Addition to an Act Entitled, 'An Act for the Due Regulation of Licensed Houses,'" *Boston Centinel*, 1 January 1817. On Philadelphia, see Robert E. Graham, "The Taverns of Colonial Philadelphia," *Transactions, American Philosophical Society* 43 (1953): 318-25.

30. *Public Statute Laws of the State of Connecticut* (Hartford, CT.: Hudson and Goodwin, 1808), sec. 7, title CLVIII, p. 644; "An Act for the Due Regulation of Licensed Houses," sec. 17.

31. William E. Nelson, *Americanization of the Common Law: The Impact of Legal Change on Massachusetts Society, 1760-1800* (Cambridge: Harvard University Press, 1975), pp. 50, 52; Douglas Greenberg, *Crime and Law Enforcement in the Colony of New York, 1691-1776* (Ithaca, N.Y.: Cornell University Press, 1976), pp. 38-39.

32. John A. Krout, *The Origins of Prohibition* (New York: Alfred A. Knopf, 1925), pp. 44-45.

33. Ibid.

34. Earle, *Customs and Fashions*, p. 196; Sydney Nathans, *Daniel Webster and Jacksonian Democracy* (Baltimore: Johns Hopkins University Press, 1973), pp. 9-10.

35. See "Fifth Annual Report of the Massachusetts Society for the Suppression of Intemperance," appendix to Samuel Worcester, *The Drunkard a Destroyer: A Discourse, Delivered before the Massachusetts Society for the Suppression of Intemperance, at Their Anniversary Meeting, May 30, 1817* (Boston: J. Eliot, 1817), pp. 21-22; Ebenezer Porter, *The Fatal Effects of Ardent Spirits* (Concord: New Hampshire Tract Society, 1813), p. 21; [Heman Humphrey], "On the Ruinous Effects of Ardent Spirits," pt. 2, *Panoplist*, n.s. 5 (March 1813): 442-44.

36. Harrison Hall, *Hall's Distiller, . . . Adapted to the Use of Farmers as Well as Distillers . . .* (Philadelphia: John Bioren, 1813), p. 12; Crowgey, *Kentucky Bourbon*, pp. 80-82; *Journal of Humanity*, 26 January 1832.

37. Cole, *Wholesale Commodity Prices*, pp. 129-97, 291.

38. Timothy Pitkin, *A Statistical View of the Commerce of the United States of America* (Hartford: Charles Hosmer, 1816), pp. 101-02.

39. Krout, *Origins of Prohibition*, pp. 44-45; Crawford, *Social Life*, pp. 139, 391-93.

40. Sumner G. Wood, *The Taverns and Turnpikes of Blandford, 1733-1833* (The author, 1908), p. 157.

41. *Hartford City Directory for 1828* (Hartford, CT.: Ariel Ensign,

Sobering Up

1828); *Worcester Village Register, April 1828* [Worcester, 1828]; Emma F. Waite, "Old-Time Taverns of Worcester," Worcester Society of Antiquity, *Collections,* 19:70-82.

2

MEN OF MODERATION

It is customary to date the emergence of the antiliquor crusade from the second decade of the nineteenth century when the first societies devoted to the suppression of intemperance arose in the northeastern United States. In New York, Connecticut, Pennsylvania, and indeed in most other northern states, these societies did not limit their activities to the liquor question and were usually termed "societies for the suppression of vice and the promotion of morality."[1] In Massachusetts, however, the first society directed specifically toward the problem of intemperance was formed in 1813. The Massachusetts Society for the Suppression of Intemperance (MSSI) declared that its objective would be "to suppress the too free use of ardent spirits, and its kindred vices, and to encourage and promote temperance and general morality." By 1818, the society had reached its peak strength of more than forty auxiliaries claiming an average of one hundred members each. The parent society had two hundred and six carefully chosen members.[2]

It is equally conventional to explain this novel movement as a product of displaced clergy and Federalist decline.[3] An analysis of the tactics and membership of the MSSI shows that this premier temperance society of the period was indeed dominated in large part by Congregationalist clergy and the eastern Massachusetts Federalist elite; the emergence of temperance agitation did have something to do with the collapse of deference and the decline of political federalism. From these facts the reputation of the early temperance agitation as a surrogate Federalist crusade for social control has been largely based.

Yet the MSSI crusade had an extremely limited character and impact, both geographic and social. The group arose as a makeshift response to temporary circumstances created by the War of 1812. Once those circumstances had changed, its agitation rapidly declined even though the problem of intemperance remained severe. Thus the MSSI was in many ways a failure, a false start to the temperance agitation. The temperance movement succeeded in mobilizing the American population insofar as it quickly shed the domination of the Federalist elite illustrated in the activities of the MSSI. The tactics of the MSSI, so far from pointing to the approaches the temperance movement would utilize during the antebellum period, merely illustrated the collapse of the customary eighteenth-century system of regulating the liquor traffic.

The Erosion of Established Elites

The formation of temperance societies between 1812 and 1818 owed much to the social and economic dislocation caused by President Thomas Jefferson's embargo policy and the War of 1812. The first temperance reformers pointed alarmingly to evidence of economic decay, poverty, and social upheavals, which they frequently attributed to the effects of strong drink. They did not need to exaggerate the economic evidence, even if the connection with intemperance was not always so self-evident. The impact of embargo and war depressed New England's shipping industry, its import trade, the fishing industry, and the lumber industry. Hardest hit were coastal towns like Newburyport, Salem, Marblehead, and Portland. For Newburyport, the War of 1812 delivered an economic blow from which the town did not recover until the 1840s. The value of property fell 50 percent between 1807 and 1817 and declined still further by 1820. The town's population fell from 7,634 in 1810 to 6,852 in 1820. In Portland, prosperity depended on the export trade in fishing and lumber. This was so severely disrupted by the embargo that the Reverend Edward Payson wrote:

A large number of the most wealthy merchants have already failed, and numbers more are daily following, so that we are threatened with universal bankruptcy. Two failures alone have thrown at least three hundred persons, besides sailors, out of employ; . . . The poor house is already full, and hundreds yet [are] to be provided for, who have depended on their own labor for their daily bread. . . .4

The specter of pauperism remained to threaten the sober citizens of Portland, Newburyport, and other seaboard cities long after the initial causes of economic dislocation had disappeared. The reality of the problem is further indicated in the fragmentary but suggestive evidence of rising expenditures on paupers in many coastal towns and cities. The number of poor in Salem's Alms House rose from 547 in 1818, to 668 in 1820, and to 706 in 1821. Town expenditures on paupers were $8,972 in 1810; they rose steadily to a maximum of $15,795 in 1814 out of a total town budget of $23,468. In New York City, the number of paupers and the expenditure on them rose in a similar fashion during and just after the War of 1812.5

At this time, the temperance societies found their strongest support in the eastern seaboard towns hit hardest by the economic crisis. The societies attracted the old, established merchants whose interests in trade, shipping, and finance were damaged by the war.6 These merchants were alarmed by rising tax rates for the support of paupers and by the social problems accompanying unemployment. Merchants knew that the war created the depressed economic conditions in the coastal towns, but they believed intemperance would compound the problem of pauperism. In Portland, the Overseers of the Poor pressed the town selectmen to warn retailers not to sell their liquor "to that class of persons who are reputed *common drunkards*, . . . mispending [sic] their time and estate where spirituous liquors are sold."7

If one aim of temperance reformers was to prevent intemperance from adding to a pool of poverty at a time of general economic distress, another was to prevent men made idle by the economic situation from contracting bad habits in such abodes of idleness as the local taverns. The temperance society of Newburyport, noting that idleness was "an avenue to vice" and industry "a principal assistant and guide to virtue," appointed a committee "to devise means to employ the poor, especially those who are of virtuous character, or who show signs of reformation from vice."[8]

The war's effects were psychological and social as well as economic. In New England, the Congregational clergy had opposed the war from the start, and American military reverses reinforced their belief that the war was immoral and unjust. Were not "the calamities of war" only "the judgments of Heaven" on a wicked people who sustained such a war? This interpretation was wholly intelligible to men nurtured in the tradition of the Puritan jeremiad.[9] Yet while the war provided reason enough to bolster the moral fiber of the nation through temperance reform, the war merely confirmed the clergy's belief that morals had deteriorated; the "growing immorality" of the American people served to explain the clergy's suspicion that the community no longer accepted them as the moral preceptors of society.

The clergy's fears had much deeper roots than the war itself. Even before the turn of the century, the Congregational clergy of New England had felt their influence waning at the expense of the secular politicians who had usurped the position of the clergy as community spokesmen. Jeremy Belknap, himself a convinced temperance reformer, complained against "a monopolizing spirit in some politicians, who would exclude clergymen from all attention to matters of state and government."[10] The feeling of exclusion from secular power grew in the new century as Americans rejected the Federalists as a national political force in favor of the deist Jefferson, and then moved to a dangerous confrontation with Great Britain. At home in New England, even the Federalist politicians, preoccupied with the development of their secular political organizations, seemed to pay less and less attention to the wishes of the clergy.

New England's Congregationalism suffered also from internal bickering. The orthodox and liberals wrangled with each other over doctrine, while the dissenting sects reaped a harvest of converts from those repelled by the doctrinal controversies.[11] The Methodist and Baptist churches expanded rapidly in New England after 1800, and these dissenting groups allied themselves in the political arena with

Jeffersonian Republicanism to secure the virtual disestablishment of Massachusetts Congregationalism in May 1811. Henceforth public taxes could be paid for the support of any religious group. The practice of forcing dissenters to contribute to the coffers of the Congregational church had ended. The creation of the first temperance societies followed very soon upon the act of 1811. While Massachusetts Congregationalists gave no indication that this political reverse directly spurred the clergy toward temperance reform, it seems likely that the erosion of the clergy's privileged position reinforced what the larger religious picture in the state already suggested. Congregationalists would have to support voluntary efforts to stimulate morality and religion among the indifferent or lose more ground to secularism and dissent.[12]

Convinced of growing immorality in society and concerned for the future of their own social influence, the Congregationalists of New England sought a comprehensive solution to their plight in a crusade for sobriety. At its meeting in June 1811, the General Association of Massachusetts Congregational Churches attacked intemperance among professed Christians and urged Congregationalists to take the lead in the battle against "this national sin."[13] The General Association appointed a committee to investigate what Congregationalists could do, and the efforts of this committee led directly to the organization of the Massachusetts Society for the Suppression of Intemperance in 1813. In Connecticut, the Congregationalists followed the lead of Massachusetts and openly expressed the connection between the social concerns of the clergy and the aims of the Connecticut Society for the Promotion of Good Morals. The Connecticut clergy recognized the gravity of the attack "on our religious institutions and civil order" but believed that the challenge could be met by a vigorous assertion of temperance and morality among Christians.[14] In both states, the influence of orthodox Congregationalism was considerable. Even in Massachusetts, where Unitarianism flourished, orthodox clergy supplied one-quarter of the members of the state temperance society—the largest single religious bloc—and the most active workers in the local auxiliaries as well.

Nevertheless the first temperance societies had a broader appeal than to religious orthodoxy. In addition to clergymen, the society also attracted many Federalist politicians and lawyers, doctors, merchants, and country gentlemen whose motivation was social rather than religious. [15] Moreover Unitarians cooperated in the work of the MSSI and submerged their doctrinal differences with the orthodox to do so. Fully 15 percent of the members of the Massachusetts society consisted of Unitarian ministers, and lay Unitarians were equally numerous. In noting this cooperation between liberals and the orthodox, it must be made clear that only the exceptional circumstance presented by the dislocation of the War of 1812 could temporarily override the mutual and growing suspicions between the two branches of Massachusetts Congregationalism. The removal of those temporary circumstances after the war, together with the emergence of the liberal-evangelical split into an irrevocable doctrinal and power struggle after 1815, greatly accelerated the decline of the MSSI. [16]

Yet during the War of 1812, it was still possible to get agreement that intemperance threatened the established social order, and a common commitment to the preservation of that order held the otherwise disparate membership of the Massachusetts society together. The members sensed a loss of social and political power. Their chief complaint was that the "best men," meaning themselves, no longer ruled in state and local politics. [17] They attributed this loss of power to a decline in public morality. In their view, more people desecrated the Sabbath through work or drinking, more people swore within earshot of the respectable, more people became drunk in public places. Although the jeremiads of the reformers may have exaggerated the immorality of the times, a decline in social deference toward the moral standards of the respectable probably did occur, in part simply because cheap liquor was becoming so readily available but possibly also as a social manifestation of the decline in political deference which undoubtedly took place in the first decade of the nineteenth century.

One indication of declining deference was the increased popular participation in politics. While the state's population rose only by one-quarter, voter turnout more than doubled in Massachusetts between 1800 and 1812, and the rise took place without any change in the property qualifications for voting. [18] Partisan competition and a new assertiveness among the common people explain the increased turnout. Massachusetts had been solidly Federalist before 1800, but party competition was intense in the new century. The Republicans had become a powerful force in state politics, as the four gubernatorial contests they won between 1807 and 1812 demonstrated. To enhance their electoral prospects, the Republicans had appealed to assertive yet previously underprivileged social groups. Dissenters, for long the frustrated and dispossessed in Massachusetts society, rallied to the Republican cause to alleviate their religious disabilities and political subordination.[19] No longer was political power confined to local oligarchies, and established patterns of social deference went by the board.

One obscure member of the MSSI best illustrated the drastic consequences which the new assertiveness and partisan competition had for the men who had previously ruled Massachusetts. Bailey Bartlett left no record of his reason for joining the MSSI. Bartlett was not conspicuous as a temperance reformer, and he was not especially prominent in the political affairs of his state, but nothing of any consequence happened in Haverhill, Massachusetts, without his concurrence. Bartlett was not quite the wealthiest man in the town, but he was the most important. Like his father, Bartlett was a prosperous import merchant. He served in the state legislature and for two terms in the United States Congress, yet he derived most of his power and prestige from his appointment as sheriff of Essex County in 1789. Sheriffs occupied an office of primary importance and influence in the counties of Massachusetts; they "granted favors, set bail, packed juries, . . . and appointed 'scores of Deputies, Appraisers, Keepers of Goods, and jailors of citizens.'"[20] Bartlett exercised his power with generosity. He was "firm, fearless, and immovable" when he dealt with serious infractions of the law. At the same time, he was "kind and indulgent almost to a fault" with debtors, and "his purse often paid the exactions of the unfeeling creditor." Bartlett was "decided" in his commitment to the Federalist cause, yet he opposed the spirit of political partisanship and did not "suffer political feeling to enter into his official duties."[21] Although this old-fashioned gentleman dealt generously with friends and political opponents alike, he did so only while his official authority in Essex County remained unchallenged. Bartlett held the office of sheriff until his death in 1830, except for the period from December 6, 1811, to June 20, 1812. The Republican-controlled legislature had given the governor the authority to appoint new sheriffs and county clerks. Bailey Bartlett became one of the victims of Governor Elbridge Gerry's appointments policy.

Although Bartlett left no record of his reasons for joining the MSSI, his removal from office by the Republican administration supplied an ample motive. The incident demonstrated that the Federalists, who had controlled Massachusetts politics, were no longer invulnerable to political attack. Bartlett was one of scores of Federalists who joined the temperance societies. Over half the Boston members of the MSSI were active Federalist political workers, and perhaps nine-tenths favored the Federalists in politics. In marked contrast, no Jeffersonians have been found in the ranks of the societies at all. [22] Magistrates, justices of the peace, local legislators, country doctors and lawyers, retired gentlemen and merchants, all of them Federalists, swelled the ranks of the Massachusetts Society for the Suppression of Intemperance after its founding in 1813.

Like the clergy in the sphere of religion, these Federalists were used to the unchallenged exercise of power. The new assertiveness in politics and the political reverses they suffered seemed to indicate the disintegration of the social and moral order. These Federalists believed that a commonly accepted code of morality underlay the acceptance of their authority by the lower classes in the colonial period. But this public morality had broken down in the years following the American Revolution, and consequently the common people no longer accorded their betters the deference they customarily had received. [23] Many Federalists blamed intemperance, which, "by corrupting the publick morals, relaxes or dissolves the only bond which can retain, in one compact, well-organized mass, the discordant materials of which society is composed." [24] They joined the temperance societies to restore the moral basis of their social and political authority.

Conservative Tactics for Conservative Reformers

The Federalist and elitist character of the first temperance reformers is well known; yet the specific tactics the MSSI used have not received sufficient attention. An examination of the tactics of the MSSI is especially important because it reveals the extremely limited character and impact of temperance reform in Massachusetts in the second decade of the nineteenth century and, moreover, supplies additional evidence that these reformers sought to reassert social control over their own communities. Rather than seek self-reform, MSSI temperance reformers focused on the drinking habits of the mass of common people, whose manners and morals the temperance advocates no longer seemed to control. The sins of intemperance, warned Daniel Clarke Sanders, a Boston Unitarian minister, were especially prevalent among "the lowest classes" of society, who "yield themselves up to the misrule of sordid appetite."[25] While education promoted self-control among the more enlightened and privileged elements of society, the poor lacked such inhibitions and so drank prodigiously. The absence of constraints upon the drinking habits of the poor encouraged not only intemperance itself but also a host of attendant evils: pauperism, Sabbath breaking, profane swearing, and stealing. If these vices were dangerous because of their immediate cost to the community, they were doubly abhorred by temperance reformers as symptoms of that decay in the "publick morals," which must have serious consequences for the entire social and political order. Habits of intemperance threatened, in the view of Henry Warren, a Roxbury lawyer, to unleash terrible passions on society by "nourishing among us that idle and mischievous species of population called in Europe the mob."[26] Although temperance reformers hoped that "the laboring class" would be "the strength of the nation," they believed that its strength was "rapidly . . . becoming weakness" under the baleful influence of intemperance.[27]

One goal of the first temperance reformers was to avert such potential threats to the existing social structure by influencing the common people. For this purpose, the Massachusetts society devoted much of its energy to the prevention of excessive drinking among laborers in both urban and rural areas. Members were alarmed at the common practice of giving laborers a rationing of spirits as part payment for their work. They reasoned that the ration fostered the appetite for strong drink among the laboring poor and contributed to their notorious intemperance. The MSSI therefore set as one of its foremost tactics of reform "a friendly concert of merchants, sea captains, and wharfingers, of respectable farmers, mechanics, and manufacturers; in a word, of all hirers of labour, not to furnish ardent spirit to their labourers."[28]

Temperance societies did not condemn moderate drinking because it was practiced by too many of their supporters. But they did criticize "immoderate drinking" or the "too free use" of spirits among members, in the hope that reform of their own drinking practices might help restore some of the authority and influence they believed they had lost in society. The Massachusetts Society for the Suppression of Intemperance did warn the respectable that "intemperance is most prevalent among the labouring classes," but "it is not confined to them. This ill bred vice finds its way into other company." Many "gentlemen of talents and distinguished respectability in civil life, and in the learned professions, have been ruined by intemperance."[29] Singled out for special condemnation was the custom of equating a gentleman's hospitality with his furnishing spirits for all visitors. Social drinking spread intemperance "in high places" and sapped the wealth and influence of the natural leadership of society.[30]

Although the temperance organizations made specific demands of both higher and lower ranks of society, they did not think that reform could be accomplished through voluntary action alone. The reformers knew that the American states had inherited from the colonial period a long tradition of regulation of the liquor trade. They assumed that the liquor laws had been properly enforced in the years before the Revolution by "our forefathers," those "wise, and moral, and pious, and venerable men, who founded and settled that admirable system of social regulations under which we enjoy all that is left us of order and security in our civil state."[31] Because the first temperance reformers were so close in time and temperament to the men of the eighteenth century, they could not envisage a wholly new solution to the problem of intemperance. They instinctively looked back to the years of social homogeneity when the social elite had controlled the regulatory system. The Reverend Ebenezer Porter, for example, admitted the need for taverns: "In all civilized society, there must be houses of entertainment for strangers, and for the accommodation of men who meet on necessary business." But such establishments must be in the hands of the respectable: "Those who are entrusted with the business of selling spirits in small quantities, are in a sense entrusted with the morals and lives of their fellow men. Their situation is highly responsible. They ought to be men of strict integrity."[32]

The first temperance societies believed that intemperance had become a major social problem because the restrictions on the liquor trade were no longer enforced. Rather than attempt something new, reformers sought merely to restore the old system of legal controls. They did not, like later temperance reformers, try to eliminate the liquor traffic but sought to regulate it in the manner intended by colonial Americans. Through the pressure of temperance societies, the moral part of the community would persuade town selectmen to license only those "men of strict integrity" who would obey the restrictions on the sale of liquor envisaged in the state license laws.[33] At the very least, the temperance societies hoped that violators of the law would be punished and that no one who violated the law would be able to renew his license when the local licensing authorities, the selectmen or the county commissioners, made their annual reviews of licenses.[34]

In Massachusetts, reformers emphasized the enforcement of "the good and wholesome laws of the Commonwealth."[35] Liquor sellers were urged to suspend the sale of liquor to minors and to habitual drunkards. The welfare of these groups was officially protected under the state law of 1787, which specifically forbad such sales.[36] Selling liquor on the Sabbath, gambling in taverns, and rowdy behavior in the vicinity of licensed houses all came under attack. The first temperance reformers especially railed against the sale of liquor by the drink to local townspeople in small retail shops licensed only to sell for consumption off the premises. Such shops the temperance reformers designated dramshops and reserved for them their harshest epithets. Unlike the taverns, no socially useful purpose of providing refreshment for the weary traveler could redeem the dramshop, which in the minds of these first temperance reformers existed only to corrupt the morals of the local townspeople. As a long-term solution temperance organizations urged reduction of the number of shops that could be put to such purposes, but while dramshops flourished, temperance advocates tried to convince the selectmen not to renew the licenses of violators of the law at the time of their annual review.[37]

Such were the tactics of the first temperance societies. Even though their goals were exceedingly modest, the gap between purpose and result was very apparent. The temperance reformers appealed to the public spirit of retailers and tavern keepers, implored selectmen to enforce the laws, and threatened violators with prosecution should they continue to endanger the morality of the community. Yet the exhortations and threats produced few results. Certainly there were local victories, but even these proved ephemeral. By 1820, few of the more than forty auxiliaries of the MSSI functioned, and by 1823, the leaders of the parent society openly admitted failure. [38]

On the surface, public opposition and indifference to the goals of the temperance reformers explain the failure of the Massachusetts society. Opposition and indifference were to be expected, however, because the temperance cause drew its first supporters from a restricted range of society and attracted relatively few of the middle and lower classes. But more important, temperance reform was too easily written off as a Federalist plot. The Reverend William Bentley of Salem probably expressed the sentiments of all Jeffersonians when he condemned "morals societies" as associations "formed under the garb of religion for political purposes." [39] When temperance societies spoke of restoring the "publick morals," Bentley and other Jeffersonians understood them to mean the moral influence of Federalist politicians and the authority of the orthodox Congregational church.

By a too close association with Federalism, temperance reformers ensured the indifference or opposition of many who might otherwise have joined their fight. The evangelical dissenters, especially the Methodists and Baptists, were potential allies of the Congregationalists in any antiliquor campaign. Yet virtually no dissenters were found in the ranks of the first temperance societies, and few Methodists or Baptist preachers raised their voices against the menace of liquor. It is hardly surprising that Methodists and Baptists should show little sympathy for a temperance crusade dominated by Federalists and Congregationalists, the groups that dominated Massachusetts society and opposed the disestablishment of the Congregational church. Baptists and Methodists had little to fear from the loss of social stability that so disturbed Congregationist temperance reformers because dissenters lacked social influence in the first place. It seems that the social position of the dissenters shaped their indifference to the first appeals for temperance. Because dissenting groups remained largely silent on the subject of temperance, we cannot be certain of their motivations, but the cost of their indifference was plain. Any attempt to revitalize public morality could hardly succeed while many moral and religious men held aloof. [40]

In addition to external opposition and indifference, these societies displayed some serious inner failings. Much of their support depended on the peculiar wartime conditions. When peace and political tempers returned to normal, the least dedicated supporters lost interest in the cause. The first temperance societies did not cease to function because of stunning reverses at the hands of drinkers and sellers of liquor. Their activities simply declined after the war as interest tapered off among many members. In the years after the war, the chief complaint of the MSSI was that auxiliaries no longer seemed sufficiently interested to keep up their correspondence with the state society. By 1818, only six of over forty auxiliaries reported activities to the parent society. [41]

The typical temperance advocate in the second decade of the nineteenth century was not deeply committed but a cautious and tentative reformer. While the clergy were the most zealous and often came close to advocacy of total abstinence from spirits, many of the older members did not favor total abstinence but only moderation in the use of spirits. The principle of total abstinence never became a condition of membership or a serious objective for the temperance reformers of the MSSI. The members who favored a cautious approach to reform were men like Nathan Dane, the president of the Massachusetts society and a prominent Federalist politician and lawyer. Dane was "not so sanguine as to believe, that any human means can entirely suppress" the evils of intemperance, although "the wise and virtuous of the state" might by intelligent action "very much restrain or diminish" the evils. [42] While the Nathan Danes of the first temperance societies were genuinely disturbed by the threat of intemperance, they did not have a deep and abiding commitment either to temperance reform or to the organizations they had patronized. To have launched a serious and sustained assault on the liquor problem would have meant attacking entrenched political, legal, economic, and social interests. It would have involved a radical break with established social customs and provoked serious opposition not only from the lower orders but also from within respectable and wealthy society. The first temperance reformers were prepared neither by temperament nor social standing to initiate such an assault. Though they perceived the increasing incidence of intemperance, they shrank back from a wholesale denunciation of the use of liquor, which would have reflected on their own personal conduct and that of other members of the social elite. Once the special factors created by the War of 1812 had receded from their consciousness, most of these members of the MSSI and its auxiliaries ceased to agitate for temperance reform.

A further factor limiting the scope and vigor of this first temperance agitation was a failure to perceive and to exploit the full potential of voluntary organizations for stimulating public opinion. These cautious reformers actually made little use of the societies they created. Instead of developing into a forceful organization, the Massachusetts Society for the Suppression of Intemperance relied on the initiatives of local elites as the chief method of agitation and envisioned only a limited coordinating role for the state society itself. [43] Although the society did print annual reports and addresses to the public, it made no attempt at mass circulation of such material. Samuel Worcester's address to the society in 1817 went to an edition of only twelve hundred copies, which were distributed among the society's faithful. [44] Several local auxiliaries suggested a more ambitious attempt to stir public opinion through a mass circulation of pamphlets, but the parent society rejected the idea of subsidizing a weekly newspaper and argued that such an ambitious step should not be taken until the society's local auxiliaries were numerous enough to support the venture without subsidy from the center. The leadership ruled out an active propaganda campaign to stimulate favorable public opinion. [45]

Temperance leaders failed to appreciate the crucial importance of effective organization for the success of their cause in part because they had little prior experience with organizations for the promotion of morality. The founding of temperance societies was not a planned innovation but a makeshift response to the social and economic disruption caused by the War of 1812 and the challenge to the Federalist ascendancy in New England. Few models existed for these pioneers of social reform to imitate. Church missionary activity was highly developed, but social reform was a relatively new impulse for American churches. Even in the religious field, the churches had little experience in the manipulation of public opinion through voluntary organizations. Only with the formation of the New England Tract Society in Boston in 1814 did the Congregational clergy begin to look beyond personal influence, local prestige, and their own clerical influence to circulate tracts, encourage and assemble supporters in formal organizations, and make use of the printed media generally. Even then the process began in a very small way. [46] Handicapped by inexperience, the temperance pioneers carried outmoded, eighteenth-century concepts of social influence into the temperance societies. Rather than focus on new forms of exerting influence, they relied on the social prestige of Federalists, wealthy merchants, and Congregational and Unitarian clergy. These first reformers did not make a more ambitious use of voluntary organizations in part because they did not realize at the beginning that more would be necessary to achieve their goals. [47]

External opposition as such did not kill the first temperance societies (though had reformers tried to enforce the old laws suddenly and vigorously, they would almost certainly have faced a good deal more opposition than they did, and their failure to initiate an all-out assault on drinking was in part related to fears of the controversies that such a campaign would generate). These fears, together with an absence of strong internal convictions on the liquor question and a lack of experience in the use of voluntary organizations to effect moral reform, explain the failure of the MSSI. Dilatory in their approach to reform and inexperienced in the techniques of persuasion, the leaders and members of the Massachusetts society did not have a clear strategy of reform, and they did not develop effective organizations to maximize their influence. While these men were genuinely disturbed by intemperance, they looked back to the regulatory system of the eighteenth century and to the colonial standard of moderation in the use of spirits. Yet the colonial system of regulation was gone forever, as the futile efforts of the Massachusetts society revealed. Within ten years, new organizations would emerge, which would discard the heritage of the past and attempt to exploit the potential of the voluntary organization as a vehicle for reform. Soon temperance societies would develop a vital organization, an articulate ideology, and a committed leadership with which to attack the social problems of the Jacksonian era.

Notes

1. Raymond A. Mohl, *Poverty in New York, 1783-1825* (New York: Oxford University Press, 1971), pp. 208, 214, 242, 248; report of the first semiannual meeting of the Connecticut Society for the Promotion of Good Morals, *Panoplist*, o.s. 10 (January 1814): 17-20. On morals societies in New York State, just one issue of the *Albany* (N.Y.) *Christian Visitant*, 30 December 1815, lists societies in Albany, Utica, Buffalo, Washington County, and Rochester, as well as noting forty in Connecticut and "many" in New Hampshire and Vermont; on Philadelphia, see Othniel A. Pendleton, "Temperance and the Evangelical Churches," *Journal of Presbyterian History* 25 (March 1947): 22.

I do not assert that the societies that emerged in the 1810s were the first to be concerned with the alleviation of social problems. Societies for the alleviation of poverty in New York City, for example, extended back to the 1780s. See Mohl, *Poverty in New York*, pp. 121-58. Yet the charitable societies focused on the relief of poverty until the 1810s, when new societies arose to attack intemperance and other causes of intemperance in an effort to prevent pauperism. It is true that there were a few isolated temperance societies formed before the Massachusetts society, notably the Moreau and Northumberland Temperance Society (1808), cited by Lebbeus Armstrong, *The Temperance Reformation* (New York: Fowler and Wells, 1853), pp. 22-25, but these had no influence outside their own locality and were in any case mostly quite ephemeral.

2. *Constitution of the Massachusetts Society for the Suppression of Intemperance, as Revised and Altered, Together with Their Annual Report for the Year 1818 and a List of the Officers and Members of Said Society* (Boston: Sewell Phelps, 1818), p. 4; Andrew Nichols to the Reverend Edward Payson, 21 May 1814, Miscellaneous Bound Manuscripts, MHS.

3. See esp. Joseph Gusfield, *Symbolic Crusade: Status Politics and the American Temperance Movement* (Urbana: University of Illinois Press, 1963), pp. 39-41.

4. Stephan Thernstrom, *Poverty and Progress: Social Mobility in a*

Nineteenth Century City (Cambridge: Harvard University Press, 1964), p. 10; the quotation is from Edward Payson to his father, 28 December 1807, quoted in William Willis, ed., *Journals of the Reverend Thomas Smith, and the Reverend Samuel Deane, Pastors of the First Church in Portland* (Portland, Me.: Joseph S. Bailey, 1849), p. 407. This source emphasizes the economic calamities that befell Portland throughout the 1807-1815 period. Tonnage in the port fell from 39,000 tons in 1807 to 9,000 in 1811 and did not recover until 1816.

5. Anne Farnum, "Uncle Varnum's Farm: Refuge or Workhouse for Salem's Poor?" *Essex Institute Historical Collections* 109 (January 1973): 83; Mohl, *Poverty in New York*, pp. 86, 91.

6. For example, of the sixty-six Boston-based members of the Massachusetts Society for the Suppression of Intemperance, twenty-four were merchants with interests in shipping, banking, and trade. Compiled from Boston City directories, biographical data, and the membership lists of the society, published in *Constitution of the MSSI*, pp. 24-30.

7. *Bennington* (Vt.) *Christian Chronicle*, 27 June 1818.

8. *Panoplist*, n.s. 5 (May 1813): 541.

9. "Society in the County of Worcester for the Reformation of Morals," *Worcester Massachusetts Spy*, 16 November 1814, and ibid., 2 November 1814. See also "Preamble to the Newburyport Society for Suppressing Vice and Immorality," *Panoplist*, n.s. 5 (May 1813): 539. For a history of the jeremiad, or belief that disasters were the punishment of God against erring men, see Perry Miller, *The New England Mind: From Colony to Province* (Cambridge: Harvard University Press, 1957), chap. 2.

10. Jeremy Belknap, quoted in James M. Banner, Jr., *To the Hartford Convention: The Federalist Party and the Origins of Party Politics in Massachusetts, 1789-1815* (New York: Alfred A. Knopf, 1970), pp. 157, 164-67; Joshua Bates, *Two Sermons on Intemperance Delivered on the Day of the Annual Fast, April 8, 1813*, 2d ed. (Dedham: Gazette Office, 1814), p. 4, restates the clergy's determination to speak out on secular politics.

11. The liberals were the exponents of rational religion and Arminian doctrines, which emphasized the role of human will in salvation; they ultimately broke with the orthodox Congregationalists and became Unitarians. See Conrad Wright, *The Beginnings of Unitarianism in America* (Boston: Starr King Press, 1955).

12. Benjamin Wadsworth, *Intemperance a National Evil* (Salem: Thomas C. Cushing, 1815), expresses the clergy's fear of secularism and dissent. See also *Panoplist*, n.s. 5 (May 1813): 539, and Lyman Beecher, *A Reformation of Morals Practicable and Indispensable: A Sermon Delivered at*

New-Haven on the Evening of October 27, 1812, 2d ed. (Andover: Flagg and Gould, 1814), p. 22. For the act of 1811 and its social and political implications, see Jacob C. Meyer, *Church and State in Massachusetts from 1740 to 1833* (Cleveland: Western Reserve University Press, 1930), pp. 139, 143-49, 155-57; Paul Goodman, *The Democratic-Republicans of Massachusetts: Politics in a Young Republic* (Cambridge: Harvard University Press, 1964), pp. 165-66.

13. *Panoplist*, o.s. 7 (July 1811): 86; "Report on the Intemperate Use of Spirituous Liquors," by a committee appointed by the General Association of Massachusetts, in June 1811, *Panoplist*, n.s. 5 (September 1812): 184-87.

14. Charles R. Keller, *The Second Great Awakening in Connecticut* (New Haven: Yale University Press, 1942), p. 145.

15. Membership data are from *Constitution of the MSSI*.

16. Joseph S. Clark, *A Historical Sketch of the Congregational Churches in Massachusetts, from 1620 to 1850* (Boston: Congregational Board of Publications, 1858), pp. 244-54.

17. Ebenezer Porter, *The Fatal Effects of Ardent Spirits* (Concord: New Hampshire Tract Society, 1813), p. 18; report of the Dedham Auxiliary Temperance Society, quoted in "Fifth Annual Report of the Massachusetts Society for the Suppression of Intemperance," printed as an appendix to Samuel Worcester, *The Drunkard a Destroyer: A Discourse, Delivered before the Massachusetts Society for the Suppression of Intemperance, at Their Anniversary Meeting, May 30, 1817* (Boston: J. Eliot, 1817), p. 17 (hereafter cited as "Dedham Auxiliary Report"); Daniel Clarke Sanders, *A Sermon, Preached 14th March, 1815, before the Wrentham Auxiliary Society for the Suppression of Intemperance* (Dedham: Gazette Office, 1815), p. 9; [Nathan Dane], *Report of the Board of Counsel to the Massachusetts Society for the Suppression of Intemperance, Presented at Their Eighth Anniversary, June 1, 1820* (Boston: Sewell Phelps, 1820), p. 7; Beecher, *Reformation of Morals*, pp. 17, 22-23; *Serious Thoughts on the Traffic in Distilled Spirituous Liquors* (Burlington, N.J.: David Allinson, 1811), p. 22.

18. Goodman, *Democratic-Republicans*, pp. 136-37; David Hackett Fischer, *The Revolution of American Conservatism: The Federalist Party in the Era of Jeffersonian Democracy* (New York: Harper and Row, 1965), p. xv.

19. Goodman, *Democratic-Republicans*, p. 154; Banner, *To the Hartford Convention*, pp. 211-12.

20. Goodman, *Democratic-Republicans*, p. 153.

21. George W. Chase, *The History of Haverhill, Massachusetts, from Its First Settlement, in 1640, to the Year 1860* (Haverhill: The author, 1861), p. 619.

22. Compiled from biographical data and membership lists of the MSSI in *Constitution of the MSSI*, pp. 24-30, and membership lists of the Federalist political club in *A Directory Containing Names, Places of Business, and Residences of the Members of the Washington Benevolent Society of Massachusetts, from Its Commencement* (Boston: C. Stebbins, 1813). Jeffersonians did not join the temperance societies. Despite the attraction of the clergy to the temperance movement (40 percent of the total membership of the MSSI), not one Jeffersonian clergyman has been identified. A total of eight Jeffersonians among Massachusetts Congregational clergy are listed in Goodman, *Democratic-Republicans*, pp. 90, 227, and in Banner, *To the Hartford Convention*, p. 152, but none of these joined the MSSI. For the hostile reaction of a leading Jeffersonian clergyman to the morals societies, see *The Diary of William Bentley, D.D., Pastor of the East Church, Salem, Massachusetts* (Salem, Mass.: Essex Institute, 1905), 4:22-23.

23. "Dedham Auxiliary Report," p. 17; Beecher, *Reformation of Morals*, pp. 17, 22-23.

24. [Dane], *Report of the Board of Counsel*, pp. 7-9; Porter, *Fatal Effects of Ardent Spirits*, pp. 19-21; *Serious Thoughts*, p. 22; Jesse Appleton, *An Address, Delivered before the Massachusetts Society for Suppressing Intemperance, at Their Annual Meeting, May 13, 1816* (Boston: John Eliot, 1816), p. 5.

25. Sanders, *Sermon*, p. 6; *Circular Addressed to the Members of the Massachusetts Society for the Suppression of Intemperance* (Boston: Samuel T. Armstrong, 1814), p. 10 (hereafter referred to as *MSSI Circular*).

26. Henry Warren, *An Address Delivered at Roxbury, before the Roxbury Auxiliary Society for the Suppression of Intemperance, October 25, 1821* (Boston: Russell and Gardner, 1821), p. 21.

27. Parker Cleveland, *An Address, Delivered at Brunswick, April 27, 1814, before the Brunswick, Topsham, and Harpswell Society for the Suppression of Intemperance* (Boston: Chester Stebbins, 1814), p. 11.

28. *MSSI Circular*, pp. 10-11.

29. Ibid., p. 10.

30. Cleveland, *Address*, pp. 14-15; *MSSI Circular*, p. 10; Wadsworth, *Intemperance a National Evil*, p. 15.

31. "Dedham Auxiliary Report," p. 19.

32. Porter, *Fatal Effects of Ardent Spirits*, p. 18.

33. Bates, *Two Sermons*, pp. 29-30; Beecher, *Reformation of Morals*, pp. 17-18; "Dedham Auxiliary Report," p. 21.

34. See, for example, *Report of the Society in Portland for Suppressing Vice and Immorality, . . . 1816* (Portland, Me.: A. and J. Shirley, 1816), p. 9; *MSSI Circular*, p. 13; minutes of the Massachusetts Society for the Sup-

pression of Intemperance, Records of the Board of Counsel, p. 5 (December 1816), and minutes of the Sixth Annual Meeting, p. 51 (29 May 1818), MS vol., MHS (hereafter cited, respectively, as minutes of MSSI, Board of Counsel, and minutes of MSSI, Annual Meeting).

35. [Dane], *Report of the Board of Counsel*, p. 9; "Dedham Auxiliary Report," p. 21; Bates, *Two Sermons*, pp. 29-30.

36. "Address to the Vendors of Spirituous Liquors," from the committee on the enforcement of the license laws, Newburyport Society for the Suppression of Vice, *Panoplist*, n.s. 5 (May 1813): 541-43; "Report to a Committee, Appointed at a Town Meeting on September 1, 1817, by the Town of Foxborough, to Inquire into the Causes of Intemperance," *Bennington* (Vt.) *Christian Chronicle*, 27 June 1818. The provisions of the state law of 1787 are contained in "An Act for the Due Regulation of Licensed Houses," 28 February 1787, *The Laws of the Commonwealth of Massachusetts, from November 28, 1780 . . . to February 28, 1807* (Boston: J. T. Buckingham, 1807), 1:380.

37. *Bennington* (Vt.) *Christian Chronicle*, 27 June 1818.

38. Henry Ware, *The Criminality of Intemperance* (Boston: Phelps and Farnham, 1823), pp. 17-18; minutes of MSSI, Seventh Annual Meeting, p. 52 (28 May 1819).

39. *Diary of William Bentley*, 4:306.

40. I do not assert that no dissenters cooperated in the reform, but they were certainly inconspicuous. Take, for example, the contributions of church leaders. The Methodists provided only two Methodist circuit riders, as opposed to eighty-one Congregational and Unitarian clergy. The circuit riders were Oliver Beale of Pownal and Joshua Taylor of Portland. See *Minutes of the New England Conference of the Methodist Episcopal Church, 1776 to . . . 1845* (Boston: Methodist Historical Society, 1912). I have found only one Baptist sermon disclosing cooperation with the temperance reform in Massachusetts in this period. The address comes after the War of 1812. See John Butler, *A Sermon Delivered April 28, 1817, before the Association for the Suppression of Intemperance, and the Promotion of Morality in the Town of Hanover, Massachusetts* (Boston: Lincoln and Edmands, 1817). Banner, *To the Hartford Convention*, pp. 211-12, and Goodman, *Democratic-Republicans*, pp. 164-67, deal with the hostility toward Federalists among the dissenters. See also William L. Gribbin, *The Churches Militant: The War of 1812 and American Religion* (New Haven: Yale University Press, 1973), pp. 64-65, 71-72, 78-79, 94-95, 167; *Diary of William Bentley*, 4:114-15; and Henry Wheeler, *Methodism and the Temperance Reformation* (Cincinnati: Walden and Stowe, 1882), pp. 61-71.

41. *Constitution of the MSSI*, p. 17; "Annual Report of the Massachusetts

Society for the Suppression of Intemperance," in William Jenks, *A Sermon, Delivered before the Massachusetts Society for the Suppression of Intemperance, at Their Annual Meeting, June 1, 1821* (Boston: Phelps and Farnham, 1821), pp. 19, 25.

42. [Dane], *Report of the Board of Counsel*, p. 11. On Dane, see *National Cyclopedia of American Biography* (New York: J. T. White & Co., 1893-19   ), 9:197.

43. *Constitution of the Massachusetts Society, for the Suppression of Intemperance and Report of the Board of Council, Prepared for the Anniversary of the Society, May 28, 1813* (Boston: Samuel T. Armstrong, 1813), p. 7.

44. *Constitution of the MSSI*, p. 8.

45. *Second Annual Report of the Massachusetts Society for the Suppression of Intemperance* (Boston: n.p., 1814), p. 4.

46. Clifford S. Griffin, *Their Brothers' Keepers: Moral Stewardship in the United States, 1800-1865* (New Brunswick, N.J.: Rutgers University Press, 1960), p. 32. *Proceedings of the First Ten Years of the American Tract Society, Instituted at Boston, 1814* (Andover: Flagg and Gould, 1824), summarizes the early development of the tract system.

47. "Address of the Berkshire Society for the Promotion of Good Morals," *Panoplist*, o.s. 11 (February 1815): 93; Worcester, *The Drunkard a Destroyer*, p. 13; Cleveland, *Address*, pp. 16-17.

3

THE APOSTLES OF ABSTINENCE

The mid-1820s mark the true beginnings of the organized temperance crusade. The war on drink quickly became one of the most pervasive of antebellum social reform movements as temperance sentiment spread geographically and beyond the confines of a narrow segment of society. While the new temperance movement was deeply rooted in popular discontent with the incidence of intemperance, antiliquor sentiment had to be crystallized and mobilized in a concerted effective manner if temperance were to achieve the status of an ongoing social movement. Temperance reformers needed a coherent ideology, committed leadership, and appropriate organizations to exploit the existing discontent.[1]

All these conditions emerged in the mid-1820s. The hesitant, tentative efforts of the Massachusetts Society for the Suppression of Intemperance faded before the confident campaign launched by the American Temperance Society (ATS) after its creation in 1826.[2] If the contrast between the optimism of the American Temperance Society and the pessimism of the MSSI was stark, so too was the contrast between the strategies of reform employed by the two organizations. The MSSI had tried to unite the social elite of Massachusetts directly to enforce standards of morality on the intemperate. The ATS abandoned the drunkard—indeed abandoned the attempt at social control by one group over another—and opted for self-reform. Rather than force temperance morality on social deviants, the ATS focused on the respectable and sought to regenerate the temperate part of the community.[3] To reform the temperate, the American Temperance Society announced a novel and radical departure from the Massachusetts crusade: total abstinence from alcohol.

The founders of the ATS, mostly evangelical clergy, believed that the MSSI had failed because it had temporized over the issue of abstinence, and they asserted that the only road to reform was the renunciation of hard liquor. "We have a new idea," the founders of the American Temperance Society announced. "Our main object is . . . to induce *all temperate people to continue temperate* by practising total abstinence." No moderate use, no system of regulation, no laws enforced by the best men would suffice.[4] Whereas the reformers of the 1810s asserted the personal power of men, the new societies asserted the impersonal power of an uncompromising idea. Correct principles would ultimately achieve victory because the right ideas would be the most persuasive.[5]

Divided Churches

The emergence of the American Temperance Society's crusade for total abstinence has usually been explained as a product of evangelical revivalism. Yet before we examine the contribution of evangelicalism to reform, it is important to note the divisions within the evangelical churches over the temperance question at the outset of the reform crusade in the late 1820s and early 1830s. The early reports of the temperance societies make clear that the temperance cause did not initially embrace all members of the Presbyterian, Baptist, Methodist, and Congregationalist churches. The impetus toward temperance reform came from specific groups of reformers within the churches who sought to goad the remainder into sobriety.

The opposition of some pious evangelicals is apparent from the attacks on the involvement of church members in drinking and selling liquor. Especially revealing are the detailed reports of the agents and corresponding secretaries of the Maine Temperance Society, which in the case of the 1834 report ran to 134 pages of detailed case histories of pro-liquor and antiliquor activity. These reports document the divisions within the pietistic and evangelical denominations in the state of Maine in the late 1820s and early 1830s. Free Will Baptists, Calvinistic Baptists, Methodists, and Universalists opposed the temperance societies as often as they supported them.[6] It is true that the Congregationalists of New England gave much stronger support to the ATS from the beginning than did the Methodists, or Universalists, yet even within this largely pro-temperance denomination were reported cases of indifference or opposition.[7] Similarly the Presbyterians gave strong support to the ATS, yet the General Assembly of the Presbyterian church, in the course of passing resolutions favorable to the ATS, noted the "apathy manifested by many professing Christians towards the cause of temperance" and admitted that this "sin" afflicted "some members, even officers" of the Presbyterian church.[8]

In the South and West, the opposition of some "professing Christians" was still more apparent than in the Northeast. In Kentucky, North Carolina, and Illinois, antimission Baptists opposed temperance vehemently, even to the extent of excommunicating members who joined such societies.[9] The Methodists, too, were deeply divided in these regions. The General Conference did not restore the old (and strict) Wesleyan prohibition on the use and sale of liquor until 1848, after the departure of southern Methodists over the slavery issue. The division was not purely a regional one, for not all northern delegates supported the Wesleyan rule, while "some of the warmest advocates of the temperance cause" had come from "the Southern delegations." Yet the records of the General Conferences showed that the obstruction to the restoration of the Wesleyan rule came from the South.[10]

In large part, the fact that the liquor business was so deeply entrenched in society as to involve church members explains the divisions in Christian communities. The agents of the Maine Temperance Society cited the presence of liquor sellers among Maine Baptists, Universalists, and Methodists as one important cause of the dissension within those denominations.[11] So too with southern Methodists and Baptists, among whom the use of liquor had even greater social and economic significance. Among Kentucky Baptists, for example, "the use of intoxicating liquors was so interwoven with the social habits of the people, from the earliest settlement of the country," that it "was regarded a necessity to health and comfort," not to mention its economic importance to frontier farmers.[12]

Particularly in New England, the reluctance of some Baptists, Methodists, and Universalists to join the temperance crusade in the late 1820s and early 1830s also reflected sectarian and political suspicions, which had prevented cooperation in the work of the Massachusetts Temperance Society during the War of 1812. Agents of the Maine Temperance Society met the accusation that temperance was "a federal concern" or a "political thing" or "a federal plot"; Methodists and Baptists sometimes argued that they would not join the American Temperance Society crusade because they wished "to prevent a union between church and state."[13] The long period of discrimination against Methodist and Baptist dissenters in New England and the association between political Federalism and Congregationalism in the first two decades of the nineteenth century made some Baptists and Methodists reluctant to join a temperance movement sponsored in large part by Congregationalist clergy.

Another example of these sectarian suspicions is provided at the national level by the reaction of Nathan Bangs, editor of the Methodist *Christian Advocate* in New York. Bangs resisted cooperation with the American Temperance Society because he felt that "we [Methodists] had always been a temperance society, having made abstinence from intoxicating liquors as a beverage a term of Church communion; and, therefore, to come into the measures of the American Society would be a virtual acknowledgement that we, as a Church, needed such a reformation."[14] Bangs felt that energies and money given to the American Temperance Society would be better spent by Methodists operating within the framework of their own denominational charities and church work. He conveniently ignored the fact that the Wesleyan rule had been abandoned in 1790 and that drinkers and sellers were communicants within the church.

Despite the opposition of some Methodists, many others did join the ATS campaign. Wilbur Fisk, the president of Weslyan University, engaged Bangs in a debate over intemperance in the Methodist church in the pages of the *Christian Advocate* and reported that in Connecticut, the first temperance societies under the ATS plan had been formed and led by Methodists.[15] Like many other denominations, the Methodists were divided over both the principle of total abstinence and the use of temperance societies to combat the drink problem.

The point of highlighting these religious divisions is not to imply that temperance was a secular reform movement at this time but to impress that deep piety and religiosity were not sure determinants of temperance commitment in the late 1820s. The support for temperance came in fact from particular groups within the pietistic and evangelical churches. These evangelical abstainers saw the churches as a fruitful field for their campaigns and aimed the temperance message at church members. Yet the assumption was that erring sinners would have to be brought to their senses, that Christians would have to be the first to sober up.

Ambitious Evangelicals

The leadership of the American Temperance Society came from rather different groups to the men who had launched the MSSI in 1813. Only three of the twenty-seven honorary members of the ATS were former members of the MSSI, only two of the fifteen Massachusetts-based officials and only four of the sixteen founders.[16] Certainly these figures show that there was some overlap between the two organizations, but those former supporters of the MSSI who joined in organizing the ATS had not been officials or prominent members of the older organization.

The social profile of the men who founded the ATS and shaped its strategy of reform differed in several important respects from the social profile of comparable figures in the MSSI. Bearing in mind that the numbers involved in these groups were very small (the original sixteen officeholders of the ATS and the fourteen in the MSSI) and that it would therefore be unwise to quantify too precisely, I shall summarize those differences briefly. The ATS leadership came from a somewhat younger group of reformers (by about twelve years), but the median age of the founders and officials of the ATS in 1826 was not significantly different from the median age of MSSI founders in 1813. Only half of the sixteen ATS leaders had a college education, compared to twelve of the fourteen MSSI founders. This difference reflected the greater importance of laymen in the leadership of the ATS, but there was also a significant difference in the character of the college education received by the two groups. Five of the eight of the ATS leaders with college degrees were from the evangelical schools: Williams, Yale, Union, Andover, and Brown. In contrast, Harvard, the center of theological liberalism, produced most of the members of the MSSI leadership. ATS leaders were also more deeply involved in the whole range of interdenominational benevolent reform activities. Fifteen of the sixteen ATS leaders were members of the American Board of Commissioners for Foreign Missions, and fourteen joined the American Tract Society. Most of these men served, at one time or another, as full-time professional organizers in the missionary, tract, and Bible societies; others were substantial financial contributors, and this wider involvement was in sharp contrast with the careers of MSSI leaders. [17] Only three of the fourteen MSSI founders were in the American Board of Commissioners for Foreign Missions, and only one was a member of the American Tract Society.

These were the only significant differences in the social profiles of the two groups, and as far as leadership is concerned, the evidence points toward certain religious, ideological, and organizational changes as crucial to an understanding of the creation of the American Temperance Society. If we are to understand what these new reformers stood for, what motivated them to embark on a temperance crusade, we must look at the general social ferment within which their crusade originated. In particular, we must examine the revivals of the Second Great Awakening and the place of these reformers in that context.

The influence of revivalistic religion on temperance reform should not be surprising because the Second Great Awakening was in itself a social movement of major proportions. [18] Between the 1790s and the 1830s, American religion underwent a transformation which had profound ramifications, not only for religious institutions but also for social reform. Revivals swept both the frontier areas and the established communities of the East, swelling congregations fivefold between 1800 and 1835, compared with a threefold increase of population. [19] More important than sheer numbers was the energetic and unprecedented effort to spread the word of God through preachers,

tracts, and the Bible. American religion adopted voluntary organizations as the primary means of furthering these objectives. Tract,
Bible, and missionary societies proliferated. [20]

Concurrent with the enthusiasm of the revivals, American theology gradually shed its Calvinist assumptions and adopted more
optimistic notions of the potential of all human beings for salvation.
The abandonment of Calvinism was especially noticeable in the
thought of Charles Grandison Finney, the most famous and successful of the early revivalists. Finney "rejected the Calvinist view of
God's inscrutable sovereignty and of man's ineradicable depravity
and because he did not believe that the Bible justified the view that
only a few predestined elect were eligible for salvation, he saw no
reason why the whole world might not someday be made up of converted Christians living in brotherly love."[21] But the theological
shift was not confined to western revivalists like Finney. Even the
heirs of Calvinism in New England modified their theology. While
they did not abandon their belief in a powerful and almighty God,
New England theologians and clergymen like Lyman Beecher,
Timothy Dwight, and Nathaniel Taylor began to make modest as-
sertions of man's free will and moral responsibility for his own salvation. [22] Sin now became voluntary separation from God rather than
something inherent in the ineradicable nature of man. Moreover
New England theologians modified their definition of the personal
holiness which Jonathan Edwards had regarded as a prerequisite for
salvation. Edwards's vision of "individual piety and reverence to
God" gave way to the notion of benevolence and service to mankind. Benevolence came to mean both abstaining from evil and seeking actively to root out evil in society. [23] This concept formed the
intellectual underpinning of the voluntary organizations adopted by
the evangelical churches to spread religious and moral truths to all
mankind.

The young clergy trained in the evangelical theological colleges
embraced the revival spirit, the self-searching concern for personal
holiness, and the drive toward active benevolence. These were deeply religious men, but theirs was not an otherworldly religion. Convinced that the prestige of the evangelical churches was expanding
under the influence of the revivals, they sought to use the power of
evangelical religion to solve practical social problems. In the mission

and benevolent societies, the evangelical clergy found practical outlets for their religious zeal, as well as rewarding, successful careers.
Involvement in mission, revival, and benevolent reform work did
not lessen their religious commitment, but it did impart to these men
much larger ambitions than the parochial concerns of parish clergy.
Sacraments and sermons—the traditional fare of a religious voca-
tion—could not contain their aspirations, for they wished rather to
shape "the future destinies of America" through moral reform. [24]

From men so schooled in the thought and practice of evangelical
revivalism came the architects of temperance reform, the religious
leadership which founded the American Society for the Promotion
of Temperance at a meeting in Boston on February 13, 1826. Lay
Christians of evangelical persuasion attended the foundation meeting, but the driving force behind the organization of the new society
was the Reverend Justin Edwards, a man who embodied the spirit of
evangelical reform. Edwards was born the son of a New England
farmer of Northampton, Massachusetts. The Connecticut Valley
had been the storm center of the First Great Awakening, and Northampton was the home of Jonathan Edwards, the most celebrated exponent of its Calvinistic principles. Young Justin Edwards was not
related to the great preacher, but he did share his predecessor's deep
concern with spiritual questions. Justin Edwards was already a pious
young man of nineteen in 1806 when he underwent a conversion experience and dedicated his life to Christian service. Edwards held
steadfast to this goal through the course of a forty-year working life,
as a preacher, teacher, principal of Andover Seminary, translator of
the Bible, sabbatarian advocate, and, most important of all, temperance reformer. Edwards was not content with a life of inner piety. He
longed for practical activity and influence. He yearned for the opportunity to harness the spiritual power he had discovered to change
the secular lives of men and so bring them to God. [25] As a young
clergyman in Andover, Massachusetts, Edwards was especially
stirred by the "sad influence of intemperance in steeling the heart
against the gospel." [26] In 1822, he began to preach against the "tyrant
rum," which he believed was ruining many lives in the town of Andover; in 1826, he helped to form the American Temperance Society
and became its corresponding secretary. For the next ten years, he
was to be its chief strategist and tactician. As John Tappan remarked,

[61]

he was "the pivot upon which all moved" in the early years of the society. [27]

Justin Edwards did not conform to the popular historical stereotype of a temperance reformer. He was not a fanatic or bigot but a reasonable man. His temperance tracts and sermons were logical, methodical, and learned. He believed strongly in persuasion rather than coercion to attain his goal of a temperate society. Above all, he impressed contemporaries with his "gentleness of manner." [28] "Be yourself a pattern of temperance in all things" was his oft-quoted advice to followers and his personal rule of conduct. [29] Yet his pleasant and self-effacing exterior obscured a shrewd tactician and manipulator of men. Committed to "mild persuasion," Edwards nevertheless played politics ruthlessly within the temperance societies to gain ascendancy for his point of view. He practiced compromise when necessary but knew when to insist on principles. The details of finance and organization he delegated to such capable lieutenants on the executive board of the American Temperance Society as John Tappan, the rich merchant philanthropist and brother of the more famous antislavery Tappans; Samson Wilder, a retired merchant and farmer of Bolton, Massachusetts; and George Odiorne, a wealthy Boston banker and iron manufacturer. The fifth and final member of the first executive of the American Temperance Society was Leonard Woods, a close friend and mentor of Justin Edwards. Woods taught theology at Andover Seminary, the school established to rekindle evangelical religion in Massachusetts and save the state from the "cold indifference" of the Unitarians. Besides his commitment to temperance, Woods was also influential in the councils of the American Tract Society of Boston and the American Board of Commissioners for Foreign Missions. [30]

Like the executive committee, the members of the American Temperance Society were imbued with a special moral and religious purpose. Membership in the parent society was kept exclusive at first; the society elected a total of only 118 members. [31] More than one-third of these were clergy, and the rest were doctors, college presidents (who were also clergymen), and wealthy businessmen. Like the founders of the ATS, they came predominantly (over five-sixths) from the New England region, and all were from the Northeast. The ATS was honest in naming the qualities which distinguished these men; the society carefully selected men "of known and expansive benevolence [who] could be relied on both as to correctness of sentiment, integrity and zeal."[32] Wealth and evangelical commitment, not social prominence, were the special characteristics these men possessed. Unlike the MSSI, the ATS deliberately excluded Unitarians and sought members among those of pietistic and evangelical persuasion. Presbyterians and Congregationalists predominated among the members, though Methodists, Baptists, Episcopalians, and Quakers were included among the elected.[33]

The evangelical revivals, especially of the Congregational and Presbyterian kind, had produced a corps of young and committed Christians casting about for ways of demonstrating their benevolence. Yet two questions remain: why did this religious fervor become channeled into social reform rather than missionary or other specifically Christian work, and why did it do so in the middle of the 1820s? The answers to these questions can best be begun by looking at the connections between the American Temperance Society and the American Tract Society, which demonstrate the blend of religious enthusiasm and personal ambition that produced the ATS campaign for total abstinence.

Tract operations can be traced back to the first two decades of the nineteenth century, but these were fairly small-scale regional and local operations. Among them was the Massachusetts-based New England Tract Society founded in Boston in 1814. After 1817, Justin Edwards was a member of the executive committee of this society, and in 1821 he became corresponding secretary. Under the energetic leadership of Edwards and Leonard Woods, the New England Tract Society quadrupled its supply of tracts, and, befitting its leadership's national aspirations, took the name American Tract Society of Boston. In 1825, however, its operations were cut short by the emergence of a larger competitor, the American Tract Society of New York, established with a $25,000 grant from Arthur Tappan and other wealthy New York merchants. The new society proposed the systematic distribution of cheaply produced tracts throughout the United States through the agencies of auxiliary organizations. The founders especially emphasized New York's central position and its commercial importance. Having exploited the wealth of evangelical New York merchants to get started, the new group hoped to use the city's central position to aid the distribution of tracts. Especially compelling in the organization of the national tract society was the opening of the Erie Canal in 1825 and the acceleration of western settlement which improved communications allowed. The tract society hoped to evangelize this emerging western society.[34] Already $1,683 in debt, the New England-based organization could not hope to compete with the new group, which had much larger financial resources and could promise a more efficient and more economical system of distribution. The New England society therefore agreed to become an auxiliary. As a sop to the Boston group, Justin Edwards was made a member of the publications committee of the New York organization.[35]

Thus after 1825 the ambitious young Boston group was left in a subordinate position within the tract empire, and it was from this conjunction of circumstances that the new temperance campaign emerged. The turn of fortunes within the tract enterprises had deprived Justin Edwards and his associates of policy-making positions and reduced Edwards's role to that of a member of a publications committee. Neither Justin Edwards nor Leonard Woods appeared to object to these changes; they applauded the chances for a much wider dissemination of the gospel through the new tract organization. But the change did leave them casting about for a new sphere of usefulness that would be complementary to the new tract society. Within six months of the removal of the tract operations to New York, Edwards, Woods, and other New England evangelicals associated with the Tract Society of Boston met to plan the temperance crusade as a complementary reform that would utilize and in some respects imitate the evolving tract system. The emergence of the national tract organization by the mid-1820s was symptomatic of the maturation of the strictly religious and benevolent reform enterprises. By and large, the religious benevolent empires were well established. For younger clergy, this process of consolidation both enabled and encouraged them to seek other causes in related areas of social and moral reform.

If internal politics within the tract empire spurred the decision to launch a new temperance crusade, the tract societies also provided proven methods of agitation which the temperance societies could adopt. In its early tactics, as in the motivations of its leaders, the

American Temperance Society bore the imprint of evangelical revivalism in general and of the tract system in particular. The ATS enthusiastically adopted the tract society's plan of flooding the country with millions of cheap tracts expressing religious and moral truths in pithy, attractive form. Indeed many of the temperance tracts were printed by and distributed through the American Tract Society of New York to take advantage of the economies of scale that the larger operation afforded. [36] This reliance on the tract society was evident especially in the publication of the *Temperance Volume* in 1831 (and 1834), which embraced "the seventeen tracts of the American Tract Society." Contributors included many of the leading polemicists of temperance—Justin Edwards, John Marsh, Dr. Thomas Sewall, and the Reverend C.P. McIlvaine. [37] The American Tract Society records show that, apart from strictly religious and scriptural concerns, literature on the temperance question exceeded any other moral issue in the volume of tracts published and distributed by the American Tract Society, especially between 1826 and 1833, the years of the early evangelical crusade against intemperance. [38]

The use of the tract system was just one example of the way in which the initial tactics of temperance reform drew on the enthusiasm and experience of benevolent evangelical reform. The American Temperance Society further imitated the efforts of revivalistic preachers and Bible and tract societies by sending to evangelical churches itinerant agents who preached the message of temperance reform. Among the men who traveled across the eastern United States in the employ of the society were Justin Edwards, the Reverend Nathaniel Hewitt, and fifteen other licensed preachers or ministers. [39] The strategy was to take the battle to the churches because church members, schooled in the language of the revivals and possessing a vocabulary of personal responsibility for sin, provided a natural audience for the message of the ATS.

These campaigns differed in several important ways from the abortive efforts of the MSSI, and the contrast makes the much larger success of the ATS more understandable. Above all, superior organization distinguished the ATS from the MSSI. Once again taking its cue from the tract organization, the ATS campaigned systematically by using its itinerant temperance agents to create a network of societies which could both raise funds and disseminate temperance propaganda. The ATS encouraged the formation of state temperance societies, but most important were the county and local organizations, because only with a network of such organizations could the temperance crusade become comprehensive and effective in its impact. With auxiliaries in every town, ATS leaders felt that the temperance message would confront the general public continually.

Financial arrangements were also more systematic than in the case of the MSSI. The ATS copied from the American Board of Commissioners for Foreign Missions a subscription system which encouraged wealthy donors by allowing them to become honorary members or directors according to the amount donated ($50 and $250, respectively). At the same time, the use of traveling agents enabled the society to garner small contributions from individual congregations. Though about two-thirds of the total donations during the first two years came from well-to-do contributors who gave more than thirty dollars each, two-thirds of the total donors were small contributors who gave less than five dollars each. [40] The ATS thus tapped both small and large contributors. Though the ATS never rivaled in its financial resources the achievement of the older mission and tract societies, its accounts showed an operating surplus each year until the mid-1830s and ever-increasing funds. Edwards complained that the society never had the resources to achieve its grandiose ambitions, but it nevertheless employed him as a full-time secretary and agent, paid the editor of the *Journal of Humanity*, funded its traveling agents, and maintained a relatively healthy financial condition, a far cry from the modest goals and achievements of the MSSI.

The financial position of the ATS in turn made possible important innovations in the use of printed materials to spread the temperance message and the influence of the ATS. The propaganda efforts of the ATS were not limited to the distribution of tracts through the American Tract Society. The temperance organization turned out annual reports, circulars appealing to such special groups as women and youths, and a weekly newspaper, the *Journal of Humanity*, which included temperance material, items on other reform and missionary causes, and general news. The ATS began, too, the use of woodcuts in temperance tracts, and other illustrative material (a trend which became much more pronounced in the 1830s). In all these ways, the

ATS strategy was to venture beyond dry and dusty annual reports to woo the public with a variety of more specialized and appealing publications.

In sum, the ATS campaign of the late 1820s and early 1830s relied on measures: paid, full-time organizers, a network of voluntary organizations, systematic financing, and the printed word as the basis of temperance propaganda rather than the spoken word from the lips of local notables. The MSSI had relied on men—the Federalist elite—to carry the brunt of the temperance message through the very force of their social prestige.

These new measures meant more than changes in the mechanics of temperance operations; equally important, they meant changes in the character and direction of the temperance message. The ATS appealed to the public on the basis of a clear-cut and novel principle of reform that cut across the ranks and hierarchies assumed in the campaign of the MSSI. The reform process drew upon a fundamental principle of the revivals of the early nineteenth century—that all believers were equal in the spirit—and applied that principle to the temperance conversion. Thus temperance reform was implicitly subversive of ministerial authority and of church dominance in social and moral matters. The appeal to the lay evangelical community could be seen most clearly in the emphasis on the recruitment of two groups excluded from effective power in the larger society: young people and women. The frank acceptance of the help of women and youths, together with the encouragement of the family as a kind of temperance society in itself, revealed the willingness of the ATS (among other benevolent organizations) to go beyond established centers of power in American communities to tap new resources for reform.

Justin Edwards himself expressed the theological and practical justifications for this course of action, especially as it affected women. He advocated women joining temperance societies because "under the light of the Gospel, which raises women, in excellence of character and ability to do good, to an equality with men, every association composed of both, will more than double its influence over the public mind, especially over the minds of youth and children." Edwards outlined a strategy of reform which would attempt to counter the influence of liquor in the larger society by giving women an enhanced role in the promotion of temperance within the family and church. He was attempting to draw on the moral resources of women, which had already been demonstrated in their activities in the missionary and tract societies. [41] The records of these benevolent evangelical societies reveal the extraordinarily large role of women in fund raising and in the swelling of membership lists. Middle-class women, increasingly deprived of meaningful economic roles, found outlets in religious and benevolent activities, and the temperance societies were not slow to include this new and growing constituency. Since few temperance membership lists survive, it is often difficult to tell the proportion of women in these societies, but in cases where manuscript records do remain, from one-third to one-half of the members were women. [42]

The example of women's participation demonstates how the ATS went about tapping the energies and resources of the lay evangelical community, though they did not do so at the expense of clerical influence. For one thing, women were not encouraged to take leadership positions but only to be followers; for another, the organizing positions were mostly monopolized by clergymen. A large degree of clerical influence was made possible by the presence at the local level of a corps of young, energetic evangelical ministers trained at the same institutions as the national leaders and holding the same values. By 1834, the American Temperance Society had elected a total of 487 local representatives as members, of whom 256 were in the northeastern states, 74 in the Midwest, and 157 in the South and border states. Of these, 213 were clergymen, most of them members of the American Bible Society, the American Tract Society, or the American Board of Commissioners for Foreign Missions. [43]

The Reverend Jonathan Going of Worcester provides an excellent example of the type of person whom the ATS used as its local carriers of reform principles. A Vermont Baptist born in 1786 and educated at Brown University, Going served as pastor in Cavendish, Vermont, before coming to Worcester, Massachusetts, in 1815 at the age of twenty-nine to be the local Baptist minister, a post he held until 1831. Subsequently Going moved to New York to become secretary of the American Baptist Home Mission Society and editor of its organ, the *Mission Record*. While in Worcester, Going had instigated religious revivals within his congregation, and "the membership of the church was very largely increased." But he did not limit himself to the religious welfare of his flock; his work in temperance, home and foreign missions, and common schools education distinguished his pastorate. [44]

The most striking aspect of Going's social profile is its similarity to those of the evangelical leaders of the ATS. Like them, he was young, ambitious, had an evangelical theological education, evinced a variety of interests in the missionary and benevolent reform fields, and ultimately joined the ranks of professional reformers. At the local level, men like Going not only shared similar values and aspirations to ATS leaders; they had very similar social backgrounds and career profiles. Such men could be relied on to carry the principles of evangelical temperance reform into their congregations and so swell the ranks of ATS supporters. In their sermons and public addresses, these clergymen echoed the sentiments and copied the arguments of the national leadership. Many of the new temperance societies were in fact organized within evangelical congregations in response to such sermons, and these ministers usually served either as presidents or secretaries of these first total abstinence societies. [45]

New Perceptions of the Drink Problem

In their leadership, systematic organization, and reform at the local level, the temperance reformers of the ATS imitated techniques of evangelical benevolent reform and tapped enthusiasms cast up by the Second Great Awakening. Given these close connections between the ATS and religious benevolent societies, it is little wonder that temperance reformers should also draw heavily on evangelical religion for their perceptions of intemperance, the language that they used, and their temperance ideology. From the evangelical doctrine of benevolence, Justin Edwards and his co-workers accepted the corollary that each person must refrain from all wrongdoing and work for the eradication of evil from society. If he did not, the sin of his failure to oppose that evil rebounded against his own prospects for salvation. [46] Justin Edwards was convinced that intemperance caused by the use of spirits was an evil that compelled vigorous action on the part of all benevolent and Christian men. It is not particularly surprising, in view of the drinking customs of colonial America and the growing extent of the drink problem between the 1780s and the 1820s, that Edwards and his fellow reformers focused on intemperance. What is most interesting is the way they perceived the problem and how their perceptions and experience shaped the solutions they proposed.

To the religious supporters of the American Temperance Society, the critical problem posed by drink seemed axiomatic. They emphasized the eternal, not the temporal, consequences of intemperance. They saw man's primary purpose as the achievement of salvation. The new religious spirit opened up the possibility of salvation to all. Receipt of God's grace depended on a willing disposition, a concern with spiritual problems, and benevolence toward one's fellow men. Only a person with such qualities could expect and receive the outpouring of the holy spirit. Intemperance blotted out man's moral sense and his rational perception of spiritual problems and thus made him indifferent to the appeals of religion. The Reverend John Marsh of Haddam, Connecticut, summarized the American Temperance Society argument in a sensational address which became a widely published pamphlet, *Putnam and the Wolf, or, the Monster Destroyed*. "Every moral and religious principle is dissipated" before the ravages of ardent spirits. "The heart becomes, under its influence, harder than the nethermill stone." Ardent spirits both hardened the heart and unleashed the passions in men. The rational faculty could no longer keep the animal instincts under control. Without the guiding rudder of a moral sense, reason "has only the power of the helmsman before the whirlwind," and consequently man was driven to heinous crimes and consigned to eternal damnation. [47] The desire to preserve man's self-control, in preparation for his salvation, led temperance reformers to attack the use of ardent spirits, which was clearly the major cause of intemperance in the 1820s.

Yet to leave the explanation there is not entirely satisfactory, since evangelical temperance reformers showed an acute concern for the social cost of intemperance, and they displayed considerable anxiety over the related problems of crime and pauperism. This aspect was seen most clearly in the space the *Journal of Humanity* gave to social deviance and to the asylum as a solution for the social problems of crime and poverty. There were, in fact, many parallels between the temperance and asylum reform movements in the 1820s and 1830s. Yet the way temperance reformers proposed to deal with social deviance was different from that proposed by asylum reformers; that important divergence illustrates the role of the social position and ideology of these evangelical temperance reformers in structuring perceptions of the drink problem and how it was to be solved. ATS reformers agreed with the supporters of the asylum movement that crime was rife. They also agreed that pauperism threatened to burden unduly the prosperous part of the community and that insanity loomed as a symptom of social disorder. [48]

Temperance reformers differed from asylum advocates not in their awareness of social disorder but in their understanding of the root causes of it. The asylum advocates attacked the obvious or external manifestations of deviancy. They took the poor, the insane, and the criminal out of society and attempted to instill them with the moral habits which would enable them to function as productive and moral citizens. The parallel for temperance reformers would have been to attack the dramshops, which were certainly the most flagrant and obvious sources of intemperance in the community. But the American Temperance Society rejected such an attack as too narrow, misleading, and self-serving a solution to the problem. Instead it emphasized the practices of respectable and Christian gentlemen who, by their actions, condoned or sustained intemperance. Whereas the Massachusetts Society for the Suppression of Intemperance had attacked the excesses of drunkenness, the evils of the dramshop, and the intemperance of the lower classes, the American Temperance Society turned the moral spotlight on the temperate or moderate drinker. This approach reflected the heightened concern with sin, guilt, and personal responsibility for evil which the new religious spirit emphasized. The American Temperance Society asserted that "the temperate were the guilty cause of all intemperance in the land."[49]

The ATS reformers thus developed a peculiar and highly original concept of deviancy. The delinquent was not so much the hopeless, confirmed drunkard as the respectable man who was indifferent to the cause of temperance reform. This view was not one that all church members shared, as the debates within the evangelical churches over organized temperance indicated. In the late 1820s, the ATS position was controversial, and it was meant to be so. The strategy was to goad the indifferent into reform. According to Charles Griswold, the president of the Middlesex County, Connecticut, Temperance Society, anyone who was "not decidedly in favor of these plans for doing good" was "decidedly against them"; as the Reverend Cyrus Mann of Worcester County, Massachusetts, warned, there was "no middle, neutral ground" and certainly no time "for lukewarmness or cold indifference."[50]

Among the most dangerous deviants were the moderate drinkers. John Marsh reasoned in *Putnam and the Wolf* that if all the effects of intemperance were immediately apparent in the form of pauperism, crime, delirium tremens, and death, the community would not tolerate so gross an evil.[51] But intemperance worked its way insidiously from seemingly harmless practices such as social drinking. Gradually the appetite for spirits hardened into an irresistible craving, which led the victims to poverty and destruction. In the earlier stages of the condition, the drinker could relinquish the habit if he would appreciate the long-term consequences of yielding to temptation. In Justin Edwards's analysis, it was "temperate drinking which gives the relish, prepares the way, and opens the door to intemperance. *Shut this door*, and it will not enter."[52] If the moderate drinker continued to take his ardent spirits, he would almost certainly develop into a habitual drunkard. Thereby he jeopardized his own chances for salvation and contributed to the pool of misery in society, perhaps leaving a wife and children to be consigned to the poorhouse. Even if he should manage to postpone or avert the "chains of appetite," the moderate drinker set the worst possible example for his fellow man. The Reverend Charles P. McIlvaine, the Episcopalian evangelical, tearfully related stories of fathers who drank spirits in moderation with "no perceptible injury."[53] Yet the moderate use in the father encouraged the immoderate use in the son. The parent, although himself temperate, had affixed to him the guilt of corrupting his drunkard son.[54]

Drunkards could not be expected to reform while the respectable condoned moderate drinking. They might for a time put away their habit, but temptation would remain around them in the daily use of spirits in all walks of life. Their powers of resistance, already weakened by the craving appetite, could not withstand temptation unless the better informed, respectable part of the community united to proscribe spirituous liquors from everyday use.[55] For a temperance reformer like the Reverend John Marsh, "all the drunkenness . . . that shall pollute our land must be traced to moderate drinkers. They feed the monster. They keep in countenance the distillery and the dram-shop, and every drunkard that reels in the street."[56]

Worse still as an example to the community was the temperate man, who lent an aura of respectability to the manufacture or sale of ardent spirits. The ATS branded distillers and retailers as traffickers in human souls and blood. The nefarious traffic in spirits would become disreputable if respectable, religious people abandoned their distilleries, taverns, and dramshops. As the Reverend Nathaniel Hewitt put it: "When upright and respectable merchants separate themselves from all participation in this traffic, it will be continued only by those who are as profligate and worthless as drunkards themselves. Then the relation between the sale of spirituous liquors and the production of pauperism, crime, madness, and death, will provoke general indignation." When the community became so enlightened, the time would have arrived to prohibit by law such part of the traffic which continued despite community resentment.[57]

Most of all, the American Temperance Society denounced Christian involvement in the liquor traffic. Justin Edwards condemned "this degrading and destructive employment" as "utterly inconsistent with the spirit and the requirements of the Christian religion."[58] A Christian who led others into the temptation of alcohol could not expect God's mercy because the traffic was the antithesis of benevolence.[59] The ATS not only attacked Christian traffickers but also leveled some of its most trenchant critiques at the failure of American churches to exclude users and traffickers from the communion table. Although the Presbyterian, Reformed, Congregational, Baptist, and Methodist churches all censured or condemned members who made, drank, or sold spirits, none actually excluded the offenders from religious sacraments. The Presbyterian church, for example, at its General Assembly of 1830, condemned church members who "feel themselves at liberty to manufacture, vend, or use ardent spirits" but "would by no means encroach upon the rights of private judgment."[60] This approach did not satisfy the American

Temperance Society. Nothing less than excommunication would expiate the guilt of the church for condoning all the inhumanity and social problems present in society.[61]

Reformers unleashed an invective on Christians out of proportion to the actual participation of church members in the traffic. No reformer alleged that church members dominated the trade; rather they argued that any involvement by church members was morally wrong. Reformers set a higher standard of morality for the church than for outsiders. Justin Edwards believed that it was "always worse for a church member to do any immoral act, and teach an immoral sentiment, than for an immoral man; because it does greater mischief." When Wilbur Fisk scornfully told his fellow Methodists who condoned the sale of alcohol that "we had indeed hoped for better things of Christians," he expressed the sentiments of many other evangelical temperance reformers.[62]

Why did the religious temperance leaders focus on the least flagrant offenders? The American Temperance Society invoked the doctrine of benevolence; yet the inward turning of temperance in this period also had roots in the social experience of the evangelical clergy. When the clergy attacked the liquor problem indirectly, they did so because other more direct attacks on the most flagrant aspects of intemperance had already proven impractical and because their experience in mission and tract work suggested new and more effective tactics and organizational techniques. The campaigns of the MSSI had made clear that enforcement of the existing liquor laws would not work. There was not sufficient backing for a stricter enforcement, and the MSSI campaign had ended disastrously. The ATS reformers confessed the impracticability of promoting temperance through legal action. "The strength of government" admitted Nathaniel Hewitt, the first general agent of the ATS, was "not adequate" to such tasks.[63] The experience of the MSSI in its drive to enforce the laws against the dramshops proved to the satisfaction of ATS reformers that "moral societies rarely *do any good* by appealing to the laws of the land." Because legal sanctions would always fail while community sentiment remained inadequate to enforce them, these reformers conceded that the community had to be persuaded of the virtues of temperance, and they advocated moral example as the best way of achieving the goal of abstinence throughout society.[64]

ATS reformers believed in the power of moral example as an alternative and more effective remedy for vice than legal restraint. Yet they did not place their hopes on example alone but on organized example. The abstainers had to impress moderate drinkers by combining in societies to display the virtues of abstinence. As Justin Edwards explained, the primary purpose of temperance societies

is not to lead their members by signing a paper, to abstain from the use of ardent spirit, and make them temperate; but it is to unite, in a visible, organized union, all that *do* abstain, and *are* temperate; in order to show, by example, the most powerful of teachers, that men of all ages and conditions, and in all kinds of business, are, in all respects, better without it.[65]

When the ATS leadership advocated the virtues of reform by organized example, it tacitly conceded the inadequacy of more traditional forms of influence. Moral exhortations, they admitted, were no longer enough to convince all the respectable, influential people in the community to abstain from spirits. Such a position would have been totally foreign to an eighteenth-century Congregational clergyman like the Reverend Nathaniel Emmons, who conceived of the local parish minister as the moral preceptor in his own community.[66] But in Jacksonian society, men formed voluntary organizations to advance their goals, be it a political office, a canal, or a moral cause. The temperance reformers were among the earliest to exploit the potential of voluntary organization in the cause of moral reform. They quickly seized the importance of the new mass techniques for mobilizing public opinion, which Jacksonian politics vividly demonstrated. "All that is wanting," the *Journal of Humanity* argued, "is for the friends of temperance to manifest the same energy in the cause, which they enlist when other interests are at stake. If an obnoxious president were to be removed, all the means which would enlist the omnipotent power of public opinion would be zealously employed." The supporters of the ATS realized that numbers, noise, and money counted most in a society which had abandoned the politics of deference.[67]

In the adoption of such techniques as the moral tract, these evangelical temperance reformers further proclaimed the obsolescence of traditional means of exerting influence. Despite vigorous efforts to train new ministers, the supply of clergy of all denominations could not meet the growth of the population and its expansion from New England into the West. Reformers like Justin Edwards responded to the danger by energetically embracing the tract as an alternative means of spreading both the gospel and temperance.[68]

Organization was a means of compensating for the inadequacy of individual example and of legal remedies for intemperance; however the ATS admitted that even the power of organized example would not reach everyone. Even with the new techniques of tracts, agents, and the phalanx of local auxiliaries, the salutary influence of the society would "extend to those only, who have a regard to their reputation in respectable and virtuous society, and who feel the force of moral obligation." The appeals of the society could not reach the sordid, habitual drunkard and his offspring who were raised "without moral and religious instruction." Over these people, "intoxicating liquors rule with absolute sway."[69] No moral appeals from the religious and respectable could reach them because they rejected the very right of the respectable to be their moral guardians. The Reverend Nathaniel Hewitt made this point in his first annual report as agent of the American Temperance Society.

Public worship they abhor. The Sabbath, by releasing them from labour, only affords them opportunity to glut themselves with uninterrupted sensuality. With those, who alone are able and disposed to promote their reformation, they have no intercourse; and will have none, because they dread and detest the very thought of repentance and amendment. Against ministers of the gospel they are violently prejudiced; and conscious that they are objects of abhorrence to the religious and respectable part of mankind, they, in turn, regard them with distrust and hatred.[70]

As Hewitt's report indicates, the attacks of ATS officials on drunkards were thinly veiled descriptions of lower-class drinking and conceded the tenuous influence of the respectable over the laboring classes. The Massachusetts society's failure to curb drunkenness was fresh in the minds of the reformers, but the American Temperance Society's inability to reach confirmed drunkards was not vital to the abstainers of the 1820s. They believed drunkards were not the chief culprits, because they could not make more drunkards. A confirmed alcoholic who failed to respond to the moral appeals of temperance would soon die of his affliction. To succeed in curbing the drunkenness among the lower orders which Hewitt had described, ATS reformers proposed a much more indirect strategy of reform than that attempted by the MSSI.

The vital part of the ATS strategy was to reach the groups which controlled the supply of liquor in the community: distillers, traders, and moderate drinkers. The vital fact shaping this ATS strategy was the presence of church members in the trade as well as drunkenness among church members. The early opposition to the ATS from within the religious community made clear the extent of church involvement. From the point of view of the ATS leadership, the church sellers and drinkers were legitimating a traffic which had become more and more dangerous in its effects. Obsessed as they were with the potential power of the churches, the ATS leadership was enraged that this power seemed to be deployed on the side of evil, cloaking with respectability a trade which caused earthly misery and brought everlasting damnation. It seemed a contradiction for churchmen to expect revivals and yet use or sell liquor. Both to clear away the obstacles to sound evangelical revivals and to solve the serious social problem which intemperance had become, the temperance reformers of the ATS labeled the respectable traffickers as deviants.

ATS reformers believed that they could never achieve their goal of a temperate, liquor-free society through direct action on the worst examples of intemperance, but, as Justin Edwards explained, the ATS hoped "to induce those that are now temperate to continue so. Then, as all who are *intemperate* will soon be dead, the earth will be rid of an amazing evil."[71] This new era of sobriety through total abstinence was the reformers' millennial vision. The view derived not from the perfectionist expectation that all men would reform but from the belief that a holding operation among abstainers, together with a reform of moderate drinkers, would usher in a total abstinence utopia.

Although the tactics used by the American Temperance Society betrayed at every step the evangelical reformers' powerlessness to shape the morals of the community through personal prestige or political power, the reformers felt that they had devised effective remedies. They feared the power of rum over the appetites of men, but they believed that the practice of total abstinence among the temperate part of the community would achieve a final victory. Hence when they presented a bleak picture of the dangers facing the religious and temperate, they contrasted the scenario with another of a happy land peopled only by total abstainers. The stark alternatives facing the temperate were characteristically put by the Reverend Wilbur Fisk, who portrayed the struggle as an elemental battle between the forces of good and evil. Should the church and its members cease to condone moderate drinking, the temperance cause would go on to a successful conclusion, the moral influence of the church would rise, and the battle for the souls of millions of sinners could then be won. But if the church failed to take a decisive stand against moderate drinking, revivals would be stayed and millions of souls lost. [72] Such a graphic description of the alternatives facing the churches borrowed heavily from the imagery of revivalism. From the revivals and from the successful promotion of the religious benevolent organizations, the American Temperance Society drew hope that the challenges of intemperance could be met. The experience of the religious revitalization was that in America, at least, men could be persuaded to support morality and religion. [73]

The faith of these men in the prospects for successful reform does not square with their historical reputation as anxious conservatives. If this appellation is to be applied to any temperance reformers, it must go to the MSSI members whom the ATS replaced. The new temperance reform movement of the 1820s did not want to stop material progress or to turn the clock back to the eighteenth century. On the contrary, the *Journal of Humanity*, the organ of evangelical temperance advocates in the late 1820s, celebrated "the progress of society," favored "the democratic principle" in government, and applauded scientific and technological innovation. They believed that moral progress ("the progress of ethics") could and would be built on the foundations of the remarkable material progress ("the progress of science") which Americans had achieved. [74] Above all, these evangelical temperance reformers were not theocratic conservatives seeking to stem the democratic tide. Rather they believed that the new republic presented the most favorable conditions in history for a successful moral revolution. American democracy encouraged in ordinary people a degree of enlightenment and virtue, which made them responsive to moral and religious campaigns. "There is nothing which ought to be done," proclaimed the Reverend Lyman

Beecher, "which a free people cannot do."[75] The early nineteenth-century revivals and the flourishing benevolent organizations all seemed to prove the point and suggested that the clergy could do much more than safeguard its social position and moral influence. The clergy could evangelize and reform the nation.[76]

Despite their fervent commitment to total abstinence, the leaders of the American Temperance Society never envisaged the elimination of spirits as an end in itself. Temperance was rather "the foundation of all reform" and a "job that *must be done*, before other benevolent plans can be prosecuted to the best advantage." When "we have absolutely *put an end* to the use of ardent spirits, our work in this cause is finished," the *Journal of Humanity* proclaimed.[77] When intemperance no longer vitiated religion and sapped America's wealth and moral purpose, the nation could turn its resources to the immensely more important task of spreading "the blessings of Christianity and civilization to the remotest and most degraded nations."[78] But before that duty could be fulfilled, temperance reformers faced the difficult task of persuading Americans to accept total abstinence. Temperance had acquired an ideology, an organization, and a determined, forceful set of propagandists at both the national and the local levels. Yet it still had to recruit a mass following among those who were disposed by currents of unrest and social change to support a temperance crusade. That task, ironically, would take the evangelical temperance reformers beyond the confines of evangelical Christianity whose cause they so forcefully defended and advanced.

Notes

1. Joseph Gusfield, "The Study of Social Movements," *International Encyclopedia of the Social Sciences* (New York: Macmillan, 1968), 14:447.
2. Although initially called the American Society for the Promotion of Temperance, this study adopts the more common title used by the temperance reformers themselves.
3. By "temperate," reformers meant all who had "formed no strong at-

tachment to ardent spirit." Thus the temperate included not only abstainers but also moderate drinkers. See Charles P. McIlvaine, "Address to the Young Men of the United States, on Temperance," p. 15, in *The Temperance Volume: Embracing the Seventeen Tracts of the American Tract Society* (New York: American Tract Society, [1834]).

4. Justin Edwards and Leonard Woods to John Tappan, quoted in William Hallock, *"Light and Love," A Sketch of the Life and Labors of the Rev. Justin Edwards, D.D.* (New York: American Tract Society, 1855), pp. 194-95. Many clergy came to the same view at about the same time. See, for example, Lyman Beecher, *Six Sermons on the Nature, Occasions, Signs, Evils and Remedies of Intemperance*, 8th ed. (Boston: Marvin, 1829).

5. Justin Edwards, "Fifth Annual Report of the American Temperance Society," in *Permanent Temperance Documents of the American Temperance Society* (Boston: Seth Bliss, 1835), p. 115.

6. *Second Annual Report of the Maine Temperance Society: Presented by the Corresponding Secretary, February 5, 1834* (Ellsworth, Me.: Robert Grant, 1834), pp. 105, 109-11.

7. Lucius M. Sargent, *Letter on the "State of the Temperance Reform," to the Rev. Caleb Stetson, of Medford, Mass.* (Boston: Damrell, 1836), pp. 24, 56-75; Ellen Larned, *History of Windham County Connecticut* (Worcester: C. Hamilton, 1874-1880), 2:482; *Permanent Temperance Documents*, p. 245.

8. Minutes, 1828, 1829, in *Minutes of the General Assembly of the Presbyterian Church in the United States of America from A.D. 1821 to A.D. 1835 Inclusive* (Philadelphia: Presbyterian Board of Publications, n.d.), pp. 244, 262.

9. Robert Torbet, *A History of the Baptists* (Philadelphia: Judson Press, 1950), pp. 279-80; George W. Paschal, *History of North Carolina Baptists* (Raleigh: General Board, North Carolina State Baptist Convention, 1955), 2:307-08.

10. Henry Wheeler, *Methodism and the Temperance Reformation* (Cincinnati: Walden and Stowe, 1882), p. 110.

11. *Second Annual Report of the Maine Temperance Society*, pp. 109-10.

12. J. H. Spencer, *History of Kentucky Baptists from 1769-1885 . . .* (Cincinnati: Baumes, [c.1885]), p. 706.

13. *Second Annual Report of the Maine Temperance Society*, pp. 29, 96, 102, 105.

14. Wheeler, *Methodism and the Temperance Reformation*, p. 72.

15. *New York Christian Advocate*, 18 September 1829. On Fisk and Bangs, see *National Cyclopedia of American Biography* (New York: J. T. White & Co., 1893-19   ), 3:177, 9:429.

16. Figures are drawn from the *First Annual Report of the American Society for the Promotion of Temperance* (Andover: Flagg and Gould, 1827), pp. 7, 11, 27-28 (hereafter cited as ATS, *First Annual Report*); *The Third Annual Report of the Executive Committee of the American Society for the Promotion of Temperance. Presented Dec. 30, 1829* (Andover: Flagg and Gould, 1830), p. 5; and *Constitution of the Massachusetts Society for the Suppression of Intemperance and . . . Report of the Board of Counsel, Prepared for the Anniversary of the Society, May 28, 1813* (Boston: Samuel T. Armstrong, 1813), pp. 10-12.

17. ATS, *First Annual Report*, pp. 7, 11, 27-28; *Constitution . . . MSSI, . . . 1813*, pp. 10-12.

18. For a suggestive treatment of the Second Great Awakening as a social movement, see Donald G. Mathews, "The Second Great Awakening as an Organizing Process, 1780-1830: An Hypothesis," *American Quarterly* 21 (Spring 1969): 25-43. See also T. Scott Miyakawa, *Protestants and Pioneers: Individualism and Conformity on the American Frontier* (Chicago: University of Chicago Press, 1964), pp. 170-73; Charles R. Keller, *The Second Great Awakening in Connecticut* (New Haven: Yale University Press, 1942), pp. 36-69; and Whitney R. Cross, *The Burned-over District: The Social and Intellectual History of Enthusiastic Religion in Western New York, 1800-1850* (Ithaca, N.Y.: Cornell University Press, 1950), pp. 3-13.

19. Charles C. Cole, *The Social Ideas of the Northern Evangelists, 1826-1860* (New York: Columbia University Press, 1954), p. 13.

20. On the benevolent and missionary organizations, there is an extensive literature. See Clifford S. Griffin, *Their Brothers' Keepers: Moral Stewardship in the United States, 1800-1865* (New Brunswick, N.J.: Rutgers University Press, 1960); Charles Foster, *An Errand of Mercy: The Evangelical United Front, 1790-1837* (Chapel Hill: University of North Carolina Press, 1960); and Cole, *Social Ideas*.

21. William McLoughlin, introduction to Charles G. Finney, *Lectures on Revivals of Religion*, ed. William McLoughlin (Cambridge: Harvard University Press, 1960), pp. xi-xii.

22. Timithy Dwight, 1752-1817, was president of Yale University, 1795-1817. Nathaniel Taylor, 1786-1858, was pastor of the First Church of New Haven, Connecticut, 1812-1822, and professor of systematic theology at Yale Divinity School, 1822-1858; Lyman Beecher, 1775-1863, was Congregational pastor at Litchfield, Connecticut, 1810-1826, at the Hanover Street Church, Boston, 1826-1831, and president of Lane Theological Seminary, 1832-1850.

23. Anne C. Loveland, "Evangelicalism and 'Immediate Emancipation' in American Antislavery Thought," *Journal of Southern History* 32 (May

1966): 176; Frank Hugh Foster, *A Genetic History of New England Theology* (Chicago: University of Chicago Press, 1907), pp. 242, 246-48, 253.

24. The phrase is taken from "Annual Report of the American Board of Commissioners for Foreign Missions, October 6, 1830," reprinted in *Journal of Humanity*, 18 November 1831. Biographical information on the early leaders of the American Temperance Society is contained in *Standard Encyclopedia of the Alcohol Problem* (Westerville, Ohio: American Issue Publishing Company, 1925-1930), and such standard biographical references as *Appleton's Cyclopedia of American Biography* (New York: D. Appleton and Co., 1888-1901). For an interpretation and further evidence supporting this viewpoint, see Lois Banner, "Religious Benevolence as Social Control: A Critique of an Interpretation," *Journal of American History* 60 (June 1973): 23-41.

25. Hallock, *Life of Edwards*, p. 56; William B. Sprague, *Annals of the American Pulpit* (New York: Robert Carter, 1857-1869), 2:582-83.

26. Hallock, *Life of Edwards*, p. 236.

27. John Tappan, quoted in ibid., p. 399. Edwards describes his own missionary activities in *Permanent Temperance Documents*, pp. 31-32.

28. Daniel Dorchester, *The Liquor Problem in All Ages* (New York: Phillips and Hunt, 1884), p. 246.

29. Hallock, *Life of Edwards*, p. 323.

30. Sprague, *Annals of the American Pulpit*, 2:438.

31. The members in 1827 resided in nine states: Maine, Massachusetts, Connecticut, Rhode Island, Vermont, New Hampshire, New York, Pennsylvania, and New Jersey. By 1829 members from Maryland and Virginia had been added. *Second Annual Report of the American Society for the Promotion of Temperance* (Andover: Flagg and Gould, 1829), pp. 27-29.

32. ATS, *First Annual Report*, p. 10.

33. Letter from Rev. Timothy Merritt, *Journal of Humanity*, 22 March 1832; Hallock, *Life of Edwards*, p. 196.

34. *The Address of the Executive Committee of the American Tract Society to the Christian Public: Together with a Brief Account of the Formation of the Society, Its Constitution and Officers* (New York: D. Fanshaw, 1825).

35. *Eleventh Annual Report of the American Tract Society, M,DCCC, XXV* (Andover: Flagg and Gould, 1825), pp. 20-21.

36. The American Tract Society was able to produce tracts increasingly cheaply because of its efficient organization, improved distribution, and the modern presses of its printer, Daniel Fanshaw. See *Fifth Annual Report of the American Tract Society, Instituted at New-York, 1825* (New York: American Tract Society, 1830), pp. 21-25; *Appleton's Cyclopedia of American Biography*, 7:101; *Thirteenth Annual Report of the American Tract*

Society (Boston) (Boston: T. R. Marvin, 1827), pp. 5-6. On changes in the printing industry generally, especially the introduction of steam printing presses in the 1830s, see James L. Crouthamel, "The Newspaper Revolution in New York, 1830-1860," *New York History* 45 (April 1964): 91-113.

37. *Temperance Volume,* passim.

38. Temperance literature exceeded in volume sabbatarian literature, for example. See *Sketch of the Origin and Character of the Principle Series of Tracts of the American Tract Society, 1859 . . .* (New York: American Tract Society, 1859), pp. 31-32. For the heavy incidence of temperance tracts in the 1826-1833 period, see the annual reports of the American Tract Society, particularly "Miscellaneous Instances of the Usefulness of Tracts," in *Sixth Annual Report of the American Tract Society, Instituted at New-York, 1825 . . .* (New York: American Tract Society, 1831), pp. 41-52.

39. *Permanent Temperance Documents,* pp. 15-32; Emil C. Vigilante, "The Temperance Reform in New York State, 1829-1851" (Ph.D. diss., New York University, 1964), p. 5. On the church-directed activities of the agents in New York City, see minutes of the New-York City Temperance Society, 9 May 1829, p. 14, MS vol., NYPL. For the same strategy, with respect to Boston, see *Journal of Humanity,* 29 March 1832.

40. ATS, *First Annual Report,* pp. 26, 28-35.

41. Justin Edwards, *The Temperance Manual* (n.p., 1836), p. 11; Barbara Welter, "The Feminization of American Religion, 1800-1860," in William L. O'Neill, ed., *Insights and Parallels: Problems and Issues of American Social History* (Minneapolis: Burgess Publishing Co., 1973), pp. 305-55; Carroll Smith Rosenberg, "Beauty, the Beast, and the Militant Woman: A Case Study in Sex Roles and Social Stress in Jacksonian America," *American Quarterly* 23 (October 1971): 562-84.

42. See, for example, minutes and proceedings, Rose Temperance Society, NYPL; ATS, *Second Annual Report,* pp. 11-13; *Temperance Herald* (Concord, N.H.), no. 9 (September 1834); *Journal of Humanity,* 17 February 1831.

43. *Seventh Annual Report of the American Society for the Promotion of Temperance* (Boston: Seth Bliss, 1834), pp. 98-101.

44. Caleb Wall, *Reminiscences of Worcester from the Earliest Period, Historical and Genealogical, with Notices of Early Settlers and Prominent Citizens* (Worcester: Tyler and Seagrove, 1877), p. 159.

45. See, for example, Levi Loring, *The Origins, Evils, and Remedy of Intemperance: An Address Delivered in Buxton, April 10, 1828* (Portland, Me.: Shirley and Hyde, 1828), pp. 1-14.

46. *Permanent Temperance Documents,* pp. 30, 245; Hallock, *Life of Edwards,* p. 328; John Marsh, *A Half-Century Tribute to the Cause of Tem-*

perance (New York: National Temperance Society Publishing House, 1851), p. 17.

47. John Marsh, "Putnam and the Wolf," pp. 7, 13, in *Temperance Volume*. In this tale, Marsh drew an analogy between an old local story from Pomfret, Connecticut, about the heroic exploits of a boy against a marauding wolf, and the modern problem of raising the alarm against and carrying the fight to a new marauding enemy, strong drink. See also Beecher, *Six Sermons*, pp. 13, 16.

48. On the asylum reformers, see David Rothman, *The Discovery of the Asylum: Social Order and Disorder in the New Republic* (Boston: Little, Brown, 1971).

49. John Marsh, *Temperance Recollections* (New York: Charles Scribner, 1866), p. 27.

50. *Journal of Humanity*, 2 December 1829, 3 November 1831.

51. Marsh, "Putnam and the Wolf," p. 14; Charles Stone, *Rev. Mr. Stone's Address before the Young Men's Temperance Society, of New Haven, Connecticut* (New Haven: S. Babcock, 1831), pp. 14-15.

52. Quoted in Hallock, *Life of Edwards*, p. 64.

53. McIlvaine, "Address to the Young Men of the United States," p. 10.

54. Ibid.; Edwards, "National Circular Addressed to the Head of Each Family in the United States," p. 3, *Temperance Volume*.

55. ATS, *First Annual Report*, p. 24.

56. Marsh, "Putnam and the Wolf," p. 14.

57. ATS, *First Annual Report*, p. 24; Justin Edwards, "On the Immorality of the Traffic in Ardent Spirit," appendix to "Sixth Annual Report of the American Temperance Society," *Permanent Temperance Documents*, pp. 198-200.

58. Justin Edwards to E. C. Delavan, 10 December 1832, Gratz Autograph Collection, Churchmen and Clergymen, HSP; statement by Justin Edwards, *Permanent Temperance Documents*, p. 113; Albert Barnes, *The Immorality of the Traffic in Ardent Spirits: A Discourse Delivered in the First Presbyterian Church in Philadelphia, April 13, 1834* (Philadelphia: George, Latimer, 1834), p. 5.

59. *Permanent Temperance Documents*, p. 113; Edward Hitchcock, "Argument against the Manufacture of Ardent Spirits," pp. 12, 21, in *Temperance Volume*.

60. *Minutes of the General Assembly of the Presbyterian Church*, p. 298. For the actions of the Congregational Associations, see *Permanent Temperance Documents*, p. 222.

61. "A Statement Made by the Corresponding Secretary of the American Temperance Society . . . ," *Journal of Humanity*, 29 March 1832.

62. *Permanent Temperance Documents*, pp. 132, 219.

63. ATS, *First Annual Report*, p. 22.

64. Quote from "Fashion," by "Luther," in *Boston Recorder and Telegraph*, 12 January 1827; Loring, *Origins, Evils, and Remedy of Intemperance*, p. 14; Lyman Beecher, *Six Sermons*, pp. 62-63; *Journal of Humanity*, 27 January 1831; ATS, *First Annual Report*, p. 22.

65. Edwards, "National Circular," p. 14; Stone, *Address Before the Young Men's Temperance Society*, p. 19.

66. See Nathaniel Emmons, *A Collection of Sermons, Which Have Been Preached on Various Subjects, and Published at Various Times* (Boston: S. T. Armstrong, 1813), esp. sermon 18, "Delivered on the Day of the Annual Fast, in Massachusetts, April 7, 1803."

67. Editorial, *Journal of Humanity*, 12 January 1832; "The Future Destinies of America, as Affected by the Doings of the Present Generation," *Journal of Humanity*, 18 November 1831; Luke Drury, *Address before the Bristol Association for the Promotion of Temperance, March 23, 1832* (Providence, R.I.: Weeden and Knowles, 1832), p. 26; and "Rum-selling in the Church," *Boston Recorder and Telegraph*, 19 December 1832. The proliferation of voluntary organizations of all types was noted by contemporary observers, especially Alexis de Tocqueville, *Democracy in America*, ed. J. P. Mayer (New York: Harper and Row, 1966), pp. 485-96.

68. *Proceedings of the First Ten Years of the America Tract Society, Instituted at Boston, 1814* (Andover: Flagg and Gould, 1824), pp. 89-91.

69. ATS, *First Annual Report*, pp. 18-19; Francis Gillett, *An Address, Delivered at Windsor (Wintonbury) Con., February 10th, 1830, before the Annual Meeting of the Temperance Society* (Hartford, CT: Augustus Bolles, 1830), p. 14.

70. ATS, *First Annual Report*, pp. 18-19.

71. Hallock, *Life of Edwards*, p. 195; Beecher, *Six Sermons*, pp. 62-83, 84-85; *Permanent Temperance Documents*, pp. 55-56.

72. "Dr. Fisk's Address to the Members of the Methodist Episcopal Church on the Subject of Temperance," *Journal of Humanity*, 31 May 1832; "The Churches of Connecticut Will All Soon Become Temperance Societies," *Journal of Humanity*, 4 November 1829; Cyrus Mann, "Report to the Annual Meeting of the Worcester North District Temperance Association," *Journal of Humanity*, 3 November 1831.

73. Editorial, *Journal of Humanity*, 8 July 1830.

74. Ibid., 24 June 1830, 24 November, 29 December 1831; Lois Banner, "Presbyterianism and Voluntarism in the Early Republic," *Journal of Presbyterian History* 50 (Fall 1972): 187-205; Perry Miller, *The Life of the Mind in America, from the Revolution to the Civil War* (New York: Harcourt, Brace and World, 1965), pp. 40-43.

75. Cf. Griffin, *Their Brothers' Keepers*, passim; Joseph Gusfield, *Sym-*

bolic *Crusade: Status Politics and the American Temperance Movement* (Urbana: University of Illinois Press, 1963), pp. 41-42; *Journal of Humanity*, 30 June 1831; Beecher, *Six Sermons*, p. 85.

76. *Journal of Humanity*, 14 July 1831; E. C. Delavan to Theodore Sedgwick, 14 September 1832, Sedgwick Papers, MHS; Banner, "Religious Benevolence as Social Control," pp. 23-41.

77. Editorial, *Journal of Humanity*, 10 March 1831.

78. Editorial, ibid., 14 July 1831.

4

THE SOURCES OF TEMPERANCE
SUPPORT IN THE 1830s

The popular response to the message of the American Temperance Society astonished its leaders. When the society first embarked on its program of reform, it expected that several years of patient effort would be needed before the idea of abstinence could generate a favorable popular response. But many local communities had begun to form auxiliaries to the society without waiting for approval or direction from the national executive or its agents.[1] Within five years of the inception of its program of reform, the American Temperance Society could point to 2,200 temperance societies in the United States, embracing 170,000 members. By 1833, there were more than 6,000 societies and a million members pledged to total abstinence from the use of spirits. Nineteen state societies had been formed, one for each state except Alabama, Louisiana, Illinois, and Missouri.[2]

The astounding growth of the American Temperance Society and its auxiliaries owed much to the support of evangelical religion. The society's agents visited Presbyterian, Baptist, Congregationalist, and Methodist churches and encouraged the formation of temperance societies within the individual congregations. General conferences of the Presbyterian and Methodist churches and of the Congregational associations all passed resolutions that urged members to abstain from the use of spirits.[3]

Yet temperance and evangelical commitment by no means coincided, since some evangelicals remained hostile to the reform, and at the same time, the temperance message spread far beyond its original evangelical constituency. As early as 1827, Nathaniel Hewitt, the first agent of the American Temperance Society, had freely admitted that support for temperance was not confined to those of evangelical religious persuasion. He disclosed that the founders of the ATS had been "prepared to toil on in our work for years, with the expectation of advancing the cause among those good men only, who, in their wisdom as well as in their benevolence, bear a likeness to Him, who sees the end from the beginning." But Hewitt quickly discovered that "the public generally will not merely endure the measures which we recommend, but is importunately calling for their speedy execution."[4] Unitarians, Universalists, Quakers, and "many distinguished persons who make no religious profession" took the pledge and joined the auxiliaries of the American Temperance Society.[5]

Increasingly in the 1830s, the temperance crusade began to draw its most prominent and energetic leaders from a broader social and geographic base to include those from outside the religious benevolent empires and from outside the New England evangelical groups which gave the crusade its initial impetus. Symbolic of these changes was the emergence of Edward C. Delavan, the secretary of the New York State Temperance Society, as a major figure in temperance agitation. Though Delavan was deeply imbued with the spirit of religious perfectionism, his background was not in the religious benevolent enterprises, and his interest in temperance reform stemmed not from the contribution which sobriety could make to the furtherance of missionary, tract, and revivalistic endeavors but from the intrinsic importance of temperance as a moral and social question. Not a clergyman or even a man with orthodox evangelical convictions—his religious views were in fact vague and eclectic—Delavan was rather a self-made businessman who had accumulated a fortune in the hardware trade in the 1820s and then retired on his investments at the early age of thirty-four to devote himself to what he called the improvement of mankind.

Why Delavan chose temperance as the object of his benevolence remains obscure, but because he had once been a wine merchant, it seems likely that he felt remorse over lives lost for his monetary gain.

To the temperance movement he brought a large ambition and a restless energy, the very qualities which had made him successful in business. For thirty years he was to finance temperance crusades, using his wealth to promote the radical causes of teetotalism and prohibition.[6] Whether this self-made man and self-righteous philanthropist was typical of temperance reformers can only be ascertained from the detailed analysis of the sources of temperance support which follows. His example, however, suggests that we must look at a wider variety of factors than evangelical religion in determining temperance support.

So too does the strong support for temperance within the medical profession; from the 1820s onward, the temperance movement enjoyed the favorable testimony of prestigious sections of the medical profession, and the American Temperance Society quickly discovered that the medical evidence was more compelling for the public than the spiritual arguments the society regarded more pertinent. In 1832, seventy-five of Boston's eighty doctors signed a declaration that *"men in health are NEVER benefitted by the use of ardent spirits"* and that "on the contrary, the use of them is a frequent cause of *disease* and *death,* and often renders such diseases as arise from other causes more difficult of cure, and more fatal in their termination."[7] Similar declarations were solicited from the doctors of the other major American cities, and in addition, doctors served in important positions in temperance organizations. In fact they constituted the largest single group on the executive of the Pennsylvania Society for Discouraging the Use of Ardent Spirits.[8]

Temperance offered a way to improve the professional, ethical, and medical standards of physicians. The drive to dissociate the medical profession from the use of ardent spirits came from the most prestigious segments of the profession—professors of medicine, eminent surgeons, college-educated doctors, and the professional associations which were trying to upgrade the standards of the medical profession.[9] Just as the medical societies attempted to discourage patent medicines and eliminate quacks during the Jacksonian era, so too did the societies seek to enhance the reputation of the physician by eliminating the use of ardent spirits as a medicine and as a beverage.[10] The Medical Society of the Western District of New Hampshire declared "the use of spirituous drinks incompatible with the duties which a physician owes to his patients, to his professional improvement, and to his health."[11] Dr. Reuben Mussey, professor of anatomy at Dartmouth and perhaps the most celebrated medical advocate of total abstinence, warned the medical profession that "ardent spirit—already under sentence of public condemnation, and with the prospect of undergoing an entire exclusion from the social circle, and the domestic fire-side—still lingers in the sick chamber." It was the duty of physicians to take the lead in eradicating ardent spirits from the community rather than to react to the exertions of the clergy. Mussey believed intemperance began through the medical use, and there it must finally be rooted out.[12]

Not all doctors agreed with Mussey that spirits had no useful place as a medicine, but many did believe that drinking hard liquor predisposed healthy people to ailments and deadly diseases. Under the influence of pioneer surgeon Benjamin Rush, doctors at Philadelphia's Pennsylvania Hospital asserted that intemperance was itself a physical disease. Their discovery was based on little objective research, but it received more and more publicity as the ATS recruited physicians and disseminated medical propaganda against the use of spirits because "the public wants the *medical reasons*" for abstaining.[13] The most effective evidence against the use of spirits came, in the opinion of many contemporary temperance men, from a Washington surgeon, Thomas Sewall. In 1842 Sewall published the results of his autopsies on drunkards who expired in the state of delirium tremens. His full-color impressions of the effects of spirits on the drunkards' bodies were extensively circulated by temperance societies as a shock tactic. The aim was to impress upon the indifferent the danger to their bodies, in the hope that such disclosure would ultimately lead the intemperate to see the greater danger to their souls.[14]

Yet if all these examples point beyond evangelicalism to the need for a more comprehensive analysis of the support for the temperance movement in its formative decades, such an inquiry cannot be undertaken until one critical difficulty is confronted: locating an issue which illuminates the divisions in American society over the temperance question. Both opponents and supporters of temperance present obstacles to this inquiry. The American Temperance Society and its supporters sought to convey the impression that by the 1830s, only the most vicious and depraved individuals resisted their entreaties. The reports of the ATS give the impression that the pro-liquor and anti-temperance forces were in constant retreat, pushed back in defeat after inglorious defeat. On the other hand, the opponents of temperance societies were loath to organize while the temperance movement remained committed to moral suasion. Indeed it was not uncommon for tavern keepers and retailers to profess support for temperance, though what remained uncertain was the meaning of *temperance*.15

The meaning of *temperance* is a still more complex question because the temperance societies of the early 1830s contained both the deeply committed and casual converts. The legislative temperance societies provide a case in point. ATS agents promoted societies within the state legislatures and in the U.S. Congress, yet the pledges solicited from prominent politicians and other public figures in these societies did not involve more than a nominal commitment to temperance reform, and in fact, the legislative temperance societies themselves had no more than a nominal existence.16 The temperance movement of the early 1830s had elicited the support of both casual converts and the deeply committed. Soon an issue would arise to divide them and to bring out into the open much of the latent opposition to temperance societies in the United States.

In the 1830s, the temperance societies of New England tried to persuade local licensing authorities to refuse licenses for the sale of liquor. Through votes of town meetings, temperance reformers sought to demonstrate community opposition to liquor licensing. These votes necessarily engendered conflict over the temperance issue because they forced men to decide whether they wished their town to proscribe the sale of liquor. In addition, such decisions were controversial because they involved a judgment on the personal conduct of men who sold or drank liquor. By the vote at town meetings, towns declared that the sale of liquor ought to be illegal and that those who sold liquor ought to be regarded as criminals. The temperance societies identified their issue with support for the no-license position and heaped scorn on those who claimed to be temperance advocates but failed to support the temperance societies on the crucial issue of no-license.

The no-license campaigns provide a means of identifying those most deeply committed to the goals of the temperance societies in the

1830s. Such an approach requires close attention to a particular case study because the no-license campaign was fought exclusively at the local level, in such Massachusetts communities as Dorchester, Roxbury, Worcester, Brighton, and Salem. The campaign in Worcester, Massachusetts, produced a confrontation between pro-liquor and anti-license forces and illustrates the division within many local communities over the no-license campaign. [17]

Temperance and Economic Change in Worcester

In the 1830s, Worcester was an average northern community. It lacked the urban development of Boston or New York and shared its ethnic homogeneity with most other American towns in the 1830s. Furthermore, like much of the rest of the United States in the 1830s, Worcester was undergoing fundamental social and economic change. Manufacturing establishments were springing up where none previously existed, commercial agriculture was developing, and canals and railroads were linking the town with the coastal markets of Boston, Philadelphia, and New York. Under the impetus of what George Rogers Taylor called the "transportation revolution," the town grew rapidly in size and industrial capacity. After becoming the largest town in the county by 1820, Worcester's population grew by 40 percent in the following decade. Although the town had virtually no manufactures in 1810, by 1840, employment was 47 percent manufacturing and by 1865, 72 percent. [18]

The first temperance society in Worcester was restricted entirely to the communicants of the orthodox First Congregational Church and was founded in 1830. When it soon became apparent that concern over intemperance touched many who were not of evangelical persuasion, a town society was formed in May 1831. In 1832 the society claimed almost half the adult population of Worcester among its subscribers. [19] That the Worcester community accepted these efforts at voluntary reform with no overt dissent is perhaps unremarkable since the town was ethnically and culturally quite homogeneous. The few foreigners in the area were Irish transients brought to the town to work on construction of the Boston and Worcester Railroad. [20] Yet despite the apparent homogeneity of Worcester in the 1830s, there were in fact bitter divisions over the temperance question just beneath the surface. The period between 1835 and 1838 saw Worcester's permanent and respectable native-born residents divide bitterly over the prohibition issue and over support for the Worcester Temperance Society.

The conflict began at the town's annual meeting in 1834. The temperance society was strong enough to push through a resolution that Worcester's selectmen not approve any licenses for the retailing of spirits by the bottle. This no-license vote made the sale of bottled spirits illegal because under Massachusetts law all sales of liquor had to be licensed. [21] Licensing decisions were actually taken by the county commissioners, but these officials usually accepted the recommendations of the town selectmen with respect to retail licenses, as the commissioners did in this case. [22] Although there was an undercurrent of discontent over the decision, no organized opposition emerged. Taverns remained licensed to serve the thirsty, and retail sales continued covertly. [23] But the following year the temperance forces determined to extend the no-license vote to include all sales of liquor, both by retail and by the glass. Now the opposition to the no-license drive came into the open.

"The town is now more full of excitement than has been known since 1812. There is a strong disposition to bring temperance into politics." So wrote Christopher Baldwin, librarian of the American Antiquarian Society, in his diary on April 6, 1835. The cause of the excitement which Baldwin saw about him was the vote at a town meeting on March 23, 1835, requesting the selectmen to refuse all applications for tavern and retail liquor licenses. [24] The selectmen yielded and refused to recommend any license applications to the county commissioners. When the existing licenses expired on April 1, the tavern keepers immediately closed their houses, arguing that they could not make a living on the charges for accommodations alone and that it would be better to go out of business entirely than to run at a loss. [25]

The no-license decision brought to the surface the divisions in the town over the temperance issue. According to Christopher Baldwin, passions flared on both sides of the dispute. Temperance partisans complained that "in more than one instance the friends of temperance were not only menaced with violence, but were assaulted on the streets."[26] Actually little violence occurred apart from a few fist-fights, but the partisans on each side spared no effort to assail their opponents verbally. The pro-license forces held a protest meeting, said to be the largest unofficial gathering in the town's history, at which the selectmen were urged to ignore the earlier town meeting and approve licenses. Just two days later, the selectmen reversed their position and issued certificates of approbation to six innhold-ers.[27]

Both pro-license and antilicense forces gathered strength for an adjourned town meeting on April 14, where the town voted by 452 to 376 to reverse its earlier decision and approved retail and tavern licenses.[28] The pro-license forces had reasserted a dominance which would persist until 1841. The town continued to grant liquor li-censes, and the pro-license forces acted in concert to keep a majority of the board of selectmen and to elect pro-license candidates to the state legislature. When the prohibitionists gained the upper hand in the early 1840s, the no-license conflict abated, but the 1830s were years of clear and illuminating conflict over the temperance issue in Worcester.

The Worcester newspapers in the 1830s published the names of the leading participants who spoke at public meetings on either side of the controversy. These lists provided an initial sample of eleven pro-hibition supporters and thirteen opponents, a restricted group of ar-ticulate leaders. But the *Massachusetts Spy* also published a list of ward committeemen for the no-license movement.[29] Although the list was not comprehensive, it did include a sampling of rank-and-file support. Altogether the lists of supporters of prohibition pro-vided sixty names.

Unfortunately no comparable list of opponents of prohibition was published in 1835, but there was a similar list of men who attended a liberal or pro-license convention in Worcester to protest the fifteen-gallon law of 1838, which prohibited the sale of spirits in quantities of less than fifteen gallons.[30] By preventing the sale of hard liquor in small quantities, the legislators hoped to eliminate the dramshops where much intemperate drinking occurred. Liquor and antiliquor forces in Massachusetts polarized sharply in their attitudes toward this law. Temperance societies made loyalty to the fifteen-gallon law a test of temperance sentiment, while opponents of the law held conventions to nominate for election to the state legislature men pledged to repeal the law. The Worcester liberal convention was one of many such conventions held in the fall of 1838. In Worcester, the principal opponents of no-license in 1835 also opposed the fifteen-gallon law. On the other hand, there was virtually no overlap between the supporters of no-license in 1835 and the opponents of prohibition in 1838. Moreover the arguments against prohibition in 1838 closely followed those against no-license in 1835.[31] All the evidence suggests that the list of opponents of prohibition in 1838 provided a control group to contrast with the supporters of no-license in 1835.

The temperance partisans in Worcester described their pro-license opponents as men of wealth, high status, and political prestige. Speakers at the no-license rally dwelled on the fact that "two of the highest dignitaries of our County" opposed their view. The speakers were referring to the county's district attorney, Pliny Merrick, and Calvin Willard, the county sheriff. In contrast, Worcester's temperance advocates pictured themselves as "the body of the people," thus implying a popular groundswell of support for no-license.[32]

How true was this picture? The first and most obvious point is that taverners and retailers were firmly opposed to the no-license position. Contemporaries noted this fact, and temperance propagandists sometimes asserted that the anti-prohibitionist group was little more than a shabby band of liquor sellers, hoteliers, and distillers. In Worcester, the panel of pro-license men shows how easy it was for temperance propagandists to develop this view. There were at least thirteen taverners, hoteliers and other retailers on the list, comprising 17 percent of the total.[33]

More important was the strong support for licenses from the merchant community generally. There were twenty-nine merchants among pro-license supporters. Some had definite connections with the liquor traffic, like Daniel Heywood and George Trumbull, who owned a distillery and a brewery, respectively. Others found their interests closely tied to the tavern business. Alvan Allen and George Jones ran stagecoaches and livery stables, callings closely tied to the prosperity of the taverns.[34] But the fact remains that all kinds of commercial men flocked to the pro-license ranks, while few were found among the supporters of prohibition. Over half of the pro-license people were in commerce (including liquor sellers). In contrast, merchants accounted for only one-tenth of the prohibitionist strength. The involvement of commercial people in the pro-license group far exceeded their numerical importance in the population (9.5 percent).[35] One reason for this preponderance of men of commerce was that merchants identified the prosperity of the town with the retail trade. They believed that the antiliquor drive would depress business generally.[36]

While people allied to the mercantile economy proved hostile to the no-license phase of the temperance movement, manufacturers and mechanics rallied to the temperance cause. In the sample of no-license supporters in 1835, manufacturers and skilled tradesmen accounted for over 40 percent of the total. Among the anti-prohibitionists, only 6 percent were involved in the town's manufacturing sector. Since manufacturing accounted for 47 percent of employment in Worcester, the pro-license group was wholly unrepresentative of the burgeoning industrial sector of the town's economy. Admittedly manufacturing was slightly underrepresented in the prohibition sample, but this arose from the predominance of a handful of articulate professional people among the speakers at temperance meetings. In the ward committees of the prohibition supporters in 1835, which more accurately represented the rank and file, manufacturers and skilled tradesmen comprised half the total membership.

It is impossible to be precise about the relative importance of employers, the self-employed, and employees in this manufacturing group because the evidence is fragmentary and because the divisions between the manufacturer and the skilled worker were slight in the Worcester of the 1830s. Nor can we be certain about the size of the operations which contemporaries called manufactories. Many were probably quite small, since early industrialization in Worcester was based on small shops, as in many other industrial centers in the 1830s. As David Montgomery points out, the average factory unit in the United States as late as 1869 employed fewer than nine workers.[37] Yet despite the often vague contemporary distinctions between manufacturers and skilled tradesmen and the uncertain employment status of some of the Worcester prohibitionists, the available evidence points to several conclusions: of the twenty-six names on the no-license list engaged in manufacturing, at least two-thirds were employers of labor, some had more than twenty-five employees in the 1830s, and more than half used some form of machinery in their shops and factories.

Though the employers of labor in the manufacturing sector were clearly on the side of the no-license campaign, the position of employees is much less certain, since there is little direct information on which to base conclusions. Some employees of no-license manufacturers may have supported the campaign of 1835, but they were certainly not prominent in the leadership or ward committees of the no-license campaign, and in fact only one of the twenty-six engaged in manufacturing—Joshua Freemen—has been positively identified as an employee (and he was a factory foreman for one of Worcester's leading pro-temperance manufacturers, Ichabod Washburn).[38] The absence of significant numbers of employees is of course, not conclusive evidence that they failed to support no-license, since we are clearly dealing with the elite of local prohibitionists in this case study. Yet together with the documentation on the sources of temperance support available within the reports of the Worcester Temperance Society, the evidence makes clear that the impetus toward prohibition came not from employees but from employers.

The campaign of Worcester employers for no-license had its origins in the economic interests and experiences of manufacturers and stemmed from changing attitudes toward work and leisure which employers were promoting. The Worcester Temperance Society reported in 1831 that many of the "farmers, mechanics, and the manufacturers" of the town had dispensed with the use of ardent spirits personally and as payment for labor. Those who had "tried the experiment uniformly assert, that their workmen are not only more constant in their attention to their business, but that they can actually perform more labor of any kind than when under the influence of any artificial stimulus."[39] The receptivity of manufacturers to the temperance cause was further underlined by the formation of temperance societies in the Blackstone Valley just south of Worcester. Here lay the mill villages which had sprung up along the banks of the Blackstone in the 1820s. When Daniel Frost, agent of the Massachusetts Temperance Society, visited the area in 1834 to recruit support for local temperance societies, he found a response exceeded nowhere in the commonwealth. "It is gratifying," commented Worcester's pro-temperance paper, the *Spy*, "to learn that the agents and proprietors of the manufacturing establishments in these, and most similar villages, have taken an active interest in the promotion of the cause, and have aided very materially the labors of Mr. Frost."[40]

Such impressionistic evidence suggests that the manufacturers were at least as important to the temperance cause as the figures for Worcester suggest. Moreover the merchants and professionals who were found among the prohibitionists had strong links with the industrial economy. For example, Oliver Harrington was a merchant in the early 1830s, but in 1835 he became master of the new Worcester railroad depot. Subsequent city directories list him as a railroad agent. Charles Hersey, another merchant prohibitionist, sold industrial real estate. Nathan Heard was a more traditional merchant, but he held canal shares and had business ties with the manufacturers Ichabod Washburn and Clement O. Read.[41] In contrast, the anti-prohibitionist merchants were grocers, hoteliers, and importers. Thus the conflict over liquor licenses was not simply merchants against manufacturers but between people who looked to the emerging industrial society and those who found their allegiance in the mercantile economy. Nor must it be assumed that the conflict was predominantly an economic one in the narrow sense. The battle was not just merchant capital versus industrial capital. The two sides had differing styles of behavior and different attitudes toward social change and the role of law in society.

The clash of values was illustrated by the strong preference of most lawyers—indeed of all people connected with the legal system—for the pro-license camp. Lawyers and court officials accounted for 20 percent of the opponents of prohibition, compared to just 6 percent of the supporters of prohibition and only 3 percent for the work force of Worcester as a whole.[42] Many of Worcester's lawyers opposed the end of licensing because they believed prohibition would upset the orderly process of justice and create more social and legal problems than it would solve. Liquor selling would continue, but it would not be under the constraints imposed by the licensing system. Instead of the respectable citizens licensed under the Massachusetts liquor laws, the trade would be continued clandestinely by the most reprehensible characters. As the Worcester pro-license meeting held in October 1838 resolved: "Instead then of the peace and good order which a well regulated system of licensed houses has a tendency to produce, there will in the end be brought in . . . disorders and irregularities which tend to bring all law into contempt, and to weaken the power of the government to secure the peace and tranquility of the community."[43] While pro-license supporters venerated the law as the foundation of social order, temperance partisans urged that the law be used to change social customs "to suit the public good."[44] Though lawyers were not entirely absent from the prohibition movement in Worcester, those in the no-license camp tended to be either nonpracticing, like the wealthy evangelical, Alfred Dwight Foster, or men who had links with the town's industrial sector, like Charles G. Washburn, a brother and business partner of the wire manufacturer, Ichabod Washburn.[45]

The cleavage over the use of law was part of a broader dispute about the pace and extent of social change. The sensitivity of the pro-license men to the legal implications of prohibition reflected a broader concern for the preservation of social harmony. Citizens opposed to the no-license policy in 1835 "regretted that the public repose should be disturbed by the agitation of a subject which ought to be considered and disposed in a dispassionate manner." They wished to "restore quiet and tranquility in place of that regretted excitement and agitation" which prevailed in the community because of the "mingling" of temperance and politics.[46]

The concern with preserving public order went to the center of the anti-prohibitionist agitation in the 1830s. Among the pro-license group were many socially prominent and respectable people who went along with the temperance society at first because they approved of the drive to end drunkenness. Several of their number actually participated in the activities of the temperance society. They opposed intemperance as a threat to social stability at a time when the industrial growth of Worcester was creating much social disorder of which the drunken behavior of the Irish working on the railroad in 1834 was a conspicuous example.[47] But the material interests and style of behavior of anti-prohibitionists inclined them toward gradual change in social customs and moderate reform rather than the sweeping plans of the no-license men.[48] They feared extreme changes in social customs and the use of law to force change.

Pro-license men saw in the direction of temperance reform an anti-traditionalism that threatened their own social rank, which was de-

rived from traditional customs and institutions. The anti-prohibitionists were far more concerned with status than were their
opponents. They were people who observed the courtesies of rank
and participated in traditional ceremonial activities. At least eighteen of the seventy-eight pro-license men commonly assumed
titles—general, colonel, captain, or esquire—compared with only
two of the sixty prohibitionists. Anti-prohibitionists were much
more likely to serve in the militia and to take the ceremonial side of
such activities seriously. Since colonial times, militia musters had
been occasions for excessive drinking, and there is little doubt that
Worcester's militia men resented temperance efforts to deprive them
of established customs and festivities.[49] But in addition, the militia
men who were prominent in the campaign against the temperance
societies between 1835 and 1838 were those of high rank and prestige
within the militia. Samuel Ward was one of the leaders of the pro-
license group in 1835. He "took great pleasure in military affairs and
was ambitious to excel and become a good disciplinarian; and he
succeeded remarkably well. He was promoted from one position to
another, till he was finally elected Colonel of the Sixth Regiment."[50]
This description could have been applied to many of the pro-license
men but few of the prohibitionists. Holding high rank in the militia
did not necessarily mean high social status, but the Worcester pro-
license men usually combined militia ranking with social respectability. Ward was "a gentlemen in his manners" who had "married into
one of the oldest and most respectable families of Worcester."[51]

The concern with ceremony and the traditional rankings of New
England society extended beyond the militia, embracing a whole
style of behavior which temperance reformers did not share. Among
the merchants and lawyers of the pro-license group were many described as dignified or gentlemanly. There was Calvin Willard, the
high sheriff, "a gentleman of dignified and precise manners," who,
when he greeted friends and acquaintances, "was careful to give
them any official title which belonged to them."[52] Another was Silas
Brooks, the town crier, and a "most estimable and upright citizen."
Benjamin F. Thomas, who took part in the prohibitionist agitation,
later described Brooks: "Crier Brooks seemed to the generation
before us a necessary part of our judicial institutions. The idea that a
court could be opened without Crier Brooks, or a jury empanelled

without the aid of his arithmetic, would have been to them prepos-
terous."[53]

The prohibitionists did not share the same respect for tradition
and ceremony.[54] The manufacturers and mechanics who endorsed
prohibition were men who had succeeded, or who hoped to succeed,
by breaking new ground in the growing industrial sector of Worcester's economy. The manufacturers among the no-license sample had
a reputation for innovation and entrepreneurial skill, as the career of
Ichabod Washburn amply illustrated. Washburn was born in Kings-
ton, Massachusetts, the son of a sea captain. After an apprenticeship
as a blacksmith, Washburn came to Worcester in 1819 where he set
up a business as a manufacturer of machinery for the textile industry. In 1822, Washburn took as a partner Benjamin Goddard, Jr.,
another temperance disciple, and they "soon employed thirty men,"
for the demand for machinery was increasing. Washburn was
constantly experimenting with new techniques and new products to
meet the expanding needs of Worcester's economy. He and Goddard
"made the first condenser and long-roll spinning jack ever made in
Worcester County and among the first in the country."[55] In the
1830s Washburn turned to wire manufacturing, which became the
basis of his fortune; although he had to borrow money to get his
start in business, Washburn left $424,000 in his estate when he died
in 1868. The Washburn and Moen Manufacturing Company, which
he founded, was eventually absorbed into the United States Steel
empire at the turn of the century. The title of Washburn's posthu-
mously published autobiography gives some insight into his social
philosophy: *Autobiography and Memorials of Ichabod Washburn,
Showing How a Great Business Was Developed and Large Wealth
Acquired for the Uses of Benevolence.* As the editor of Washburn's
autobiography noted, the Worcester industrialist "thought that the
mechanics and artisans of our American cities in successive ranks,
beginning at the bench and the forge with nothing but their labor, as
he had done, and making it a rule like himself not to spend except to
produce, should be all along lifting themselves by industry, economy, and temperance, out of the condition of labor alone into the position of capital also."[56]

Few of the Worcester temperance manufacturers and mechanics
achieved the upward mobility that Washburn did, but many aspired

to improvement. They demonstrated a capacity for innovation, a commitment to the prosperity of the town, and a devotion to voluntary organizations designed to further their material and moral improvement. More readily than their opponents, the prohibitionists joined the lyceums, mechanics institutes, and public libraries which proliferated in Jacksonian America. Of the sixteen founders of the Mechanics' Institute in Worcester, nine were supporters of prohibition in the 1830s and only two were opponents.[57] Among the officeholders of the Worcester Lyceum in the 1830s were fifteen supporters of prohibition and only two opponents.[58] The notion of improvement was as central to the lyceum and the mechanics institute as it was to the temperance society. It is little wonder that the improvement minded should patronize both.

If manufacturers favored prohibition by an overwhelming margin, farmers split over the issue, with the most enterprising and innovative farmers supporting prohibition. Farmers accounted for 32 percent of the no-license supporters in Worcester and 17 percent of the opponents of prohibition. There was no significant difference between the median landholdings of prohibitionist and of anti-prohibitionist farmers.[59] The most striking division was neither wealth nor land. Rather the prohibitionist farmers were impressive for their vigor in adopting new methods of cultivation and breeding. Of nineteen farmers in the no-license group, at least seventeen were substantial commercial farmers. At least seven of the group showed evidence of experimenting with scientific practices, and several of the farmers were characterized in biographical or contemporary references as "resourceful," "practical," or "enterprising."[60] The information from which to draw such conclusions is fragmentary, but a few examples suggest the outlook of the temperance farmers of Worcester. Darius Rice was "an active, enterprising, prosperous farmer," who "possessed an inventive genius and constructed some of the earliest implements for the saving of both time and labor in cultivating the farm."[61] Rice also served on the first Common Council of the City of Worcester after incorporation in 1848, and he promoted the development of the first water supply by gravitation in the town. Rice clearly shared in Worcester's industrial growth, both as a promoter and as one of the first farmers in the county to tailor his production specifically to the growing Worcester commercial market.

The farmers in the prohibitionist group were acquisitive in spirit. They brought land as much as they improved their acreage. There was the case of Jonathan White, who came from New Hampshire penniless in 1822. Hired as a farm laborer, he eventually married the farmer's widow and steadily acquired property in the 1820s and 1830s until he became one of the largest and most prosperous farmers in the town.[62]

Though such examples point to a connection between entrepreneurial farming and temperance activity, the association would be tenuous indeed if it rested on this fragmentary evidence alone. Fortunately there is much additional evidence to support the link between temperance and commercial farming in the agricultural press and in the proceedings and other publications of agricultural improvement societies of New England. In a speech delivered before the Anniversary Cattle Show and Exhibition of Manufactures of the Worcester Agricultural Society, Emory Washburn, a prominent town booster, advised farmers to exploit the markets created by the factories in New England. In addition to scientific farming, the men on the land who wished to benefit from "the cheerful hum of industry" which was "rising around us" must "shrink from the cup" of intemperance, for "health and industry" were the farmer's "greatest wealth."[63]

As opportunities to produce marketable surpluses in the urban and industrial areas of the Northeast increased, farmers seem to have heeded the advice of Washburn and others who exhorted them to work hard and abstain from strong drink. The columns of the agricultural papers such as the *New England Farmer* were filled with broadsides against liquor. The special focus of the attack was "the old custom of supplying a barrel of whiskey for farm workers during the harvest season."[64] Commercial farmers had to combat the still widely held notion that a ration of spirits served to strengthen laborers doing hard physical work, especially outdoors. Pressures for prohibition among employers of farm labor already evident in the 1830s would intensify still further by the 1850s as Irish immigrants began to enter the farm-labor force and as machines began to be introduced for threshing and harvesting. Drunken and inattentive farmhands could then cause grisly and costly accidents. For farmers concerned with both human welfare and the making of profits, temperance made sense.[65]

The growing support for temperance among commercial farmers

in New England was a logical outgrowth of changing market conditions and commercial opportunities. The temperance movement's appeal to farmers lay not in some collective paranoia at the growth of urban society—as the traditional interpretation of the temperance movement might suggest—but was the result of changes in work and social relations which farmers themselves were helping to promote.

This picture is further strengthened if we look at the anti-prohibitionist farmers. These men did not show the same enthusiasm for the acquisition of land or the improvement of cultivation and breeding. None of the farmers in the pro-license panel was characterized in biographical data as enterprising in the way Darius Rice or Jonathan White were. True, the thirteen farmers in the pro-license group did include the largest cattle dealers in the county, E. L. and Lewis Barnard. But Lewis Barnard also owned a tavern, a reason for his opposition to no-license. Furthermore the two Barnards were primarily traders in rather than breeders of cattle. They did not display the prohibitionists' personal interest in agricultural or pastoral improvement. [66] The farmers of Worcester thus divided along with the rest of the society according to attitudes toward the great changes in industrial development, transportation, and agriculture which began to transform the economy of Worcester in the 1820s and 1830s.

Among the manufacturers and commercial farmers, optimistic and assertive values predominated. These promoters and beneficiaries of social and economic change had developed a world view in which temperance occupied an important place, and they tried to convince the community of its validity. They wished to shape society in their own self-image; they wished to manipulate the environment to remove the obstacles to moral and material progress. Of all the impediments to personal and community advancement, intemperance seemed second to none. Accordingly the mechanics, manufacturers, and commercial farmers supported—indeed supplied the backbone of—the prohibition drive in Worcester.

Anti-prohibitionists felt the pressure of these enthusiasts for large-scale social change. They resented, even feared, the new power of the voluntary organizations which the prohibitionists patronized. Colonel Pliny Merrick, the chief organizer of the pro-license resistance in the 1830s, expressed the resentment of his followers. He disparaged the temperance reformers who "have their national socie-

ties; their state societies; their county, half-county, and town societies; their old men's, their young men's, and their female associations—all operated for the same object, by the same power—the
power of concerted action. Overloaded with these everlasting associations, they come down upon the community by concerted action,
and overpower it with their majorities."[67] Voluntary action to promote temperance he could support, but not the "concerted action,"
"menace, or coercion" of temperance organizations dedicated to
prohibition. This power of organization was now being used to
proscribe liquor retailing and tavern keeping, two occupations
of respectable status. Men of the stature of Deacon Benjamin Butman of the Unitarian church were being denounced as purveyors of
corruption simply because they wished to retail spirits along with
regular groceries. If Butman, "the principal grocer of the town" and
"an energetic, honest business man," could be so degraded, anti-prohibitionists wondered where the denunciations would end.[68]

The anti-prohibitionists saw their opponents as a threat not only
to liquor selling but also to the whole range of traditional customs.
Pliny Merrick professed temperance principles, but feared that the
temperance organizations had already gone too far. Ardent spirits
deserved censure insofar as they caused drunkenness, but Merrick
resented the temperance societies' newly discovered phobia for
wine. If wine could suddenly be proscribed, Merrick felt that the
concept of reform through organized power could be carried to
ridiculous extremes. He cited coffee, tea, and meat as possible objects of censure.

Who could tell where such organized power would lead? What
custom would be safe from visionary reformers? Merrick felt that
the reformers could be considered a potential threat to his personal
behavior. When "they say to my neighbors, as respectable as themselves, . . . you shall not have a license because you will open a 'sluice
of corruption;' . . . I will stand by my neighbor. For they infringe on
his rights; and when they trample on my neighbor, they trample on
me also." For Merrick the time had come to draw the line.[69] His
emotional attack on the interference in community affairs of highly
organized, well-financed, and omnipresent temperance societies
may seem mere populist rhetoric; yet if we recall the extent of the
American Temperance Society campaign of the decade after 1826

and the goal of saturating the country with temperance societies and their pamphlet literature, Merrick's call to resist this expanding organizational empire must have had considerable appeal for pro-license voters.

Merrick was an eloquent and persuasive public speaker with his finger on the public pulse, but two questions remain open: why did so many share his fears of the temperance societies, and who were the nameless opponents of no-license? The anti-prohibitionist list included only about one in five of those who actually cast a vote against the no-license stand of the Worcester Temperance Society. Of the others, little is known; their motives and purposes must be inferred from fragmentary evidence. Because town meetings did not vote by ward and because the town officials kept no record of the individual votes, the rank and file of the anti-prohibitionist campaign in Worcester must remain obscure. Nevertheless the temperance newspapers hinted at the composition of the anti-prohibitionist forces, alleging that the propertyless had supported Pliny Merrick. The Worcester correspondent of the *Boston Recorder* blamed the defeat partly on the illegal voting of the propertyless, "some of them men of whom a tax could not be collected," who "were made voters previous to the meeting by having their taxes paid" by interested parties.[70] It seems obvious that the men who voted with Merrick wanted to preserve their right to drink freely. But were temperance reformers correct in alleging the lower-class origins of many of the silent opponents of prohibition? Evidence from Worcester and elsewhere indicates that some groups of workers did resist the temperance societies' attempts to regulate moral conduct in the 1830s. Bruce Laurie suggests that in Philadelphia, skilled workers in traditional crafts tended to oppose temperance in the 1830s as part of their resistance to the regimen of the factory; but there is considerable evidence that temperance agitation in the United States also provoked opposition from many rural workers and from the unskilled and semiskilled generally.[71]

Temperance agents reported resistance from the laboring classes when the total abstinence pledge was first introduced. Edward C. Delavan, the secretary of the New York State Temperance Society, believed that temperance societies did not have "the confidence of the laboring classes" because the temperance movement seemed self-serving and hypocritical in its standards. According to Delavan, the early reluctance of temperance reformers to attack the use of wine as they did the use of spirits condemned the movement in the eyes of the poorer classes. [72] The Massachusetts Temperance Society, meeting at Worcester in 1833, admitted that the poor would not sign the pledge until the "better classes" had provided the "lower orders" with a spotless example. [73] Yet despite the testimony of temperance supporters, the chief impediment to reform among workingmen was not the example of the upper classes but the weight of tradition. Colonial social customs insisted that drink was an aid to physical labor. It was extremely common for laborers to drink spirits on the job to relieve fatigue and to bolster their reserves of energy. The use of drink, widespread among workers in preindustrial American society, was inimical to the regular work patterns demanded by the nineteenth-century factory. But workers in the 1830s clung stubbornly to their traditional customs, drank widely on the job, and resisted the efforts of entrepreneurs to impose upon them the sober, disciplined work habits manufacturers considered appropriate to an industrializing society. [74]

The use of spirits was widespread enough among workmen to alarm many factory owners. In New York, manufacturers complained of *"blue* Mondays, which run pretty well into the week," caused by "the intemperance of workmen." [75] In East Dudley, Massachusetts, three factory owners refused to sell liquor in factory stores because "the profit derived from the sale of liquor was nothing, when compared with the losses they occasioned, in time spent by their workmen in drinking, in bad debts, etc., to say nothing of the poverty and misery, the scenes of riot and wickedness thus produced." [76] The concern of employers in Pennsylvania with the intemperance of workers in mines and foundries was such that the state legislature passed numerous acts forbidding the sale of liquor within three miles of specified industrial sites. [77] When Michel Chevalier, the French traveler and social commentator, visited the Lowell, Massachusetts, textile mills in the 1830s, he noted that the rules of the Lowell Manufacturing Company "prohibited all ardent spirits from the company grounds." [78] The concern of entrepreneurs with the drinking practices of workingmen clearly extended wherever the industrial system was emerging in the United States, and Worcester was no exception.

As early as 1831, twenty-six "mechanics shops," in Worcester and six "manufactories" embracing over "two hundred hands" forbad the employment of intemperate workmen and banned the use of spirits during working hours. [79] And if the Worcester no-license agitation gives any indication, the concern of manufacturers with the intemperance of workingmen intensified in the 1830s.

The enthusiasm of employers for temperance may have made factory operatives and common laborers even less inclined to support the antidrink crusade than they otherwise would have been. Horace Greeley observed of New York State in 1844 that "many of our Workmen are taught in the grogshops they frequent that it is a test of independence and spirit to vote right or wrong, contrary to those whom they work for." [80] There is no direct evidence on this point from the Worcester of the 1830s, but Ichabod Washburn made some suggestive observations on the habits of Worcester workingmen. In 1829 when Washburn raised the first house built in Worcester without providing spirits for the laborers, he found that only a few of his "own workmen at the shop [were] willing to help. The others were within sight, and by their jeers, ridiculed the undertaking, and did their best to make it a failure." [81] Whether some groups of workers in Worcester projected hostility toward employers into the public controversy over licensing is uncertain, but it does seem that the temperance reformers correctly gauged the lower-class origins of some of their opponents in Worcester. Certainly the liberal convention meeting in Worcester in 1838 lent further credence to such a view; the liberal campaign in Worcester focused in large part on the discriminatory nature of the fifteen-gallon law, which, by barring sale to those who could not afford to buy in large quantities, threatened to establish "odious distinctions between different classes in society." [82]

The opposition to no-license, then, came from both respectable gentlemen and not-so-respectable tavern keepers and retailers, with some support from workers who resented the incursions of employers on their drinking habits. The anti-prohibitionist group linked men with a direct economic interest in the liquor traffic and those who wished to preserve their traditional customs against self-righteous, self-appointed custodians of community morality.

The evidence examined so far suggests a split over the temperance issue on social and economic lines, but it is possible that other variables significantly influenced the vote. How far, for example, did partisan loyalty intrude? Data on the attitudes of Whigs toward the no-license question suggest that party affiliation was not an independent variable, at least for Whigs. The Whig town committee of 1837 was used in one test of party affiliation and support for prohibition. The total of 103 names on the town committee provided 27 prohibitionists and 29 anti-prohibitionists. The attitudes of the remainder are unknown.[83] Because the Whig party of Worcester split down the middle over the no-license issue, prohibition and temperance in the town never became purely partisan struggles. At the same time there was a strong connection between Democrats and those who opposed the no-license movement. All of the prohibitionists whose party connection is known (60 percent) were Whigs. There were no Jacksonians of any prominence in the ranks, and the town's Democratic leaders were active anti-prohibitionists. Jubal Harrington, the editor of the Jackson paper, Isaac Davis, the perennial Jackson candidate for Congress, and Maturin L. Fisher, later to be the appointee as postmaster of Worcester, were all among the leaders of the pro-license and anti-prohibitionist movement. Democrats in Worcester posed as the protectors of individual liberties against moral regulation by the state. Such an appeal was directed toward the tavern keepers and retailers whose livelihood was at stake and toward the drinkers whose individual liberty was threatened by prohibitionists.

The evidence from Worcester thus supports in some respects the larger picture of the Democratic party which Lee Benson has drawn.[84] Democrats attracted groups opposed to legal interference with social customs. Yet the alignment of Democrats with opposition to prohibition was by no means universal or immutable. A minority of Massachusetts Democrats always supported no-license, while the opposition of party spokesmen to prohibition was in large part an opportunistic maneuver, designed to capitalize on the split over the issue in the Whig party. Although less sympathetic toward prohibition than the Whigs, Massachusetts Democrats in fact responded to the political demands of both anti-prohibitionists and no-license advocates. As the no-license campaign became dominant in Massachusetts politics in the 1840s, Democratic opposition became more spasmodic as Democrats themselves began to split over the liquor question.[85] Democratic party leaders did not determine voting patterns but responded to popular fears and followed closely behind changes in public opinion. Explanations of public attitudes toward prohibition must go beyond partisan affiliation.

If party allegiance was not an independent determinant of attitudes toward the no-license issue, the question remains how far religion motivated the reformers who committed the temperance movement to prohibition. Just 56 percent of the prohibitionists and 33 percent of the anti-prohibitionists either belonged to a particular church or publicly expressed a religious preference.

The opponents and supporters of no-license displayed one decisive difference in religious affiliation. Twenty-five of the pro-license people expressed a religious preference, and no fewer than twenty of these were Unitarians. Only one orthodox Congregationalist was on the list. The absence of the evangelicals was most striking when compared with their presence in the prohibitionist group. Of the thirty-four identified by religion among the prohibitionists, nineteen were members of the orthodox churches. These figures do suggest that the link between evangelical religion and temperance sentiment remained important at the local level as the temperance movement shifted to its no-license phase. But three important qualifications are clear. First, there were nine Unitarians among the temperance supporters, a number large enough to suggest that evangelical religion did not preempt the field of temperance support. Among the eleven leaders of the no-license group in 1835 were four Unitarians, more than any other religious group. Unitarians in Worcester (and throughout Massachusetts) provided a substantial portion of reform leadership and thus confounded the common assumption that temperance was a purely evangelical crusade. Second, some of the no-license people probably had no religious affiliation at all; and third, the persistence of involvement in temperance among evangelicals does not show that evangelical religion was the cause of temperance support at the local level. Rather evangelical religion and temperance tended to occur together as part of the same response to the social and economic changes which were transforming Worcester in the 1830s.

An excellent example of the common roots of temperance and evangelical religion is provided by the career and religious life of Ichabod Washburn, a deacon of the orthodox Union Church in Worcester after its formation in 1837. Washburn was in fact a committed temperance reformer and secretary of a temperance society before he became a communicant of the Congregational church, though he had been a regular church attender before. Despite his nominal preference for orthodox Congregational doctrines, Washburn was actually quite eclectic in his religious views. He patronized the town's Methodist church, provided a home for its pastor, George Pickering, and worshipped on occasion in the Methodist church along with Samuel Perry, another Congregational deacon and no-license supporter. Washburn's sympathies for Methodism may have reflected the fact that the Methodist church was strong in Worcester among the factory operatives, and Washburn, a paternalistic employer, sought to provide for the spiritual as well as material needs of his employees. Certainly Washburn gave heavily for the support of working-class religion in Worcester, in particular through his funding of the Congregationalist Mission Chapel.[86] There was, indeed, a pronounced utilitarian streak in Washburn's religion, which he openly confessed at the end of his life in his *Autobiography*. Washburn told the mill owners of America to follow his example and provide churches for the benefit of their factory operatives. "If your mill owners want to make good dividends," he advised, "let them see to it that they have a plenty of good orthodox preaching, a good minister well housed, and . . . it will prove to be the best part of their investment; for godliness is profitable to all things."[87] For entrepreneurs like Washburn, both temperance and religion were part of a pattern of good community relations, good labor relations, and good factory management.

Aside from these functional economic considerations which appealed to upwardly mobile entrepreneurs, evangelical religion was emotionally and intellectually satisfying to the same men. Both temperance and the varieties of evangelical religion patronized by Worcester temperance reformers had similar styles and emotional and intellectual appeals. Both stressed personal responsibility for wrongdoing, and both gave man an important place in the process of conversion. The religion which Worcester temperance reformers supported was not that of the helpless sinner in the hands of an angry God; the religion of these men included room for works as well as for faith and gave some place to the doctrine of human ability. The Arminian doctrines which gained strength in the Congregational church in the early nineteenth century were congenial to the improvement-conscious manufacturers and farmers who provided the backbone of temperance support in Worcester in the 1830s. These men believed from their own experience in the individual's role in the transformation of his own destiny by manipulating the conditions of life around him. It is not surprising, therefore, that they should find appropriate a religion emphasizing human endeavor and material improvement as a sign of inner grace. In Worcester, fourteen of the nineteen prohibitionists who belonged to orthodox churches favored the evangelical churches which emphasized Arminian doctrines. And of those fourteen, thirteen were entrepreneurs whose occupations were linked to the emerging market economy. [88]

If the entrepreneurs who dominated the temperance movement from the 1830s found the doctrines of evangelical religion attractive, they also shared identical views of technological change with the evangelical clergy who formed the American Temperance Society. Evangelical temperance reformers hoped to exploit the social and economic changes taking place in the Jacksonian era and sought to harness changes in technology to the end of strengthening evangelical religion and morality. The fulcrum of this approach for the religious reformers was the use of the press. Through the printed word they hoped to flood the country with tracts and so save mankind from intemperance and damnation. In their use of technology and their development of organizations to deploy the message of temperance, the clergy were spiritual promoters. Their activity paralleled the more secular efforts at moral improvement which came from the industrial entrepreneurs. Both groups sought to manipulate the environment through the use of technology; both welcomed material progress as the basis of moral improvement; and both looked forward to the universal regeneration of mankind. By their appeal to rationality, technology, and organization to achieve reform, the evangelical clergy who participated in the temperance crusade had become, by the 1830s, as thoroughly subversive of tradition and rank as the upwardly mobile mechanics were. Justin Edwards of the American Temperance Society wrote that

the present age is marked with strong and auspicious peculiarities. One of them is, increasing numbers of people are disposed to inquire, with regard to every moral principle and practice, "Is it right?" It is less satisfactory now, than in former times, that a thing is pleasant merely, that it is popular, has been practised a long time, by respectable men, or even by good men. The question is, and with numbers increasing continually, "Is it right?"[89]

Such a view was as fundamentally rationalistic and anti-traditional in its approach to the customs of society as were the aspirations of the mechanics and manufacturers of Worcester.

Common aims and styles of behavior thrust the religious reformers and the industrial promoters together against the more traditional men who owed their allegiance to the older mercantile economy. The merchants, lawyers, tavern keepers, and respectable gentlemen who joined and led the pro-license movement felt the pressure of organized temperance societies, and they repudiated the trends in the temperance movement to teetotalism and prohibition. Never deeply committed to the temperance organizations, they now mobilized both popular opposition to changes in traditional social customs and fear of domination by well-organized and socially ambitious reformers.

The Implications of the Worcester Study

The wider relevance of the Worcester study can only be determined by a detailed investigation of support for temperance in all regions and sections of the United States. Yet a broad range of evidence suggests that Worcester provides a reliable guide to the sources of temperance support in the northeastern states in the 1830s. The temperance movement began and flourished in the northeastern states in the antebellum period. Eastern Massachusetts, in particular, proved remarkably receptive to the temperance crusade in the period from 1820 to 1860, and the movement there "was strongest in rising manufacturing and farming towns, weakest in port cities."[90] So too in Connecticut. Ellen Larned's useful county history of Windham County provides much detail explicitly linking the founding of the first temperance societies in the county with manufacturers concerned with both personal advancement and a supply of predictable, sober factory workers. The Connecticut Temperance Society's reports merely add to the examples.[91] Perhaps it is not surprising that Connecticut, with a pattern of industrial development similar to Worcester's, should parallel the course of its temperance agitation. Yet further afield in western and central New York, the same generalizations hold true. In New York State, Whitney Cross found temperance and similar reform enthusiasms weakest in underdeveloped counties and commercial centers, strongest in manufacturing towns and among the urban middle classes of prosperous, developed communities along the Erie Canal route. Towns such as Utica, Rochester, Troy, Syracuse, and Oswego favored temperance, while Albany and Buffalo did not.[92] And it was employers of labor—especially manufacturers and commercial farmers—who were the strongest supporters of temperance in these areas. When traveling agent Daniel Axtell formed fifty ATS auxiliaries in western New York in 1829, he reported that "a considerable majority of the members [were] influential heads of families (many of them large farmers—mechanics—master-workmen, etc.) who will of course extend the principles of the [American Temperance] Society over their families and labourers."[93] Thus in the areas which sustained the majority of temperance societies and members in the 1830s— New England and New York—the pattern of support was similar to that of the Worcester case study.

The nation's largest cities provide still further evidence for the thesis that temperance was closely bound up with changes in attitudes toward work and leisure which accompanied industrial and commercial development. Though New York City as a whole lagged in its support for temperance, questionnaires circulated by the New-York City Temperance Society in 1830 and 1837 make clear that within the nation's largest city, as in smaller, industrial centers, manufacturers strongly backed the temperance agitation. The "Mechanics' Circular" sent to many employers in the city called forth many responses detailing the concerns of the city's manufacturers with intemperance among workmen. These reports document initiatives of manufacturers to control the supply of liquor on the job through their own hiring and firing practices and in the larger society through support for the New-York City Temperance Society and the American Temperance Society. In contrast (and as in Worcester), merchants were much slower to organize in support of temperance societies. The manufacturers of New York had had their own temperance society (the Mechanics' Apprentices) ten years before merchants organized a similar Merchants' Temperance Society.[94]

In Philadelphia, too, support for temperance ran strong among entrepreneurs and promoters who had an interest in manufacturing industries. Just as Worcester had its Ichabod Washburn, Philadelphia's temperance movement had its archetypal self-made man in Matthias Baldwin, the founder of the Baldwin Locomotive Works. An exponent of the gospel of improvement, Baldwin embraced evangelical religion and antislavery as well as temperance. Baldwin patronized the First Presbyterian Church where Albert Barnes preached against liquor sellers and slaveholders alike. Barnes's congregation was full of self-made and upwardly mobile men like Baldwin, and Barnes's message of self-improvement and salvation through temperance and evangelical conversion ideally suited the congregation.[95] A detailed study of temperance in Philadelphia confirms the impression of temperance support which the examples of Baldwin and Barnes suggest. Membership in the city's leading temperance societies, the Pennsylvania Society for Discouraging the Use of Ardent Spirits, and the Mechanics and Workingmen's Society, demonstrates that temperance found its strongest support among evangelical clergy, doctors, and the elite of the city's entrepreneurs.[96]

Each of these cases—Worcester, New York, and Philadelphia—points to the central importance of the improvers in the temperance crusade in the 1830s. Men who had achieved or who wished to achieve self-improvement embraced temperance. They reasoned that sobriety and self-discipline produced individual improvement, and they projected their own standards for success as the solution for society's ills. The importance of the upwardly mobile entrepreneurs and all those concerned with self-improvement does not negate the moral and religious drive of temperance reformers; nor does it disparage the evangelical commitment of many reformers. Nevertheless the improver in the temperance ranks exerted a dominant influence on the goals and ideology of temperance agitation as they took shape in the 1830s.

Notes

1. *First Annual Report of the American Society for the Promotion of*

Temperance (Andover: Flagg and Gould, 1827), pp. 14-15 (hereafter cited as ATS, *First Annual Report*).

2. *Permanent Temperance Documents of the American Temperance Society* (Boston: Seth Bliss, 1835), pp. 38-39.

3. Church resolutions against the traffic are listed in ibid., pp. 17-18.

4. ATS, *First Annual Report*, pp. 14-15.

5. *Minutes of the General Assembly of the Presbyterian Church in the United States of America from A.D. 1821 to A.D. 1835 Inclusive* (Philadelphia: Presbyterian Board of Publications, n.d.), p. 262.

6. John Marsh, *Temperance Recollections* (New York: Charles Scribner, 1866); *Standard Encyclopedia of the Alcohol Problem* (Westerville, Ohio: American Issue Publishing Company, 1925-1930), 2:779. Delavan (1793-1871) left no collection of papers, but he wrote more letters than any other prominent temperance agitator, and many of these have been retained in the Gerrit Smith Miller Collection, SU, and in the John H. Cocke Papers, UV.

7. The widespread support for temperance among physicians is noted by James H. Cassedy, "An Early American Hangover: The Medical Profession and Intemperance, 1800-1860," *Bulletin of the History of Medicine* 50 (Fall 1976): 405-31. The quoted declaration is printed in *Journal of the Proceedings of the Massachusetts Temperance Convention, Begun and Held at Worcester, on Wednesday, September 18, 1833* (Boston: Ford and Damrell, 1833), p. 36; *Report of a Committee, Appointed by the Philadelphia Medical Society, January 24, 1829 . . .* (Philadelphia: John Clarke, 1829), p. 21.

8. See *The Anniversary Report of the Managers of the Pennsylvania Society for Discouraging the Use of Ardent Spirits Read on the 27th May, 1831* (Philadelphia: Henry H. Porter, 1831).

9. For example, in Worcester, Massachusetts, all the doctors signed a declaration similar to the one signed by the Boston doctors. "Declaration of Sixty-five Physicians of Worcester County," *Twenty-first Annual Report of the Massachusetts Temperance Society, Presented by the Council, at the Annual Meeting in Boston, May 29, 1834* (Boston: Ford and Damrell, 1834), p. 32. Six of the eight who signed were college educated. See also, Daniel Drake, *A Discourse on Intemperance; Delivered at Cincinnati, March 1, 1828, before the Agricultural Society of Hamilton County* (Cincinnati: Looker and Reynolds, 1828), p. 27.

10. On the problem of quackery and the medical profession's attempts to deal with it, see Henry B. Shafer, *The American Medical Profession, 1783 to 1850* (New York: Columbia University Press, 1936), pp. 224-25, 229.

11. *Boston Recorder and Telegraph*, 8 June 1827.

12. "Extract from a Prize Essay, by Reuben D. Mussey, M.D.," *Permanent Temperance Documents*, pp. 494-506; *Report of a Committee, Ap-*

pointed by the Philadelphia Medical Society, p. 25; Drake, *Discourse*, p. 27.

13. Samuel Emlen, "Remarks on the Mischievous Effects of Spirituous Liquors on Society, and the Means of Preventing Them," *North American Medical and Surgical Journal* 3 (1827), quoted in ATS, *First Annual Report*, p. 20; Leonard Woods to J. C. Warren, 20 April 1829, John C. Warren Papers, MHS.

14. Daniel Dorchester, *The Liquor Problem in All Ages* (New York: Phillips and Hunt, 1884), pp. 578-81. Edward C. Delavan "gave to the public eight large drawings of Dr. Sewall's, on a grand lithograph, nine times the size of a common stomach. They were extensively taken at ten dollars a set, and hung in public institutions and temperance halls for the use of public lectures. He also commenced a preparation of a small set to be placed in every school in the state [New York], confident that no parent would withhold his mite for such an object." Marsh, *Temperance Recollections*, p. 100.

15. See, for example, *Fourth Annual Report of the New-York State Society for the Promotion of Temperance* (Albany: Packard and Van Benthuysen, 1833), pp. 54, 56, 94, and Dawson Burns, *Temperance History: A Consecutive Narrative of the Rise, Development, and Extension of the Temperance Reform* (London: National Temperance Publication Depot, n.d. [c. 1881]), p. 99; J. E. A. Smith, *The History of Pittsfield, (Berkshire County), Massachusetts, from the Year 1800 to the Year 1876* (Springfield, Mass.: C. W. Bryan, 1876), p. 394; "The Tavern Keepers and Retailers of Hampden, to Their Friends and Fellow Laborers in the Same Occupations in Worcester," *Worcester Republican*, 15 April 1835; J. Conrad to Roberts Vaux, 24 August 1832, Roberts Vaux Papers, HSP; *Pittsfield Sun*, 10 April 1834.

16. Keith L. Sprunger, "Cold Water Congressmen: The Congressional Temperance Society before the Civil War," *Historian* 27 (August 1965): 498-515.

17. See *Boston Daily Advertiser*, 11 April 1835, and *Temperance Journal* (April 1834) for accounts of the many local clashes over the no-license issue. A brief and speculative early statement of some of the themes developed in this chapter appears in my "Temperance and Economic Change in the Antebellum North," in Jack S. Blocker, Jr., ed., *Alcohol, Reform, and Society: The Liquor Issue in Social Context* (Westport, CT.: Greenwood Press, 1979).

18. The economic changes of the Jacksonian era are well treated in George R. Taylor, *The Transportation Revolution, 1815-1860* (New York: Holt, Rinehart and Winston, 1951). On Worcester's economic development, see Charles G. Washburn, *Industrial Worcester* (Worcester: Davis Press, 1917).

19. Caleb Wall, *Reminiscences of Worcester from the Earliest Period*,

Historical and Genealogical, with Notices of Early Settlers and Prominent Citizens (Worcester: Tyler and Seagrove, 1877), p. 122; *Worcester Massachusetts Spy*, 11 May, 26 October 1831; "Report of the Worcester Massachusetts Temperance Society," *Journal of Humanity*, 17 May 1832.

20. "Report of the Executive Committee of the Worcester Temperance Society," *Worcester Massachusetts Spy*, 22 October 1834. In April 1834, there were four Catholic families and about twenty single Catholics in Worcester in a population of over four thousand. William Lincoln, *History of Worcester, Massachusetts, from Its Earliest Settlement to September, 1836; with Various Notices Relating to the History of Worcester County* (Worcester: Charles Hersey, 1862), p. 186. This volume was printed together with Charles Hersey, *History of Worcester, Massachusetts, from 1836 to 1861, with Interesting Reminiscences of the Public Men of Worcester* (Worcester: The author, 1862) (hereafter cited as Lincoln and Hersey, *History of Worcester*).

21. The distinction between retailing and tavern licenses is made in chap. 1.

22. *Worcester Massachusetts Spy*, 5 March, 2 April 1834; *Laws of the Commonwealth of Massachusetts, Passed by the General Court, . . . One Thousand Eight Hundred and Thirty-two* (Boston: Dutton and Wentworth, 1832), ch. 166.

23. *Worcester Massachusetts Spy*, 22 October 1834.

24. Nathaniel Paine, ed., *Diary of Christopher Columbus Baldwin, Librarian of the American Antiquarian Society, 1829-1835* (Worcester: American Antiquarian Society, 1901), p. 347; Franklin P. Rice, ed., *Worcester Town Records, 1833-1848* (Worcester: Worcester Society of Antiquity, 1895), p. 61. The vote was 325 for no-license and 272 for licenses.

25. *Worcester Palladium*, 8 April 1835. Only Porter's Temperance House remained open for travelers.

26. *Temperance Journal* (May 1835).

27. *Worcester Palladium*, 8 April 1835; *Boston Daily Advertiser*, 11 April 1835.

28. *Worcester Town Records, 1833-1848*, p. 63; *Worcester Massachusetts Spy*, 15 April 1835.

29. *Worcester Palladium*, 8 April 1835; *Worcester Massachusetts Spy*, 8 April 1835.

30. The list is published in *Worcester National Aegis*, 3 October 1838. To obtain a control group of opponents of prohibition, I added this list to the list of eleven opponents of no-license in 1835, and together, the lists provided me with seventy-nine names.

31. Only one supporter of prohibition in 1835 was an anti-prohibitionist in 1838. He was John F. Clarke, the keeper of the House of Correction. Al-

though biographical information on Clarke suggests that he should be placed among the opponents of prohibition, his name has been deleted from both the supporters' and opponents' lists, and after deletion, there are sixty supporters of prohibition and seventy-eight opponents. For anti-prohibitionist arguments, see "The Address of the Convention held at Worcester, on Thursday, the 4th of October, 1838," *Worcester Palladium*, 24 October 1838, and ibid., 15 April 1835.

32. *Temperance Journal* (May 1835); *Worcester Massachusetts Spy*, 6, 8 April 1835.

33. All figures computed from biographical data. See appendix for the lists of prohibitionists and their opponents.

34. Worcester tax list, 1832, WHS; Nathaniel Paine, *Random Recollections of Worcester, Massachusetts, 1839-1843* (Worcester: Privately printed, 1885), p. 29.

35. Computed from *Compendium of the Enumeration of the Inhabitants and Statistics of the United States, . . . from the Returns of the Sixth Census . . .* (Washington, D.C.: Blair and Rives, 1841).

36. *Worcester Massachusetts Spy*, 29 March 1837.

37. David Montgomery, *Beyond Equality: Labor and the Radical Republicans, 1862-1872* (New York: Alfred A. Knopf, 1967), p. 8; see also Robert Doherty, *Society and Power: Five New England Towns, 1800-1860* (Amherst: University of Massachusetts Press, 1977), pp. 24-25.

38. See Worcester Society of Antiquity, *Collections*, 9:59.

39. *Worcester Massachusetts Spy*, 26 October 1831.

40. Ibid., 24 September 1834.

41. *The Worcester Almanac, City Directory and Business Advertiser for 1844* (Worcester: Henry J. Howland, [1844]); Worcester tax list, 1832; Washburn, *Industrial Worcester*, p. 143.

42. Computed from *Compendium of the Sixth Census*.

43. "Address of the Convention Held at Worcester on Thursday the 4th of October, to the People of Worcester County," *Worcester Palladium*, 24 October 1838; *Worcester Palladium*, 8 April 1835.

44. Statement by Ira Barton, ibid., 15 April 1835.

45. George H. Haynes, *The Life of Charles G. Washburn* (Boston: Houghton Mifflin, 1931), pp. 6-7. For Foster, see *Reminiscences and Biographical Notices of Eighteen Members of the Worcester Fire Society, Prepared by a Committee of the Society, 5th Series* (Worcester: Printed for the society, 1887), pp. 49-50.

46. Resolutions of a public meeting of citizens opposed to the no-license vote of the town meeting, *Worcester Palladium*, 8 April 1835; editorial, ibid., 1 April 1835; resolution of the pro-license meeting, ibid., 15 April 1835.

47. *Worcester Massachusetts Spy*, 22 October 1834.

48. "The late attempt to instruct the selectmen has awakened many fears that the leaders of the temperance reform design to make it a political subject. Several who were members of the Society for promoting Temperance have directed their names to be withdrawn." Paine, ed., *Diary of Christopher Columbus Baldwin*, p. 347.

49. On militia drinking, see Horace Greeley, *Recollections*, quoted in Alice Felt Tyler, *Freedom's Ferment: Phases of American Social History since Colonial Times* (Minneapolis: University of Minnesota Press, 1944), p. 310; and W. A. Newman Dorland, "The Second Troop Philadelphia City Cavalry," *Pennsylvania Magazine of History and Biography* 49 (January 1925): 78.

50. On Ward, see *Reminiscences of Past Members of the Worcester Fire Society, 4th series* (Worcester: Printed for the society, 1874), p. 43.

51. Ibid.

52. *Reminiscences and Biographical Notices of Eighteen Members of the Worcester Fire Society*, p. 37.

53. *Reminiscences of Past Members of the Worcester Fire Society, 3rd Series* (Worcester: Printed for the society, 1874), p. 25.

54. Ibid. As Benjamin F. Thomas himself observed, "Our fathers discovered more worth in forms and external observances than their children."

55. Washburn, *Industrial Worcester*, p. 143.

56. Ibid., p. 161; Henry T. Cheever, ed., *Autobiography and Memorials of Ichabod Washburn Showing How a Great Business Was Developed and Large Wealth Acquired for the Uses of Benevolence* (Boston: D. Lathrop, 1878), pp. 117, 170.

57. Washburn, *Industrial Worcester*, p. 301. Prohibition men among the founders of the Mechanics Institute were Ichabod Washburn, Anthony Chase, Henry W. Miller, William M. Bickford, William A. Wheeler, Rufus Dunbar, John P. Kettel, James S. Woodworth, and Albert Tolman. The opponents of prohibition were Joseph Pratt and Levi Dowley.

58. Worcester's Temperance Convention applauded "the love of reading and the taste for knowledge fostered by Lyceums and social Libraries, and every institution designed to make men think for themselves, and reflect upon their social duties and ultimate destinies." *Worcester Massachusetts Spy*, 22 November 1837.

59. For prohibitionists, 119 acres; for anti-prohibitionists, 117 acres. Computed from Worcester tax list, 1832.

60. The seven were Francis Thaxter, Walter Bigelow, Jonathan White, Darius Rice, Ebenezer Read, Paul Goodale, and George T. S. Curtiss. Evidence drawn from *Worcester Massachusetts Spy*, 6 September 1835, 12 April, 30 November 1837; Henry M. Wheeler, "Early Roads in Worcester,"

Worcester Society of Antiquity, *Proceedings* 20:96, 101-02; "Flagg Family in Worcester," Worcester Society of Antiquity, *Proceedings* 19:207; Wall, *Reminiscences of Worcester*, p. 388; Worcester tax list, 1832.

61. "Flagg Family in Worcester," p. 207.

62. Wheeler, "Early Roads in Worcester," p. 96.

63. Emory Washburn, *Address, Delivered before the Worcester Agricultural Society, October 11, 1826; Being Their Eighth Anniversary Cattle Show and Exhibition of Manufactures* (Worcester: Charles Griffin, 1827), pp. 13-14.

64. Albert L. Demaree, *The American Agricultural Press, 1819-1860* (New York: Columbia University Press, 1941), p. 77. See also Sumner G. Wood, *The Taverns and Turnpikes of Blandford, 1733-1833* (n.p.: The author, 1908), p. 325.

65. "Annual Report of the Worcester Temperance Society," *Worcester Massachusetts Spy*, 26 October 1831; *Journal of Humanity*, 17 January 1831; *New England Farmer*, 4 February 1825, 17 January 1826; David E. Schob, *Hired Hands and Plowboys: Farm Labor in the Midwest, 1815-60* (Urbana: University of Illinois Press, 1975), pp. 98-101, 247-48, 254. This work has larger implications than its title suggests; it contains a useful summary of labor conditions and mechanization trends in antebellum New England.

66. Wheeler, "Early Roads in Worcester," p. 83; Worcester tax list, 1832.

67. *Worcester Palladium*, 15 April 1835.

68. *Reminiscences and Biographical Notices of Twenty-one Members of the Worcester Fire Society, 6th series* (Worcester: Printed for the society, 1889), p. 76.

69. *Worcester Palladium*, 15 April 1835. On Merrick, see Lincoln and Hersey, *History of Worcester*, pp. 208, 343; and Wall, *Reminiscences of Worcester*, p. 315.

70. *Boston Recorder*, 24 April 1835. The Worcester tax list for 1832 shows that more anti-prohibitionists were not assessed than prohibitionists: thirty out of seventy-eight as opposed to nineteen out of sixty. The anti-prohibitionists also had three times as many assessed under $1,000 (twelve versus four). The evidence tends to support the *Boston Recorder*, yet the tax list is too early to prove the point conclusively.

71. Bruce Laurie, "'Nothing on Compulsion': Lifestyles of Philadelphia Artisans, 1820-1850," *Labor History* 15 (Summer 1974): 344-45.

72. E. C. Delavan to J. H. Cocke, 13 March 1835, Cocke Papers, UV.

73. *Journal of the Proceedings of the Massachusetts Temperance Convention*, p. 20.

74. Paul Faler, "Cultural Aspects of the Industrial Revolution: Lynn, Massachusetts, Shoemakers and Industrial Morality, 1826-1860," *Labor*

History 15 (Summer 1974): 367-94; Laurie, "'Nothing on Compulsion,'" pp. 39-40.

75. "Circular of the City Temperance Society to the Manufacturers and Mechanics of the City of New-York," Appendix to *Eighth Annual Report of the New-York City Temperance Society, . . .* (New York: D. Fanshaw, 1837), p. 51. This problem was common in early industrializing America, as Herbert Gutman makes clear in "Work, Culture, and Society in Industrializing America, 1815-1919," *American Historical Review* 78 (June 1973): 531-83.

76. *Journal of Humanity*, 3 February 1830.

77. Asa E. Martin, "The Temperance Movement in Pennsylvania Prior to the Civil War," *Pennsylvania Magazine of History and Biography* 49 (July 1925): 213-14.

78. Michel Chevalier, *Society, Manners, and Politics in the United States: Letters on North America*, ed. John W. Ward (New York: Anchor Books, 1961), p. 140.

79. *Worcester Massachusetts Spy*, 26 October 1831. There is no reliable information on the total number of manufacturing establishments until 1840.

80. Lee Benson, *The Concept of Jacksonian Democracy: New York as a Test Case* (Princeton, N.J.: Princeton University Press, 1961), pp. 162-63.

81. Cheever, ed., *Autobiography and Memorials of Ichabod Washburn*, p. 57.

82. "Address of the Convention Held at Worcester on Thursday the 4th of October, to the People of Worcester County," *Worcester Palladium*, 24 October 1838. Not until the Washingtonian societies of the 1840s challenged the dominance of the affluent and evangelical among the temperance reformers were any laborers found in the ranks of the town's temperance societies.

83. The Whig committee list is printed in *Worcester Massachusetts Spy*, 7 October 1837. There is no comparable list for Democrats in the town for the same time.

84. Benson, *Concept of Jacksonian Democracy*.

85. For Democratic support for both no-license and prohibition, see *Norfolk* (Dedham, Mass.) *Democrat*, 9 November 1839; *Salem Register*, 18 May 1835; Edward Everett to J. H. Clifford, 24 June 1839, John H. Clifford Papers, MHS; John A. Bolles, *An Oration Delivered July 4, 1839, at Medfield, Mass., at a Temperance Celebration, in Which the Citizens of Medfield and Eight of the Surrounding Towns United without Distinction of Party* (Boston: Whipple and Damrell, 1839), p. 24. The Democratic party in Massachusetts was a minority party in the 1830s both in Worcester and

throughout the state, and the split within the Whigs over prohibition presented a good opportunity for political success. See A. B. Darling, *Political Changes in Massachusetts, 1824-1848: A Study of Liberal Movements in Politics* (New Haven: Yale University Press, 1925), p. 240.

86. Cheever, ed., *Autobiography and Memorials of Ichabod Washburn*, p. 59; Alfred S. Roe, *Worcester Methodism: Its Beginnings* (Worcester: Franklin P. Rice, 1889), p. 19; D. Hamilton Hurd, *History of Worcester County, Massachusetts, with Biographical Sketches of Many of Its Pioneers and Prominent Men* (Philadelphia: J. W. Lewis and Co., 1889), 2:1463.

87. Cheever, ed., *Autobiography and Memorials of Ichabod Washburn*, p. 74.

88. Hurd, *History of Worcester County*, 2:1460-63. The fourteen who supported these churches included five tradesmen, four manufacturers, and three commercial farmers. The other five prohibitionists who supported orthodoxy belonged to Old South, the most conservative and Calvinist of Worcester's Congregational churches. My conclusions support Robert Doherty, "Social Bases for the Presbyterian Schism of 1837-1838: The Philadelphia Case," *Journal of Social History* 2 (Fall 1968): 69-79, that in Philadelphia, evangelical religion tended to find its support among the upwardly mobile mechanics and manufacturers.

89. *Permanent Temperance Documents*, p. 339.

90. Faler, "Cultural Aspects," p. 369. For the distribution of temperance societies and their concentration in the Northeast, see John A. Krout, *The Origins of Prohibition* (New York: Alfred A. Knopf, 1925), pp. 129-31.

91. Ellen Larned, *History of Windham County, Connecticut* (Worcester: C. Hamilton, 1874-1880): 2:480-89; *Journal of Humanity*, 24 June 1830.

92. Whitney R. Cross, *The Burned-over District: The Social and Intellectual History of Enthusiastic Religion in Western New York, 1800-1850* (Ithaca, N.Y.: Cornell University Press, 1950), pp. 75-76. For corroborating evidence from temperance sources, see J. Marsh to J. H. Cocke, 16 August 1855, Cocke Papers, UNC, and E. C. Delavan to J. H. Cocke, 10 May 1847, Cocke Papers, UV.

93. *Second Annual Report of the American Society for the Promotion of Temperance* (Andover: Flagg and Gould, 1829), pp. 16-17.

94. *Eighth Annual Report of the New-York City Temperance Society*, pp. 47-58; *First Annual Report of the New-York City Temperance Society. 1830* (New York: Sleight and Robinson, 1830), pp. 19-30; *JATU* 5 (September 1841): 136, and ibid., 5 (October 1841): 148.

95. On Baldwin and Barnes, see Doherty, "Social Bases for the Presbyterian Schism," pp. 69-79.

96. The executive of the Pennsylvania Society for Discouraging the Use

of Ardent Spirits, a body composed exclusively of Philadelphians, was dominated by doctors (twelve of forty-three), manufacturers (nine), and clergy (seven). This society represented the elite of wealthy temperance supporters in the city. See *Anniversary Report . . . Pennsylvania Society for Discouraging the Use of Ardent Spirits*; Laurie, "'Nothing on Compulsion,'" pp. 352-54. For the social composition of the Mechanics and Workingmen's Temperance Society, see Albert Barnes, *The Connection of Temperance with Republican Freedom: An Oration Delivered before the Mechanics and Workingmen's Temperance Society of the City and County of Philadelphia* (Philadelphia: Boyle and Benedict, 1835), p. 28. Philadelphia city directories and biographical directories too numerous to cite were used to assess the social backgrounds of the known members of these societies.

5

THE IDEOLOGY AND SOCIAL
OUTLOOK OF MAINSTREAM
TEMPERANCE

The temperance reform attracted from its beginnings ambitious and upwardly mobile men whom I shall call improvers. These entrepreneurs and evangelical reformers continued to dominate the mainstream temperance organizations, the American Temperance Society, the American Temperance Union, and their affiliates until the Civil War. One thing ought to be plain from the Worcester case study and from the larger pattern of studies linking temperance with economic change: temperance reform from the 1830s to the 1850s was not the reactionary, provincial movement of popular belief and historical interpretation, nor was it the property of rural backwaters seeking to reassert traditional values on a changing society.[1] On the contrary, temperance reformers sanctioned the acquisitive and individualistic economic order developing in America, and they optimistically predicted the improvement of the moral state of society on a firm basis of material progress. Viewed from the perspective of hindsight, temperance reformers appear as apologists for economic change; they were men who were working to create a society of competitive individuals instilled with the virtues of sobriety and industry.

Viewed from the perspective of these reformers, however, the antidrink crusade was the work of liberators of humanity, not fearful conservatives who wished to restrict the possibilities for human development. Profoundly influenced by the spirit of romantic perfectionism which permeated antebellum social thought, the men who were most strongly committed to temperance reform in the late 1830s expressed a deep and abiding faith in man's potential for improvement. The belief that society could be transformed through the eradication of liquor became more pervasive as these men gained power in the temperance movement.

The commitment to human improvement was not restricted to the successful economic entrepreneurs who supported the temperance societies in the antebellum decades. The improvers' ranks included those who hoped for upward mobility, although they might be dismal personal failures, as well as clergy and intellectuals who hoped to build a more moral world on the foundation of material improvement. The idea of human perfectibility undoubtedly had intellectual and religious origins, as John Thomas has argued, yet also contributing to the success and currency of the idea was the fact of material improvement, which seemed to illustrate remarkable possibilities for human development.[2]

The link between ideas of moral perfectibility and material improvement is illustrated by the reception of technology among reformers. The machine offered men liberation from their age-old dependence on manpower and animal power, and through the machine, the industrial revolution illustrated that men need not be passively subject to the dictates of environment; the environment could be reshaped to suit human purposes. The influence of this by now commonplace idea on early nineteenth-century social thought is difficult to overestimate. For moral reformers, the lesson was plain; the progress of technology made reformers more conscious that social customs could be changed, and even radically transformed. The machine and mass-production techniques of the industrial revolution encouraged the idea not of gradual change (an Enlightenment concept) but of drastic ruptures in the social fabric. Temperance reformers of the 1830s and 1840s spoke in sermons and speeches of "breaking the cake of custom"; Justin Edwards's injunction "Is it right?" was of the same tenor, implying a sharp break with past experiences and practices.[3] The language of discontinuity which these reformers used mirrored what was happening in the world of work with the disruption of established preindustrial work patterns by the machine and by mass-production, factory-type techniques.

That these mainstream temperance reformers shared an optimistic view of social change and derived this faith from changes in technology and business organization can be seen in both the beliefs they frequently espoused and in their actions and backgrounds. This optimism was often derived from personal experience. It must be remembered that the men who came to dominate the temperance movement in the 1830s were frequently innovators in business, religion, or professional life. We have already noted this pattern in Worcester, where the leading temperance reformers were those with a hand in the work of inventions and of innovations in factory and machine production. Examples of the involvement of temperance reformers of the 1830s in the process of technological change and industrialization could be multiplied on the national level. Industrial entrepreneurs were common among the most prominent promoters of temperance reform. John Hartwell Cocke of Virginia, for example, who served as president of the American Temperance Union from 1836 to 1843, and Christian Keener of Baltimore, the chief financial backer of the Maryland Temperance Society, were partners in copper smelting enterprises and in railroad and canal investment; Anson Phelps in New York was one of the wealthiest of the captains of industry, specializing in iron ore mining and copper smelting.

Some of these men were especially notable not only for their vigorous promotion of economic change but also for their capacity for innovation in business and industrial organization. Matthias Baldwin of Philadelphia was not merely a successful entrepreneur but also prominent in the improvement of locomotive design. Daniel Fanshaw, the printer for both the New-York City Temperance Society and the American Tract Society, was the first to introduce machinery into the New York book publishing business, even before regular commercial publishers did. The example might also be cited of the Tappans, whose innovation was not strictly technological but rather organizational. The credit rating system which they initiated showed how people who became involved in temperance and other reform movements made innovations which ultimately revolutionized business organization; the Tappans' credit system displayed the same demand for a rational (in the Weberian sense) and predictable universe which temperance reformers espoused and which they hoped to bring about by creating a world of moral, self-disciplined, sober individuals.[4]

These innovators in business and professional life assumed an equal ability to transform the moral world. A society which could build canals and railroads and harness the immense energies of steam to industrial production could, Gerrit Smith and Edward C. Delavan both agreed, surely devise a better and more moral world. "We think it quite likely," one temperance journalist wrote, "that the moral world is to be changed and elevated, as the physical has been, by means and instruments as simple and old-fashioned as the long neglected steam power."[5] The imagery of the machine, and of steam power in particular, dominated reformers' statements of moral as well as material progress. These reformers believed that the development of the steam printing press and the creation of more efficient networks of communication with the spread of canals and railroads would enable the temperance movement to saturate the country with millions of cheap temperance pamphlets. Distributed by ever more efficient organizations, the pamphlets would emulate the conquests of steam. "Like the movement of a mighty steam engine, steady, true, irresistible," the temperance reformation would spread the message of total abstinence across the land.[6] The effusive praise which temperance reformers showered upon technology reveals their attitudes toward socioeconomic change and the developing industrial-commercial society. Men who are so often depicted by historians as deeply conservative were in fact encouraging and exploiting change.[7]

These enthusiastic promoters of social change had great confidence in the ability of individuals to improve themselves, yet at the same time they did not feel content to adopt a purely laissez-faire attitude in matters of morality. They placed the principal blame for intemperance on society, not on individual drinkers. And they accepted an active responsibility for the eradication of intemperance throughout society—by persuasion if possible, by force if necessary.

The entrepreneurs among the temperance reformers thus present a puzzling picture of men who had succeeded economically through personal effort yet rejected a self-help philosophy. Society had rewarded them materially, yet they remained dissatisfied with the basic condition of society. They were certainly not defenders of the status quo. The reformers' puzzling urge to transform the moral condition of society arose from the uneasy juxtaposition of human misery and a sense of social and political power. Despite the optimism of reformers that their message would ultimately succeed, much poverty and despair remained around them. As the Reverend Albert Barnes told his prosperous Philadelphia congregation, there were still 200,000 paupers "in a land abounding in all the wealth that the richest soil can give, and under all the facilities which the most favored spot under the whole heaven can furnish for acquiring a decent and honest subsistence." Similarly Horace Mann noted that "in the midst of all this munificence and prodigality of Heaven, a degree of want and suffering abounds."[8] Temperance reformers such as Mann did not accept the responsibility for the creation of the social problems they saw around them, but they did accept responsibility for the elimination of those problems. As one popular writer of temperance pamphlets, Henry D. Kitchell, remarked, temperance reformers could not allow "this horrid business . . . any beyond the least degree of legal toleration to which we could reduce it." Otherwise reformers were "fearfully implicated in its guilt."[9]

Stanley Elkins has argued that antebellum reformers acquired a deep sense of guilt and responsibility for the evils in society because they lacked the power to dissipate their guilt through less moralistic and more pragmatic solutions to social problems. The reformers were, in Elkins's view, deeply alienated from the basic institutions of society.[10] Yet the example of temperance reformers suggests that their sense of power derived from their professional and business achievements, and their manifold involvement in the institutions of society made them feel responsible for the eradication of society's defects.

When reformers focused on intemperance as the cause of social disorder, they ignored the more obvious contribution of economic change to the creation of such problems as pauperism. For example, they discounted low wages and the influence of banking and trade fluctuations when they discussed the causes of poverty. In an analysis of the depression of 1837, one Worcester temperance convention expressed its sympathy with "the distress of the poor," but it could

offer no solution except "to unite with us in abstaining from all intoxicating drinks."[11] In the liquor trade and in the custom of drinking, temperance reformers found an explanation for social disorder
which lay outside their own roles as entrepreneurs and apologists for
economic change. By denouncing the liquor business as illegitimate
and unproductive, these men simultaneously and quite self-con-
sciously legitimated the acquisition of property through other forms
of business activity, which they labeled "the useful and honest em-
ployments of life." Drink was, as Jesse Goodrich of Worcester put it,
an "unnatural influence" which prevented the triumph of "Cold
Water, —Capital, —Enterprise, —Industry, —Morals, —and   Religion." Since liquor had no function in the society the improvers were
trying to create, the only justification for it lay in the fact that it had
always been used in colonial society.[12]

This is not to say that these reformers naively ignored obvious
sources of immorality which modern society had spawned. They
were aware that economic growth and personal mobility had created
extreme wealth, luxury, and greed. They believed that the large
cities—Boston, New York, and Philadelphia—created temptations
of their own for unsuspecting young immigrants from rural areas.[13]
But the temperance improvers saw no reason to add to the inevitable
stimuli of modern society by sanctioning the persistence of what
they believed was an irrational social custom.

If the "manufacture of drunkards" were not given sanction and respectability through law and if individuals could be persuaded to renounce liquor, reformers felt confident that lyceums, mechanics'
institutes, and other literary and educational organizations would
help individuals develop the mental and moral culture necessary to
avoid the remaining moral pitfalls in modern society. By eradicating
the liquor traffic, the reformers of the 1830s believed they would remove the chief obstacle to the progress of both individuals and the
whole society along what Neal Dow, the famous Maine prohibitionist, would call "the highway of prosperity."[14]

The men who dominated the mainstream temperance reform societies in the antebellum decades were optimistic about the prospects
for social change and espoused a forward-looking ideology. They
had acquired a set of beliefs which explained disparate reality, diag-
nosed social ills, and provided a key to action which promised to

transform society. The goal of these reformers was to make the United States into a total abstinence republic. They would achieve this purpose by eliminating the drinking customs which prevented Americans from attaining moral improvement to match their startling material growth. The committed temperance reformer found in his ideology the promise of a better future; equally important, he acquired at the same time a new set of values which shaped his present conduct. [15] The immediate impact of ideology on the temperance movement was to create intense pressure within the temperance societies to adopt tactics consistent with the social purpose and ideological position of temperance reform. In concrete terms, this internal debate pushed the temperance crusade toward the adoption of teetotalism.

As the notion of human improvement gained currency among temperance reformers in the 1830s, attention shifted from preserving the temperate to reforming the intemperate as well. The improvers believed that no man was beyond reform, and consequently they began to tackle the reformation of drunkards. But the reform of the inebriate would demand a more radical pledge than the old pledge against ardent spirits, which allowed the use of wine. Temperance workers quickly discovered that the use of wine among reformed drunkards often led them back to the bottle. The attempt to reform drunkards in the 1830s thus provided one of the primary reasons for the adoption of the teetotal pledge.

Notes

1. John G. Cawelti, *Apostles of the Self-Made Man* (Chicago: University of Chicago Press, 1965), pp. 48-50, does not specifically mention the temperance reformers but asserts that "the popular exponents of self-improvement in the age of Jackson and Lincoln" reaffirmed "the traditional virtues of temperance, industry, frugality, honesty, and perseverance." He ignores the crucial distinction between "temperance" and total abstinence, which was emphatically not a traditional value. Histories which depict the American temperance movement as rural and provincial in origin include Brian Harrison, *Drink and the Victorians: The Temperance Question in England, 1815-1872* (London: Faber and Faber, 1971); Andrew Sinclair,

Prohibition: The Era of Excess (Boston: Little, Brown, 1962), pp. 18-22; Richard Hofstadter, foreword to Sinclair, *Era of Excess*, p. vii; and Alice S. Rossi, *The Feminist Papers: From Adams to de Beauvoir* (New York: Columbia University Press, 1973), p. 270.

2. On romantic perfectionism, see esp. John L. Thomas, "Romantic Reform in America, 1815-1865," *American Quarterly* 17 (Winter 1965): 658-81.

3. Chester Dewey, *An Appeal to the Friends of Temperance, Delivered in Pittsfield, Mass. on Sabbath Evening, October 7, 1832* (Pittsfield: Phineas Allen, 1832), pp. 7-8; "C.S." writing in *Temperance Recorder* 1 (August 1832): 42; Samuel F. Cary, ed., *The National Temperance Offering, and Sons and Daughters of Temperance Gift* (New York: R. Vandien, 1851), esp. Phillip S. White, "Retrospect of the Past, and Contemplation of the Future," pp. 13-17; *Permanent Temperance Documents of the American Temperance Society* (Boston: Seth Bliss, 1835), p. 339.

4. Christian Keener to John H. Cocke, 26 November 1845, Cocke Papers, UV; Moses Beach, *The Wealth and Biography of the Wealthy Citizens of the City of New York*, 12th ed. (New York: The Sun Office, 1855), p. 61; *Appleton's Cyclopedia of American Biography* (New York: D. Appleton and Co., 1888-1901), 1:149, 7:101; Bertram Wyatt-Brown, *Lewis Tappan and the Evangelical War Against Slavery* (Cleveland: Case Western Reserve University Press, 1969), pp. 229, 236.

5. Editorial, *New York Organ*, 8 September 1849; E. C. Delavan to Gerrit Smith, 28 April 1851, box 10, Gerrit Smith Miller Collection, SU; *Journal of Humanity*, 24 November, 8 December 1831; Azor Taber, "Address Before the Fourth Annual Meeting of the New-York State Temperance Society," *Fourth Annual Report of the New-York State Society for the Promotion of Temperance* (Albany: Packard and Van Benthuysen, 1833), pp. 16-17.

6. Editorial, *New York Organ*, 9 July 1849; E. C. Delavan to Gerrit Smith, 25 April 1851, box 10, Gerrit Smith Miller Collection; editorial, *New York Genius of Temperance*, 31 July 1833; editorial, *Worcester County Cataract*, 27 September 1843; Christian Keener to J. H. Cocke, 26 November 1845, Cocke Papers, UV. On the developments in the printing industry, see James L. Crouthamel, "The Newspaper Revolution in New York, 1830-1860," *New York History* 45 (April 1964): 91-113.

7. See Rowland Berthoff, *An Unsettled People: Social Order and Disorder in American History* (New York: Harper and Row, 1971), pp. 267-70. Through the analysis of Joseph Gusfield, *Symbolic Crusade: Status Politics and the American Temperance Movement* (Urbana: University of Illinois Press, 1963), this interpretation has become the generally accepted view of the early temperance movement.

8. Albert Barnes, *The Immorality of the Traffic in Ardent Spirits: A Discourse Delivered in the First Presbyterian Church in Philadelphia, April 13, 1834* (Philadelphia: George, Latimer, 1834), p. 8; Horace Mann, *Two Lectures on Intemperance* (New York: Funk and Wagnalls, 1859), p. 17 (first delivered in 1835).

9. Henry D. Kitchell, *An Appeal to the People on the Liquor Traffic* (New York: Oliver and Brother, 1848), p. 24. This was one of the most widely acclaimed of the temperance tracts. The Sons of Temperance awarded it a special prize of $200, and the American Temperance Union used it in the campaign against liquor licensing. Its arguments became in effect those of the American Temperance Union, and I have used Kitchell's *Appeal* as one indication of the ideology of the American Temperance Union leadership in the 1840s.

10. Stanley Elkins, *Slavery: A Problem in American Institutional and Intellectual Life*, 2d ed. (Chicago: University of Chicago Press, 1968), pp. 157-64.

11. Worcester County Temperance Convention, *Worcester Massachusetts Spy*, 22 November 1837; speech of Horace Mann, *Temperance Journal* (March 1835); E. C. Delavan to J. H. Cocke, 10 January 1837, Cocke Papers, UV.

12. *Worcester County Cataract*, 12 July, 9 August 1843; *Permanent Temperance Documents*, pp. 339, 358-59; Dewey, *An Appeal to the Friends of Temperance*, p. 7; White, "Retrospect of the Past," pp. 14-15; Kitchell, *Appeal*, p. 35.

13. Robert M. Hartley, *Intemperance in Cities and Large Towns: Showing Its Physical, Social, and Moral Effects; Also the Means for Its Prevention and Removal* (New York: John F. Trow, 1851), pp. 105-06; *Report of a Committee of the Massachusetts Society for the Suppression of Intemperance Adopted at a Meeting of the Society, June 3, 1831* (Boston: Power Press, 1831), p. 4; Edward Everett to unidentified correspondent, 14 December 1833, Otis Norcross Papers, MHS; *JATU* 14 (December 1850): 184.

14. *Eighth Annual Report of the New-York City Temperance Society* (New York: D. Fanshaw, 1837), pp. 32-33; *Proceedings of the Convention of the Young Men of Massachusetts, Friendly to the Cause of Temperance, Held at Worcester, July 1 & 2, 1834* (Boston: Ford and Damrell, 1834), pp. 10, 17; "Address by Professor Packard before the Second Annual Meeting of the Maine Temperance Society," *Second Annual Report of the Maine Temperance Society: Presented by the Corresponding Secretary, February 5, 1834* (Ellsworth, Me.: Robert Grant, 1834), pp. 5-6; "An Oration Delivered Before the Maine Charitable Mechanic Association, at Their Triannual Celebration, July 4, 1829, by Neal Dow," Neal Dow Papers, MeHS; Neal Dow, *The Reminiscences of Neal Dow, Recollections of Eighty Years*

(Portland, Me. : Evening Express Publishing Co., 1898), p. 177; *Massachusetts Cataract*, 17 July 1851.

15. The term *ideology* has several meanings in the social sciences. Here it is used to mean "that synthesis of ideas and representations designed to state an ideal and to motivate action. It may be true in some of its parts; but it is a gross oversimplification both of history and of the existing situation, the true recognition of which would not be in accord with the feelings and interests of the men who advance the ideology." Merrill D. Petersen, *The Jeffersonian Image in the American Mind* (New York: Oxford University Press, 1960), p. 21.

6

THE ORIGINS OF TEETOTALISM

When temperance organizations took a radical turn and embraced the teetotal pledge in the 1830s, reformers vowed to exclude all intoxicating beverages from daily use and championed the benefits of nature's own beverage, cold water. Beer, wine, and cider joined spirits on the list of condemned alcoholic temptations that reformers held responsible for drunkenness and misery throughout the land. The word *teetotal* is of uncertain origin but was probably the accidental creation of a stammering English plasterer named Richard (Dickie) Turner, who denounced the old pledge as a partial rather than a total abstinence position. At a public meeting of the Preston, Lancashire, Temperance Society in 1833, Turner announced in most emphatic terms: "I'll have nought to do with this moderation, botheration pledge. I'll be right down tee-tee-total forever."[1] The term soon won favor among supporters of the new pledge in England, and by 1840 it had come to signify in America a radical and rigorously applied commitment to the doctrines of total abstinence.

If the term was imported to the United States, the phenomenon of teetotalism was an indigenous product of tactical and ideological pressures operating upon temperance reformers. Although teetotalism became identified with radicalism in the temperance ranks, the adoption of teetotalism did not involve an abrupt change in social groups or classes controlling the temperance movement. The leaders of the American Temperance Society fully supported and directed the adoption of the teetotal pledge. Not social class but commitment to the temperance reform and involvement in the organizing drives of the temperance societies impelled the ATS agents, temperance journalists, lecturers, and corresponding secretaries of the temperance societies to adopt teetotalism. Their experiences in the temperance organizations convinced them that the cold water pledge was essential to the success of the crusade for sobriety.

Principled Teetotalers

For committed temperance workers who espoused teetotalism, the new pledge was a question of principle and the only firm foundation for the temperance agitation. They spoke as if God had decreed the new pledge from Mt. Sinai. Rather than court "public favor," the teetotalers trusted "simply to the rectitude of their principles and to the goodness of their cause."[2] The sincerity of these deeply committed men remains beyond question, yet they adopted teetotalism because the tactical needs of their temperance organizations demanded the new pledge. As Gerrit Smith, the Peterboro, New York, reformer argued, "If our old principles do not meet the necessities" of reform, then "let us substitute principles which do; and let us not be ashamed to own that the developments of Providence, in the course of the temperance reformation, have instructed us."[3]

The American Temperance Society and its auxiliaries and agents had defined ardent spirits as the cause of intemperance, but victory did not come as easily as the ATS had implied. When the temperance societies failed to achieve a quick and complete victory, temperance organizers blamed the use of wine and beer, arguing that fermented liquors whetted the appetites of drinkers and prepared them for stronger drinks. Elisha Taylor, an agent of the New York State Temperance Society, claimed that "intemperate habits are formed—the love of alcoholic drinks induced, by the habitual use of these 'lighter beverages.'"[4] Reformers even went so far as to suggest that liquor sellers deliberately adulterated wine with spirits to ensnare unsuspecting drinkers in the grip of appetite. "As to wine," wrote Dr. Samuel Woodward of Worcester, "it is no substitute" for hard liquor, "but only a form in which alcohol is disguised. I see no difference at all in the danger of wine and spirit-drinking at this time, for no wine is found that does not contain from one quarter to one half brandy or spirits."[5] In addition, temperance reformers began to blame even unadulterated wine and beer for more of the intoxication around them. "Daily experience convinces us," argued John Tappan of Boston, "that we must include all intoxicating drinks in our pledge, or the excepted drinks will perpetuate drunkenness thro' all coming generations." In part, this perception was a realistic appraisal of the trend of liquor consumption. As Lucius M. Sargent of Boston correctly observed, "The consumption of malt liquors [had] prodigiously increased, since the spread of the temperance reform, and beyond the ratio of the increase of our population."[6]

The increasing use of fermented liquor was in fact creating a new drinking problem, which warranted the extension of the pledge to include beer and wine. In 1810, the drink problem had been created almost exclusively by spirits, the consumption of which was five times larger than the consumption of fermented liquor. Yet by 1840, total consumption of spirits was only 1.78 times the consumption of fermented liquors. A 500 percent rise in the total consumption of beer and wines had occurred, while spirit drinking rose only 60 percent. On a per-capita basis, spirit drinking actually declined precipitously from 4½ to 2½ gallons, while the consumption of fermented liquors rose from 1 to over 1½ gallons.[7] Moreover licenses for the sale of fermented liquor expanded, thus providing increased facilities for drinking of wine and beer. The licensing authorities in Massachusetts, for example, responded to the pressure of temperance societies by reducing the number of licenses for hard liquor; but to satisfy retailers, they granted more licenses for the sale of wine alone.[8] From the perspective of temperance agitators, the authorities took away with one hand what they gave in the other. After 1845, the immigration of Germans and other beer-drinking Europeans would send the consumption of fermented liquor soaring, but already in the 1830s, the temperance reformers had discovered the bewildering variety of alcoholic temptations. It was clear that the increased consumption of wine and beer would demand a new pledge. As Lyman Beecher remarked, "We attacked first what we met first, and that was the van of the enemy's power. It came on under the banner of ardent spirits, and we drove it back at the point of the bayonet. But no sooner had we put the enemy to flight, than we found that he had a great many auxiliaries, whose power we never were aware of, until the main body was gone."9

Yet the new pledge was not merely a desperate ploy to explain the failure of the old pledge, and it was more than a pragmatic response to the changing nature of the problem of intemperance. If the problem was changing, the more important transformation took place in the minds of reformers: their goals in the 1830s were broader and more ambitious than when the ATS was founded in 1826. Reformers now wanted to do much more than "keep the temperate temperate." The ideology of improvement impelled temperance advocates to seek the reform of all men, including drunkards. Because the improvement-minded teetotalers had little contact with heavy drinkers and no personal experiences of the bottle, they had no realistic conception of what would be necessary to win inebriates to the temperance movement. Yet the fitful and imperfect efforts to get drunkards to renounce hard liquor soon convinced temperance men that the old pledge would not suffice in their mission.

When the temperance movement began to accept the responsibility for the reform of drunkards, it took on a goal which was enormously difficult to achieve. When the temperance reformers preached largely to the sober, the movement easily achieved a measure of success. Little real danger of temptation or backsliding existed. But the reformed drunkard, on the other hand, was constantly in danger of violating the pledge. He was, if only by his past history, a man susceptible to the influence of strong liquor.10 Abstention from spirits was clearly not enough to secure the reformed man from a possible relapse. Teetotal advocates pointed to the numerous examples of reformed drunkards within their experience who had lapsed back into the use of ardent spirits after drinking wine, beer, or other fermented liquor. "Cider, cider, cider," wrote Gerrit Smith, the Peterboro, New York, landowner and philanthropist. "This is one of the grand difficulties in the way of the reformation of drunkards." Smith wrote a celebrated pamphlet in which he detailed the life histories of the intemperate in Madison County, New York. These cases starkly asserted the connection between teetotalism and permanent reformation, between the partial pledge and permanent degradation.[11] Justin Edwards, John Marsh, and Edward C. Delavan hailed Smith's pamphlet because it showed the possibility of reforming drunkards yet demonstrated how the path to sobriety was fraught with danger for the inebriate. Only teetotalism could save him.[12]

If the drunkard must adopt teetotalism to save himself, the committed reformer must practice it to save others as well as himself. Teetotalers insisted on the adoption of the new pledge as a means of setting the intemperate "an example which they may follow with safety."[13] In addition, the teetotal pledge would remove a glaring inconsistency in the practice of temperance men. As teetotalers pointed out, the old pledge proscribed spirits, the drink of the poor, but left untouched wine, the drink of the affluent. Moses Stuart of Andover despaired "whether it can ever be possible to persuade the lower classes of men to abstain from ardent spirits . . . while the upper classes consume the like quantities in the form of mixture with the juice of the grape." William Goodell of New York realized that reformers faced ridicule from critics who pointed to the "inconsistency" and "hypocrisy" of "wine-bibbing temperance men."[14] One such critic was C. C. Baldwin, librarian of the American Antiquarian Society, who observed the delegates at a meeting of the Worcester County South District Temperance Society:

The delegates from many of the towns sat down at the public dinner table. They have signed the constitution of the Society, and profess to be samples of sobriety and regularity. I observed, however, that every one of the Society drank very freely of Cyder, and that which was of the very worst and most unpalatable sort. . . . I should regard myself as not much better than a drunkard to be found drinking such intolerable stuff as this Cyder.[15]

Such attacks on the sincerity and sobriety of temperance reformers were standard retorts to the moral crusade of the temperance societies. In New York, Edward C. Delavan testified that he faced the charge of inconsistency from liquor dealers in Albany and, equally important, could not make any headway among the "laboring classes" in the state until the New York Temperance Society had adopted a teetotal pledge in 1835. Only then did his critics see "that we are sincere in our temperance, that we are willing to make sacrifices for them."[16] Temperance reformers were acutely sensitive to the charge of hypocrisy precisely because the ideology of the temperance movement emphasized the personal example of the man who had taken the pledge. In addition, the American Temperance Society had stressed avoiding temptation by practicing total abstinence from hard liquor. Yet if the danger lay in the moderate use of alcohol rather than in the abuse, it seemed logical for temperance reformers to exclude all alcohol in beverages and so avoid the most insidious form of temptation. The practice of the American Temperance Society was clearly inconsistent with the ideology of the movement. When the gap between ideology and practice became apparent through public debate on the temperance question, committed temperance reformers moved quickly to provide a "consistent and efficacious example."[17] For the committed temperance reformers, teetotalism was a logical extension of the goals and ideals of the first phase of the total abstinence movement.

New Converts

Though the teetotal leadership came in large part from a group of temperance agitators who were identified with the older established temperance societies, the new pledge drew much of its support from new converts: from the young men's temperance societies and from the successful improvers such as the men who backed no-license in Worcester, Massachusetts. The first societies to adopt the teetotal pledge in a community were typically the mechanics' and young men's temperance organizations. In New York City, teetotalism first appeared in the Apprentices' Temperance Society in 1833, while the "city legitimates" of the regular temperance society lagged badly. The latter finally went teetotal in 1840. The Apprentices' Temperance Society in New York was in fact controlled not by "the journeymen and apprentices" but by their employers—the "leading mechanics"—who enrolled their workers from the city's factories and shops.[18] In Philadelphia, too, the inception of a separate temperance society for mechanics in 1835 saw immediate adoption of the teetotal pledge. As in New York, the mechanics' temperance societies in Philadelphia attracted successful entrepreneurs whose concern with social discipline and self-improvement made them hostile to any possible temptation and disposed them to seek eradication of every source of intoxication in the community.[19]

A similar preoccupation with the sources of temptation disturbed the socially ambitious and improvement-conscious reformers of the young men's temperance societies which were found in the vanguard of the teetotal movement. In Massachusetts the Young Men's Temperance Convention of 1834 was the first public body to express "a decided opinion in favor of abandoning the use of wine as an article of common drink."[20] In New York City, in New Haven, Connecticut, in Harrisburg, Pennsylvania, in Washington, D.C., in Albany, New York, in Worcester and Springfield, Massachusetts, the young men's temperance societies adopted the teetotal pledge while it remained only a visionary reform within the temperance movement as a whole.[21]

The young men's temperance societies displayed more clearly than any other part of the temperance movement the faith of reformers in the individual's capacity for material and moral improvement. These societies attracted supporters who enthusiastically accepted the American ideal of a career open to talent. They pictured the United States as "a country where every thing invites and stimulates to honorable enterprize and effort, where the road to the highest eminence and most enviable distinctions is thrown open equally to all."[22] The men who joined these societies did so because the groups expressed their own aspirations for material and moral improvement. Success in antebellum America would come through the application of industry and merit. And to seize the opportunities which American society presented, young men had to avoid the temptations and pitfalls around them. They had to be temperate, sober, and virtuous in their habits because they relied on their own exertions for upward mobility. They lacked the advantages of large property or high rank, which in other societies gave some youths a decided start in the race of life. As the Massachusetts Young Men's Temperance Convention explained, "We must, unaided, work out our own character, . . . our own destiny."[23] It matters little how fanciful a view the young men took of their own mobility or of the society around them. What mattered was their commitment to the ideal of personal advancement and their belief that man could manipulate the conditions of life around him to improve himself and society.

Although the young men's temperance organizations explicitly championed improvement, they did not limit the concept to personal mobility. Far from being totally preoccupied with self-advancement, they wanted to perfect the whole of American society; they professed a desire to promote "the moral prosperity of this nation and of the world."[24] This high-minded rhetoric was typical of the idealism of the younger teetotalers, but even the inexperienced young improvers could see the gap between the rhetoric of human perfectibility and the social realities of poverty, crime, insanity, and inequality in the Jacksonian era. The young teetotalers noted that not all young men took advantage of the opportunities for improvement which American society seemed to offer. Yet rather than indict the economic system they so enthusiastically endorsed, the young reformers reasoned that the defect must lie in faulty social customs which led the innocent down the path of personal, moral ruin. By eliminating the practice of drinking intoxicating liquor, teetotalers would preserve the benefits of material progress and make the process of social change "wholly rational and moral."[25]

The young men's temperance supporters proclaimed the belief that youth had the power to achieve its moral as well as its material goals. "There is a noble spirit of enterprise in the character of American young men," wrote one group of reformers. "If it receives a right impulse, and be directed to the right objects, the moral aspect of society here and throughout the world will rapidly improve."[26] Teetotalism was the impulse which the young reformers sought. The desire to universalize moral improvement, as much as a desire for personal advancement, impelled the young men to teetotalism.

By no means did all young American men favor teetotalism or even temperance. A glance at the activities of these young men's societies shows that they were not intended to compete directly with the lower-class tavern culture so much as to provide a refuge for literate, respectable, and evangelical youths. Activities included lectures, debates, and the provision of reading rooms. The example of the New York Young Men's Temperance Society illustrates their limited role. This society's activities included scripture reading; semimonthly meetings "to read original essays upon literary subjects, and adopt all laudable means for the increase of general scientific information"; and "to find out and recommend to young men visiting the city, boarding-houses where no immorality is tolerated, and to secure, as far as possible, their separation from vicious society and influences."[27] Thus these groups fulfilled some of the functions of the lyceums, debating societies, and young men's political clubs, though without the alcohol associated with the latter. In addition, some of the societies in New York and Baltimore, for example, enrolled women as well, so they served as places where respectable and pious youths might meet the opposite sex.

The literary and evangelical cast of the young men's societies would not have attracted lower-class youths, and indeed, an analysis of the support for the temperance movement in the young men's societies shows a heavy bias in favor of the professional and business occupations and in favor of students from evangelical colleges.[28] Both opponents and supporters of the temperance movement agreed that the young men's societies attracted "many young men of respectability, talent, and intelligence." Even Christopher Baldwin grudgingly spoke of "young gentlemen of great respectability" when he described the delegates to the Massachusetts Young Men's Temperance Convention held at Worcester in July 1834.[29]

If social background distinguished the young men from the general community, so too did the parental and educational influences which impelled these young men to seek sobriety. Much of the young men's agitation was prompted by the exhortation and example of their elders in the regular temperance societies. The first Young Men's Temperance Convention held in Massachusetts, for example, was organized by the regular temperance societies, not by the young men's organizations. It was, too, the temperance regulars who encouraged temperance among the young by creating organizations to cater to the special needs of children, juveniles, and college students. Especially in the evangelical colleges was the influence of the temperance regulars apparent. At Amherst, Williams, Union, and Andover colleges, among others, the faculties indoctrinated students with temperance principles and encouraged the whole student population to join college temperance societies.[30]

The young men who joined temperance societies and formed their own youth organizations were not uncritical and passive supporters.

Whenever and wherever the young men's temperance societies emerged, they expressed impatience and irritation at the slow pace of reform dictated by the temperance elders. The young men's societies frequently attacked expediency or compromise over the adoption of teetotalism. "When *will* it [teetotalism] be expedient?" asked one exasperated group of young temperance supporters in Albany, New York.[31] The new converts had enthusiastically accepted the rhetoric and ideology of the older temperance reformers, but the young men applied their temperance principles with a rigor which was often absent from the actions of their elders. This youthful idealism pushed the young men's temperance societies into the vanguard of the teetotal movement.

Teetotalism, then, was fostered by a group of activists within the older temperance societies who made common cause with the young men's societies, improvers, and other teetotal groups. When the established leaders felt that they commanded majorities in state and local temperance societies, they began to demand the teetotal pledge as a requirement of temperance membership. The adoption of teetotal pledges and resolutions accelerated in 1835 and 1836, beginning in state temperance conventions in New Hampshire, Massachusetts, and New York and culminating in the adoption of the teetotal position at the National Temperance Convention at Saratoga, New York, in the summer of 1836. Edward C. Delavan, Justin Edwards, and Lyman Beecher took the initiative in the conversion to teetotalism at Saratoga. The American Temperance Union (ATU), established by the convention as the new national temperance society, adopted the teetotal pledge, and the *Journal of the American Temperance Union* attacked all intoxicating liquor from its first issue in 1837.[32]

Satisfied that the American temperance movement now stood upon sound principles, Justin Edwards retired from active participation in temperance reform after eleven years' hectic service. In his place as chief tactician for teetotalism came John Marsh, a fiery Congregational clergyman from Haddam, Connecticut. As secretary of the new American Temperance Union and editor of the society's *Journal*, John Marsh technically possessed an authority and prestige rivaling that of Justin Edwards. Yet Marsh never had the influence which Edwards had exerted. The reasons for the declining influence of the national leadership of the temperance movement lay primarily in the fragmentation of power and purpose within the temperance organizations. The temperance movement had become too big, too socially diverse, and too decentralized to be dominated by a coterie of national leaders. Power was rapidly decentralizing, and one vital centrifugal force was the teetotal pledge, which both Edwards and Marsh had championed.[33]

Teetotal Controversies

Although the teetotal leaders had achieved the victory they believed essential to the long-term success of the movement, the immediate result was to create bitter controversy within temperance ranks. Teetotalers attacked the use of wine in the communion service and so threatened to alienate the religious groups which had been the basis of temperance agitation. The most outspoken and radical teetotalers, who included Gerrit Smith, agreed that the Bible sanctioned the use of fermented liquor but urged Americans to abandon outmoded biblical practices. Jesus Christ had drunk liquor, Smith conceded, but why, he urged, should Americans of the 1830s follow that erroneous practice? Smith explained that Jesus Christ lacked the "better knowledge of our times," which discoveries in chemistry and physiology had provided.[34]

Smith's position was not an irreligious or anti-Christian one; he wished rather to make Christian practice conform to the spirit of the Christian gospels, not to the letter of the biblical texts. Smith was critical chiefly of religious hypocrisy within the organized Christian churches. This renunciation of religious practice and denunciation of religious hypocrisy within the churches would broaden in scope in the 1840s, as lower-class Washingtonians entered the temperance ranks, and would thus produce serious divisions over temperance tactics and over the meaning and direction of temperance reform itself.

But few of the earliest teetotalers adopted so radical a position as to renounce organized Christianity as some Washingtonians would soon do. The first teetotalers were mostly deeply religious men who were too attached to the mainstream evangelical traditions to take a step so subversive of clerical control of the temperance movement. Men like Justin Edwards, Moses Stuart, John Tappan, and other tee-totalers were pillars of evangelical orthodoxy and products of the crusades of the missionary and benevolent societies. They believed that the Christian churches must provide the backbone of temperance or any other moral reform movement. If teetotalism were to triumph, Edward C. Delavan believed that Christians must be persuaded that the example of Christ demanded the complete renunciation of liquor. "So long as the Savior of the world is held up as a maker and dispenser of intoxicating wine," Delavan argued, "the cause you advocate will make but slow progress."[35] Like Delavan and Justin Edwards, most teetotal leaders in the 1830s concentrated on proving that the Bible did not sanction the use of fermented liquor. Edwards believed that the wine sanctioned in the Bible was not fermented, and he urged churches to distinguish "between 'the fruit of the vine' & 'the fruit of fermentation.'" He doubted whether biblical scholars would ever prove that "*fermented* wine was used at the passover, by divine direction, or that our Lord used it in the sacrament of the supper or created it, at the Marriage of Cana."[36] Teetotalers were prepared to rewrite or retranslate the Bible to prove Edwards's point. One of the foremost biblical scholars of the day, Moses Stuart of Andover Theological Seminary, poured over ancient Hebrew and Greek manuscripts to produce elaborate textual justifications for the teetotal position.[37]

The propaganda campaign of the teetotalers persuaded few church congregations to renounce fermented wine for communion purposes. Only three hundred churches in New York State (approximately 7 percent of the total number of congregations) used unfermented wine in 1840.[38] Part of the resistance stemmed from practical difficulties. Unfermented wine was difficult to get: grape culture was not widely disseminated, and given the absence of refrigeration and the long distances over which grape juice often had to be carried, it is hardly surprising that churches failed to conform to the expectations of teetotalers.

There was also opposition of a very articulate kind to the radical teetotal position on scriptural and theological grounds. The communion wine issue made radical teetotalers seem ridiculous and blasphemous to many opponents. While some individual congregations of Baptists, Presbyterians, and Congregationalists adopted the use

of unfermented wine before the Civil War, general church conferences refused to tackle this divisive and explosive issue. Even the
Methodist church, which was well in the forefront of the teetotal
movement, did not outlaw the use of fermented wine in the communion service until 1880.[39] The teetotalers' attack on communion
wine confronted and contradicted traditional church practice and
the plain language of the Bible, so it is little wonder that many Christian congregations resisted the teetotalers' demands. The "juice of
the grape" made no progress at all among the ritualistic and tradi-
tional-minded Episcopalians, Lutherans, and Roman Catholics, but
in addition, Calvinistic (Old School) Presbyterians and Baptists, as
well as Methodists and Congregationalists, proved slow to conform
to radical teetotalism on the communion issue. The Reverend James
Alexander of Princeton expressed the sentiments of Old School Presbyterians when he wrote: "The bible speaks well of wine, even as an
exhilarant."[40] Despite their religious rhetoric and despite their attempts to find biblical sanction for the total exclusion of wine, teetotalers betrayed a hostility toward existing church practice and
beliefs which disturbed many churchgoers and ministers.[41]

The dispute over the communion question was of the utmost importance to the more extreme teetotalers, or ultras, who valued "correct principles" above all else because they believed that success
would come to the movement if its principles were correct. As Edward C. Delavan explained, "I consider the holding up the truth . . .
to be the only effectual method of advancing the cause."[42] The
Young Men's Temperance Society of Worcester, Massachusetts,
agreed that right principles would secure victory. The society did not
fear a hostile reaction from the adoption of the teetotal pledge: "We
trust in the righteousness of our cause for success, and fear a reaction only from the remissness of the friends of the cause, and not
from our too strenuous efforts."[43] To put the temperance reform
movement on the "correct principles," the ultras did not hesitate to
agitate the communion question, even if such action risked the alien-
ation of religious support for the American temperance movement.
It was more important to the ultras that the temperance movement
renounce the use of liquor under any circumstances than that reformers should enhance their short-term public appeal. Exactly the
same tactical stance was adopted by the ultras on the other vexing
question which teetotalism raised: should reformers condemn men

who would sign only the old pledge? To the ultras it was axiomatic that they must condemn the old pledgers to separate the temperance movement from any connection with intoxicating liquor. E. C. Delavan denounced the old pledgers as worse than the most unprincipled liquor sellers because the old pledger made "the wine bibber respectable."[44]

By no means all temperance reformers meekly accepted the dominance of the ultra position. Yet much of the opposition to ultraism within the temperance societies argued a compromise position on the issue of teetotalism; it denied not the efficacy of the teetotal pledge but the wisdom of exclusive reliance on it. To make the cold water pledge the sole criterion of loyalty to temperance reform would, some teetotalers believed, alienate "many excellent people who cannot go the whole way."[45] This view, which the ultras dubbed the expediency doctrine, was best articulated by the New-York City Temperance Society. The New York City society circulated both pledges and argued that the way to introduce men to teetotalism was to wean them first from the use of spirits. The society took the position that "few converts have been made to the *new pledge* except from the ranks of those who had tried the *old one*." When men "have abandoned the use of ardent spirits *because* it produces intemperance, if they are honest, it only remains to convince them that wine and other fermented drinks are fruitful sources of intemperance, and they will give their personal example against these." Even if they did not reach the "summit level of cold water," their support remained valuable because ardent spirits was a greater cause of intoxication than wine or beer.[46] The society argued that to insist on teetotalism as a prerequisite of temperance membership would jeopardize the achievements of the early 1830s and set the temperance cause back many years.

Although the ultras labored to belittle both the arguments and the support for the doctrine of expediency, the New York City society's stand was a widely held and respectable position within the temperance movement in the 1830s. At the Saratoga National Temperance Convention in 1836, the opposition to the ultra position came from men like Professor Alonzo Potter of Union College, who argued that outright condemnation of fermented liquors would deprive the temperance movement of many erstwhile supporters.[47]

Support for expediency came partly for tactical reasons through fear of the divisiveness of the teetotal position. Yet behind this divisiveness lay two factors: religion and social class. The teetotal pledge, especially the efforts of the ultras to denounce alcohol in the most vitriolic and unequivocal terms, disturbed many churchgoing temperance reformers for precisely the same reason that they deplored the communion controversy. For some religious temperance men, particularly the Old School Presbyterians, low church Episcopalians, and Reformed Dutch temperance supporters, the expediency position enabled them to accept teetotalism without denouncing the use of liquor under all circumstances. They could thus avoid taking a position on the wine issue which they regarded as unscriptural. These men were critical of radicalism in temperance reform, but they generally remained within the temperance societies and attempted to fight what they saw as dangerous ultra tendencies. Examples were two Princeton professors, Dr. John McLean and the Reverend James Alexander, who refused to adopt the teetotal pledge in 1838 but by 1841 had signed to give a good example to their students. Yet both still refused to accept the ultra position that to take even a tiny drop of alcohol was a sin against God. [48]

In contrast to these reformers who doubted the expediency or the scriptural authority of the ultra position, the other main opposition to adoption of the teetotal pledge came from men whose temperament or social class made them hostile to teetotalism on principle. Included were wealthy supporters of the Massachusetts Temperance Society, the New-York City Temperance Society, and the Maine Temperance Society. The position which these men, often merchants, lawyers, or politicians, took was clearly articulated by Edward Everett of Massachusetts and William King of Maine. Everett, the governor of Massachusetts between 1836 and 1838, did what he could "to promote temperance," which he regarded "as a practicable Christian virtue, in contradistinction to teetotalism," which he was "compelled to regard as an ascetic Utopian vision." Everett had given lectures on the subject of temperance, but he was in no sense a committed or zealous temperance agitator. He frequently counselled discretion and moderation in the "application of moral principles." [49] Men like Everett were unwilling to make the personal sacrifices for the cause that teetotalism involved.

In addition to a social temperament which eschewed controversy and extremism these opponents also shared an extremely high social status, and they moved in social and political circles where the use of wine was obligatory—a matter of social etiquette as much as personal preference. William King, the wealthy ex-governor of Maine and the most prominent opponent of teetotalism in the Maine Temperance Society, defended the use of wine as "essential to the intercourse of gentlemen." Edward Everett refused to exclude wine whenever he entertained his social equals because its use was "the custom of society." As Edward Delavan recognized, "Good men . . . attached the idea of good society to the use of wine."[50] Temperance for men such as Everett and William King connoted social responsibility, but teetotalism seemed to subvert social institutions and social hierarchies.

The result was disillusionment among some of the wealthy and respectable groups which had supported the American Temperance Society and its auxiliaries and the consequent loss of money and prestige for the temperance movement. In both Maine and Ohio, the old temperance societies disbanded and were replaced by teetotal societies, while the Massachusetts Temperance Society continued on but was practically moribund after 1838. Disapproving of the radical turn in temperance thinking, many of the members of these societies either dropped out of temperance reform entirely or ceased to take an active role.[51]

Yet although teetotalism did alienate some socially exclusive supporters of temperance, the impact of internal divisions on the temperance movement in the 1830s has been exaggerated.[52] A sharp pause in the activities of all American temperance societies did occur between 1837 and 1839, but temperance records make clear that this hiatus resulted more from the financial depression than from tactical disputes. Like all other major benevolent crusades, the temperance movement suffered from the crash of 1837, which depleted the assets of such wealthy supporters as Arthur Tappan, Isaac Lloyd of Philadelphia, and Christian Keener of Baltimore.[53] To be sure, adoption of teetotalism did compound the problem by shattering the organizational unity of the temperance movement; but the new pledge did not impair the numerical support for temperance societies, except in the very short term. It is true, for example, that the New York State Temperance Society lost 40 percent of its members between 1836 and 1838, but by 1840, the society's quarreling factions had called a truce, and the state organization reported even more members than in 1836, despite its insistence on the teetotal pledge. The process of agitation and debate in fact won over many reluctant teetotalers within the New York temperance movement by 1840.[54]

All this is not to deny the divisive impact of teetotalism on the temperance organizations. Yet if we are to comprehend fully the character of the divisions within temperance reform, the analysis must extend beyond the 1830s to take in the upheaval in temperance support and tactics that occurred in the 1840s. Much of the dissaffection among upper-class temperance reformers over the course of temperance agitation came after 1840. The New-York City Temperance Society, for example, did not disband in the 1830s even though it had for a time led the fight against the new pledge. In fact, the society eventually adopted the pledge of teetotalism in 1840 and continued to operate until 1842. The ultimate demise of the society came about not principally because of controversy over teetotalism but as a result of controversies generated by the subsequent Washingtonian movement.[55] Although upper-class temperance reformers were disturbed by the radical trend in temperance thinking and by the denunciation of wine, the subsequent agitation of the Washingtonians was still more alarming to them. The argument so far has revolved around temperance tactics within the older and established temperance societies and among men who usually shared a common background of either wealth, or evangelical commitment, or respectability. Teetotalism espoused by respectable and evangelical reformers did not arouse quite the same degree of unease as that elicited by lower-class drunks and artisans when they formed their own temperance societies and began to dispute the authority of temperance regulars in the 1840s. The disillusionment of many wealthy and respectable reformers with the course of temperance agitation was in fact a cumulative process which had begun in the 1830s, but accelerated with changes in the class composition of temperance societies during the Washingtonian revival of the 1840s.

Notes

1. There are widely divergent accounts of the exact origin of the term *teetotal* used to describe the new pledge. August F. Fehlandt, *A Century of*

Drink Reform in the United States (Cincinnati: Jennings and Graham, 1904), pp. 80-81, asserts that the term originated in Hector, New York, in 1827. In the Hector society, those who signed the comprehensive or new pledge placed the letter *T* after their names to designate total abstinence from all intoxicating liquor. By explaining this designation on the roll, that *T* stood for total, such persons were directly referred to as *T-totalers.* John A. Krout, *The Origins of Prohibition* (New York: Alfred A. Knopf, 1925), p. 158, gives essentially the same story but attributes the origins of the term to Scottish teetotalers of the early 1830s. Daniel Dorchester, *The Liquor Problem in All Ages* (New York: Phillips and Hunt, 1884), pp. 323-24, gives an alternative explanation, which Brian Harrison, in *Drink and the Victorians: The Temperance Question in England, 1815-1872* (London: Faber and Faber, 1971), p. 126, also supports. Dorchester wrote that at a meeting of the Preston, Lancashire, Temperance Society, "a simple, eccentric, but honest and consistent drunkard" had coined the term when he blurted out an emotional denunciation of the old pledge. Whatever the origins of the term, the word *teetotal* does seem to have been used first in England. Contrary to Fehlandt, the first notice of its use in the United States comes in 1835, in *Permanent Temperance Documents of the American Temperance Society* (Boston: Seth Bliss, 1835), p. 477 in a report on the Preston teetotalers.

2. *Proceedings of the Annual Meeting of the Young Men's Temperance Society of the City of Albany: Together with the Address to the Young Men of the United States, 1836* (Albany: Hoffman, 1836), p. 9. See also John Tappan to Reverend Calvin Duffy, of Dedham, Massachusetts, 12 February 1842, Miscellaneous Manuscripts, NYHS; E. C. Delavan to Gerrit Smith, February 1838, box 10, Gerrit Smith Miller Collection, SU; Justin Edwards to E. C. Delavan, 1 October 1835, Gratz Collection, HSP.

3. See, for example, Gerrit Smith to Samuel Hopkins, 25 March 1836, in Samuel Hopkins, *Correspondence on the Principles of Right Reasoning Applicable to Temperance* (Geneva, N.Y.: n.p., 1836), p. 7.

4. Justin Edwards, *Letter to the Friends of Temperance in Massachusetts* (Boston: Seth Bliss, 1836), pp. 12-13, 29; Gerrit Smith, *Letter of Gerrit Smith to Samuel M. Hopkins, January 26, 1837* (n.p., 1837), p. 8.

5. Samuel Woodward, *Asylums for Inebriates* (Worcester: n.p., 1838), p. 15. On the question of adulteration of liquors, there was an extensive propaganda campaign. See Edward C. Delavan, "Adulteration of Liquors," in Samuel F. Cary, ed., *The National Temperance Offering, and Sons and Daughters of Temperance Gift* (New York: R. Vandien, 1851), pp. 56-69.

6. Tappan to J. H. Cocke, 28 March 1835, Cocke Papers, UV; Lucius M. Sargent, *Letter on the "State of the Temperance Reform," to the Rev. Caleb Stetson, Medford, Mass.* (Boston: William S. Damrell, 1836), p. 47.

7. *Compendium of the Enumeration of the Inhabitants and Statistics of the United States, . . . from the Returns of the Sixth Census . . .* (Washington, D.C.: Blair and Rives, 1841), p. 358; and Tench Coxe, *A Statement of the Arts and Manufactures of the United States of America for the Year 1810* (Philadelphia: A. Cornman, 1814), sec. 1, table 22. During the decade 1850-1860, production of fermented liquors rose 300 percent, while spirit production rose 87 percent. In 1860, production of fermented liquors exceeded production of distilled spirits for the first time. See J. D. B. De Bow, *Statistical View of the United States . . . Being a Compendium of the Seventh Census . . .* (Washington, D.C.: A. O. P. Nicholson, 1854), p. 182, and Joseph C. G. Kennedy, *Preliminary Report on the Eighth Census, 1860* (Washington, D.C.: Government Printing Office, 1862), pp. 178-79.

8. *Temperance Recorder* 4 (May 1835): 38.

9. Dorchester, *Liquor Problem in All Ages*, p. 266; Dawson Burns, *Temperance History: A Consecutive Narrative of the Rise, Development, and Extension of the Temperance Reform* (London: National Temperance Publication Depot, n.d. [c.1881]), p. 99; E. C. Delavan to J. H. Cocke, 3 March 1837, Cocke Papers, UV.

10. The reform of drunkards is discussed by Justin Edwards, in *Permanent Temperance Documents*, p. 265; and in E. C. Delavan to Gerrit Smith, 5 September 1833, box 10, Gerrit Smith Miller Collection.

11. Gerrit Smith to William Goodell, 5 October 1833, letterbook, vol. 1, p. 14, Gerrit Smith Miller Collection; *Communication from Gerrit Smith, to Edward C. Delavan, Esq, on the Reformation of the Intemperate*, republished from the fourth number of the *American Temperance Magazine*, art. VI, Peterboro, September 11, 1833 (n.p., n.d.), p. 16.

12. Edwards to Smith, 13 March 1839, box 20, and E. C. Delavan to Smith, 5 September 1833, box 10, Gerrit Smith Miller Collection.

13. *Proceedings of the Pennsylvania Young Men's Temperance Convention, Held at Carlisle, Nov. 4, 1834* (n.p., n.d.), p. 12.

14. Moses Stuart, *Essay on the Prize-Question, Whether the Use of Distilled Liquors, or Traffic in Them, Is Compatible at the Present Time, with Making a Profession of Christianity* (New York: John P. Haven, 1830), p. 61; *New York Genius of Temperance*, 31 July 1833.

15. Nathaniel Paine, ed., *Diary of Christopher Columbus Baldwin, Librarian of the American Antiquarian Society, 1829-1835* (Worcester: American Antiquarian Society, 1901), p. 182.

16. E. C. Delavan to J. H. Cocke, 13 March 1835, 3 March 1837, Cocke Papers, UV. For other expressions of the criticism of wine drinking, see letter to editor, *Worcester Massachusetts Spy*, 4 April 1832; Josiah Bissell to Gerrit Smith, 28 April 1830, quoted in Ralph V. Harlow, *Gerrit Smith: Philan-*

thropist and Reformer (New York: H. Holt, 1939), p. 72, and *An Address to the Leaders of the Abstinence Enterprise: By a Friend of Temperance and Equal Rights*, 3d ed. (n.p., 1831), p. 3.

17. Harlow, *Gerrit Smith*, pp. 76-77; Samuel Pond's speech, *Temperance Journal* (April 1835); *JATU* 1 (December 1837): 181; George C. Shattuck to Lucy B. Shattuck, 26 October 1834, Shattuck Family Papers, MHS.

18. *New York Genius of Temperance*, 30 October 1833; E. C. Delavan to Gerrit Smith, 2 December 1839, box 10, Gerrit Smith Miller Collection; minutes of the New-York City Temperance Society, 8 May 1840, p. 200, NYPL; *Second Annual Report of the New-York Apprentices Temperance Society, February 1832* (New York, 1832), pp. 9, 13; *Sixth Annual Report of the New-York City Temperance Society, Presented May 15, MDCCCXXXV* (New York: H. R. Piercey, 1835), pp. 12-14.

19. *Philadelphia Inquirer*, reported in *Boston Daily Advertiser*, 25 March 1835; Albert Barnes, *The Connection of Temperance with Republican Freedom: An Oration Delivered before the Mechanics and Workingmen's Temperance Society of the City and County of Philadelphia* (Philadelphia: Boyle and Benedict, 1835), p. 25; *Second Annual Report of the Maine Temperance Society: Presented by the Corresponding Secretary, February 5, 1834* (Ellsworth, Me.: Robert Grant, 1834), p. 15.

20. *Proceedings of the Convention of the Young Men of Massachusetts, Friendly to the Cause of Temperance, Held at Worcester, July 1 & 2, 1834* (Boston: Ford and Damrell, 1834), p. 16.

21. *New York Genius of Temperance*, 26 June 1833; John Marsh, *Temperance Recollections* (New York: Charles Scribner, 1866), p. 56; *Constitution of the New-York Young Men's Total Abstinence Society, to Which Are Added the By-Laws of the Board of Directors: With a List of Officers, Managers and Committees* (New York: Osborn and Buckingham, 1836); communication from "Aristides," *Worcester Massachusetts Spy*, 12 March 1835.

22. *Proceedings of the Convention of the Young Men of Massachusetts*, pp. 11-15.

23. Ibid., p. 15.

24. *Proceedings of the Annual Meeting of the Young Men's Temperance Society of the City of Albany*, p. 11.

25. *Proceedings of the Young Men's Temperance Meeting Held at Harrisburg, April 20, 1833* (n.p., 1833), pp. 1-5; James M. Lincoln et al. to J. C. Warren, 15 November 1845, Warren Papers, MHS; *Proceedings of the Convention of the Young Men of Massachusetts*, p. 17; Azor Taber et al., "Address to the Young Men of the United States," *Proceedings of the Annual*

Meeting of the Young Men's Temperance Society of the City of Albany, pp. 21-22.

26. Taber, "Address to Young Men," p. 19.

27. *Journal of Humanity*, 1 September 1831; *Eighth Annual Report of the New-York City Temperance Society,* . . . (New York: D. Fanshaw, 1837), p. 19; *New York Genius of Temperance*, 22 June 1831.

28. If the Boston delegation to the Massachusetts Young Men's Temperance Convention in 1834 gives any indication, the Boston young men's temperance societies attracted primarily young professionals, businessmen, and artisans. Representative of the delegation were George Stillman Hilliard, a rising young attorney and friend of Charles Sumner; Amasa Walker, a leather goods merchant and railroad promoter; and Elisha Tower, a gilder representing the Laboring Young Men's Temperance Society. On Hilliard, see James S. Loring, *The Hundred Boston Orators, Appointed by the Municipal Authorities and Other Public Bodies* . . . (Boston: John P. Jewett, 1852), pp. 548-51. For the office-holders and directors of the Boston Young Men's Temperance Society, see *Address of the Young Men's Temperance Society to the Young Men of Boston: to Which Is Annexed the Constitution of the Society* (Boston: Garrison and Knapp, 1832); *Boston Recorder*, 15 August 1832. The most active and prominent members of the Young Men's Temperance Society in Worcester seem to have come from backgrounds similar to those of older teetotalers in Worcester. Of twenty-eight leaders, there were twelve tradesmen or industrial entrepreneurs; twelve professionals (three lawyers, three clergymen, five teachers, and the superintendant of the Worcester State Asylum); three merchants; and one farmer. For membership lists, see *Worcester Massachusetts Spy*, 20 January 1836, and appendix to the *Proceedings of the Convention of the Young Men of Massachusetts*.

29. The *Temperance Journal* (August 1834) called the delegates to the Young Men's Temperance Convention in Worcester "the *elite* of the land." Paine, ed., *Diary of Christopher Columbus Baldwin*, p. 313.

30. For encouragement and support from regular teetotal groups for the young men's societies, see *Youth's Temperance Advocate*, no. 1 (1839): 1-2; Edward Hitchcock, *An Essay on Temperance, Addressed Particularly to Students and the Young Men of America*, 2d ed. (Amherst: J. S. and C. Adams, 1830), p. 22; and Edwards, *Letter to the Friends of Temperance in Massachusetts*, p. 3. The favorable reception given to the Massachusetts Young Men's Temperance Convention is illustrated in *Temperance Journal* (July, August 1834) and the favorable reception in Worcester, in communication from "Aristides," *Worcester Massachusetts Spy*, 12 March 1834.

31. *Proceedings of the Annual Meeting of the Young Men's Temperance Society of the City of Albany*, p. 6. See also *Proceedings of the Pennsylvania Young Men's Temperance Convention, Held at Carlisle*, pp. 12-13, and *Worcester Massachusetts Spy*, 18 March 1835.

32. Dorchester, *Liquor Problem in All Ages*, pp. 264-65; Marsh, *Temperance Recollections*, p. 44; report of the national temperance convention, *New York Observer*, 20 August 1836.

33. Marsh (1788-1866) was born in Wethersfield, Connecticut, and died in Brooklyn, New York, after thirty years of service as secretary of the American Temperance Union. Before his appointment, Marsh had been educated at Yale; he became a clergyman in Haddam, Connecticut (1818-1832), secretary of the Connecticut Temperance Society (1828-1832), and secretary of the Pennsylvania Temperance Society (1833-1837). On the life of Marsh, see his *Temperance Recollections* (1866).

34. Smith to E. C. Delavan, 29 July 1839, Smith Family Papers, NYPL.

35. P. T. Winskill, *The Comprehensive History of the Rise and Progress of the Temperance Reformation from the Earliest Period to September, 1881* (Crewe, Eng.: Mackie, Brewtnall & Co., 1881), p. 204.

36. Justin Edwards to Edwin James, 1 October 1835, Gratz Collection, HSP.

37. Moses Stuart, *Scriptural View of the Wine Question, in a Letter to the Reverend Dr. Nott, President of Union College* (New York: Leavitt, Trow, 1848). Stuart's views were first published in the *Albany Temperance Intelligencer* of August 1835. See also Eliphalet Nott, *Lectures on Temperance* (New York: Sheldon, Blakeman, 1847). These lectures were delivered at Union College, Schenectady, New York, in 1838 and 1839; they were first published in 1846.

38. Burns, *Temperance History*, p. 99. The number of congregations in the state of New York is based on De Bow, *Statistical View of the United States*, p. 133, which gives figures for 1850, the earliest year for which census information is available on this question.

39. For churches adopting unfermented wine, see *JATU* 5 (January 1841): 10; and Records of Meetings of the Membership and Presbytery of the Congregational Church of Malta, New York, p. 89, NYHS. On Methodist attitudes, see Henry Wheeler, *Methodism and the Temperance Reformation* (Cincinnati: Walden and Stowe, 1882), pp. 236-38.

40. James W. Alexander to John Hall, 14 January 1842, *Forty Years' Familiar Letters of James W. Alexander, D.D., Constituting, with the Notes, a Memoir of his Life. Edited by the Surviving Correspondent, John Hall, D.D.* (New York: Charles Scribner, 1860), 1:346. See also *Minutes of the General Assembly of the Presbyterian Church in the United States of Amer-*

ica: with an Appendix. A.D. 1837 (Philadelphia: Lydia R. Bailey, 1837), p. 507.

41. William B. Sprague, *Sprague's Reply to Professor Stuart's Letter Addressed to Him Through the American Temperance Intelligencer of August 1835, Relative to His Late Sermon on the Exclusion of Wine from the Lord's Supper* (Albany: Packard and Van Benthuysen, 1835), pp. 1-28; David M. Reese, *Humbugs of New-York: Being a Remonstrance Against Popular Delusion Whether in Science, Philosophy, or Religion* (New York: John S. Taylor, 1838), p. 135; report of the national temperance convention, speeches by John McLean, David M. Reese, and Alonzo Potter, *New York Observer*, 20, 27 August 1836; Whitney R. Cross, *The Burned-over District: The Social and Intellectual History of Enthusiastic Religion in Western New York, 1800-1850* (Ithaca, N.Y.: Cornell University Press, 1950), p. 216.

42. Edward C. Delavan to Gerrit Smith, February 1838, box 10, Gerrit Smith Miller Collection.

43. *Worcester Massachusetts Spy*, 18 March 1835. On the psychology of ultraism and its application to temperance and teetotalism, see Cross, *Burned-over District*, pp. 211-17.

44. E. C. Delavan to Gerrit Smith, 2 December 1839, box 10, Gerrit Smith Miller Collection; Delavan to J. H. Cocke, 20 October 1838, Cocke Papers, UV; Cross, *Burned-over District*, pp. 212-13.

45. *JATU* 1 (March 1837): 44.

46. *Eighth Annual Report of the New-York City Temperance Society*, p. 39.

47. *New York Observer*, 27 August 1836; Krout, *Origins of Prohibition*, p. 156; Marsh, *Temperance Recollections*, p. 45.

48. George William Hawkins, *Life of John H. W. Hawkins* (Boston: John P. Jewett, 1859), p. 141.

49. Edward Everett to Professor McCoy, 1 December 1855, vol. 105, p. 131, and Everett to Edward Brooks, 27 June 1839, vol. 68, p. 293, Everett Papers, MHS. For his temperance views, see Edward Everett, *Address of the Hon. Edward Everett, before the Young Men's Temperance Society of Salem, Massachusetts, June 14, 1833* (Boston: Dutton and Wentworth, 1833), p. 16. For another example, see the case of Samuel Ward, a New York City merchant. *JATU* 4 (January 1840): 16.

50. Frank L. Byrne, *Prophet of Prohibition: Neal Dow and His Crusade* (Madison: Wisconsin State Historical Society, 1961), p. 24; Everett to J. C. Warren, 21 June 1850, vol. 93, pp. 63-64, Everett Papers; Delavan to J. H. Cocke, 20 February 1837, Cocke Papers, UV.

51. *Augusta* (Me.) *Age*, 11 February 1837; Neal Dow, *The Reminis-*

cences of Neal Dow: Recollections of Eighty Years (Portland, Me.: Evening Express Publishing Company, 1898), p. 233; *JATU* 1 (March 1837): 39, 44; Krout, *Origins of Prohibition*, p. 161.

52. Cf. Krout, *Origins of Prohibition*, pp. 159-62.

53. See E. C. Delavan to J. H. Cocke, 5 November 1837, Cocke Papers, UV, on the financial woes of the American Temperance Union and Lloyd's financial difficulties; *JATU* 5 (April 1841): 60; Allan Nevins and Milton Halsey Thomas, eds., *The Diary of George Templeton Strong: Young Man in New York, 1835-1849* (New York: Macmillan, 1952), p. 131; William M. Thayer, *Charles Jewett: Life and Recollections* (Boston: James H. Earle, 1880), p. 150; and minutes of the New-York City Temperance Society, December 1840, p. 216, NYPL.

54. Burns, *Temperance History*, p. 188; Krout, *Origins of Prohibition*, p. 161; E. C. Delavan to Gerrit Smith, 2 December 1839, box 10, Gerrit Smith Miller Collection; Winskill, *Comprehensive History*, pp. 191-92.

55. Minutes of the New-York City Temperance Society, 8 May 1840, p. 200, and circular, March 1842, p. 273, NYPL.

7

THE WASHINGTONIANS:
ARTISANS AND ALCOHOL

Alongside the evangelical and well-to-do supporters of the American Temperance Union, a new and less affluent group of teetotalers emerged in the 1840s. The older evangelicals had lacked personal experience of drink and sought converts chiefly among the already sober; the new group of reformers focused the attention of the temperance movement on the drinkers themselves. Foreshadowed in the temperance benefit societies established by artisans between 1837 and 1840, the new trend became pronounced after 1840 with the emergence of the Washingtonian temperance movement among reformed alcoholics of the lower-middle and working classes. For the first time, humble artisans formed their own temperance societies, and equally important, women began to take an independent and more prominent role in temperance agitation. The exploits of the reformed drunkards, artisans, and women spurred renewed public interest in the antiliquor crusade, and temperance societies proliferated.

This novel movement began quietly in May 1840 when six casual drinkers gathered in a Baltimore tavern. After lamenting their too-fond regard for whiskey, they decided to take a pledge against the use of all intoxicating liquor and formed a new society to carry out the pledge, the Washington Temperance Society of Baltimore. The founders probably took Washington's name for their society as a patriotic symbol, yet the use also reflected the teetotaler's own image of himself. Washington had delivered the country from its political oppression; the teetotalers believed they would liberate Americans from the greater social oppression of alcohol.[1] The new society made a deliberate effort to convert drunkards to the pledge of teetotalism, and by the end of 1840, the converts numbered about three hundred.[2] News of the Washingtonian success in Baltimore spread rapidly to New York, and the original Washingtonians were invited there in March 1841 to spread the message of self-reform. Wherever they went, the Washingtonian speakers attracted enormous attention because they underlined the growing conviction among temperance supporters that drunkards could be saved. By the end of 1841, Washingtonians claimed 12,000 adherents in Baltimore, 10,000 in New York, 5,000 in Boston, and a total of 200,000 throughout the North. By 1843, they claimed with heady enthusiasm that their following numbered in millions. Leaving aside the undoubted exaggerations of the new teetotalers, the reality was that the Washingtonians had acquired a mass following without precedent in the history of temperance reform.[3]

The Washingtonian movement was not socially homogeneous; it embraced lower-middle-class as well as lower-class people, employers as well as employees, ex-alcoholics and men and women who were lifelong abstainers, the thoroughly respectable and the not-so respectable, evangelicals and those of a more secular disposition. The disparate character of the new movement makes more intelligible its rapid rise and enormous support, but the diversity of the Washingtonians' appeal did create friction within and between the various Washingtonian societies. Between 1843 and 1845, the Washingtonian movement fragmented into a bewildering variety of societies, reflecting the social diversity of the self-help temperance groups. While the fragmentation of the Washingtonian movement had many causes, there was one overriding issue: the character of the relationship between the Washingtonians and the older temperance regulars.

At first glance, the style and tactics of the Washingtonians and temperance regulars might seem so divergent that one may legitimately question whether they were ever part of the same movement.

Washingtonians often seemed indifferent to the evangelical religion which the temperance regulars espoused. Moreover Washingtonians advocated moral suasion, while regulars strongly favored prohibition. The relationship between temperance regulars and Washingtonians was, however, exceedingly complex. It would be wrong to exaggerate the autonomy of the early Washingtonian revival and to depict the new societies as entirely separate from the regular temperance organizations. There were, in fact, important organizational, personal, and financial links between them. Most striking is not the absence of links but a pattern of uneasy cooperation, uneasy because the temperance regulars soon sought to control the Washingtonians and to shape the movement in directions acceptable to the old societies. It was the response of Washingtonians to this power struggle which split the Washingtonians between 1843 and 1845.

Washingtonians of more middle-class status or aspirations tended to ally themselves with the wealthy and evangelical temperance groups, which emerged again in the middle of the 1840s to demand prohibition. On the other side were Washingtonians, usually reformed men or people of predominantly lower-class backgrounds, who resisted the alliance with the temperance regulars in a variety of ways. Thus the Washingtonian revival had essentially two phases within its short history: the creation of new and innovative temperance societies among lower- and lower-middle-class people, and then the fragmentation of those societies because of conflict both within the Washingtonian movement and between Washingtonian societies and the temperance regulars.

Before examining the relationship between the larger temperance movement and the Washingtonians, we must explore what might be called the inner history of the Washingtonian movement. The analogy with the study of slavery may be helpful. Historians of slavery have become increasingly aware in recent years of the independent life of the slaves and of a vital slave community culture distinct from, although related to, the culture and society of their masters. Certainly no one would assume that the interests and aspirations of slaves and masters were the same. So too historians of working-class culture have begun to examine the independent lives and culture of artisans and working-class communities generally.[4] This trend involves historians of temperance, for in the 1840s occurred the first profound divisions within the temperance movement on the basis of social class. The very same people whom temperance entrepreneurs sought to reform in the 1830s, their workers, were among those reforming themselves in the Washingtonian societies of the early 1840s. Yet though these lowly people were in a general sense responding to a temperance agitation they had not created, we cannot assume that Washingtonians displayed the same concern for upward mobility, social control, and power in their communities which animated the earlier societies. To understand the spectacular success of the reformed men in the early 1840s, we must look at the social and psychological appeals of the Washingtonian societies to the artisan classes which created them.

Socioeconomic Roots of the Washingtonians

The ranks of the Washingtonians were not limited to former drinkers. In fact, a substantial proportion—possibly as many as half—had never touched a drop of alcohol. The Worcester society, for example, had about 550 members in June 1841. Of these, about fifty had been "hard cases" of habitual intemperance; another fifty were known to have been drunk occasionally. Two hundred had been moderate drinkers before taking the Washingtonian pledge, and some 250 were previously total abstainers. Of 4,200 pledges in Boston, about 2,000 were those of the habitually intemperate. Another thousand were reported as occasionally drunk, and the remainder were either light drinkers or abstainers. In Raleigh, North Carolina, only 50 to 60 of the 230 members of the local Washingtonian society were reformed men; in Baltimore, the home of the original Washingtonians, the figure was two-thirds of the total membership.[5]

But the presence of reformers who had never touched the bottle did not change the fact that a new element had been infused into the temperance ranks. The change was apparent in the methods of organizing the new societies and in the conduct of temperance meetings. Rank-and-file members now participated in temperance meetings to an extent unknown among the earlier temperance societies. Whereas the older societies often convened merely to hear an address from a visiting speaker, a dozen or more members commonly spoke at Washingtonian meetings. [6]

The new methods of conducting temperance meetings were part of a much broader shift in the tactics of teetotalism which occurred as the reformed men and other teetotalers of low status moved into the temperance ranks. The Reverend John Marsh recognized that the Washingtonian methods substituted emotional and psychological appeals for the rational arguments against liquor which older temperance reformers had stressed. "Men are not to be reasoned out of drinking," Marsh admitted. Intemperance had "no rational defense and will not be reasoned with. It must be met by a different weapon, and masses of men must throw off the monster evil, either in a spirit of indignation, or in a jovial hurrah." [7]

By far the most distinctive contribution of the Washingtonian movement to American temperance was the experience meeting. A product of English working-class teetotalism of the 1830, the experience meeting gave audiences the opportunity of hearing reformed men relate their battles with the bottle. The Baltimore Washingtonians first introduced the genre to the United States, hoping to make their meetings attractive to potential converts. [8] Washingtonians believed that only reformed teetotalers could appeal successfully to the intemperate. "A reformed man has the best access to the drunkard's mind and heart," wrote John Zug, a Baltimore Washingtonian, "because he best knows, and can enter into a drunkard's feelings." [9] The man who would not accept the censorious moralizing of the sober and respectable would cheerfully embrace the message of a brother in suffering.

The success of the experience meetings and the insatiable demand for experience speakers suggested that the strategy was both realistic and effective. The experience speeches which have survived indicate the powerful impact of the reformed men upon their audiences. Among the accounts of such meetings is one written by Benjamin Estes, a liquor retailer who reported the experience of a Mr. Bond from Brooklyn, when he spoke at a Washingtonian meeting in New York in the early 1840s.

He stated that he had been a confirmed drunkard for fifteen years, and that he had been brought to the lowest depths of degradation and misery, insomuch that he wanted to die, and had almost been tempted to put an end to his life. He stated that for years he had loafed around the markets and wharves without any regular means of subsistence, sleeping in the markets and on the side-walks, almost without clothes, or friends, and that all he sought for was rum; and that his appetite was so craving that he would stoop to the meanest calling to obtain a little rum. He also stated that he was a father, and his intemperate habits had brought on his family all the misery and wretchedness that could be inflicted by a drunken father. He also stated that his wife, after living and enduring poverty and misery to the greatest extent, would cling to him with affection and love, and did so for years, but at last was compelled to leave him and seek protection among her friends; and that they had been separated for seven years by that foul monster, rum. He then made a solemn pause; after which, he said, gentlemen, you can here see me as I am. And indeed he was a man well-clothed, and a very respectable looking man, and I imagined I could see love and benevolence beaming in his countenance. [10]

The contrast between past degradation and present respectable condition which the reformed man presented on the stage carried tremendous dramatic force. The stark alternatives—poverty then, respectability now—were embodied in the person of the reformed man. Here was living proof that a personal moral and physical transformation could be made.

Although popular, the drunkard's tale was too stereotyped to represent the reality of his condition. The narratives often grossly exaggerated the poverty and degradation of the drunkard before he took the pledge in order to maximize the dramatic effect of conversion. The Washingtonians were not quite the moral dregs they often claimed to be in their sensationalist propaganda nor were they really quite the social dregs which that propaganda might also indicate. The occupations of the six founders of the Baltimore Washingtonians do not suggest the bottom of the social scale. A tailor, a carpenter, a blacksmith, a wheelwright, a coachmaker, and a silverplater began the Baltimore Washingtonians. [11] The reformed men who spoke at the experience meetings in New York and Boston were predominantly artisans: William Wisdom, a blacksmith, John Hawkins, a hatter, William K. Mitchell, a tailor, William Rich and Joseph Johnson, shoemakers, Samuel Holbrook, a sea captain, Mr. Shaw, a bricklayer, and Charles T. Woodman, a baker. John B.

Gough, perhaps the most famous reformed drunkard of them all, was a Worcester bookbinder before he took the pledge.[12]

A closer examination of the support for the Washingtonian societies in New York bears out the contention that artisans dominated this new movement. Yet the Washingtonian revival was not exclusively restricted to artisans. The new societies were often quite eclectic in support and ranged from unskilled laborers through journeymen and small independent tradesmen to professionals—doctors, lawyers, clergy, and teachers—and entrepreneurs. Nor would it be true to depict the Washingtonians as restricted to wage-earning groups alone, since Washingtonians encompassed both employers and employees, both lower-middle- and lower-class groups. The bias of the movement, though, was toward the skilled trades, toward the small shops where master craftsmen and journeymen worked together, where the sense of identification and loyalty was toward the trade or craft, and where the interests of employers and employees were not clearly distinguished. This was the world of the artisan classes, but it was a world in process of rapid transformation. These men were not the social dregs they sometimes claimed to be but men (and women) seeking to avoid becoming dregs through drink.

Take, for example, the thirty-eight Washingtonian organizations which participated in a procession in March 1842 to commemorate the first anniversary of the visit of the Baltimore Washingtonians to New York.[13] Of these thirty-eight societies, five were trade based: the Hatters' Temperance Society, the Bakers' Temperance Benefit Society, the Shipwrights' and Caulkers' Temperance Society, the Franklin Temperance Society (for printers), and the Butchers' Temperance Benefit Society. Three others had a quasi-trade appeal: the Neptune Temperance Benefit Society and the Marine Temperance Society (for seamen) and the Fireman's Temperance Society. (In addition, at least two more such societies existed in the city—the cartmans' and the carpenters' societies—but did not take part in the procession.) It is not clear, however, that membership in any of these trade societies was restricted to wage earners. The Franklin, which has left the most information in print (perhaps because it was a society of printers), opened its doors to "printers, publishers, bookbinders, and the public generally." Its lists of officers and speakers show that publishers, master printers, and journeymen participated in the organization.[14] The same seems to be true of the Shipwrights' and Caulkers', while the Marine Temperance Society, which actually predated the Washingtonian crusade in its origins, had 2,170 members, "including about 140 shipmasters, 120 mates and 1,100 seamen." Its meetings were addressed "chiefly by captains and seamen."[15] So far as the available evidence tells us, these societies were organized on a trade basis with journeymen and masters, wage earners, and (mostly small-scale) employers cooperating within them in the early 1840s.

Though the other twenty-nine societies participating in the procession of 1842 did not have a trade or quasi-trade bias, they too failed to distinguish between employers and employees, but found their strongest support within the artisan classes. The mixed character of these Washingtonian societies is evidenced by a study of eighty-three Washingtonians named in two pro-temperance newspapers as attending Washingtonian meetings in 1842 and 1843.[16] Of fifty-three names traced, twenty were artisans (it was impossible from the city directories to determine the exact employment status of many of these). But there were also eleven professionals (five doctors, four lawyers, and two clergymen), at least five unskilled and semiskilled workers, five small merchants and shopkeepers; the editors of three temperance newspapers, three publishers, a broker, an auctioneer, a phrenologist, two marshals, and a clerk to the New York City police.

Though the names traced suggest both the strong artisan support for the Washingtonians and the existence of professional and petit bourgeois involvement, these figures may understate the importance of unskilled and semiskilled workers. The newspapers tended to report the most articulate Washingtonians, and lower-class groups were notoriously underrepresented in the city directories. Thus many of the thirty who could not be traced may have been transients (often unskilled and propertyless workers) who drifted out of the city quickly and were never recorded in the directories. We know, too, of distinctly plebian elements within the Washingtonians from other literary evidence and especially from the kinds of tactics which Washingtonians pursued. The fact that the Washingtonians deliberately and successfully drew members from the dock areas, the slums, and the houses of correction and encouraged ex-felons to join their societies suggests a lower-class, unskilled component. The houses of correction, for example, were full of laborers and other unskilled and semiskilled workers. [17]

Yet unskilled workers do not seem to have provided the core of Washingtonian support. The experience speeches, the lists of founders, and local case studies of Washingtonian groups all point to the artisan basis of the movement. In Worcester, for example, it was the practice, until 1844, to draw the officers and committee representatives from obscure and new converts to teetotalism. Of thirty-six such men elected in 1843, artisans made up one-third of the total number, or twelve of the twenty-nine identified; yet the Worcester Washingtonians also clearly crossed class boundaries between the working and the lower-middle classes in the town, for they included clerks, grocers, merchants, and even a few manufacturers. While there were wage earners in this group—possibly as many as ten— many were either self-employed, in partnerships, or were small-scale employers of labor, while at least two were manufacturers by Worcester standards, employing more than fifteen workers each. [18]

What distinguished the Washingtonians of the early 1840s, then, was not the employment status of its members and leaders, for both employers and employees were present. Rather it was the relative absence of the older evangelicals and wealthy and upwardly mobile captains of industry from controlling positions in the new societies. These people—by and large the leaders of the old temperance movement—were either entirely missing from the Washingtonian movement or else they took a back seat for a time in the early 1840s. The Washingtonian movement was essentially a creation of the artisan classes.

The forces which impelled the artisan classes, both master craftsmen and journeymen, both small businessmen and employees, to enter the Washingtonian societies lay in the changing character of American manufacturing. The late 1830s and the 1840s were years of increasing economic dislocation for many American artisans. In many industries, the unit of production became larger as factories emerged under the control of merchant capitalists and as mechanization began to undermine the demand for various types of skilled labor. Instead of small, independent proprietors, merchants began to dominate many manufacturing industries. In such cities as Philadelphia, New York, and Baltimore, master craftsmen often could no longer maintain their independence and were forced to accept work as journeymen or as foremen in the larger manufacturing establishments. The opportunities for journeymen to become manufacturers in their own right were fast declining.

To be sure, these changes worked in vastly different ways from one trade to another and within trades, depending on the structure of the particular industry concerned. While the traditional artisan craft of shoemaking was hit hard by mass production in factory conditions, some skilled workers were in fact better off as new industries emerged or as industrial expansion created demands for new types of skilled labor. Thus the emergence of the iron and steel industry in Worcester created new jobs for skilled machinists. [19] Yet even prosperous artisans were affected by the uncertain and unsettled economic climate for both skilled and unskilled labor. In addition to the disruptive threats imposed by large-scale manufacturing were the inevitable short-term hardships imposed upon many artisans by cyclical and seasonal fluctuations in economic activity. Especially severe in its effects was the economic depression of 1837-1843, which threw many thousands of artisans out of work. [20]

These larger social and economic changes wrought their disruptive impact on the men who formed the first Washingtonian societies. All of the experience speakers mentioned economic distress, and three of the early leaders, John B. Gough, John Hawkins, and John W. Oliver, complained of lack of work during the depression. "The financial difficulties of 1837 compelled" John W. Oliver to relinquish his business as a printer "and go to work as a journeyman." [21] John Hawkins "found but little to do at his trade" of hatting because "the manufacture of fur hats was rapidly declining." [22]

One response of the artisans to their hardships was to form temperance benefit societies. The appearance of the first such societies in Philadelphia and New York in 1837 coincided with the onset of the depression. Dominated by artisans and designed to provide members with mutual protection against financial hardship, these societies were essentially primitive insurance cooperatives. [23] Benefit societies had, as E. P. Thompson has shown, a long tradition in the history of English artisan culture as proto-trade unions and as fraternal and beneficial associations. In America, these societies did not exclude alcohol from their meetings. The New-York City Temperance Society, surveying intemperance among artisans in 1837, found that "the beneficial societies among mechanics" were "a prolific source of intemperance" because of the almost universal practice of meeting in taverns. [24] Under the impact of both the worsening employment position of artisans in the late 1830s and the stimulus and example of teetotal societies among mechanics in such cities as New York and Philadelphia, artisans themselves initiated the novel merger of temperance and beneficial principles. If artisans were to survive in the hostile economic climate, they would have to practice sobriety and frugality. Although initially quite distinct, these temperance benefit societies became incorporated into the more general artisan activity of the Washingtonian revival. Some of the early artisan benefit societies, in fact, became Washingtonian affiliates while retaining their beneficial principles. If the temperance benefit society was one early indication of the artisan's sensitivity to social and economic distress, it was only part of what became the Washingtonian movement for self-help through sobriety.

The Washingtonians sensed the economic roots of their precarious social condition, yet they blamed drink, not the banking system. William K. Mitchell spoke often in his experience speeches "about hard times, made very hard by whiskey bills." [25] Captain Lane of Baltimore urged his audiences to take care of intemperance, and providence would take care of the currency. [26] William Wisdom, "a hard laboring smithy," owned his own business but found saving impossible because he drank too much. [27] Charles T. Woodman, a baker, believed that he "might have done well, had it not been for [my] old habit reviving." As a result of his indulgence, Woodman allowed himself "to be taken in, and incurred bad debts." His business was ruined, and he had to flee Boston for Philadelphia to escape his own creditors. [28]

Washingtonians naturally blamed drink for their misfortunes because many among their number had already been corrupted by alcohol. Although the Washingtonians contained only a small proportion of men who had literally dragged themselves from the gutter, they did include many men who had suffered personally because of liquor. And many other Washingtonians knew of cases of relatives or friends who were the victims of alcohol. Washingtonians who were not themselves ex-drinkers sometimes related in experience speeches their tearful tales of drunken relatives. In Worcester, one teetotaler explained before a packed meeting of the Washingtonian society that he "had resolved to be a teetotaler, or rather not to carry a rum jug for the members of an intemperate family, at the early age of ten years,—had been whipped repeatedly for his firm adherence to his resolution, and from that time to the present," he had held steadfast to his cold water principles. [29] Henry Wilson, the Natick cobbler and self-made man who later became vice president of the United States under President Grant, liked to address Washingtonian audiences on the searing experience of his intemperate upbringing. Wilson "hated alcoholism for he could never remember a time when the tragedy of drink was not present" in his house. [30]

So pervasive was the knowledge and the reality of temptation for the artisan classes that the message of reformed men hit home at Washingtonians, both the ex-alcoholics and lifelong abstainers. Samuel Hazelwood, a reformed man of Dedham, Massachusetts, "drew a picture of his home as it was when alcohol ruled, and of the peace and joy which reigned there now, which will never be forgotten by those who heard him." [31] John Hawkins, the famed experience speaker, had a similar impact on his Boston audiences: "He came to us with a story of misery unparalleled in interest, and told with a simplicity, a natural eloquence, that cannot be surpassed. You saw all around, your own eyes filled with tears, weeping men, women, and children." [32] Such reports of experience meetings make clear that the audiences endorsed the values and the aspirations of the reformed men.

If the experience speeches document the social aspirations of reformed men, they also illuminate the social outlook of the listeners. The melodramatic tales of the Washingtonians had several functions for the more respectable among the audiences. They reinforced the belief that poverty and social distress were the products of personal failure rather than flaws in the nature of society. Middle-class audiences could identify with the poor and at the same time assure themselves that something was being done to alleviate social ills.

In addition, the tales of drunkenness reminded artisans that in a society which placed the emphasis for well-being and personal improvement on the individual, only personal restraint could ensure survival, especially in times of economic distress and depression. For respectable and sober artisans, it seemed that only teetotalism separated them from the possibility of physical and mental ruin. When John W. Oliver returned to his native Baltimore, the scene of his early indulgence with liquor, he was struck with the "poverty and degradation" which had befallen so many of his former friends and fellow artisans. In Oliver's view, only teetotalism had saved him from the same fate. [33]

For the reformed men themselves, self-respect rather than upward mobility was of paramount importance. They wished to be accepted back into the society they had forsaken; they wanted to restore their domestic happiness. William Collier of South Boston conquered his intemperance and became once again "a kind father, an affectionate husband, and an obliging friend." [34] Charles T. Woodman emphasized that through the pledge he had been restored to his "forfeited station in society." [35] After signing the pledge, "Mr. Field, of Dorchester" found that he quickly regained "the respect and confidence of his fellow townsmen." [36]

One of the central themes in the speeches of these ex-alcoholic artisans, which deeply touched their audiences, was the desire to preserve or to restore their precarious status as respectable artisans. They did not expect great material success in their new lives. Washingtonians wanted only a "competence" of "this world's goods" so that they could live peacefully and comfortably. They believed they could attain this goal provided they did not waste their money on liquor. One reformed man, Charles T. Brush of Wayne County, New York, found that after signing the pledge, "he had enough of this world's goods and these, with a peaceful conscience, and regained self-respect, are enough." [37] The Washingtonians' pretensions to economic prosperity were restricted by their limited social circumstances and experiences. When Washingtonians did display an interest in their own economic prosperity, they dreamed, for example, of owning two houses and renting one; they did not expect vast wealth and power. If economic success should come, then well and good, but such success was not their primary concern, only a concomitant of their quest for a sober style of life. [38]

Psychological and Material Benefits

If the quest for self-respect led artisans to embrace the temperance cause, it also led the early Washingtonians to shape new tactics of reform quite independent of those advocated by the older temperance leaders. This novel approach stemmed directly from the experiences of artisans who appreciated, better than did older temperance reformers, the attractions of drink and how they could best be overcome. The first and most important innovation of the Washingtonian movement was to assert an unqualified faith in the ability of drunkards to reform. William E. Wright, a reformed man from Baltimore, expressed the primary message of the Washingtonian movement to the habitually intemperate: "We do not know what it is to despair. The word FAIL is not in our vocabulary."[39] This declaration of optimism among reformed men on the speaking platform represented a personal conviction of the effect of the Washingtonian message on their lives. They desired, as all other zealous converts do, to convey this new hope to their fellow sufferers.[40]

The presence of reformed men on the stage, proclaiming the possibility of reform, spurred the early success of the Washingtonian movement. Only the reformed drunkard could say, "*I* have done it; *you* may do the same," and this optimistic message proved infectious wherever it was applied.[41] When the Baltimore Washingtonians brought the story of their success to New York in 1841, their public meetings were punctuated by spontaneous conversions as derelict alcoholics and moderate drinkers streamed down the aisles to sign the pledge and proclaim their allegiance to the cold water army. As the New York meetings demonstrated, the Washingtonians elicited responses from their audiences akin to those of a religious revival. Like revivalist preachers, reformed experience speakers offered their audiences personal regeneration through a radical break with past behavior. Reformed inebriates underwent a secular equivalent of a religious conversion. For faith in God, reformed men substituted faith in self; for belief in ultimate salvation, they substituted belief in immediate reform.[42]

The attraction of the Washingtonians did not end with the pledge signing. The Washingtonians designed psychological supports for ex-inebriates to help give them a new sense of inner purpose. Converts were encouraged to recant their hedonistic past through the medium of the experience speech, a tactic that served to reinforce the ex-inebriates' resolve. By publicly confessing sins, reformed men felt a sense of atonement for their past. They could put their sins behind them and assert their new sobriety. [43] A Mr. Shaw, who was converted at the New York meetings, "felt relieved; I woke from my wretched course [and] felt like a man who had been seven years asleep." Similarly John B. Gough experienced a "feeling of relief" after his public recantation, not because "there was any supernatural power in the pledge" but because of "the honest desire to keep a good resolution." [44]

Besides the new purpose which reformed men derived from their public recantations, the Washingtonians provided a new sense of group solidarity to bolster converts through their follow-up procedures. Washingtonians visited new converts to provide encouragement, advice, and supervision. John B. Gough, who became a famed temperance lecturer, regarded the genuine interest taken in him by fellow Washingtonians after his conversion as the crucial factor in his personal battle to break free from the "chains of alcohol." When Jesse Goodrich, Worcester's most virulent opponent of alcohol, visited Gough immediately after the latter's teetotal conversion in Worcester in 1842, Gough found that "I was not alone in the world; there was a hope of my being rescued from the 'slough of despond,' where I had been so long floundering." [45] Newly reformed drunkards needed the companionship of like-minded individuals to bolster their resolve. In the Washingtonian movement they found friends who shared the same concerns, men who would not tempt them to drink but would encourage their persistence in the teetotal course because they were undergoing the same experience. John Hawkins, another famed temperance lecturer, emphasized the intercession of his teetotal friends in his successful conversion: "My friends took me by the hand. They encouraged me. They did right." [46] Hawkins felt the obligation to extend the hand of friendship to others, just as it had been given to him. The Washingtonians strengthened group solidarity both by receiving and by giving advice and friendship.

The tactic of involving the newly reformed in the process of saving others gave teetotal converts a sense of purpose and direction lacking in their old drinking lives. No sooner were the reformed signed and sober than they would be inducted into some minor office in the local society and sent out to reclaim drinkers under the slogan, "Every man brings a man." [47] Thus the reformed became secular missionaries for Washingtonian principles. Observers of the reformed men commented on the zeal of the Washingtonian missionary. Benjamin Estes wrote of the Washingtonians that

their whole souls seemed to be engaged for the benefit of their fellow-men, and when attending their meetings they would contribute liberally for relieving the distresses of the poor drunkard, and their labors were wonderful, for they would work hard through the day—this did not prevent them from spending their evenings at some of the temperance meetings, and this generally every evening in the week and Sundays. . . . Here was a mystery to me and to the world, for there never has been such a set of men that have acted upon such disinterested principles since the days of the apostles.[48]

But the Washingtonians did not act upon merely disinterested principles; these missionaries had a personal investment in the cause. They had become swept up in the organization's effort to save drunkards. By saving others, they simultaneously saved themselves.

Nowhere was the personal investment in the success of Washingtonianism greater than among the temperance lecturers. Experience speakers with a gift for public lecturing soon discovered the demand for their talents.[49] And so the Washingtonian revival became a means of upward mobility for some, like John B. Gough, who progressed from intemperate bookbinder in Worcester, Massachusetts, to experience speaker, then temperance lecturer, and finally to international celebrity. Grateful to receive seventy-five cents a lecture in 1843 at the start of his career, Gough could demand twelve guineas during his tour of England in 1857. By the 1870s, he had amassed a sizable fortune from his platform oratory in support of the temperance cause.[50]

Public lecturing could bring success only to the talented few, but nevertheless there were definite material as well as psychological rewards for many ex-alcoholics who joined the Washingtonians. The severe character of the economic depression which still beset the United States in the early 1840s made the Washingtonians deeply conscious of the sources of want in their midst.[51] In a fashion unprecedented among earlier reformers, the Washingtonians extended material assistance to needy converts and so became the first temperance group to launch a positive campaign to uplift the habitually intemperate.[52] The campaign was all the more impressive because the resources of the Washingtonians were slim. Despite their meager means, welfare work was not confined to a few societies but was in fact rather widely practiced.

Roving Washingtonian missionaries scoured the docks and low dives of Boston, New York, and Philadelphia for derelict alcoholics to induce them to sign the pledge in return for shelter and food. Ever alive to the connection between intemperance and crime, Boston Washingtonians provided a cab service between the house of correction and Washingtonian headquarters. Newly released convicts could be brought immediately into the protective custody of the Washingtonians and thereby be prevented from slipping back into their familiar, corrupting environment. [53] The Washingtonian halls in Boston and New York served as antebellum versions of the settlement house, halfway house, or crisis center. Relief workers responded to pleas for help from the poverty stricken and emotionally disturbed by visiting problem drinkers in their homes and attempting to alleviate their economic distress. An account of such home visitations by the Boston Washington Total Abstinence Society reveals the social ethic behind the Washingtonian welfare work.

In all cases poverty and wretchedness in the extreme are depicted in every countenance—the wife miserable and haggard, the children in most cases ragged and pale. No furniture, no provisions, no clothing, but all around is filth and misery. . . . The visitor enters and commences his work by inquiring the cause of so much poverty—in some cases the woman bursts into tears and then tells of better days, before her husband became a drunkard—the hand of friendship is extended to the miserable husband—the pledge is introduced—the blessing, the happiness and peace, which will follow if the pledge of total abstinence is signed and kept, are held out—hope lightens up the eye—the pledge is signed . . . another tenement is provided—articles of furniture are furnished—clothing for the man and his whole family are immediately supplied, and everything assumes a new aspect. [54]

The Washingtonians unabashedly attached their offers of material assistance to the signing and keeping of the pledge, and to reinforce the decision to abstain, some Washingtonians even went so far as to provide a convert with new housing and a job with teetotal employers. Through such material assistance, drunkards received positive incentive to reform and to embrace the goals of respectability and self-help.[55] Because the founders and leaders of the Washingtonians came from the artisan classes, they recognized the environmental roots of the drink problem among the lower-middle and working classes. Unless the immediate material wants of the ex-drinker were provided and unless a drink-free environment were created to bolster his resolve, the convert would soon return to his former habits and haunts.

The primary purpose of benevolent work was to uplift drunkards, but the Washingtonian welfare workers, too, benefited from their own charitable acts. Whether a reformed man seeking to atone for his past or a teetotaler with no past to atone for, the Washingtonian missionary gained personal respectability from benevolent activity. The Washingtonians depicted themselves as doers rather than talkers. They saw themselves as the "practical philanthropists" or "Good Samaritans" of the temperance reform who did not pass to the other side of the street when they met the gaze of the destitute and needy.[56] They chastised the many wealthy citizens who did not join in the benevolent work, and they took comfort in the observation that moral worth did not depend on wealth. All could demonstrate their concern for their fellow man by joining in the practical work of the Washingtonians. Not all men could be rich, but "morally and intellectually, we may all of us be rich, and learned, and elevated."[57]

Alternative Amusements

While charitable assistance to reformed men was one side of the Washingtonian work, equally important was the emphasis on positive social entertainments to supersede the attractions of alcohol. During the Washingtonian phase, temperance reform shed its dull image and adopted a more lighthearted aspect. Temperance fairs, picnics, concerts, balls, and processions abounded in the 1840s. These social attractions fulfilled the demand of artisan teetotalers for more innocent social entertainment divorced from the threat of alcohol.

Earlier temperance reformers had urged drunkards to abstain but had not provided alternative forms of recreation for the drinking public. Yet almost every form of entertainment in antebellum society involved the temptation of drinking. Theater licenses commonly allowed the sale of liquor on the premises, and theaters were considered places to drink as much as places to enjoy music or drama. Bowling, a popular form of recreation in the 1840s, went hand in hand with tippling. Alleys (like billiard rooms) almost invariably included bars.[58] But for most Americans, particularly in the smaller towns and rural areas, recreation centered around the local tavern just as it had done in colonial times. The attractions remained essentially the same: informal entertainments, a center for gambling and for the conducting of cockfighting, boxing, and other popular sports.[59] Grogshops were major social centers for workingmen in an era before organized sports, public libraries, and the like provided alternative sources of entertainment. Because earlier reformers were largely removed from the experience of the bottle, their proposed solutions did not show how reclaimed men were to survive in a society in which drink and social entertainment were closely interrelated. The Washingtonians were the first to provide artisans with "suitable means of enjoyment and improvement of the leisure hours." They were the first to provide alternatives to the dramshops.[60]

One positive alternative was to improve the minds of the reformed men. When a Washingtonian society was organized, one of its earliest actions was to provide reading rooms stocked with suitable temperance and general literature. Mental idleness "begat intemperate habits" as much as did physical idleness. "A new direction" had to be given to the reformed man's "thoughts as well as his habits."[61] But the addition of reading rooms could hardly have countered the appeal of alcohol and its allied attractions. Washingtonian halls had a barren, uninviting appearance, which probably would have attracted only those with no money to seek entertainment elsewhere. In Boston, for example, "Hall No. 1 was furnished with newspapers from various towns, as well as nearly all the publications of our own city. A table was prepared, and the seats arranged in the form of a reading room; a fountain of cold water, and a desk containing the pledge, occupied another part of the room."[62]

Rather than restrict their social activities to the improvement of mental culture, Washingtonians placed much more emphasis on social entertainment. They popularized the ubiquitous temperance fairs, processions, and picnics. One essential event for every Washingtonian group was the Fourth of July picnic, complete with games, feasts, toasts (in cold water), and bombastic orations on the "second declaration of independence," not against a political foe but that greater tyrant, "King Alcohol."[63] Such activities were not intended primarily to convert the intemperate; their function was largely recreational. Temperance picnics and processions provided the teetotalers with pleasant summertime recreation divorced from the temptations of alcohol. In the winter, concerts and temperance balls replaced the outdoor entertainment in the larger centers such as New York and Philadelphia. A single weekly issue of the *New York Crystal Fount* often listed a half-dozen temperance concerts; one such meeting in December 1842 attracted over 4,000 persons, although attendances of around six hundred were more common at such functions. The Washingtonian concerts served the respectable and improvement-conscious lower-middle-class teetotalers as much as they did the reformed men. At a shilling a head, the poorer classes were excluded from such concerts. But the Washingtonian societies sometimes held free concerts to attract the largest possible crowd.[64]

Singing added a major new attraction to the teetotal movement in the 1840s. The touring temperance singer arose as the counterpart of the experience lecturer. Messers. Covert and Dodge, the "two famous temperance glee singers from New York," were in constant demand, and they attracted packed houses in New England and New York.[65] Washingtonians thrilled to such popular numbers as "I've Thrown the Bowl Aside," written by "a reclaimed inebriate," and "Sparkling with Light Is the Water Bright," which never failed "to afford much gratification to a temperance audience."[66] Temperance songs were usually lighthearted or melodramatic numbers that attacked King Alcohol in an almost jovial manner. Audiences loved the "comic temperance song," performed "in so *feeling* a manner as to convulse the whole audience with merriment."[67] Although the lyrics were invariably doggerel, the taste of the composers conformed to that of the audiences, as the commercial success of the temperance melodies demonstrated. Washingtonian newspapers responded to the enthusiastic demand for temperance songs by devoting increasing space to such material, while the most profitable business for Washingtonian publishers was the printing of collections of teetotal melodies.[68] Temperance singing, too, could become as lucrative a profession as experience speaking for the talented and ambitious few. Ossian E. Dodge was one who made the complete transition by the 1850s to property and respectability. In fact, in an 1851 tour of New England, appearing before middle-class audiences, he netted the phenomenal sum of $11,000.[69]

Women in the Washingtonians

Neither the charitable work nor the lighter entertainments of the Washingtonians could have flourished without the zealous contribution of women. Alongside the Washingtonian societies for reformed men, parallel Martha Washingtonian organizations emerged and soon rivaled the men's societies in both commitment and numerical support. In Wilmington, Delaware, the Jefferson Reformed Men's Society had 222 members; the Female Society had 528. In New York City, Washingtonian women usually outnumbered men at temperance functions. Of 4,000 who turned up at a temperance concert in December 1842, over 2,500 were women. Washingtonians freely admitted their growing dependence on women for their charitable activities and entertainments in New York.[70]

The growing involvement of women in temperance reform was one of the most striking developments of the era. Though women had joined temperance societies in the 1820s and 1830s, they were meant to be seen and not heard.[71] Now, for the first time, they played a prominent role in temperance reform through the Martha Washingtonian societies. In New York City alone, over forty Martha Washingtonian societies had enrolled 6,000 members by 1842. Societies sprang up as far away as Rochester, New York, Portland, Maine, and Pittsburgh, Pennsylvania.[72] In addition to the formation of a large number of women's temperance societies, the Martha Washingtonians began to speak out on the temperance platform and so gave women's temperance reform a degree of publicity almost entirely absent from the earlier phases of the temperance agitation.

The surge of women's activity in the Washingtonian societies was part of a much larger expansion of woman's role in nineteenth-century benevolent organizations. Excluded from full participation in the political and economic life of the nation, the energies of middle- and upper-middle-class American women were channeled into a host of voluntary organizations from church clubs to antislavery and temperance societies. What was distinctive about the Washingtonian women within the ranks of the larger temperance movement among women was their modest means. Far from being the stereotype of the upper-middle-class woman freed to do charity work because servants took care of the housework, these Washingtonian women were of lower-middle and working-class origins, and some were working women.

Although the new women's societies did contain a smattering of well-to-do reformers, most members were probably the wives of artisans or small entrepreneurs. There are no extant membership lists for the Martha Washingtonians, and even the leaders of New York's Martha Washingtonian societies proved difficult to trace. When Washingtonian newspapers mentioned the leaders of the women's societies, they did not give the first names and addresses of married women. [73] But of seventeen names traced successfully, one was the wife of a physician; the rest were wives of coopers, sailors, clerks, bookbinders, blacksmiths, auctioneers, and tailors. Of the four who were unmarried, one was a teacher, one a laundress, one a milliner, and the other ran a fancy goods store. [74]

These artisan women seized the opportunity to participate in the temperance movement more actively and more independently than they had previously done. What gave them the opportunity was the reformed man's need for clothing, money, and shelter. Benevolent and charitable work had long been assigned to women by society, but women could now use the traditional function to achieve their own aspirations.

Women quickly asserted a dominant role in the welfare work and a prominent role in the general activities of the men's societies. They supplied most of the funds for the social activities of the Washingtonians, as well as for the material needs of the reformed men. To raise the money for these purposes, they organized temperance bazaars and concerts. In addition, they supplied at least half of the audience at a typical Washingtonian experience meeting. [75]

More important, women used their growing participation in the Washingtonian movement to vent their frustration at the intemperance of men. The Washingtonian women of Worcester, Massachusetts, paraded at the annual Washingtonian processions with banners which read, "Teetotal or No Husband."[76] The Washingtonian women of Vermont were "said to kiss the lips of Temperance men to ascertain whether they keep their pledges."[77] Although the Martha Washingtonians did claim to reform women, their chief object was to reform men.

Women had good reason to be incensed with the intemperance of men because excessive drinking was predominantly a male vice. The premium attached to the womanly virtues of piety and purity by the "cult of true womanhood" made the heavy-drinking woman a rarity.[78] More important, though, the intemperance of men vitally affected women, because the law gave women no protection against a drunken husband. Some of the Martha Washingtonians had personal experience of drunken husbands. Margaret L. Davis of Boston had married "a merchant in the city of New York." At the time, "there was every prospect of future prosperity and happiness." Yet within five years, he who had been "a kind husband and an affectionate father, had become a terror to those whom it was his duty to protect, and they subjected to privations which can better be imagined than described." Mrs. Davis turned to temperance lecturing after her husband's death and narrated her own experiences to impress upon others the defenseless position of women whose husbands had become intemperate.[79] By no means every Martha Washingtonian had personally experienced the poverty associated with intemperance, but the example of women like Mrs. Davis reminded them all that the social problem of drinking could destroy a woman's world at any time.[80]

When women organized the Martha Washingtonian societies, they sought protection from women against drinking husbands, fathers, and brothers. They would accomplish this purpose by reforming men and by providing mutual aid for the women and children who were the innocent victims of men's intemperance. The women's aim was to "make comfortable the domestic circle of the . . . inebriate, and to restore him again to society. To relieve the distressed mother and helpless children is our aim."[81]

The Martha Washingtonians took their appointed role in antebellum culture seriously.[82] They accepted the thesis of the cult of true womanhood that women had a special social function as preservers of the family and guardians of morality. What frustrated these women was the gap between the idealized family structure and the grim reality for many American women. In the Martha Washingtonian societies, women sought to fulfill their social function, though not through the submissive role accorded them by the cult of true womanhood. Instead of remaining within the family circle, women would preserve the domestic fireside through active participation in social reform. [83]

So novel was the idea of an active role for women in social reform that the Martha Washingtonians couched the defense of their involvement in wholly traditional terms. Charity, benevolence, and sympathy for the downtrodden supposedly lay deeply rooted in women. No more compelling object existed for the outlet of these natural womanly urges than the victims of intemperance. "Although duty does not call us to the battle field, or the strife of politics," explained the Martha Washingtonians, "yet we cannot congeal the gushing fountain of our heart's sympathy for a cause which has for its object the restoration of tranquility to the sanctuary of home."[84] The rhetoric of the Washingtonians, and the essentially charitable functions of their organizations, did underscore the persistence of the cult of true womanhood. Yet the fact remained that women did speak at temperance meetings, they did form their own societies, and they did become involved in the teetotal movement to an unprecedented extent. In the light of the prevailing mores of the 1840s, women had made a substantial breakthrough in temperance participation.

The work of Washingtonian women illustrated how the Washingtonians made the most of their limited resources by tapping converts from social groups either neglected entirely by earlier temperance reformers or given only limited roles within the confines of an evangelical temperance movement dominated by men. The increasing role accorded women in the temperance movement in the 1840s was only one example of the broadening of temperance support and of the shifts in temperance tactics which accompanied this process of change.

By the middle of the 1840s the temperance movement had been visibly altered by the Washingtonian crusade. Teetotalers were much more numerous than they had been in the late 1830s, new entertainments had been added to the repertoire of temperance agitators, a more popular, democratic image had been imparted, and a new vitality was apparent. Much of this enthusiasm had been supplied by the energies of the new groups of lower-middle and lower-class teetotalers who joined and led the Washingtonian societies. These new groups did not bring teetotalism to the temperance movement, for the evangelicals and their allies of the 1830s had done that. Rather temperance reformers had begun to address themselves to the practical questions of supplying alternatives to the grogshop for the drinking classes. Both the psychological and the physical needs of the reformed men had been catered to as never before. Some of these changes would remain stocks in trade of the temperance crusade. In particular, the popularization of reform through drama, comedy, song, and procession would continue to be significant for the dissemination of the temperance message for decades to come.

Regulars of the American Temperance Union and its affiliates regarded this resurgence of temperance interest with considerable pride and yet at the same time fear. The changes which the Washingtonian crusade both effected and threatened made the popularization of reform a two-edged sword. The challenge to the old tactics implied a challenge to the old leadership. Quickly the Washingtonian crusade became marred by a struggle for power between the old and the new temperance groups.

Notes

1. One Washingtonian editor made plain the patriotic symbolism: "We labor in a cause of freedom, from a greater tyrant than British taxation—a slavery that binds both body and mind—and could Washington speak to us from his starry home, he would bid us go on, as worthy sons of noble sires." *New York Crystal Fount*, 22 February 1843. See also Jesse W. Goodrich, *A Second Declaration of Independence; or, the Manifesto of All the Washington Total Abstinence Societies of the United States of America* (Worcester: Spooner and Howland, 1841). Soon every patriot from the Revolutionary period was represented among the names of the new societies, but the movement as a whole continued to be called the Washingtonian movement.

2. George William Hawkins, *Life of John H. W. Hawkins* (Boston: John P. Jewett, 1859), p. 67.

3. *The New Impulse, or Hawkins and Reform* (Boston: Samuel N. Dickensen, 1841), p. 18.

4. See esp. E. P. Thompson, *The Making of the English Working Class*, 2d ed. (Harmondsworth, Middlesex: Penguin Books, 1968), and John W. Blassingame, *The Slave Community: Plantation Life in the Antebellum South* (New York: Oxford University Press, 1972). Jill Siegel Dodd, "The Working Classes and the Temperance Movement in Ante-Bellum Boston," *Labor History* 19 (Fall 1978): 510-31, appeared while this work was in proof.

5. Jesse W. Goodrich to William K. Mitchell, 5 June 1841, *Worcester Massachusetts Spy*, 21 July 1841; *Proceedings of the Third National Temperance Convention, Held at Saratoga Springs, July 27, 1841* (New York: S. W. Benedict, 1841), pp. 11-13; *Salisbury Carolina Watchman*, 8 January 1842.

6. John Zug, *The Foundation, Progress and Principles of the Washington Temperance Society of Baltimore, and the Influence It Has Had on the Temperance Movement in the United States* (Baltimore: John D. Toy, 1842), p. 14.

7. *JATU* 6 (September 1842): 138.

8. Ibid., (June 1842): 92.

9. Zug, *Washington Temperance Society of Baltimore*, p. 43.

10. Benjamin Estes, *Essay on the Necessity of Correcting the Errors Which Have Crept into the Washington Temperance Movement and of Its Bringing to Its Aid the Church of God* (New York: Job Printing Office, 1846), p. 6.

11. *The Washingtonian Almanac for the Year of Our Lord 1844* (New York: E. Kearney, 1844), p. 10.

12. Ibid.; *JATU* 5 (April 1841): 49-52; Hawkins, *Life of Hawkins*, pp. 61, 87, 89. By artisans, I mean skilled workers, including apprentices, journeymen, master craftsmen, and small, independent tradesmen. For an excellent discussion of the world of the artisans, especially its social and cultural context, see Thompson, *Making of the English Working Class*, pp. 234-68.

13. *New York Daily Tribune*, 28 March 1842; *New York Washingtonian*, 21 May 1842.

14. *New York Daily Tribune*, 11 March 1842; *New York Crystal Fount and Rechabite Recorder*, 13 January 1844.

15. *New York Crystal Fount and Rechabite Recorder*, 16 December 1843; *Eighth Annual Report of the New-York City Temperance Society, . . .* (New York: D. Fanshaw, 1837), p. 19; *JATU* 6 (January 1842): 8.

16. *New York Daily Tribune* and *New York Crystal Fount*, October

1842-April 1843. These randomly selected names have been traced in the city directories and in the manuscript population schedule (New York), Seventh Census, 1850, microfilm, National Archives.

17. See the reports of the Boston Prison Discipline Society, for example, *Twenty-seventh Annual Report of the Board of Managers of the Prison Discipline Society, Boston, May 1852* (Boston: T. R. Marvin, 1852), p. 60. In Worcester, 80 percent of the inmates of the house of correction were laborers; the rest were semiskilled workers and artisans. See manuscript population schedule (Worcester), Seventh Census, 1850.

18. Of the thirty-six elected officials of the Worcester Washingtonian Total Abstinence Society in 1843, drawn from the files of the *Worcester County Cataract*, seven are either unknown or their occupations cannot be established; twelve were artisans; two were employed as clerks in the manufacturing industries; two were the proprietors of manufacturing establishments; seven were grocers or small merchants; one was a lawyer and editor of the *Worcester County Cataract*; one was a teamster; one was a clerk in the Boston and Worcester Transportation Company office; one was a teacher (and book publisher and printer); one worked for the registrar of deeds; and one was a farmer. While the leadership of the Worcester Washingtonians is not an infallible guide to the movement's sources of support, the procedures for electing the leadership ensured that the rank and file would be represented. In the absence of adequate membership lists, no better guide to the membership could be obtained.

19. Robert Doherty, *Society and Power: Five New England Towns, 1800-1860* (Amherst: University of Massachusetts Press, 1977), pp. 23-26.

20. The analysis in the preceding paragraph is drawn from Stuart Blumin, "Mobility and Change in Ante-Bellum Philadelphia," in Stephan Thernstrom and Richard Sennett, eds., *Nineteenth Century Cities: Essays in the New Urban History* (New Haven: Yale University Press, 1969), pp. 165-208; John R. Commons, "American Shoemakers, 1648-1895: A Sketch of Industrial Evolution," *Quarterly Journal of Economics* 24 (November 1909): 39-81; Norman Ware, *The Industrial Worker, 1840-1860* (New York: Hart, Schaffner and Marx, 1924), pp. 26-70; Paul Faler, "Cultural Aspects of the Industrial Revolution: Lynn, Massachusetts, Shoemakers and Industrial Morality, 1826-1860," *Labor History* 15 (Summer 1974): 388; Bruce Laurie, "'Nothing on Compulsion': Lifestyles of Philadelphia Artisans, 1820-1850," *Labor History* 15 (Summer 1974): 344; Samuel Resneck, "The Social History of an American Depression, 1837-1843," *American Historical Review* 40 (July 1935): 662-87; Hawkins, *Life of Hawkins*, pp. 55, 59.

21. Samuel F. Cary, ed., *The National Temperance Offering, and Sons and Daughters of Temperance Gift* (New York: R. Vandien, 1851), p. 297.

On Gough see John B. Gough, *Autobiography and Personal Recollections of John B. Gough, with Twenty-six Years' Experience as a Public Speaker* (Springfield, Mass.: Bill, Nichols, 1870), p. 81, and Carlos Martyn, *John B. Gough: The Apostle of Cold Water* (New York: Funk and Wagnalls, 1893), p. 74.

22. Hawkins, *Life of Hawkins*, p. 58. A group of over 150 Danbury, Connecticut, hatters wrote to Hawkins in 1842, "The times are very much against us, as most of our men are out of employment, and can get nothing to do. But they hold on finely to the Car of Temperance." Ibid., p. 204.

23. *Constitution and Laws, of the Temperance Beneficial Association* (New York: Piercy and Reed, 1838); *Constitution of the Female Branch, No. 1, Temperance Beneficial Association, Southwark. Instituted November, 1837* (Philadelphia: W. F. Geddes, 1838), p. 2; *JATU* 4 (February 1840): 18.

24. Thompson, *Making of the English Working Class*, pp. 199, 561, 459.

25. *JATU* 5 (April 1841): 52.

26. Ibid. 6 (March 1842): 40.

27. *Washingtonian Almanac*, pp. 19-20.

28. Charles T. Woodman, *Narrative of Charles T. Woodman, A Reformed Inebriate, Written by Himself* (Boston: Theodore Abbot, 1843), p. 37.

29. *Worcester County Cataract*, 21 June 1843.

30. See Ernest McKay, *Henry Wilson: Practical Radical: A Portrait of a Politician* (Port Washington, N.Y.: National University Publications, Kennikat Press, 1971), p. 11.

31. *Norfolk* (Dedham, Mass.) *Democrat*, 30 December 1842.

32. Hawkins, *Life of Hawkins*, p. 89. See also *The New Impulse*, p. 15; and *JATU* 5 (April 1841): 49-53, and ibid. (February 1841): 29, for other general accounts of the excitement stimulated by the experience speeches in Baltimore and New York.

33. Cary, ed., *National Temperance Offering*, p. 297.

34. *Norfolk Democrat*, 21 May 1841.

35. Woodman, *Narrative*, pp. 120, 132.

36. *Norfolk Democrat*, 21 May 1841. See also Estes, *Necessity of Correcting the Errors*, p. 6; speeches by Mr. Brush and Mr. Bishop, *Third National Temperance Convention*, pp. 12-14.

37. *Third National Temperance Convention*, p. 12. The idea of gaining a competence was pervasive in the thought of nineteenth-century artisans. See, for example, Woodman, *Narrative*, p. 194; Laurie, "'Nothing on Compulsion,'" p. 358.

38. Hawkins, *Life of Hawkins*, pp. 84-85, and *JATU* 5 (April 1841): 49-53.

39. *Third National Temperance Convention*, p. 19.

40. Speech of Mr. Bishop in ibid., p. 14; speech of Mr. Shaw, *JATU* 5 (April 1841): 51.

41. *New York Crystal Fount*, 26 October 1842.

42. See Hawkins, *Life of Hawkins*, pp. 78-90, for descriptions of Washingtonian meetings that strongly resemble revivals. Brian Harrison, *Drink and the Victorians: The Temperance Question in England, 1815-1872* (London: Faber and Faber, 1971), p. 131, finds the same phenomenon in English teetotalism.

43. Hawkins, *Life of Hawkins*, pp. 78-90. *Norfolk Democrat*, 21 May 1841, reports an experience meeting of the South Boston Washington Total Abstinence Society, which notes that all six drunkards who appeared on the stage "acknowledge their willingness to appear in a public manner, and confess they had once been drunkards, now reformed."

44. *JATU* 5 (April 1841): 50; Gough, *Autobiography*, pp. 131-32, 139-40.

45. Gough, *Autobiography*, p. 135.

46. *JATU* 5 (April 1841): 49.

47. Zug, *Washington Temperance Society of Baltimore*, pp. 16, 48-49.

48. Estes, *Necessity of Correcting the Errors*, p. 12.

49. Woodman, *Narrative*, pp. 126, 132, 135; Hawkins, *Life of Hawkins*, passim.

50. Harrison, *Drink and the Victorians*, pp. 154, 212-13; Gough, *Autobiography*, pp. 137-44; *The Cyclopedia of Temperance and Prohibition* (New York: Funk and Wagnalls, 1891), p. 193.

51. *New York Crystal Fount*, 12 October 1842, reported that "owing to the unparalleled depression of the times there is more absolute want and distress apparent this fall than we ever recollect of seeing."

52. Statement by Mr. Whitaker, *Norfolk Democrat*, 16 December 1842.

53. Hawkins, *Life of Hawkins*, pp. 114-15; *Boston Evening Mercantile Journal*, 1 June 1841; *First Quarterly Report of the Auditor of the Washington T.A.S., with the Address of the President* (Boston: Henry P. Lewis, 1841), pp. 11-12; Estes, *Necessity of Correcting the Errors*, p. 12; *New York Crystal Fount*, 1 February 1843.

54. *First Quarterly Report . . . Washington T.A.S.*, p. 14.

55. Ibid.; Lorenzo Johnson, *Martha Washingtonianism, or a History of the Ladies' Temperance Benevolent Societies* (New York: Saxon and Miles, 1843), p. 32; *New York Crystal Fount*, 1 March 1843; *New York Olive Plant*, 1 September 1842; *Temperance Offering* 1 (January 1846): 45; report of the East Walpole Washington Total Abstinence Society, *Norfolk Democrat*, 7 October 1842.

56. Rechabite column, *New York Crystal Fount*, 8 March 1843; speech

by Maria Jenkins, *Worcester County Cataract*, 27 September 1843; Johnson, *Martha Washingtonianism*, pp. 32-33; *The New Impulse*, p. 21.

57. *Maine Washingtonian Temperance Journal and Family Reader*, 24 August 1842.

58. "The Causes of Intemperance in Large Towns," in Albert Barnes, *The Immorality of the Traffic in Ardent Spirits: A Discourse Delivered in the First Presbyterian Church in Philadelphia, April 13, 1834* (Philadelphia: George, Latimer, 1834), pp. 25-26; Francis Trollope, *Domestic Manners of the Americans*, ed. Donald Smalley (New York: Alfred A. Knopf, 1949), p. 133; *Massachusetts Cataract*, 17 May 1849.

59. On the absence of entertainments to counter the grogshop, see *The British Mechanic's and Labourer's Hand Book and True Guide to the United States: with Ample Notices Reporting Various Trades and Professions* (London: C. Knight, 1840), pp. 61-73; "Long Evenings," *Worcester Daily Spy*, 26 September 1850; and Carl Bode, *The American Lyceum: Town Meeting of the Mind* (New York: Oxford University Press, 1956), p. 33.

60. "History and First Annual Report of the Jefferson Temperance Society of Wilmington and Brandywine, Del.," *New York Crystal Fount*, 16 November 1842.

61. *Columbia* (Hudson, N.Y.) *Washingtonian*, 30 March 1843; *Norfolk Democrat*, 16 December 1842; *Worcester Massachusetts Spy*, 18 August 1841.

62. *First Quarterly Report . . . Washington T.A.S.*, p. 10.

63. *New York Crystal Fount*, 4 July 1842; Hawkins, *Life of Hawkins*, pp. 84-85; *Worcester County Cataract*, 12 July 1843.

64. *New York Crystal Fount*, 14 December 1842.

65. "To the Editor," by a Washingtonian, *Norfolk Democrat*, 20 January 1843.

66. Ibid., 25 June 1841, 20 January 1843; *New York Crystal Fount*, 24 August 1842.

67. *Norfolk Democrat*, 25 June 1841.

68. Collections included the *Washingtonian Harp* (New York: Saxon and Miles, 1842). See *New York Crystal Fount*, 13 July 1842.

69. *Biographical Sketch of the Life of Ossian E. Dodge* (Boston: Wright and Potter, [1856]), p. 4.

70. *New York Crystal Fount*, 14 December 1842.

71. In Massachusetts, there were only four women's temperance societies out of a total of 185 reported in the census of temperance organizations made in 1831. In Pennsylvania, only three of the ninety societies catered exclusively to women. *Journal of Humanity*, 17 February 1831. The male leadership of the ATS wished to enlist the moral support of women for temperance in the 1830s but would go no further than to encourage women to join tem-

perance societies. They did not invite women to shape the policies of their auxiliaries or to speak on temperance platforms. Justin Edwards, "National Circular," pp. 15-16, in *The Temperance Volume: Embracing the Seventeen Tracts of the American Tract Society* (New York: American Tract Society, [1834]).

72. *JATU* 6 (September 1842): 138.

73. A "Mrs. Johnson," for example, could be the wife of any one of a hundred by that name.

74. Thirty-five names were checked in the New York City directories. All names were drawn from the lists of participants in Martha Washingtonian functions in 1842-1843, listed in the *New York Crystal Fount*. Those listed represent only a fragment of the membership.

75. "First Annual Report of the Lady Washington T. A. Society," *New York Crystal Fount*, 14 December 1842; speeches by Zenas Hyde and Mrs. Mallison, *New York Crystal Fount*, 21 September 1842; editorial, *New York Crystal Fount*, 23 November 1842; Johnson, *Martha Washingtonianism*, pp. 8, 35, 40-41.

76. *Worcester County Cataract*, 9 August 1843.

77. *Norfolk Democrat*, 27 May, 15 July 1842.

78. Travelers pointed to male intemperance. See, for example, Trollope, *Domestic Manners of the Americans*, pp. 298-99, and George A. Sala, quoted in Edgar W. Martin, *The Standard of Living in 1860* (Chicago: University of Chicago Press, 1942), p. 78. The constraints on public immorality among women are analyzed by Barbara Welter, "The Cult of True Womanhood, 1820-1860," *American Quarterly* 18 (Summer 1966): 151-74. Social surveys show that even today women are less likely to drink than men (60 percent as opposed to 77 percent), and heavy drinking is four times as common among men as it is among women. See Don Cahalan, Ira H. Cisin, and Helen M. Crossley, *American Drinking Practices: A National Study of Drinking Behavior and Attitudes* (New Brunswick, N.J.: Rutgers Center of Alcohol Studies, 1969), p. 20.

79. East Walpole Washington Total Abstinence Society meeting, *Norfolk Democrat*, 9 December 1842. Mrs. Davis met and married C. T. Woodman after the death of her first husband. Woodman, *Narrative*, p. 195.

80. Editorial, *New York Crystal Fount*, 23 November 1842; speech by Isobella Gray, *New York Crystal Fount*, 30 November 1842; Johnson, *Martha Washingtonianism*, pp. 10, 26.

81. *New York Crystal Fount*, 14 September 1842; Marie E. Jenkins speaking at the Ladies' Washingtonian Fair, *Worcester County Cataract*, 27 September 1843; Johnson, *Martha Washingtonianism*, p. 10.

82. Speech by Marie Jenkins; Welter, "Cult of True Womanhood."

83. Cf. Carroll Smith Rosenberg, "Beauty, the Beast, and the Militant

Woman: A Case Study in Sex Roles and Social Stress in Jacksonian America," *American Quarterly* 23 (October 1971): 562-84.

84. Speech by Marie Jenkins; Johnson, *Martha Washingtonianism*, pp. 40-41.

8

COOPERATION AND CONFLICT IN
TEMPERANCE AGITATION, 1840-1850

Despite the differences between the old and new temperance societies, the early reaction of the temperance regulars to the Washingtonians was not rejection but ostensibly strong support. Indeed
this support played an important part in the proliferation and early
success of the Washingtonians. What is most striking in the reception of the Washingtonians by temperance regulars between 1840
and 1842 is the enormous publicity given to the reformed men by the
older teetotalers. Favorable reports of Washingtonian meetings and
of the phenomenon of reformed men fill the pages of the *Journal of
the American Temperance Union* between 1840 and 1842.[1] Here,
initially at least, was a pattern not of conflict but of cooperation.

The reasons are not difficult to find. Temperance regulars initially
viewed the Washingtonian movement as a vindication of the teetotal
pledge that had been adopted in 1836. The doomsday predictions of
the decline of temperance reform which opponents of the new pledge
had made in 1836 now seemed ludicrous and completely refuted by
the new and growing teetotal movement among the artisan classes.
Temperance regulars in fact went further than this to perceive the
new movement not as a threat but as a culmination of their years of
labor. Repeatedly they used the biblical imagery of the sower and the
reaper. They, the pioneers of reform, had "sown the seed broad-

cast," and now the field stood "white to the harvest."[2] Men who fifteen years before would have been regarded as hopeless alcoholics were now being reclaimed. If these could reform, who could not? The temperance millennium now seemed a practicality.

That the Washingtonian societies were not, at least initially, entirely independent of the larger temperance movement and of the older temperance societies is made especially clear by the circumstances in which the original Washingtonians spread their message beyond Baltimore. The old New-York City Temperance Society gave $500 to finance the trip of the Baltimore Washingtonians to New York, provided publicity, and helped them organize the first Washingtonian societies in New York. The New-York City Temperance Society in fact boasted that the first president of the New York Washingtonians had been chosen by the secretary of the NYCTS, Robert Hartley.[3] In terms of patronage and influence, the New York example was not an isolated one, since the first visit of the Baltimore Washingtonians to Boston had been similarly supported by the regular teetotal organization, the Massachusetts Temperance Union. Temperance regulars were also active in giving the Washingtonians financial support to help set up Washingtonian newspapers, particularly the *New England Washingtonian*, financed by Moses Grant, a wealthy Boston temperance reformer.[4] Without the support of wealthy teetotalers, it is unlikely that the Washingtonian temperance movement would have spread as quickly or as successfully as it did.

If wealthy temperance regulars made an important early contribution to the proliferation of the Washingtonian message, it is equally clear that the Washingtonians themselves valued, under certain circumstances and under certain conditions, the financial and organizational assistance of the older reformers. Several of the Washingtonian editors, including James H. Aikman of the *Crystal Fount*, Henry Clapp of the *Lynn Pioneer*, and Virginia Allen of the *New York Pearl*, solicited funds either directly from the American Temperance Union or from wealthy supporters of the regular temperance societies. Even the original Washingtonians acknowledged the assistance and patronage of Christian Keener, a wealthy Baltimore businessman and secretary of the Maryland Temperance Society, in the formation and expansion of the Washingtonians in the city of Baltimore.[5]

The complex pattern of relations between the regulars and the Washingtonians is suggested by the actions of the very editors who called upon temperance regulars for assistance. Those Washingtonians who were most solicitous of financial contributions from temperance regulars were often the same men and women who spoke out most strongly in criticism of the measures adopted by the older temperance societies. Virginia Allen, the editor of the *New York Pearl*, the most militant of artisan temperance publications in New York, hurled abuse upon the mainstream temperance reformers and yet called on the benefactors of that movement for financial aid, privately soliciting support from John Hartwell Cocke, a former president of the American Temperance Union, in 1847. Moses Grant of Boston was mortified at "the abusive attack" launched upon him and his friends by the *New England Washingtonian*, printed on, as his friend Cyrus Morse pointed out, "the very press" which "he lent them the money to buy."[6] Most Washingtonian editors were more circumspect and conciliatory than this, but even those like James Aikman of the *New York Crystal Fount*, who strongly believed in cooperation between the different wings of the temperance crusade, were quick to assert their independent views on the tactics of temperance agitation.[7] Willingness to cooperate did not mean blind subservience to the interests and aspirations of temperance regulars.

Behind these ambiguities lay the critical problem in the relationship between the temperance regulars and the Washingtonians. When the older reformers gave the reformed men assistance, they did so almost invariably with strings attached; the price was some kind of supervision or control over the Washingtonian work. Thus when the NYCTS gave the Baltimore Washingtonians funds to come to New York to continue their work, it was with the express stipulation that "the formation of all or any new organization be under the direction of this society, and auxiliary to the city society."[8] For their part, Washingtonians desired and solicited the aid of temperance regulars in the battle against what Washingtonians believed to be a common enemy, drink. Yet they did not want temperance regulars to dominate the new movement. (Thus the NYCTS overture in 1841 to supervise the Washingtonian work was ignored by the early Washingtonian societies which grew out of the visit of the Baltimore group.) While there were personal, financial, and organizational considerations cutting across class and intersociety rivalries to promote a measure of cooperation between the old and new societies, the very pattern of that relationship was fraught with friction. When conflict did erupt between the old and the new societies, it actually grew out of the ambiguous and reciprocal relationship between the Washingtonians and temperance regulars.

The character of this conflict can best be conveyed by a single incident, insignificant in itself and yet illustrative of the larger relationship between old and new temperance reformers. In October 1842, Isaac Covert, the "temperance glee singer," advertised a concert sponsored by the Columbian Temperance Society of New York and held in a Congregational church hall hired by the society on a weekly basis for Washingtonian meetings. The deacons of the Free Congregational Church seemed anxious to help the Washingtonian cause as an extension of their support for the American Temperance Union. Yet when the deacons discovered that church property was to be used by this Washingtonian group for such an "idle amusement," they locked the Washingtonians and their audience out of the hall on the night of the meeting. The reformed men were especially annoyed since the concert was a benefit affair for Covert, who had given many free concerts in aid of the cause of the reformed men. The Columbians were incensed that the church had over the course of the year, taken a weekly rent of five dollars for the use of the hall and had now denied the use of their facilities to a needy Washingtonian and had attempted to censor a Washingtonian activity. The church had, Columbia Washingtonians believed, committed a "very unchristianlike and uncharitable action."[9] The Washingtonians had apparently used the church for convenience; at five dollars a night, it was cheap in comparison with a commercial rent of thirty dollars for a suitable hall. Yet so affronted were they at the actions of the church deacons that they resolved never to meet in the church again, and the society held its subsequent meetings in Military Hall on Broadway. Yet to underscore the complexity of relations between old and new societies, the Ladies Columbian Temperance Society, the auxiliary to the men's society, continued to meet in the church hall.

The incident illustrates many points at issue between Washingtonians and temperance regulars, especially Washingtonian attitudes toward institutional religion and evangelical temperance reformers, the tone of some Washingtonian entertainments, and subtle

social distinctions between different groups of temperance reformers. Yet as both the Isaac Covert incident and the question of the
funding of Washingtonian activities indicate, the very attempts at
cooperation between the different societies often generated this dis-
agreement because of the very different interests and aspirations of
old and new societies.

Each of the three major areas of conflict between Washingtonians
and temperance regulars—religion, entertainment, and the relative
merits of moral suasion and coercion—documents the often divergent views of the meaning and direction of temperance reform between temperance regulars and sections of the Washingtonian movement, and illustrates the emerging struggle for power between these
different groups of reformers. From an initial position of cooperation, relations deteriorated when the temperance regulars tried to
direct the Washingtonian societies in ways acceptable to mainstream
temperance. It was this power struggle within the temperance movement which split the Washingtonian societies and brought increasingly acrimonious relations between reformed men and the older
reformers.

The Attack on the Washingtonians

The first aspect of the Washingtonian agitation to receive condemnation from temperance regulars was the quality of social entertainments at some Washingtonian meetings. Ezra Stiles Gannett, the
Boston Unitarian minister and temperance advocate, deplored
"meetings in which the object appeared to be more to create amusement than to produce conviction, processions which had very little
purpose except to gratify a love of excitement, and various factitious
inducements to join the ranks of the reformed."[10] An excellent example of the amusements which temperance regulars opposed was
Charley White's Jim Crow entertainment. White became one of the
best-known Broadway theater entrepreneurs of the 1840s, but he got
his start at Teetotaler's Hall, the Washingtonian headquarters,
where his Kentucky Negro Minstrels first played in the early 1840s,
much to the chagrin of Horace Greeley and other more respectable
teetotalers.[11]

What these reformers found especially objectionable in Washingtonian entertainments was a too-close association between temperance and the low life of the grogshop. As John Marsh admitted, "Many families of refinement and seriousness have at times felt that [Washingtonian temperance music] was too low; too much like the grog shop for them and their children to hear." Horace Greeley hinted at much the same point when he wrote that many temperance concerts had "no more to do with temperance than what you saw in any porter house or circus."[12] It was the desire of regular teetotalers like Marsh and Greeley and the middle-class constituencies they represented to separate themselves socially and economically from the tavern culture and from lower-class life in general. The coarser types of Washingtonian entertainment were offensive because they reminded middle-class teetotalers of the very social situation they wished either to avoid or forget. Moreover temperance regulars feared that the vulgarity of the Washingtonians would taint the entire temperance movement, thus destroying the middle-class teetotaler's desire for respectability and self-improvement. Although the Washingtonians, too, hoped for respectability (and believed themselves to be respectable), the reformed men's idea of respectability differed from that of the temperance regulars. By pointing to the levity and vulgarity of some Washingtonian meetings, the older teetotalers revealed the social distance separating them from the lower-status groups within the new societies.

The quality of Washingtonian entertainments was not the only issue separating temperance regulars from the reformed men. Especially important was the issue of religion. Temperance regulars objected fundamentally to what they saw as the irreligious tendencies of Washingtonians.[13] In reality, however, some of the fears which evangelical reformers expressed were gross misunderstandings of Washingtonian attitudes and practices. It is not true, as it was sometimes alleged, that many Washingtonians were anticlerical or atheistic. Evangelical temperance reformers generalized these fears from a few isolated anti-evangelical papers, such as the *Lynn Pioneer*, edited by Henry Clapp. Yet even Clapp, who specialized in baiting the evangelical clergy, was not anti-Christian but rather a Christian anarchist, an associate of a group of New England come-outers that included Nathaniel P. Rogers. What Clapp constantly admonished in the orthodox clergy was what he believed to be the failure of the clergy and their congregations to do much in a practical way to help drunkards. Clapp depicted himself as a practical Christian, in contrast to those "Pharisees" who neglected the needy in the community.[14]

It is true that prayers were excluded from the meetings of the original Baltimore Washingtonians, a fact which alarmed some temperance regulars. But this practice reflected, as in the case of the *Lynn Pioneer*, not hostility to Christianity but a mistrust of the motives of evangelical temperance reformers. The Baltimore Washingtonians feared, on the basis of past experience, that evangelical temperance men would attempt to use the Washingtonian meetings to get converts for their own denominations. Because the Washingtonians in Baltimore attracted men of many different denominations and those of no particular religious affiliation, they feared that the introduction of what Washingtonians called "sectarianism" would divide their movement and distract Washingtonians from the task of saving drunkards.[15]

Evidence that Washingtonianism was compatible with evangelical religion can be found in the drunkards' experience speeches. Ex-drunkards often pointed out to their audiences that one of the benefits of signing the pledge had been the effect it had had on their religious experience. The ultimate and happy consequence of taking the temperance pledge for at least some Washingtonians was Christian conversion. John Hawkins, who became a pious Methodist, reminded his audiences that the pledge was nothing without a "change of heart; strip me of my salvation and I am gone."[16]

Yet if Washingtonians were generally neither atheistic nor irreligious, the old guard had good reason to suspect reformed men of putting self-help before religious salvation. The superficial resemblance of the experience meeting to a religious revival did not obscure the fact that teetotalers asserted a radical change in their morals (and material condition) through the human agency of the pledge. Some religious temperance men frowned on the exaggerated claims of self-reform which often accompanied the experience speeches of reformed men. The Reverend Samuel Babcock of St. Paul's Episcopal Church in Dedham, Massachusetts, favored total abstinence. But he believed that intemperance was "the outward manifestation of a corrupt heart," and the only sure means of reformation lay in a spiritual transformation. He had no confidence "in the temperance of men who made no professions of religion."[17] In a similar vein, John Marsh chided reformed men who thought that they could maintain their new sobriety without God's offer of salvation, while Justin Edwards wrote from retirement that "the sanctions of religion as well as morality . . . must be brought to bear on the hearts of men" if intemperance were to be conquered.[18]

At issue here was not so much professions of religion among Washingtonians, for there were plenty of examples of religious zeal, but the order in which these changes in the lives of men could and should occur. For the older temperance regulars, temperance and religion had to go hand in hand through the leadership of religious temperance men. According to the ATU, it had to be the evangelical clergy and their allies who led the crusade for moral and social change.

The secular tendencies of temperance reform, of which so many temperance regulars complained in the 1840s, were in fact manifest before the advent of the Washingtonian revival, though they did not create widespread alarm among temperance regulars while a religious rhetoric pervaded the reform movement and while evangelical clergy and their allies controlled the major temperance organizations. Lyman Beecher, Justin Edwards, and John Marsh had not objected to the trend of temperance thought in the 1830s to stress such secular issues as the medical benefits of temperance, even though critics of reform movements like John Henry Hopkins clearly delineated certain secular implications of temperance agitation. In 1835 when Hopkins, bishop of the Vermont Episcopal diocese, accused the temperance reformers of usurping the role of the church in the moral reformation of men, religious temperance men had been deeply offended.[19] Yet it was true, as Hopkins had correctly perceived, that temperance leaders exhorted respectable non-Christians, as well as Christians, to join their societies. Temperance men had formed organizations in which religious faith was not an article of membership, so that the faithful and the unfaithful met as equals and were judged according to their sobriety, not their piety. The same exaggerated claims of human improvement were made by the religious temperance men of the 1830s as by the Washingtonians.

Yet in the 1830s, evangelical temperance reformers like John

Marsh and Justin Edwards believed that their own clerical leadership would keep temperance reform on the correct path. They would direct the benevolent work to the ultimate task of saving souls. When Marsh insisted that temperance must "come with all the authority of God, speaking through his works, and providences, and word," he actually asserted at the same time his own claim to interpret the providential plan for man's universal sobriety. The Washingtonians caused Marsh alarm because they challenged the evangelical and clerical leadership of the American Temperance Union. [20]

The contest between Washingtonians and temperance regulars reflected in part the challenge to clerical leadership from lay members of churches; but equally important, the conflict also revealed the changing power and position of different denominations within the temperance movement. The churches which most strongly sustained the Washingtonians were the Methodists, Baptists, and such lesser (and largely lower-class) denominations as the Primitive Methodists and the Universalists. The churches which spoke out against the secular trends within the Washingtonians were mainly Presbyterian and Congregationalist. Interdenominational rivalry was especially evident in the case of Universalist participation. The doctrines of universal salvation which the latter denomination espoused were, in the opinion of John Marsh, little better than atheism. [21] The controversy over the role of religion within the Washingtonian movement reflected such persistent denominational tensions.

The American Temperance Union also clashed with the Washingtonians over the issue of prohibition. While temperance regulars had adopted general prohibition as the ultimate aim of reform by 1840, the Washingtonians renounced all reliance on legal measures. Their pledge required abstinence from the use of liquor as a beverage, but unlike the ATU pledge, it did not demand personal abstinence from the manufacture and traffic in liquor. Under the Washingtonian pledge, it was possible for liquor sellers to join the teetotal society, though the Baltimore Washingtonians assured alarmed temperance regulars that a seller who did not soon renounce his business would hardly continue to be welcome at Washingtonian meetings. [22]

Washingtonians did not like liquor sellers any more than temperance regulars did, but the social backgrounds of many Washingtonians and their experiences in the Washingtonian meetings led them to take a more tolerant view of the retailers' plight. Unlike the more middle-class reformers and evangelicals who had little direct experience of drink and the taverns, many reformed men could not simply dismiss sellers as distant demons. They knew better than temperance regulars the complexities of the liquor trade at the retail level. This was especially true of liquor sellers who joined the Washingtonians and then renounced the drink business, as Phillip Miller of Franklin, Massachusetts, did. (Ex-retailers often opened coffeeshops and temperance eating houses to serve the growing temperance clientele desiring places of entertainment and refreshment separate from the temptations of alcohol.) Such repentant sellers offered themselves as evidence that moral suasion actually worked for sellers as well as drinkers. Thus Washingtonians were more likely than supporters of mainstream temperance societies to admit that the liquor seller was a man who depended for his own livelihood, and for the maintenance of his family, on the liquor trade. Rather than emphasize the punitive or coercive policy of prohibition—the jailing of retailers especially—Washingtonians favored persuading sellers to renounce the business and sought to find them alternative employment.[23]

The experience of mainly lower-class ex-drinkers with legal and penal systems also colored their view of the efficacy of legal action against the liquor traffic. Reformed men viewed prohibition in the same light that they viewed the laws against drunkenness. Both types of law were instruments of coercion which would tend to corrupt rather than reform their unfortunate victims. Some of the Washingtonians had been imprisoned for drunkenness, and their experience convinced them that law was useless as a means of rehabilitation. C. T. Woodman's experience in prison made him hostile toward all institutional methods for reforming men. In his view, the house of correction served as a means of controlling deviants and did not have a rehabilitative function. Woodman "had been incarcerated seventeen times in the House of Correction for intemperance— he was sent there by the laws of his country, and he might at this moment be still there had not a chord in his heart been touched by the law . . . of *moral suasion*."[24] Whether the Washingtonian had been a victim of the law or not, the early success of the reformed drunkards' campaign convinced many Washingtonians that moral suasion was superior to consigning drunkards "to houses of correction to become the companions of criminals." Moral suasion had accomplished in two years what license laws and laws against drunkenness had not done in two hundred years to solve the problem of intemperance.[25]

By no means all Washingtonians opposed legal action, but the supporters of legal action were mainly long-standing teetotalers who had joined the Washingtonian organizations.[26] The reformed men and their fellow artisans tended to oppose prohibition or were indifferent toward the temperance regulars who called for prohibition in the early 1840s. Since the temperance regulars had decided that legal action was necessary to end the traffic, the Washingtonians' commitment to moral suasion threatened to thwart the designs and tactics of the temperance regulars by channeling the enthusiasm of teetotalers away from legal action. The regulars had good reason to be alarmed at the early success and sensational appeal of the Washingtonians.[27]

Each of these issues—religion, entertainments, prohibition—involved the question of who would control the Washingtonian movement: the evangelical and wealthy reformers or the lowly artisan groups. And behind that problem lay the fears of temperance regulars: if the Washingtonians were allowed to go their own way, they might subvert the authority, arguments, and strategies of mainstream temperance and might threaten to take over control of the entire temperance movement should their support continue to expand. The demise of the New-York City Temperance Society provided alarming evidence to substantiate such fears. Peeved at the monopoly of publicity accorded to the reformed men, annoyed that Washingtonians did not prove especially grateful to the older reformers for their help in 1841, and deprived of funds by the dissaffection, death, and retirement of its wealthy supporters, the New-York City Temperance Society disbanded in July 1842. In a final blast, the society's secretary, Robert Hartley, accused temperance reformers of concentrating too much on reformation rather than what he believed to be the more important task of preventive measures.[28]

While the New York City society responded to the rise of the Washingtonians by retiring petulantly from the field, John Marsh proposed to fight to reassert the dominance of the American Temperance Union. Because the Washingtonians seemed to be defying or ignoring the collective wisdom of temperance regulars, the early enthusiasm for the cause of the reformed men quickly gave way to hostility within the ATU. John Marsh discovered between 1840 and 1842 that his evangelical temperance constituency did not like what it called the excesses of the Washingtonians. Thus in late 1842, with the support of the American Temperance Union, Marsh began a counterattack. In October both Marsh and Horace Greeley of the *New York Tribune* began to chide the Washingtonians for holding temperance meetings on the Sabbath and for mixing their meetings with much material of a dubious and "vulgar" nature. Early in 1843 the quality of music sung at temperance meetings came under repeated assault, and then in September 1843, a broadside was launched, charging infidelity and atheism in the temperance ranks. By October 1844 Marsh had proclaimed the Washingtonian movement dead and advised a return to other tried and tested tactics of the temperance regulars. In particular he advocated a resurgence of prohibitionist activity. [29]

More important than these verbal assaults on the Washingtonians were the efforts of temperance regulars to take over the Washingtonian societies in New York City and drive out the recalcitrants who refused to alter their old Washingtonian ways. In December 1843 Greeley made overtures to the Washingtonian societies to join them in a general federation of New York City temperance societies which would be under the leadership and direction of the temperance regulars. Greeley especially linked his call for a general council of temperance societies to the issue of prohibition. Despite the Washingtonian movement, he pointed out, there were still three thousand licensed drinking houses in New York City alone, evidence that the Washingtonian movement itself could not solve the larger problem of excessive consumption of alcohol. Greeley urged all temperance societies in New York to work together to get rid of this "evil". [30]

The responses of reformed men to these various attempts to shape and control the Washingtonian movement were mixed. Many Washingtonians seem to have ignored the efforts of both the NYCTS and Greeley to sponsor a city-wide temperance alliance—perhaps they were ignorant of such broader power struggles—and some went so far as to denounce the efforts of temperance regulars to dominate the Washingtonian movement. There was, reported the Washingtonian press, talk of "the silk stocking gentry" attempting to turn "the rich against the poor" within the New York City temperance movement. [31] Such fragments of information, vague though they are, provide evidence of a profound social conflict developing between the temperance regulars and some elements within the Washingtonian societies. The *Crystal Fount*, though failing to identify the sources of opposition to temperance regulars, referred to "a jealousy" among "the pioneers" of the Washingtonian work, directed against those men "who have never been drunkards." These original Washingtonians, the *Crystal Fount* reported, "would almost prefer to have the work cease, rather than have anybody else to perform it." [32] The *New York Organ*, the Sons of Temperance journal, later confirmed that the overture of temperance regulars in 1843 for a city-wide temperance council had been opposed by elements within the Washingtonian societies, which the *Organ* referred to only as "blabbermouths," who refused to countenance any but "reformed drunkards" in the Washingtonian societies. [33]

There was also evidence of a growing split within the Washingtonian movement. The more respectable and more middle-class Washingtonians whose aspirations lay in the direction of self-improvement gradually separated themselves from the more "vulgar" and lower-class elements within the Washingtonian societies and, more important, responded favorably to the appeals for reforms within the Washingtonian societies which would make those societies more acceptable to temperance regulars. Especially important were the efforts of certain Washingtonians to reform Washingtonian amusements. John Marsh himself commended James Aikman of the *Crystal Fount* for his efforts "to elevate, chasten and improve" the quality of Washingtonian music by publishing more respectable tunes and words in his temperance newspaper. [34] It became common in 1843 for Washingtonian societies to advertise their engagements, as the Lady Margaret Wallace Temperance Benefit Society did, as "Intellectual Temperance Entertainment," or as the Mitchell Society did, as "superior speaking." [35] In this way, these societies sought to ensure respectable readers and members, as well as the temperance regulars, that they would not be offended by the entertainment.

The leaders of the New York Sons of Temperance were particularly active in this campaign to make the Washingtonian societies more respectable. The Sons of Temperance was a new fraternal temperance lodge with mutual benefit provisions founded in 1842 in New York by John and Isaac Oliver and fourteen other Washingtonian artisans. Though the Oliver brothers had been journeymen printers during the 1837-1839 economic recession, the business generated by the Washingtonian revival—particularly the demand for temperance music, handbills and other job printing and later the contracts for Sons of Temperance printing and the *New York Organ*, the order's journal—gradually turned the brothers into successful businessmen who identified their interests with the mainstream temperance organizations.[36] The *New York Pearl*, a paper bitterly opposed to the course adopted by the Olivers and their allies, noted this change in the interests of the editors of the *New York Organ*. "There are men in this city," the *Pearl* noted, "whom moral suasion and the beneficial influence of Washingtonianism took literally from the gutter of drunkenness, and who now stand upon the highest pinnacle of the Temple of Temperance, who seem to be inclined to kick over the ladder by which they rose, instead of assisting others to mount it."[37] The *Pearl* complained not only of the excessive respectability and exclusiveness practiced by the Olivers, Ephraim L. Show, a business associate, and others allied with the *Organ*, but also described their motives as a combination of political and economic aggrandizement. The *Pearl* pointed out that these men had made money from the old Washingtonian movement through newspapers and job printing; moreover their support for prohibition reflected, in the opinion of the *Pearl*, an attempt "to make the temperance reform a hobby horse to ride into public favor and distinction."[38] Perhaps personal malice inspired the *Pearl*'s vitriol, yet the Oliver brothers did indeed do well out of the temperance agitation. By 1850, they were well-known general printers whose business extended far beyond the original temperance constituency which had given them their start.[39]

Respectable middle-class teetotalers like the Olivers took over most of the Washingtonian societies between 1844 and 1845 and purged them of their coarse experience speeches and "vulgar music." In the process, most of the older Washingtonians who would not dress and act like middle-class teetotalers were barred from the Washingtonian meetings in New York. John Marsh noted the change which had come over the movement of reformed men in New York "under the direction of Mr. Oliver" by December 1845. "It is very crowded every Thursday evening," Marsh wrote of the New York Washingtonian Temperance Society's weekly meetings, "yet very orderly. Much care is taken in the selection of speakers, and the singing is done by the whole audience standing, from cards distributed having songs and odes of a good character. Numbers mightily take the pledge."[40] Marsh's description showed that the spontaneity of the Washingtonian societies had been replaced by an orchestrated, middle-class respectability. The temperance regulars had not wrought this change, but the character of the Washingtonian revival had been changed from inside by the more respectable and middle-class Washingtonians themselves.

The takeover of the Washingtonian movement went beyond the issue of respectability. Once the Oliver group had gained control of the New York Washingtonian societies, it proceeded to alter the fundamental tactics of the reformed men by acceding to the demands of temperance regulars for a united city temperance movement devoted to the cause of prohibition. From Oliver's *New York Organ* came the initiative for a city-wide General Temperance Council in which Sons of Temperance and Washingtonians participated with the evangelicals and wealthy temperance regulars. Thus the objectives advanced by Horace Greeley in 1843 were now a reality. Significantly the General Temperance Council campaigned in 1846 for a no-license provision for the city of New York. [41] The no-license stance of the city-wide council and its support by the Washingtonian Temperance Society of New York reflected both the changing class composition of the Washingtonian movement, to a more respectable, middle-class base, and its emerging alliance with the well-to-do and evangelical reformers.

The New York case is important in itself, since the city boasted over sixty thousand Washingtonians by 1843, the nation's largest concentration of reformed men. It also mirrored a national trend. The same pattern occurred in Worcester, where wealthy manufacturers and clergy from the mainstream temperance movement gradually assumed more control within the Washingtonian society between 1843 and 1845. In alliance with likeminded skilled tradesmen, clerks, and small shopkeepers, they introduced regular addresses by clergymen and installed as president John M. Earle, the wealthy

Quaker editor of the *Spy* and a member of a prominent manufacturing family in Worcester. More important, the society supported the concept of a coalition of all the temperance societies in the town to get a statewide prohibitory law passed in Massachusetts. [42]

In response, a splinter group of Washingtonians left to form a "society of true Washingtonian reformers," devoted to the perpetuation of moral suasion and self-help. Within the first three months, four hundred members, a mixture of small employers, self-employed tradesmen, and wage earners, had been enrolled but not a single one of Worcester's manufacturing elite or evangelical clergy ever joined. [43] Significantly, too, all of the eight founders had been ex-drunkards. As in the New York case, reformed men tended to distrust those who had no personal experience of alcohol and resented the efforts of evangelical and middle-class teetotalers to take control of the Washingtonian societies.

Patterns of Washingtonian Dissent

Both the Worcester and the New York cases suggest that the split within the Washingtonian societies—and between the reformed men and the older teetotalers—involved issues of social class. Further evidence for the social bases of these conflicts can be found by looking at the patterns of dissent from middle-class dominance of temperance throughout the North. The question of the fate and the motives of dissident Washingtonians is not easy to determine because many appear to have dropped out of the temperance movement entirely, leaving no record of the character or purpose of their defection. Yet the main causes of defection seem to have been related either directly or indirectly to the social and economic circumstances of reformed men. Though there was much backsliding (or breaking of the pledge), these renunciations of the pledge were not random but followed distinct patterns derived from the structure of artisan life.

Two of the major periods of backsliding coincided with the congressional and presidential elections of 1842 and 1844, and Washingtonians frequently admitted that one major cause of defections was the persistence of election treating. Political loyalties, camaraderie, and the presence of large quantities of free liquor triumphed over the pledge for many Washingtonians. [44] Political excitements and the temptations to drink that they presented were especially damaging to the Washingtonian movement because of the movement's peculiar constituency. Treating was a time-honored technique used by politicians to generate popular support at the polls and had long been a feature of the preindustrial drinking culture of the lower classes. The tavern keepers played an important role in this process of political mobilization, for taverns were meeting places for political clubs, polling often took place there, and political elites used tavern keepers as ward captains of their political organizations in the larger cities. Once they had broken the pledge with free liquor supplied by the tavern keepers at election time, many Washingtonians appear to have slipped back into their old associations and drinking customs. Because they had come from humble origins and because the tavern played a critical part in their social, economic, and political lives, many Washingtonians found it difficult to sustain their pledges despite the special innovations of their societies.

The element of social class which operated in the form of backsliding could also be detected in the defection of Washingtonians to labor agitation. The Washingtonian movement lost some of its artisan support after the middle of the 1840s because of larger social changes which altered the interests and aspirations of the men and women who had contributed so much to the temperance movement in the first years of the Washingtonian revival. After about 1844 the temperance societies faced increasing competition from resurgent labor organizations which promised to improve the condition of workers in more direct ways than that promised by Washingtonian orators. The 1845-1855 period was one of renewed labor militancy, provoked by a somewhat tighter market for labor and by steeply rising prices. Through the development of a variety of labor organizations, workers and their allies among reformers sought to cope with these changes. [45]

The involvement of some Washingtonians in labor reform can be traced quite closely in the Worcester case. The artisans who formed the "society of true Washingtonian reformers" in Worcester after wealthy temperance regulars and prohibitionists took control of the old Washingtonian society in 1844 sent delegates to the New England Workingmen's Convention and proclaimed their support for the struggle "to arrest the progress of capitalists in the reduction of the price of labor."[46]

When Washingtonians entered labor agitation, as some in Worcester did after 1844, they often took their temperance principles with them. Many of the labor cooperatives, unions, and labor reform organizations formed after 1844—such as the Iron Casters' Cooperative of Cincinnati, the Workingmen's Protective Union of Boston, the Mechanics' Mutual Protection Association in New York State, the Lynn Cordwainers' Association and the National Reform Association—all gave some play to temperance principles and demonstrated the persistence of Washingtonian ideas among artisans who were in the process of being transformed into industrial workers. To protect and preserve funds, as well as to advance the moral and social condition of its artisan members, the Boston Workingmen's Protective Union restricted its membership to workers who do "not use intoxicating drinks as a beverage." Although the Iron Casters of Cincinnati did not exclude drinkers from membership in their cooperative, the society allowed no liquor to be sold "within a long distance of the union," and, observed Horace Greeley of the *New York Tribune*, "there is little or no demand for any."[47] Not all of these organizations made clear distinctions between employees and employers, not all used the language of class, and some, like the National Reform Association, attempted to erect new panaceas for the troubles of the laboring classes. Yet the organ of the National Reform Association, the *Workingman's Advocate*, praised teetotalism and the Washingtonian program, even though the society believed the "land monopoly" to be the root of all evils, including intemperance.[48]

Although temperance influenced these labor reform organizations in the 1840s, it does not follow that they supported prohibition. From the evidence of pro-labor periodicals and newspapers, as well as the absence of specific commendation of prohibition from labor reform organizations, it seems that prohibition was not strongly favored. The Worcester "True Reformers" affiliated with the New England Workingmen's Association opposed "coercive measures," and so did the *New York Workingman's Advocate*. The latter paper denounced Sunday closing, for example, arguing that enforcement of the law did not stop all drinking on Sundays but merely discriminated against the "small rum shops" frequented by artisans. In their attitudes toward the tactics and strategies of temperance agitation, labor reformers were reminiscent of the Washingtonian sentiment that moral suasion was the most effective tactic of reform.[49]

Employers increasingly supported statewide prohibition as a way to create a society of disciplined and predictable individuals. Yet while the evangelical and well-to-do temperance regulars proclaimed legal coercion as the road to national sobriety, at least some workingmen defined the meaning of temperance in different ways. Washingtonians (and their successors in the labor unions of the 1840s) accepted the temperance message originally devised by wealthy and upwardly mobile temperance regulars without bowing to the authority and the will of those individuals and groups determined to force prohibition on their communities. In the early Washingtonian societies, and in the influence of temperance principles on the nascent labor organizations of the 1840s, there is evidence that workers turned temperance principles to their own purposes in the battle to survive amid those very industrial processes which had produced the temperance movement in the 1820s and 1830s.

But if some artisans left the Washingtonian agitation for the labor movement, there is also evidence that the old Washingtonian principles of self-help, moral suasion, and concern for drunkards persisted into the 1850s within organized temperance societies. The most important of the societies to perpetuate Washingtonian principles was the Rechabites, a fraternal and beneficial order founded in England in 1835 and brought to the United States in 1841. (The order took its name from a biblical sect which abstained from alcohol.) It is difficult to estimate the number of Rechabites because of the absence of a national, controlling body; hence appraisals of the order's strength in the late 1840s vary wildly from twelve to one hundred thousand. Nevertheless the fact that this order refused to adopt prohibition as part of its program suggests that within the artisan communities which supported the temperance beneficial societies, some resisted the trend of temperance agitation toward prohibitionist solutions.[50]

Similarly the Order of the Good Samaritans in New York City perpetuated the Washingtonian concern with drunkards; this society
was said to have enrolled more ex-drunkards than any other in the
city.[51]

The Rechabites and Good Samaritans were not militant, class-
conscious groups of artisans. They talked rather of brotherly love
and practical Christian charity, and they condemned the "coercion-
ists" who violated these principles. Like the original Washingtonians, these societies were influenced by Baptist and Methodist impulses toward lay control of moral reform and revivalism. Like the
original Washingtonians, too, the Rechabites and Good Samaritans
were suspicious not merely of Presbyterian and Congregational clergy but also of any reformers bent on manipulating the temperance
movement to advance their own sectarian, political, or economic
interests. It is understandable, therefore, that these old-fashioned
Washingtonians should find suspect a strategy of reform sponsored
by temperance regulars. But in addition, Rechabites and Good Samaritans resisted making prohibition part of their strategy because
they believed moral suasion was the most effective way of reforming
drunkards and because they feared that political action would split
their organizations and distract their energies from this central and
original task of Washingtonian temperance societies.[52]

Though not class conscious, these societies did reflect the factor of
social class in their internal structures and in the strategies of reform
they adopted. These temperance lodges were only two of a bewildering variety of societies to emerge in the wake of the Washingtonian
movement. Yet the groups which perpetuated Washingtonian principles of moral suasion were those with the most plebian origins and
the least social pretensions. The Good Samaritans specialized in re-
claiming as members distinctly disreputable, mainly lower-class
drunks; the Rechabites' main selling point was its "internal economy" (unlike its rival fraternal and beneficial societies, the Sons of
Temperance and the Temple of Honor, it did not spend money de-
corating its meeting halls, did not support paid officials, and eschewed expensive regalia).[53] That this dissent from prohibition had
plebian roots is further supported by the association between these
moral suasionist groups and the *New York Pearl*. The *Pearl*, which
proclaimed itself the champion of "the laboring interests," praised

the Rechabites and Good Samaritans as "true Washingtonians." In turn, the moral suasionist groups reciprocated by placing their advertising with this outspoken, pro-labor temperance publication in New York.[54]

A Partial Reconciliation

By the middle of the 1840s the temperance movement was not only split between Washingtonians and temperance regulars; a profound schism had occurred within the Washingtonian movement. Some reformed men either left the temperance movement entirely for the labor movement or the taverns, or they persisted in moral suasionist activity on the Washingtonian model in the Rechabites and Samaritans. Still others were assimilated into the mainstream temperance movement and increasingly into its prohibitionist phase. The survival of independent artisan temperance activity has already been charted above. It remains now to detail the gradual accommodation of part of the old Washingtonian movement and the temperance regulars. This process of accommodation can best be described through the changing character of the most important of the fraternal lodges, the Sons of Temperance, the most numerically and politically significant of the orders growing out of the Washingtonian movement.

The initial and central purpose of the Sons of Temperance was to provide more effective support and incentives for reformed men. The organization was a pragmatic response to the problem of backsliding Washingtonians, and its founders were Washingtonian artisans who hoped that their new order would "bind those who have been so unfortunate as to acquire the insatiate thirst for alcoholic drinks, more securely to the paths of rectitude and honor." The new order would secure the reformed men from the temptations around them by strengthening the material attractions and social entertainment provided by the temperance societies.[55]

To attract both reformed men and confirmed teetotalers, the Sons of Temperance offered mutual benefits to contributing members. In return for five-cent weekly payments, members could draw on the Sons of Temperance for sickness and funeral payments for themselves or their wives. The idea of combining the benefit principle with a requirement of teetotalism was not new in 1842, but the Sons of Temperance popularized it, extended it throughout the United States, and enrolled 221,578 members by 1849.[56]

At the same time, the Sons of Temperance imitated the fraternal societies such as the Freemasons in order to enlarge the social attractions of teetotalism. Because the Sons of Temperance recognized that intemperance was "peculiarly a social evil," they sought to "resist its terrible power by a social and fraternal combination."[57] Passwords, initiation rites, regalia, fraternal mottoes and symbols, and honorific titles—all these the Sons borrowed from the fraternal orders. The founders designed the ritual to give temperance a visual and emotional appeal. Their assumption was that most men required external symbols to reinforce their allegiance to teetotalism; they needed "to have truth impressed and excitement produced through the eye and ear, and should not be left wholly to unaided mental introversion."[58]

In addition, the fraternal system would strengthen a teetotaler's resolution to keep the pledge by creating a stronger sense of group solidarity than other temperance organizations maintained. The symbols, ceremonies, and ideology of the order all emphasized fraternal cooperation and unswerving loyalty to the organization. Members were expected to help brothers who had violated the pledge regain their sobriety and self-control. The secrecy surrounding division meetings was designed in part to prevent public knowledge of backsliders. In the opinion of the Sons of Temperance, such publicity damaged the reputation of the order and contributed nothing to the reform of erring brothers. Rather than censure backsliders, the Sons stressed private assistance and fraternal support. The fraternal order of the Sons of Temperance was designed to be a "circle of sobriety" in a world full of temptation. The Sons could not immediately reform those who remained outside the sober world in miniature, yet by extending the organization throughout the United States, the circle of sobriety could be enlarged until it encompassed the entire Union. Such was the grandiose ambition of the founders.[59]

One of the great ironies of artisan temperance in the 1840s was that while the Sons of Temperance designed and promoted their order as a means of making the Washingtonians more respectable, more honorable, more acceptable to the temperance movement as a whole, some aspects of the new order produced a hostile reaction from temperance regulars. Although the Sons of Temperance viewed the fraternal features of their order as unobjectionable devices to attract support, the older evangelical leaders regarded the same features as subversive of temperance and religion. Anti-Masonic agitation in the United States had subsided by the 1840s, but the fears of Masonry lingered among the evangelical Protestants who had provided the initial impetus toward temperance reform in the 1820s and 1830s. [60] Evangelicals like the Reverend John Marsh condemned fraternal orders because they demanded that members give their primary allegiance to the secular organization and thus threatened to interfere with the individual's Christian duties. Like all the other fraternal orders, the Sons of Temperance fostered through their oaths of secrecy and loyalty "a spirit of dependence on something besides obedience to the gospel of Christ for salvation." They led men to say "temperance is religion enough for us."[61]

In the rituals of the fraternal temperance orders, the evangelicals found much more to criticize. The emphasis on ceremony in the fraternal orders gravely offended the evangelicals, who stressed individual commitment to Christ, not external observances, as the test of faith. For the evangelicals, the ritual of the fraternal temperance orders conjured up images of both Masonry and the Catholic church. Several critics of the Sons of Temperance warned that "the individual entering this Order . . . sells himself, body and soul, to an irresponsible oligarchy," while the Reverend John Marsh denounced fraternal orders as "the POPERY OF TEMPERANCE." In his opinion, fraternal and ceremonial paraphernalia had no part to play in the propagation of the temperance gospel, which must rest primarily on the rational appeal to man as an accountable moral agent. [62]

In response to such criticism, the Sons of Temperance abandoned its quasi-Masonic fraternal grip in 1844. The use of fraternal signs outside the order rooms handicapped the expansion of the order in the strongly evangelical burned-over district of New York where many temperance men "refused to become members on account of the existence of signs."[63] But perhaps more important, the signs gave "great dissatisfaction to many highly respectable and influential members of the Order." The Sons faced criticism of their ritual from evangelicals within as well as outside the order. Lyman Beecher and Ezra Stiles Ely were among the evangelical clergy who joined the Sons of Temperance because they believed it to be the most effective temperance organization then in existence. Yet they would support the organization only if it avoided the charge of Masonry.[64]

To appease the evangelicals, the Sons of Temperance kept its ritual spartan in comparison with the elaborate ceremonies and symbols of the Masons and Odd Fellows. Although at least four or five degrees or rankings were commonly used in other fraternal orders, the national leadership of the Sons of Temperance resisted pressure from a minority of its supporters who wanted a more elaborate ritual. The leadership preferred to let the advocates of more ritual secede from the order to form the rival Temple of Honor rather than continue to offend evangelicals. Increasingly the policy of the Sons of Temperance became one of smoothing over differences with the evangelicals and reassuring them that the order had no ulterior purpose beyond advancing the temperance cause.[65]

Behind evangelical attacks on the Sons of Temperance lay the same fear which the Washingtonians had provoked: that the new fraternal orders would erode the power of the older organizations. John Marsh felt bound to attack the Masonic tendencies of the new orders because "they come forward to take the reins into their own hands." The fraternal orders seemed to threaten the religious leadership of the temperance movement just as the Washingtonians had done. In Marsh's view, the fraternal orders frightened evangelicals from the temperance movement and drained men and money from the regular organizations.[66]

The factor of power in evangelical temperance opposition to the Sons of Temperance was closely related to the issue of prohibition. As its critics charged, the purpose of the Sons of Temperance was not initially to advance the cause of prohibition but to protect individual members from temptation. Although the individual men who had founded and led the organization in New York were deeply implicated in the no-license strategy of the General Temperance Council, nationally (and as an organization) the Sons tried at the outset to avoid an issue as divisive as prohibition. But in the late 1840s, the various state divisions, particularly in the North, began endorsing legal action, claiming that moral suasion had "outlived its time." In response to this growth of prohibitionist sentiment within the Sons of Temperance, the attitudes of temperance regulars to the order began to change. [67]

Because the organizational support of the Sons of Temperance was expected to be so valuable in the prohibition campaigns, John Marsh dropped his opposition to the fraternal orders. The overwhelming desire of the evangelical leaders for legal action triumphed over their distrust of fraternalism. Once the Sons of Temperance began to attack the traffic, Marsh began to find new virtues in the fraternal orders. He now noted that the Sons of Temperance had "spread over the length and breadth of the land embodying a vast amount of wealth and energy and talent."[68] Marsh was now prepared to submerge his differences with the order over organization and ritual in return for their commitment to prohibition.

By 1850 a partial reconciliation between the warring factions of the temperance movement had occurred, with the most important society of temperance regulars—the ATU—allied with the most important remaining artisan temperance organization, the Sons of Temperance. The truce between the temperance regulars and elements within the old Washingtonian coalition clearly showed that some of the erstwhile enemies of the 1840s now became allies in the campaigns for statewide prohibition which were beginning in the Northeast.

The simplest and most superficially appealing explanation of the shift of artisans into the prohibitionist movement is nativism. Many artisans feared the competition for jobs from the predominantly German and Irish immigrants who entered the country in increasing numbers after 1845. Particularly in Philadelphia and other large cities, this antagonism toward immigrants drove many artisans into support for political nativism. In the 1840s it occurred through the American Republican party in Philadelphia and through support for James Harper's municipal reform ticket in the New York City mayoral election of 1844; and later, in the 1850s, it occurred on the national level through the Know-Nothing party. Perhaps prohibitionist sentiment among artisans was linked to this surge of nativist feeling; perhaps through suppression of the liquor trade, native-American artisans could assert American cultural values over and express hostility toward immigrant groups. [69]

There are, however, difficulties with this interpretation. Though it is true that prohibition and nativism became closely intertwined during the 1850s, there were important splits within the native-born artisan classes over the prohibition issue. Despite the competition for jobs and despite considerable animosity toward immigrants within artisan communities, some groups of Washingtonian artisans resisted the alliance with the wealthy and evangelical temperance reformers who sought prohibition. The *New York Pearl*, for example, could at the same time be in favor of protection from "the fearful flood of foreign emigration" and violently opposed to prohibition. The *Pearl* blamed "the rich manufacturer" for both. Similarly it was not the increasingly prohibitionist Worcester Washingtonian Temperance Society but the breakaway and moral suasionist group of wage earners and small tradesmen in the True Washingtonian Reformers which became allied with the Native American party after its formation in Worcester in 1845.[70] More important, opposition to adoption of prohibition came principally from Washingtonians who were likely to experience economic competition from immigrant labor: from wage-earning Washingtonians and petty tradesmen, from the Washingtonians who entered the labor unions, and from fraternal lodges which catered to workingmen.

The prohibitionists stand in sharp contrast. The prohibitionist movement of the late 1840s and 1850s involved above all else an alliance of property and middle-class respectability against the specter of pauperism and urban crime. Though many of the enemies of middle-class temperance were foreigners, the division over prohibition was never simply between native born and foreign born, nor was the prohibitionist issue articulated in these terms. The division was pre-eminently one of class rather than ethnicity. The Washingtonians who came to endorse prohibition tended to be the most successful, the most competitive, the most concerned with their respectability in the eyes of temperance regulars, and those with loyalties to the mainstream evangelical denominations and their clerical leaders.

It was the Sons of Temperance, the fraternal order which endorsed prohibition, which also bowed to evangelical pressure over the use of degrees and fraternal grips in its lodges because these practices displeased evangelicals within and outside the order. But not only did the Sons of Temperance come to an accommodation with mainstream temperance over religion and prohibition. In addition, the general social philosophy of the order became more closely identified with the interests of employers. The *New York Organ*, the Sons of Temperance weekly magazine, expressed alarm in 1850 at the emerging labor organizations in New York City. It attacked "the labor movements," which through "the injudicious and wild speeches of their own advocates" set employees against employers in New York City. The *Organ* argued that instead of seeking higher wages, these militant workers should take the pledge and so make themselves more acceptable to their employers.[71]

The changing character of the Sons of Temperance was also visible in the gradual decay of the beneficial principle. The system of benefits for contributing members had been the mainstay of all the temperance lodges with artisan support. But from the 1850s onward, the Sons of Temperance began to phase out benefit payments and contributions. Though the system had been a major attraction for struggling artisans, the provision of mutual benefits was increasingly irrelevant to Sons of Temperance who were now more interested in imposing sobriety on others than in the self-help principles of the Washingtonians. The decline in the mutual benefits system signified the gradual change in the status, social class, and aspirations of the Sons of Temperance constituency.[72]

The men who led this Sons of Temperance organization and controlled its policies were, by 1850, respectable teetotalers in alliance with temperance regulars. They included John W. Oliver, the publisher of the *New York Organ*, who used the Washingtonian revival as an avenue to property and respectability (in much the same way as John B. Gough, the temperance orator, and Ossian Dodge, the temperance glee singer did), and Samuel Fenton Cary of Cincinnati, Ohio, who employed a family inheritance to devote his energies fulltime to the task of putting the Sons of Temperance in the prohibitionist column.[73] These Sons of Temperance who pushed prohibition were either respectable, middle-class teetotalers in the first place or men who had divorced themselves from the artisan drinking culture and achieved personal respectability and prosperity through sobriety. Largely because of their personal experiences and aspirations, they embraced the idea of self-improvement, which animated the larger mainstream temperance movement. These men now saw their interests as similar to those of the older teetotalers, and they joined evangelical and well-to-do reformers in imposing their conception of social order on both recalcitrant Washingtonians and German and Irish immigrants.

To be sure, this social conflict over prohibition, which soon divided the whole community, was to some extent also fought out within the Sons of Temperance, where there was evidence of splits over prohibition and related issues. When the prohibitionists gained the upper hand by 1850 and then turned the Sons of Temperance toward the campaign for Maine Law prohibition, the numerical support for the order began to decline, dropping from a peak of 238,902 in 1851 to 134,000 by 1855. Many diverse issues produced this decline—controversies over the admission of women and blacks, the decay of the benefit system, and personal rivalries—but Sons of Temperance officials like John Stearns conceded that prohibition had brought both dissension within the ranks and defections among those who disagreed with the dominant policy of an alignment with the middle-class and evangelical temperance societies.[74] Those whose interest in the order had been its fraternal and beneficial features rather than the larger political issue of prohibition dropped out.

Though some Washingtonians came, through the Sons of Temperance, to endorse prohibition in 1852, they did so only after statewide prohibition was already in force in Maine, and after local prohibition had proved politically powerful throughout New England. The dynamics of the prohibitionist movement must be sought outside the internal politics of the Washingtonians and all of the other fraternal and beneficial temperance societies of the 1840s. To understand the logic of the decision to seek prohibitory laws, we must turn to the origins of the no-license agitation in New England.

Notes

1. See, for example, *JATU* 5 (April 1841): 49-53.
2. John Tappan, in *Proceedings of the Third National Temperance Con-*

vention, Held at Saratoga Springs, July 27, 1841 (New York: S. W. Benedict, 1841), p. 14.

3. Minutes of the New-York City Temperance Society, 15 March 1841, pp. 227-28, and circular, March 1842, p. 270, NYPL.

4. Cyrus E. Morse to John H. Cocke, [6] July 1846, Cocke Papers, UV.

5. John Zug, *The Foundation, Progress and Principles of the Washington Temperance Society of Baltimore, and the Influence It Has Had on the Temperance Movement in the United States* (Baltimore: John D. Toy, 1842), pp. 28-29.

6. Cyrus E. Morse to John H. Cocke, [6] July 1846, and John Marsh to John H. Cocke, 17 February 1847, Cocke Papers, UV; see also *Lynn Pioneer*, 9 April 1845.

7. *New York Crystal Fount*, 12 October, 14 December 1842, 15 March 1843.

8. Minutes of the New-York City Temperance Society, 15 March 1841, pp. 227-28.

9. *New York Daily Tribune*, 26, 27 October 1842; directory of Washingtonian societies, *New York Crystal Fount*, 26 October 1842.

10. Ezra Stiles Gannett, *The Temperance Cause: A Discourse Delivered before the Boston Young Men's Total Abstinence Society, on Sunday Evening, November 8, 1846* (Boston: William Crosby and H. P. Nichols, 1846), p. 14.

11. Alvin Harlow, *Old Bowery Days: The Chronicles of a Famous Street* (New York: D. Appleton, 1931), p. 272; *New York Daily Tribune*, 26 October 1842.

12. *JATU* 7 (February 1843): 25; *New York Daily Tribune*, 26 October 1842.

13. *JATU* 8 (April 1844): 57, and ibid. 7 (September 1843): 137.

14. *Lynn Pioneer*, 18 June 1845; on Clapp, see James R. Newhall, *History of Lynn, Essex County, Massachusetts . . .* (Lynn: Nichols Press, 1897), 2: 129-30.

15. Zug, *Washington Temperance Society of Baltimore*, pp. 59-63; see also minutes of the New-York Washington Temperance Society, in *New York Crystal Fount*, 16 November 1842.

16. *Worcester County Cataract*, 26 April 1843.

17. *Norfolk* (Dedham, Mass.) *Democrat*, 15 April 1842.

18. William Hallock, *"Light and Love," A Sketch of the Life and Labors of the Rev. Justin Edwards, D.D.* (New York: American Tract Society, 1855), p. 498; *JATU* 6 (December 1842): 182; see also *Infidelity and Benevolent Societies: A Discussion between the Rev. William Watson, and the Editor of the Waterbury American* (Waterbury, CT: E. B. Cooke, 1848), p. 9.

19. John Henry Hopkins, *The Primitive Church, Compared with the Protestant Episcopal Church of the Present Day* (Burlington, Vt.: Smith and Harrington, 1835), pp. 126-52.

20. *JATU* 12 (November 1848): 170; Hallock, *Life of Edwards*, pp. 497-98.

21. See the directory of Washingtonian meetings in the *New York Crystal Fount*, 26 October 1842; *Lynn Pioneer*, 26 March 1845; statement by Ira Steward, in *Boston Investigator*, 28 April 1852; *JATU* 7 (February 1843): 25.

22. *New York Crystal Fount*, 23 November 1842; Zug, *Washington Temperance Society of Baltimore*, p. 4.

23. *Columbia* (Hudson, N.Y.) *Washingtonian*, 13 April 1843; *Norfolk Democrat*, 14 January 1842; *New York Crystal Fount and Rechabite Recorder*, 27 March 1847.

24. Speech by Woodman, *Norfolk Democrat*, 30 December 1842; Charles T. Woodman, *Narrative of the Life of Charles T. Woodman, A Reformed Inebriate, Written by Himself* (Boston: Theodore Abbot, 1843), p. 12, 48-49, 59-72, 87; editorial, speech by Henry Clapp, and memorial to the Massachusetts General Court on the subject of an asylum for inebriates, *Lynn Pioneer*, 12 March 1845; John B. Lecraw, *A Sketch of the Life, Travels, and Sufferings of a Reformed Man . . . Written by Himself* (Pawtucket, R.I.: B. W. Pearce, 1844), pp. 24-27.

25. Edwin Whitaker and James Dorr, reported in *Norfolk Democrat*, 30 November 1842; Lorenzo Johnson, *Martha Washingtonianism, or a History of the Ladies' Temperance Benevolent Societies* (New York: Saxon and Miles, 1843), p. 32; *Columbia Washingtonian*, 23 February, 13 April 1843; *New York Crystal Fount*, 18 May, 24 August 1842.

26. See the prohibitionist statement by one of Worcester's leading spokesmen for the Washingtonians, Jesse W. Goodrich, *Worcester County Cataract*, 9 August 1843; editorial, *Maine Washingtonian Journal and Temperance Herald*, 30 November 1842; Norfolk County Washingtonian Total Abstinence Convention, *Norfolk Democrat*, 16, 30 December 1842.

27. *JATU* 7 (July 1843): 106-07; ibid. 6 (July 1842): 105.

28. Minutes of the New-York City Temperance Society, July 1842, pp. 277-78, and circular, March 1842, p. 270.

29. *New York Crystal Fount*, 26 October 1842; *JATU* 6 (October 1842): 154, ibid. 7 (February 1843): 25, ibid. 7 (September 1843): 137, ibid. 8 (October 1844): 154; *New York Daily Tribune*, 26, 27 October 1842; John Marsh to Gerrit Smith, 15 May 1841, box 31, Gerrit Smith Miller Collection, SU.

30. *JATU* 7 (December 1843): 185.

31. *New York Crystal Fount*, 15 March 1843; *Columbia Washingtonian*, 18 March 1843; *Lynn Pioneer*, 23 April, 4 June 1845.

32. *New York Crystal Fount*, 18 January, 1 March 1843.

33. *New York Organ*, 9 November 1844.

34. *JATU* 7 (February 1843): 25.

35. *New York Daily Tribune*, 21 November 1842, 24 March 1843.

36. Samuel F. Cary, ed., *The National Temperance Offering, and Sons and Daughters of Temperance Gift* (New York: R. Vandien, 1851), pp. 293-300. On the Sons of Temperance organization, see "Proceedings of the New York Division, No. 1, S. of T. from the Commencement of the Order until the Formation of the Grand Division of the State of New York," pp. 11-12, in *Journals of the Proceedings of the National Division of the Sons of Temperance, First to Sixth Annual Sessions* (Philadelphia: S. Douglas Wyeth, 1844-1849). The artisan founders of the Washingtonians and their aims and aspirations are discussed in Donald W. Beattie, "Sons of Temperance: Pioneers of Total Abstinence and Constitutional Prohibition" (Ph.D. diss., Boston University, 1966), pp. 29, 30-31.

37. *New York Pearl*, 13 February 1846.

38. Ibid., 30 March 1847.

39. *New York Organ*, 23 February 1850.

40. *JATU* 9 (December 1845): 185; *New York Organ*, 16 October, 9 November 1844, 21 June 1845.

41. *New York Organ*, 30 August 1845, 31 January 1846.

42. *Worcester County Cataract*, 15 July, 20 December 1843, 1 May, 21 August, 17 September 1845.

43. *Worcester Reformer and True Washingtonian*, 8 October 1844.

44. *New York Crystal Fount*, 25 January 1843; *New York Daily Tribune*, 22 November 1844; James Watson to John H. Cocke, 31 January 1845, Cocke Papers, UV.

45. Norman Ware, *The Industrial Worker, 1840-1860* (New York: Hart, Schaffner and Marx, 1924), chaps. 13-15.

46. Ibid., p. 205; *Worcester Reformer and True Washingtonian*, 8 October 1844; *Worcester County Cataract*, 20 December 1843, 1 May, 21 August 1844.

47. John R. Commons et al., *A Documentary History of American Industrial Society* 2d ed. (New York: Russell, 1958), 8:126, 171-72, 197, 233, 261-62, 314; Paul Faler, "Cultural Aspects of the Industrial Revolution: Lynn, Massachusetts, Shoemakers and Industrial Morality, 1826-1860," *Labor History* 15 (Summer 1974): 393; Ware, *Industrial Worker*, p. 212; *New York Workingman's Advocate*, 13 May, 8 June 1844; *Lynn Pioneer*, 19 November 1845.

48. *New York Workingman's Advocate,* 18 May, 29 June 1844.

49. Ibid., 18 May, 14 September 1844; *Worcester True Reformer and Washingtonian,* 8 October 1844. See also Ware, *Industrial Worker,* p. 212, and *New York Pearl,* 24 April, 29 May 1847.

50. *The Beauties of Rechabism* (Philadelphia: J. and J. L. Gihon, 1851), pp. 8-9, 38; *Laws of the Order of the Sons of the Rechabites . . .* (Philadelphia: W. F. Geddes, 1842), pp. 1-12; *New York Crystal Fount and Rechabite Recorder,* 23 September, 21 October 1843; *Standard Encyclopedia of the Alcohol Problem* (Westerville, Ohio: American Issue Publishing Company, 1925-1930), 3:1294; John A. Krout, *The Origins of Prohibition* (New York: Alfred A. Knopf, 1925), p. 211.

51. *An Occasional Paper* [of the Good Samaritans] (New York), 11 September 1870, p. 8; *New York Organ,* 8 February 1851.

52. *The Beauties of Rechabism,* p. 38; "Independent Order of Good Samaritans and Daughters of Samaria," *New York Organ,* 8 February 1851.

53. *New York Crystal Fount and Rechabite Recorder,* 9 September 1843.

54. Ibid., 18 September 1847; *New York Pearl,* 17 October 1846, 17 April 1847.

55. *New York Organ,* 9 November 1844.

56. "Constitution of the Subordinate Divisions of the Sons of Temperance," p. 14, in *Journals of the Proceedings of the National Division of the Sons of Temperance; Journal of the Proceedings of the National Division of the Sons of Temperance: Sixth Annual Session* (Philadelphia: S. Douglas Wyeth, 1849), p. 24.

57. *Blue Book for the Use of the Subordinate Divisions, of the Order of the Sons of Temperance* (Cincinnati: C. Clark, 1853), p. 21.

58. Phillip S. White and Ezra Stiles Ely, *Vindication of the Order of the Sons of Temperance* (New York: Oliver and Brother, 1848), p. 45.

59. Orlando Lund, *The Order of the Sons of Temperance,* 2d ed. (Rochester: E. Shepard, 1847), pp. 13-14; Phillip S. White and H. R. Pleasants, *The War of Four Thousand Years; Being a Corrected History of the Various Efforts Made to Suppress the Vice of Intemperance* (Philadelphia: Griffith and Simon, 1846), p. 276; *Blue Book,* p. 18.

60. The evangelical reaction against Masonry is treated in Whitney R. Cross, *The Burned-over District: The Social and Intellectual History of Enthusiastic Religion in Western New York, 1800-1850* (Ithaca, N.Y.: Cornell University Press, 1950), p. 117, and Ronald P. Formisano, *The Birth of Mass Political Parties: Michigan, 1827-1861* (Princeton, N.J.: Princeton University Press, 1971), pp. 222-38.

61. Editorial, *JATU* 9 (June 1845): 90; "Report of the Third Presbytery of New York, on Secret Societies, April, 1845," *JATU* 9 (June 1845). For other

attacks on the Sons of Temperance by evangelicals, see *New York Observer*, 15 November 1845; *A Discussion of the Order of the Sons of Temperance between Rev. W. R. DeWitt D.D., of Harrisburg, and Rev. W. Easton, of Smyrna, Pa., together with a Letter from Rev. W. Easton, in Reply to Rev. H. Harburgh, on the Same Secret Order* (Philadelphia: T. R. Simpson, 1847), pp. 97, 107; J. Blanchard, *Secret Societies, A Discourse, Delivered in the Sixth Presbyterian Church, Cincinnati, September 7th, 1845* (Cincinnati: C. Clark, 1845), pp. 11-12; *Maine Washingtonian Journal and Temperance Herald*, 1 February 1843.

62. *JATU* 9 (June 1845): 90. The Masonic threat is emphasized by Easton, *Discussion of the Order of the Sons of Temperance*, p. 107; by Blanchard, *Secret Societies*, pp. 7, 16; and in *JATU* 7 (April 1843): 58.

63. *Journal of the Proceedings of the National Division of the Sons of Temperance: Second Annual Session* (Philadelphia: S. Douglas Wyeth, 1845), p. 44; report of the Rochester Division, no. 36, of the Sons of Temperance, February 25, 1848, in Sons of Temperance, records, accounts, reports, and miscellaneous papers of the Mantauk Division (Long Island), 1848-1856, NYHS.

64. *Journal of the Proceedings of the National Division of the Sons of Temperance: Second Annual Session*, p. 44; *New York Organ*, 8 November 1845. Ezra Stiles Ely, 1786-1861, was minister at the Northern Liberties Presbyterian Church in Philadelphia from 1844 to 1851.

65. Dissidents within the Sons of Temperance who demanded a more elaborate ritual formed the Temple of Honor in 1845 but tried to retain an affiliation with the Sons. However, after four years of discussion between the two orders, the Sons rejected the Templars' request for affiliate status, and the two organizations became completely separate. *Templar's Magazine* 1 (1850): 19; *Journal of the Proceedings of the National Division of the Sons of Temperance: Sixth Annual Session*, pp. 36-37, 78-79. For a general discussion of fraternal orders, which illustrates the central role of ritual and documents the elaborate ritual of the Masons and Odd Fellows, see Noel P. Gist, "Secret Societies: A Cultural Study of Fraternalism in the United States," *University of Missouri Studies* 15 (October 1940): 67-126.

66. *JATU* 8 (May 1844): 66; ibid. 9 (June 1845): 90.

67. Ibid. 8 (September 1844): 138; "Proceedings of the Grand Division, S. of T. of the State of New York," pp. 45-47; *Proceedings of the Quarterly Session of the Grand Division of the Sons of Temperance, of the State of Ohio; Held at Zanesville, April 25, 1849* (Cincinnati: Hastings, Yerkes, 1849), pp. 14, 37; *One Hundred Years of Temperance* (New York, 1886), pp. 494-97; *Proceedings of the Grand Division of the Sons of Temperance, of the State of Vermont . . .* (Montpelier, Vt.: Ballou's Press, 1849), p. 28.

68. *JATU* 13 (December 1849): 182; ibid. 13 (November 1849): 166; ibid. 14 (July 1850): 99.

69. David Montgomery, "The Shuttle and the Cross: Weavers and Artisans in the Kensington Riots of 1844," *Journal of Social History* 5 (Summer 1972): 411-46; Joseph Gusfield, *Symbolic Crusade: Status Politics and the American Temperance Movement* (Urbana: University of Illinois Press, 1963), pp. 55-57. See also Bruce Laurie, "'Nothing on Compulsion': Lifestyles of Philadelphia Artisans, 1820-1850," *Labor History* 15 (Summer 1974): 356-57, for a somewhat different view. On New York, see Ira Leonard, "New York City Politics, 1841-1844: Nativism and Reform" (Ph.D. diss., New York University, 1965), pp. 409-45.

70. *New York Pearl*, 27 June 1846; *Worcester Sentinel and Reformer*, 12 July, 8 November 1845; Caleb Wall, *Reminiscences of Worcester from the Earliest Period, Historical and Genealogical, with Notices of Early Settlers and Prominent Citizens* (Worcester: Tyler and Seagrove, 1877), pp. 318-19.

71. *New York Organ*, 17 August 1850; see also ibid., 7 June 1851.

72. *Journal of the Proceedings of the National Division of the Sons of Temperance of North America* (New York: Isaac J. Oliver, 1857), p. 5; Beattie, "Sons of Temperance," pp. 80-82.

73. For Cary, see Cary, ed., *National Temperance Offering*, pp. 28-31, and Jed Dannenbaum, "The Crusader: Samuel Cary and Cincinnati Temperance," *Cincinnati Historical Society Bulletin* 33 (Summer 1975): 139.

74. John N. Stearns, ed., *Temperance in All Nations* (New York: National Temperance Society and Publication House, 1893), 1:37-38; Robert M. Foust to Daniel S. Hill, 22 April 1856, Daniel S. Hill Papers, DU; *Journal of the Proceedings of the National Division* (1857), pp. 5-6; Beattie, "Sons of Temperance," p. 398.

9

THE LOCAL ORIGINS OF
PROHIBITION

As the conflict between the Washingtonians and the regular temperance organizations demonstrates, evangelical and wealthy temperance societies had already opted for prohibition by 1840. The Washingtonian movement proved to be an obstacle to the plans of temperance regulars, who saw the activities of the reformed men as divisive tactics undermining the authority, energies, and arguments of the prohibitionists. Only after considerable controversy and a protracted and acrimonious power struggle was this obstacle partially overcome by the merger of the regular organizations with parts of the Washingtonian movement. This merger brought the wealthy and evangelical societies into an alliance with the more respectable and more middle-class elements within the old Washingtonian societies. From this constellation of social forces came the massive campaigns for prohibition which made the decade of the 1850s distinctive in the history of antebellum temperance agitation.

Yet though the scale of political activity was unprecedented, the adoption of statewide prohibition in the 1850s did not represent a dramatic break in the tactics of temperance reformers. The shift from persuasion to coercion was a continuous and cumulative experience which had begun in the 1830s. Twenty years before the prohibitory legislation of the 1850s, many temperance supporters assumed that communities had the right to suppress the liquor traffic and had begun to experiment with prohibition at the local level. Local prohibition was a spontaneous social movement without central direction from the American Temperance Society or from professional agents of any of the other temperance societies. Rather than the creation of a few radical ideologues, it was the product of practical experience with the working of the liquor regulation system; this experience drove local groups at widely separated points toward legal action to end the sale of liquor. Although spasmodic at first, their efforts gradually coalesced in a profound and far-reaching movement, which culminated in the massive phase of statewide prohibition in the 1850s.

The sources of this early prohibitionist impulse were the same as those analyzed in the Worcester of the 1830s. In the towns of New England where the local prohibition campaigns began, the upwardly mobile entrepreneurs and their clerical and evangelical allies favored regulating community morality through law. This chapter will focus on how these wealthy and influential people came to choose prohibition as the solution to the drink problem. Such an analysis of the evolution of antiliquor tactics from temperance to stringent prohibition is essential to an understanding of the Maine Law impulse, the culminating phase of both antebellum temperance and the drive for power on the part of prohibitionists.

The political and legal experience of local prohibitionists between 1830 and 1850 impelled them to shift the focus of their tactics toward more stringent and comprehensive legal remedies. At first they tried to influence the town selectmen, who recommended applicants for liquor licenses to the county commissioners. But gradually their concern moved outward from the local level to the county, and from the county to the state level, as they discovered the magnitude and the complexity of obtaining legal solutions for intemperance. Prohibitionists hoped initially to destroy the liquor traffic by utilizing the existing license laws, but quickly discovering that the old laws were hopelessly inadequate, they began to seek newer and stricter laws. By 1850 temperance reformers were ready to launch a campaign for statewide prohibition.

Local prohibition flourished in most states of the Northeast in the 1830s and 1840s, but the process of reform was most clearly defined

in Massachusetts, where a substantial number of temperance reformers favored prohibition in the early 1830s, even though the
American Temperance Society still remained committed to moral
suasion. This is not to say that all temperance reformers supported
prohibition in the 1830s, even in Massachusetts. The no-license campaign split the temperance societies, and the Washingtonian slogan
of moral suasion won considerable support in the 1840s. Nevertheless the prohibitionist solution came to dominate the temperance
movement by the late 1840s, and the subsequent strategies and tactics of prohibitionists in the northern states were deeply influenced
by the experience with local action over the previous two decades.

The Logic of Local Action

The champions of prohibition in Massachusetts did not regard
legal action as a drastic last resort for men who had failed to persuade their communities to be temperate. Instead they looked on
prohibition as a natural and logical course for them to pursue. These
temperance reformers found prohibition congenial because they
grew up in a system of local government in which communities were
constantly using law to regulate the behavior of individuals in the
interest of the public good. As Tocqueville noted, the municipal
magistrates of New England, the selectmen, were charged with the
responsibility of executing the laws of the state and with the promul-
gation of "regulations necessary for public health, good order, and
morality of the citizens."[1] Temperance reformers constantly drew
on the New England tradition of community and on the reality of
New England town government. As Ira Barton, a Worcester lawyer
and prohibitionist, argued, "Every individual who incorporates
himself in the mass of civil society necessarily yields up such rights,
as in their exercise would conflict with the general welfare."[2] This
was a widely held view among local prohibitionists: the community
had the right and the obligation to regulate the morality of the individual through law.

In addition to the general tradition of New England town government, temperance reformers had the much more specific experience
of the license laws in mind when they proclaimed the right of the

community to regulate individual behavior. From the operation of the license laws, prohibitionists fashioned their view of the role of law in the temperance crusade. The licensing system, inherited from colonial times, allowed selectmen to recommend to the county commissioners men "of good moral character" for the purposes of selling liquor by retail (for consumption elsewhere) or in small quantities to be drunk in licensed houses or taverns.[3] Not all applicants of good character need be granted licenses. Indeed the law assumed that the number could be limited for the public good by the selectmen and by the county commissioners. Behind the licensing system lay the assumption that an excessive number of licensed houses would tend to corrupt the morals of the community.

Since temperance men had a long acquaintance with the use of law to regulate the traffic, it was only a short step for them to advocate legal action to suppress the sale of liquor altogether. The licensing authorities were constantly deciding who should and who should not be empowered to sell, and no-license advocates believed that the same power could be used to prevent anyone from selling. As Mark Hopkins, president of Williams College, pointed out, "What the law has a right to authorize and to regulate for the public good, it must have the right to prohibit for the same reason."[4]

Undoubtedly coercion of the seller was one motive in the minds of prohibitionists, but in the 1830s this was not the dominant aim behind legal action. More important was the educative value of a no-license decision. Prohibition would remove the aura of respectability from the licensing system. Thereby prohibitionists hoped to make the traffic disreputable as well as criminal. Asahel Huntington, the district attorney for Essex County and a zealous prohibitionist, praised legal action against the traffic "not so much for its effect in putting a stop to the traffic in ardent spirits, as for exerting a moral influence of the highest importance, on the people of the State. The law no longer recognized the deceiving doctrine that ardent spirit is a benefit to the community—*a public good*."[5] Temperance reformers sincerely believed their no-license rhetoric because they made several attempts, all unsuccessful, to abolish the license laws without seeking prohibitory laws to take their place. Huntington stated that he "would rather there would be no law, than that a law of the Commonwealth should teach such an egregious falsehood" as the public utility of liquor shops.[6] When the Essex Temperance Society and the Temperance Society of Salem petitioned the state legislature in 1834 and 1835, they demanded not a prohibitory law but the abolition of all license laws. Petitioners wanted the state legislature to remove the "sanction" and "countenance" which they believed the license laws gave to the liquor trade.[7]

Reformers believed that the law gave a cloak of respectability to a traffic in which many tavern keepers and retailers did not abide by the formal restrictions placed upon them. James T. Austin, Suffolk County attorney and later attorney-general of Massachusetts, told the state temperance society as early as 1830 that the "existing laws . . . were evaded by many and rarely enforced by the proper officers."[8] While many retailers traded entirely without licenses, Judge David Daggett of Connecticut expressed special concern that local selectmen did not even ensure the "good moral character" of those who were granted licenses.[9] Like Daggett, John Marsh hoped that the no-license strategy would remove this respectable facade, which the laws maintained, and, by exposing the trade, set the "index of public morality" in the township or county. Respectable people would then avoid both the liquor trade and the grogshop. Rum selling would, in the words of Jesse Goodrich of Worcester, be placed "on the level of brothel-keeping. No one making pretensions to respectability would be seen at a grog-shop, sooner than at a brothel."[10]

Even if the liquor traffic were outlawed by the state legislature, prohibitionists in Massachusetts expected it to continue for there would always be men who defied the law; but the selling would be "driven into corners and secret places" and left to the most "depraved and vicious" traders.[11] When the respectable abandoned the traffic, its ill effects would be laid bare and the work of converting the public to total abstinence made much easier.[12] Prohibitionists did not see law as an alternative to moral suasion but as a means of reshaping community sentiment in conjunction with the tools of persuasion. The notion that licensing gave sanction and respectability to the traffic was first fashioned in the 1820s and 1830s. Until the 1820s, respectable society viewed the licensing system as a means of promoting the public good. Antebellum reformers shaped the new view of licensing from their own experiences of the system in operation and from their own impulse to remake the moral world of the early nineteenth century.

Most early advocates of prohibition did not rule out eventual legal aid from the state, but for a variety of reasons, they preferred to begin at the local level. Prohibitionist sentiment varied greatly from one locality to another, and local action offered reformers a means of obtaining relief from the licensing of liquor shops in particular areas while statewide or county-wide action remained politically impossible. As Dr. Charles Jewett, the Massachusetts temperance lecturer, remarked, "The laws as they now exist, enable each town . . . to refuse licenses altogether; and in all greatly to restrain its sale. And there are communities so far advanced in temperance as to be able to take this stand."[13] Moreover local prohibition could provide the building blocks of a broader prohibition. No-license advocates such as the *Boston Christian Watchman*, a Baptist paper, believed that outlawing the traffic would enhance the prosperity of the no-license towns. Other towns would follow suit as the moral and material advantages of prohibition became apparent. "If some towns should vote to license, and others should refuse, let the morals of the license and anti-license towns be compared," and "a triumphant revolution" would occur in "municipal economy" and in public opinion.[14] Some reformers, like Justin Edwards, clearly viewed local action as a means of building prohibitionist sentiment, which would ultimately result in statewide laws.[15] But most local reformers merely struck out at the local manifestations of the problem of intemperance and left obscure their attitudes toward statewide prohibition. Whatever the merits of statewide or county-wide prohibition, no-license advocates wished to protect their local communities and do everything in their power to eradicate intemperance. Where a town favored no-license, prohibitionists asserted that "the will of the people" ought to be respected. "Is it not monstrous," asked the Essex County Temperance Convention of 1835, "that a grog shop shall be forced upon such a community against its will?"[16]

If the principle of self-determination supplied one reason for local action, beginning at the local level was also logical and natural because it was the local selectmen who gave sanction to the traffic by recommending men for licenses.[17] The reformers' first tactic was to urge selectmen to refuse to recommend applicants for licenses to the county commissioners. Since no one could sell liquor legally without a license, a no-license decision amounted to an indirect prohibition. The most obvious way to impress upon the selectmen the opposition of the community to the liquor traffic was to carry no-license votes at annual town meetings. Temperance reformers adopted this tactic despite the fact that such votes were not binding on selectmen under Massachusetts law. The licensing laws made no direct provision that selectmen must ascertain the wishes of the town before recommending men for licenses to the county commissioners. Yet because they were elected annually, selectmen rarely defied the vote of a town meeting. In Hampshire County, the selectmen in twelve of twenty-six towns had outlawed the traffic by 1833, and in Worcester County, twenty of the fifty-five towns voted no-license in annual town meetings in 1834. In the southeastern counties, the no-license campaign was even more successful. As early as 1831, all the towns of Plymouth had voted no-license, and by 1835 the traffic was illegal in each of the six southeastern counties of Norfolk, Plymouth, Barnstable, Bristol, Dukes, and Nantucket.[18] In none of these cases did selectmen prove a serious obstacle to no-license.

The county commissioners, not the selectmen, threatened to block the antiliquor crusade. The law gave them a discretionary power in the granting of licenses. Aggrieved licensees could appeal to the county commissioners against the refusal of selectmen to approbate them. If the town wished to persist in its refusal, selectmen were required to appear before the commissioners to demonstrate that the plaintiff should not be licensed. However, the county commissioners could license the plaintiff anyway.[19]

The use which commissioners made of their discretionary power differed from county to county. In the southeastern counties, the commissioners were sympathetic to temperance and acceded to the dominant no-license sentiment. In addition, the commissioners for Essex and Hampshire refused retail licenses; and Worcester's county commissioners quickly deferred to the wishes of the towns in the matter of retail licenses wherever the town meetings voted against licenses.[20] Thus the licensed grocery or grogshop was quickly outlawed in these three counties, but the commissioners reserved the right to approbate tavern keepers over the expressed wish of no-license towns. The county commissioners argued that innkeepers catered to a wider traveling public and that only the commissioners could weigh the broader interest against the wishes of the local community. In Essex County, the commissioners licensed innholders "to entertain strangers and travellers, because we think there should be some places in all our principal towns, where such persons may have the right to demand such entertainment,—and where they can be under the protection of the law in their persons and property."[21] Even though the Essex commissioners wished to license innkeepers without granting them liquor licenses, no legal provision for separation of tavern keeping and the sale of liquor existed in Massachusetts law. Ever quick to respond to such tactical obstacles, prohibitionists sought an amendment to the licensing laws which would give county commissioners explicit authority to license temperance inns. The objective was achieved in an amendment passed without opposition by the general court in the 1837 legislative session.[22]

Perhaps this amendment met no objection in the legislature because it left untouched the broader problem posed by the discretionary power of the county commissioners. In several counties, the commissioners licensed both retailers and tavern keepers over the recommendations of selectmen. In the mid-1830s, Hampshire, Franklin, Berkshire, and Middlesex counties all ignored the selectmen.[23] The refusal of commissioners to heed the wishes of the towns angered temperance reformers. "The people," wrote one frustrated prohibitionist, "have no voice in granting licenses. For in whatever way they may be consulted, their compact is not necessary. The power is in other hands."[24] The *Massachusetts Spy*, seeking to frighten county commissioners into compliance with the popular will, warned them that their "frequent disregard of the wishes of the people" on the subject of liquor licenses created "much dissatisfaction throughout the state" and generated popular demands that commissioners no longer be appointed by the governor-in-council but elected by the people.[25]

Yet despite popular dissatisfaction, prohibitionists did not seek the election of county commissioners. Instead they urged amendment to the licensing laws so that the people of each town could "determine the temperance question for themselves." With effective local control, "the inhabitants who are suffering" would have the final vote on the question of local morality.[26] The preference for local control stemmed in part from the prohibitionists' perception that their power varied greatly from locality to locality and hence that county-wide tests of strength might be inexpedient.[27] Moreover many of the temperance men were Whigs who feared that if county commissioners were elected, candidates would be judged solely by their attitudes toward liquor licensing. With county politics assuming "a marked temperance character," the important administrative tasks of the commissioners might be neglected. Election of county commissioners would lead to "partisan conflict," less qualified candidates, "less decision of character, less independence of feeling," and "less justice" in the administration of law.[28] Since state law assigned to the commissioners the important tasks of preparing county budgets, dividing taxes voted by the legislature, and building and repairing county roads, the fears of Whigs were not groundless. Whigs wished to keep the commissionerships in safe hands, by which they meant Whig hands. As long as commissioners were appointed by the governor, who was almost inevitably a Whig, Whigs monopolized this important county office.[29]

The prohibitionists concentrated their legislative energies on the securing of local option from the general court during the sessions of 1834 and 1835. Prohibitionist representatives each year secured in committee an amendment to the license bill which would place the power over the sale of distilled spirits in the hands of the townspeople. No licenses would be granted unless the inhabitants, at their annual town meetings, voted that licenses should be granted.[30] Yet each year the bill failed to pass, largely because many legislators roundly denounced the requirement that the licensing decision be made by vote of the town meeting. The Reverend Sylvanus Cobb of Malden, a Universalist clergyman, and several others condemned the amendment to the licensing bill of 1834 as "casting a fire brand into the towns, which would create great excitement." Samuel McKay of Pittsfield feared that the local option provision would "lead to the formation of parties which would carry [temperance] into all political action." Given the bitter town battles over the no-license issue which had occurred during 1834 and 1835 in Worcester, Dorchester, Brighton, Roxbury, and Salem, the divisive effects of local option seemed irrefutable to many legislators.[31]

The no-license advocates did not win the local option they desired in the mid-1830s, and the passage of a law in 1835 making the county commissionerships elective offices ensured that prohibitionists would be drawn into political campaigning on the county level. The drive for the election of county commissioners came mostly from the southeastern counties, where prohibitionists had already secured no-license decisions from the commissioners. It was, in fact, the opponents of prohibition, not the supporters, who were the most insistent advocates of elective county commissioners. Many of the petitions calling for election of county commissioners expressed dissatisfaction with the prohibitionist victories. The pro-license residents of Pawtucket, in Bristol County, objected strenuously to the refusal of their county commissioners to grant licenses and contended that commissioners could discriminate among applicants for licenses but could not refuse every applicant. Pro-license men felt that such a construction of the licensing power by county commissioners exceeded the boundaries of their authority. By making the office elective, anti-prohibitionists hoped to prevent such "arbitrary acts" on the part of commissioners.[32]

The bill for election of county commissioners won legislative support, partly because the pro-license discontent coincided with other, wholly unconnected sources of dissatisfaction with the existing system. Many petitions to the general court emphasized discontent with the commissioners' performance of their administrative and financial duties.[33] In response to the popular pressure, the general court provided that after May 1835, the commissioners would be elected every three years. There would be three county commissioners and two special commissioners who would act as county commissioners in the event of the incapacity of the commissioners themselves.[34]

Just as a good deal of the impetus for elective commissioners had come from the opponents of prohibition, it was the opponents who took the initiative to organize politically once the new laws were in force. With the first election scheduled for May 1835, supporters of licensing began to organize "liberal tickets" in Essex, Plymouth and Bristol counties. Quick to sense the importance of the election, temperance partisans responded by nominating prohibitionists to run against the liberals. Temperance tickets emerged victorious in all three counties, and in Barnstable, Norfolk, and Hampshire counties as well. In Berkshire and Hampden, Democratic tickets committed to a liberal licensing policy won election.[35]

Although prohibitionists were initially reluctant to test their strength in the commissioner elections, the success achieved in 1835 induced more and more political campaigning by no-license advocates. Henceforth the county commissioner elections in Massachusetts became, as the Whigs had predicted, inextricably connected with the temperance question. "Our County Commissioners," wrote one prohibitionist, "are now elected almost solely on the ground of their opinion in regard to the utility of the retail traffic in intoxicating liquors."[36] Prohibitionists were drawn into the political contests to protect the counties they had already won and to extend prohibition to the remaining counties. Despite their early professions of support for local control by each town, prohibitionists found obvious advantages in the county licensing system. Provided they could attain a majority in a county, they could impose no-license on every town and so prevent a single pro-license town from undermining the no-license strategy in dry towns. Prohibitionists justified this county-wide prohibition with the same argument that they used to suppress individual license holders: "To promote the best good of the community, individual wishes and preferences must yield to the wish of majorities and to circumstances."[37]

Pro-temperance commissioners inferred their legal authority to refuse all licenses from the discretionary power given to county commissioners. Before 1835 prohibitionists had condemned the "arbitrary and tyrannous" discretion of the commissioners, but in the counties controlled by temperance commissioners after 1835, they invoked the argument of discretionary power to defend the imposition or prohibition on unwilling towns.[38] Pro-license forces insisted that under the acts of 1787 and 1832, the licensing authority could discriminate among potential licensees but could not reject all applicants. Although temperance commissioners denied this argument, temperance reformers again resorted to political pressure to put the matter beyond dispute. They won from the legislature in 1837 an amendment to the license laws that made clear the legal grounds for refusal of all licenses by county commissioners.[39]

Success at the county level bred confidence in legal solutions and spurred new demands for statewide prohibition. If the public good did not require licenses in some towns and counties, prohibitionists began to argue that the public good did not demand them anywhere. The Suffolk County Temperance Society pointed to the success of no-license forces in outlawing the traffic "in neighboring towns and counties" whose economic and social condition favorably contrasted with that of Boston. It was now possible for temperance reformers like Moses Grant, a wealthy Boston merchant, to argue that prohibition was not a dangerous experiment but a tested formula whose benefits ought to be extended throughout Massachusetts by state law.[40] To prohibitionists it was unquestionably wrong to allow the traffic to continue anywhere in the state if reformers had the power to eliminate it. By 1837 the political success of no-license at the town and county level convinced prohibitionists that they did have the power to implement their principles. Horace Mann confidently predicted in 1837 that "the entire prohibition of the sale of ardent spirits as a drink" would soon be accomplished, while the *Christian Watchman* announced that "the time has come when public opinion will sustain such a law."[41] Such views were not uncommon at a time when local gains encouraged euphoric proclamations of the impending triumph of statewide prohibition.

If success bred faith in legal action, it also exposed the inadequacy of the existing laws for the elimination of the liquor traffic. While prohibitionists won their local victories in the southeastern counties, illegal selling continued. "There are many selling without a license," reported the Nantucket Temperance Society.[42] "It is painfully obvious," observed prohibitionists in Dedham, that "violations are now frequently practised. One can hardly be in almost any tavern in the county a half hour, without witnessing it."[43] The Essex County Temperance Society called a state convention in February 1838 to consider "what measures are necessary to secure a more general execution of the law."[44] The outlawing of the traffic had removed respectable dealers, as reformers had predicted, but others had taken their places.[45] In response, the emphasis shifted gradually from the use of the law to educate the public to the use of law to enforce temperance morality. Temperance societies in Dedham, Beverly, and Roxbury formed vigilance committees to investigate and prosecute violations of the law.[46] But the main thrust of the agitation shifted to petitioning for a general prohibitory law.

The Fifteen-Gallon Law

Support for general prohibition was strong enough and vocal enough to convince the representatives in the general court to pass the fifteen-gallon law during the session of 1838 to prohibit the sale of spirits, except for medicinal and mechanical purposes, in smaller quantities than fifteen gallons.[47] While prohibition had been gathering forces in Massachusetts for several years, the sudden victory of 1838 was largely the product of superior organization rather than secure majority support in the community. The Massachusetts Temperance Union churned out a formidable stream of propaganda setting out the alleged benefits of statewide prohibition. The liquor sellers were ill prepared for the prohibitionist onslaught. Opponents of the law of 1838 could manage only to defer its application for a year in the hope that opposition could be organized before the law came into force. John Marsh of the American Temperance Union hailed the new law as the sign that public opinion would now support general prohibitory laws, but Marsh and the Massachusetts temperance reformers were utterly misled by the no-license campaign. Despite its easy passage, the fifteen-gallon law proved to be an abortive and ineffective start on the road to statewide prohibition.[48]

Opposition to the law was slow to emerge, but when the anti-prohibitionists did organize, they sabotaged enforcement and achieved repeal within two years. The obvious opponents of the law—distillers, tavern keepers, and retailers—held local and county conventions and threatened political retaliation against prohibitionist legislators. More important, the law raised opposition from respectable people who opposed legal coercion on principle. The law severely divided the Whig party and led to the nomination of liberal Whig tickets in the 1838 election.[49]

With the Whig party divided, Democrats seized the opportunity to overcome their permanent position as the minority party in Massachusetts. Aside from the motive of political expediency, there were other considerations stemming from the social support for and the political attitudes of Democrats. Democrats in Massachusetts, as in other states, were less likely than Whigs to endorse prohibition. Democrats tended to oppose the interference of legislatures in matters of community morality and adopted a laissez-faire attitude toward the liquor problem.[50] Furthermore the party's constituency in Massachusetts included many from the erstwhile dissenting groups. While many Baptists and Methodists were increasingly receptive to the idea of abstinence, some were suspicious of—and sometimes completely hostile to—prohibition measures sponsored by Congregationalists and Unitarians.[51]

Thus the Democratic party could please its supporters and garner the votes of dissatisfied Whigs by stressing support for temperance while at the same time intimating hostility toward the fifteen-gallon law. Marcus Morton, the gubernatorial candidate, was ideal for blurring the issue on temperance since he had served as president of the American Temperance Society between 1827 and 1829. Morton combined platitudes on temperance with silence on the fifteen-gallon law. It was widely rumored, though, that a vote for the Democrats was a vote against the prohibitionists. Certainly Edward Everett, Morton's incumbent Whig opponent, shared this view and feared the political effects of the law. Everett charged that Democrats "avowedly advocated" Morton "on the ground, that he is against the license law, which I am denounced for signing."[52] Sensing the growing unpopularity of the fifteen-gallon law, Everett tried to divest himself of the albatross of prohibition during the final election campaign by calling into question the practicality of the law, but the effort failed. Morton defeated Everett with an absolute majority of one vote.[53] Everett polled only 917 fewer votes than he had received in 1838, and the Democrat won because he attracted 9,239 votes more than he received the previous year. The fifteen-gallon law apparently brought to the polls many who did not normally vote.[54]

More important than Morton's victory was the election of a pro-license majority to the general court. Liberal Whigs split the Whig vote at the polls and allowed a coalition of Democrats and liberal Whigs to control the legislature during 1840, thus opening the way for the repeal of the license law. When repeal came, the *Temperance*

Journal, the organ of the Massachusetts Temperance Union, blamed party prejudice for the setback and vowed not to rest "till we get prohibition in an effectual form and power." [55]

Defeat of the fifteen-gallon law taught prohibitionists an important lesson: local gains must be consolidated before attempting statewide action. State and national temperance leaders urged a return to the local campaigns which had proved so successful before 1838. John Marsh of the American Temperance Union concluded from the Massachusetts experience that local option was the most effective course for prohibitionists. At the local level, "a free vote" could be taken "separate, as it cannot be in legislative bodies, from political considerations." [56] Marsh was certain that prohibition would prevail once divorced from the partisan rivalry which had determined the fate of the fifteen-gallon law. After the National Temperance Convention endorsed this view in 1841, local action became the standard policy of the American Temperance Union and remained so until the end of the 1840s.

Organizing Locally for State Prohibition

The abortive campaign of 1838 should not obscure the steady progress which prohibitionists made at the local level. Massachusetts adopted prohibition by 1850 not through statewide laws but by a gradual takeover at the county level. With the fifteen-gallon law repealed, the license laws existing before 1838 came into force again, and legal prohibition remained in effect in the eight counties which had refused licenses in 1838. But prohibitionists did much more than hold the ground they had won. Within three years of their disastrous defeat, no-license advocates had won prohibition in Worcester, Middlesex, and Berkshire counties. Suffolk and Franklin fell into line in 1847, and only Hampden still granted licenses. That lone county fell to the prohibitionists in the county commissioner election of 1850. [57] The victories of the 1840s were not only more extensive geographically; they were more comprehensive. At first, in the early 1830s, the no-license activity had been directed solely toward the sale of spirits, but by the 1840s, under the impact of teetotalism, local prohibitionists demanded, and received, from county commissioners rulings against all intoxicating liquors, including wine and beer.

In part, superior organization enabled the no-license men to prevail at the county level. As they gained experience in the no-license campaigns, they learned the value of thorough agitation; they became more skilled in the tactics of persuasion and more adept at manipulating the county commissioners. Temperance societies labored continuously to demonstrate before the commissioners the strong public support for the no-license policy. The prohibitionists organized petition drives, in addition to no-license votes at town meetings, and sent as many representatives as possible to the commissioners' sessions to present the no-license case. When the commissioners of Middlesex and Berkshire refused licenses in 1843, temperance agent Nathan Crosby rejoiced that "the *people* had literally assembled before the Commissioners, remonstrating against the granting of licenses."[58]

Yet elaborate propaganda campaigns meant little unless prohibitionists could win majorities in the elections for county commissioners. They succeeded because they had the votes which county and local officials respected. In Berkshire County, the no-license decision brought with it an impressive display of prohibitionist sentiment and its influence on the regular politicians. When the temperance representatives argued the no-license case before the county commissioners, they presented petitions from two-thirds of the county's legal voters. The Whig and Democratic candidates for congressman from the Seventh District could not ignore the prohibitionist sentiment, and both appeared before the commissioners to argue against licenses.[59]

The expanding public support for no-license was based on the hope that local prohibition would solve the pressing social problems facing Massachusetts. Temperance society petitions and the no-license decisions of the county commissioners all focused on poverty, crime, delinquency, and immorality in the local communities. No-license advocates claimed to have a solution to social disorder, and support for the prohibitionist cause was predicated on this claim, as the no-license triumph in Berkshire County suggests. In the 1820s and 1830s, Berkshire had been one of three agrarian counties in western Massachusetts which lagged behind in adopting local pro-

hibition. But in the 1840s, Berkshire, Hampden, and Franklin all endorsed prohibition. The social changes which had earlier affected the
southeastern counties had reached western Massachusetts. From
1810 to 1840, the predominantly agricultural communities of Berkshire had shifted from subsistence and small-scale farming to sheep
culture to serve the growing textile industry of the county. But
"Berkshire did not prove as well adapted to sheep-culture as the
more enthusiastic expected, and those who made it their sole dependence had cause to regret it. . . . Gradually under the increasing competition of the more favored regions of the West, the raising of sheep
[became] a comparatively insignificant item with the Berkshire
farmer."[60] The competition of western agriculture first hit hard in
the 1840s, as Percy Bidwell has pointed out. Sheep herds declined 50
percent between 1840 and 1850 and another 30 percent from 1850 to
1860.[61]

Although agriculture did not decline precipitously in western
Massachusetts, economic distress did occur. In response, farmers
sought more efficient means of production and cultivation to meet
the challenge of western agriculture. Along with an increasing devotion to improved methods of grazing and farming, Massachusetts
farmers abandoned the practice of dispensing liquor for their personal use and for rural laborers, an important change because it indicates the drift and the sources of local prohibition in Berkshire County.[62] The success of prohibition in the western, rural counties in the
1840s did not represent an anti-urban animus nor did it stem simply
from the moral dimensions of the temperance issue. Rather the support for prohibition represented a growing commitment on the part
of farm entrepreneurs and their small-town allies that temperance
would be economically and socially beneficial to the whole community. Just as changes in the character and conception of work in the
factories shaped the support for and the direction of temperance agitation, a similar process of economic change was occurring on the
farm. The disruptive effects of the commercialization of agriculture
created the social and economic problems which local prohibitionists claimed they could solve.

Economic dislocation produced social disorder, which in turn
could be exploited by the zealous petitioning and political campaigning of temperance reformers to secure the no-license victories of the

1840s. But local victories did not satisfy the prohibitionists. Enforcement of the no-license decisions remained with the selectmen. Prohibitionists found that they could enforce the no-license policy only in towns which they dominated. All the indications are that liquor did become harder to obtain where strong community pressures for prohibition existed. Elsewhere the sale continued unabated. Some towns undoubtedly refused licenses to keep the temperance reformers happy and had no intention of enforcing no-license. In Boston, the city council refused licenses after 1843 but did not prosecute those who sold liquor without a license. Only when Josiah Quincy was elected mayor in 1847 on a moral reform ticket did the city begin (temporarily) to clamp down on illegal retailing and drinking.[63] Nor was the problem of enforcement confined to Boston. In Worcester County, a convention of teetotalers denounced "the traffic in intoxicating drinks still carried on within this Commonwealth in mockery of the claims of humanity and justice, and in defiance of the law."[64] Moreover even where the law was enforced, the penalty of twenty dollars for violation was inadequate to punish or to deter offenders. Henry B. Stanton told a convention of Boston teetotalers in 1846 that "as the law now is, it is utterly inadequate to suppress the traffic."[65] Charles Jewett, the traveling agent of the Massachusetts Temperance Union, reported that prohibitionists in Lowell wanted "a more efficient law, the penalties of which shall be in some degree proportionate to the magnitude of the offence—a law which shall do something more than play with the infernal system."[66] Although temperance reformers had initially viewed local prohibition as an educative device, the persistent violation of no-license created frustrations among reformers. Not content with mere symbolic legal victories at the local level, they began to demand harsher punishment for offenders.

The no-license experience led legal suasionists almost irresistibly toward new and more effective laws to prevent the sale of intoxicating drinks. If no-license campaigns had failed to eradicate the liquor traffic, they had at least exhausted the existing legal remedies and exposed their many defects. Because enforcement of no-license was both haphazard and ineffectual, prohibitionists began to demand uniform statewide laws and more stringent penalties for of-

fenders. By the late 1840s, many temperance reformers in Massachusetts were convinced of the need for statewide prohibition.

The Relevance of the Massachusetts Experience

The process of prohibitionist agitation in Massachusetts was not
an isolated case.[67] Although legal structures and local circumstances differed among states, many other northern states made
provision for county or town licensing, and temperance societies
utilized these laws to obtain local prohibition wherever possible.
The five neighboring states of New England showed the closest resemblance to the no-license movement in Massachusetts. In Connecticut, for example, 200 of the state's 220 townships had rejected
liquor licenses by 1845. By 1846, all but one of Maine's counties had
enacted local prohibition. In Vermont and New Hampshire, the
position was similar and the process the same as for Massachusetts.
Nor was the trend confined to New England. In the Middle Atlantic
states, electors had to petition their legislators to obtain special local
option laws county by county. Eighteen of Pennsylvania's counties
had gained this right by 1846, while seven-eighths of the towns of
New York voted for no-license during the brief operation of a local
option law in that state between 1845 and 1847.

The history of prohibitionist activity in the Midwest also had important parallels with the New England agitation, with no-license
campaigns spreading through Ohio, Wisconsin, Iowa, Michigan,
and Illinois.[68] Yet there were also several important departures from
the New England pattern. In the Midwest, the local prohibition
movement started later than in the Northeast and was never quite as
strong. Hence the process of prohibitionist agitation tended to become compressed; innovations in prohibitory legislation usually
began in the East and were imported into the western states by mi-
grating prohibitionists. In an important sense, midwestern agitation
for prohibition was derivative of eastern experience.[69]

The reasons for these departures from the New England pattern
were largely economic. Frontier conditions did not encourage tem-

perance and prohibitionist sentiment; prohibition in the newer states was in fact sponsored by people attempting to create a more coherent social order out of chaotic frontier conditions.[70] Also retarding the progress of prohibitionist sentiment in the Midwest (and the South) was the position of these states as major producers of corn liquor for both the larger regional markets and local consumption. In 1850 Ohio ranked first in the nation in production of distilled spirits; Indiana was fourth and Illinois fifth.[71] Particularly in the years up to the 1840s when transportation networks in the region were especially inadequate, distilling was vital to the corn economy of the Midwest. As communications gradually improved with the opening up of canals and railroads, it became possible for farmers in this region to diversify their output, dispense with distilling, and produce grain crops for the eastern urban markets. It was in the 1840s and 1850s that midwestern farmers began to seek the same discipline and market orientation from themselves and from their workers and families which earlier had generated temperance sentiments among the farmers of eastern New England.[72]

There were other related reasons for the slow growth of prohibitionist sentiment in the Midwest up to the 1850s. Early migration to this region was particularly heavy from the border states and Appalachia. These rural, mainly southern immigrants were not receptive to northern and urban reform enthusiasms, and more important, they brought with them a culture (and a subsistence farm economy associated with that culture) which accorded a central role to liquor in both social and economic life. Across Ohio, Indiana, Illinois, and into southern Iowa, a belt of counties of largely southern derivation remained hostile to prohibition agitation into the 1850s.[73] Thus it was the character of the economy and the population which made midwesterners reluctant to support prohibition until the 1850s. Only by then had majority sentiment begun to change with the influx of New England immigrants into Wisconsin, Iowa, Nebraska, and Minnesota.

By the early 1850s, then, many in the Midwest were ready to join the East in a concerted campaign for prohibition, yet it was still from New England that the initiative came. Prohibitionist attention now focused not on Massachusetts but on Maine, which had passed the first statewide prohibitory law in 1846. Because this law lacked heavy penalties for offenders and effective machinery for enforcement, the next five years saw repeated attempts to obtain a workable substitute. This battle culminated in the passage in 1851 of a prohibitory law which became the model for temperance action for a decade and the source of unprecedented political conflict. By 1851 the evolution of prohibition from local to statewide action was complete.

Notes

1. Alexis de Tocqueville, *Democracy in America*, ed. J. P. Mayer (New York: Harper and Row, 1966), p. 65.

2. Ira Barton, *Worcester Palladium*, 15 April 1835; "Address of the Temperance Convention," *Salem Register*, 15 March 1838; "Who Shall Be Licensed to Retail Ardent Spirit as a Drink?" *Temperance Journal* (February 1839). See also Page Smith, *As a City upon a Hill: The Town in American History* (New York: Alfred A. Knopf, 1966), chap. 7, and Phillip S. Paludan, "The American Civil War Considered as a Crisis in Law and Order," *American Historical Review* 77 (October 1972): 1024, 1030.

3. *Laws of the Commonwealth of Massachusetts, Passed by the General Court, . . . One Thousand Eight Hundred and Thirty-Two* (Boston: Dutton and Wentworth, 1832), ch. 166, sec. 9. Except for the period of the fifteen-gallon law (1839-1840), this act governed licensing in Massachusetts between 1832 and 1852, with only minor alterations in 1837 and 1850. Practice before 1832 was governed by "An Act for the Due Regulation of Licensed Houses" (1787). The act of 1787 remained in force, with modifications in 1807, 1816, and 1831, until 1832.

4. Mark Hopkins et al., *Address to the People of Massachusetts, in Relation to the Temperance Reformation* (Boston: Standard Press, 1846), p. 11; Ira Barton, *Worcester Palladium*, 15 April 1835; Berkshire County Commissioners' report, *Pittsfield Sun*, 27 April 1843.

5. *Investigation into the Fifteen Gallon Law* (Boston: J. T. Buckingham, 1839), p. 75; see also Neal Dow, *The Reminiscences of Neal Dow: Recollections of Eighty Years* (Portland, Me.: Evening Express Publishing Company, 1898), pp. 270-71; Gerrit Smith circular, 28 June 1841, Elizur Wright

Papers, LC; editorial, *New York Genius of Temperance*, 2 October 1833; *Permanent Temperance Documents of the American Temperance Society* (Boston: Seth Bliss, 1835), pp. 68-69.

6. *Investigation into the Fifteen Gallon Law*, p. 75.

7. *House . . . no. 37: The Memorial of Benjamin Pickman, and Five Hundred and Twenty-nine Others, of Salem, for a Repeal of the License Laws. February 7, 1834* (n.p., [1834]); *Salem Landmark*, 13 May 1835.

8. *Journal of Humanity*, 3 June 1830; "M.L.V.," *Licensed Houses: An Examination of the License Laws of the Commonwealth of Massachusetts* (Boston: J. Ford, 1833), pp. 19-20.

9. David Daggett to Cyrus Williams, 3 July 1830, Cyrus Williams Papers, NYPL.

10. *Massachusetts Cataract*, 12 October 1848; *Maine Washingtonian Journal and Temperance Herald*, 16 November 1842.

11. "Peleg Sprague's Speech before the Committee of the Massachusetts Legislature in Behalf of the Remonstrants against the Repeal of the License Law," *JATU* 3 (April 1839): 51; memorial of the Suffolk County Temperance Society, *Salem Register*, 8 March 1838; *Investigation into the Fifteen Gallon Law*, p. 75.

12. Statement by Lucius M. Sargent, *Boston Evening Mercantile Journal*, 6 February 1838.

13. *Proceedings of the Third National Temperance Convention, Held at Saratoga Springs, July 27, 1841* (New York: S. W. Benedict, 1841), p. 31.

14. Editorial, *Christian Watchman*, 21 March 1834; editorial, *Journal of Humanity*, 23 December 1830; Gerrit Smith circular, 28 June 1841, Elizur Wright Papers.

15. Henry D. Kitchell, *An Appeal to the People on the Liquor Traffic* (New York: Oliver and Brother, 1848), p. 43; Justin Edwards to Gerrit Smith, 7 October 1833, box 20, Gerrit Smith Miller Collection, SU.

16. "To the Free and Independent Electors of Norfolk," *Norfolk* (Dedham, Mass.) *Advertiser*, 24 March 1838; editorial, *Worcester County Cataract*, 5 April 1843; "Address of the Temperance Convention," *Salem Register*, 15 March 1835; letter to editor, *Salem Register*, 30 April 1835.

17. See, for example, the statements by Benjamin Thomas, Ira Barton, and Emory Washburn in *Worcester Palladium*, 15 April 1835.

18. *Journal of Humanity*, 27 January 1831; *New York Genius of Temperance*, 20 April 1833; *Pittsfield Sun*, 28 March 1833; *Investigation into the Fifteen Gallon Law*, p. 88; *Norfolk Advertiser*, 4 February 1837; *Twenty-first Annual Report of the Massachusetts Temperance Society, Presented by the Council to the Annual Meeting in Boston, May 29, 1834* (Boston: Ford and Damrell, 1834), pp. 3-8.

19. *Laws of the Commonwealth of Massachusetts,* 1832, ch. 166, secs. 6, 9.

20. *Worcester Massachusetts Spy,* 12 April, 24 September 1834; *Hampshire* (Northampton) *Gazette,* 4 May 1836.

21. *Boston Recorder,* 1 July 1836, prints the illuminating opinion of the county commissioners in the trial case of *Essex* v. *Elwell, petitioner.*

22. *Laws of the Commonwealth of Massachusetts, Passed by the General Court, . . . One Thousand Eight Hundred and Thirty-seven* (Boston: Dutton and Wentworth, 1837), ch. 242, sec. 2. The amendment allowed any innkeeper to be licensed to accommodate travelers "without authority to sell any intoxicating liquor." To encourage such licenses, the legislature exempted temperance inns from the usual licensing fees.

23. *JATU* 6 (July 1842): 107; *Hampshire Gazette,* 4 May 1836; *Springfield* (Mass.) *Gazette,* 5 April 1850; *Pittsfield Sun,* 27 April 1843; *Investigation into the Fifteen Gallon Law,* p. 88.

24. *Journal of Humanity,* 15 November 1832; editorial, *Journal of Humanity,* 8 November 1832.

25. *Worcester Massachusetts Spy,* 19 March 1834; *The Revised Statutes of the Commonwealth of Massachusetts, (1835)* (Boston: Dutton and Wentworth, 1836), ch. 14, sec. 31.

26. Editorial, *Christian Watchman,* 21 March 1834.

27. *Temperance Journal* (March 1835). See the illuminating discussions of prohibitionist tactics in the *Worcester Massachusetts Spy,* 17 March 1843, 24 February, 14 April 1841.

28. "Remonstrance of Geo. Athearn and others, against the petition of Mayhew & others, to be delivered to the appropriate committee," Papers Relating to the Laws of the Commonwealth of Massachusetts, 1835, ch. 152, MS, MSA; editorial, *Salem Register,* 7 April 1836.

29. For the coolness of the Whig press to the election of county commissioners, see *Boston Daily Advertiser,* 19 May 1835; *Worcester Massachusetts Spy,* 20 May 1835; and *Salem Register,* 7 May 1838. Fears for the neglect of administrative duties are expressed in "Address to the People by Andrew Nichols, Asahel Huntington, and Daniel Lord," *Salem Register,* 17 April 1835. The administrative functions of the commissioners are set out in Tocqueville, *Democracy in America,* p. 68.

30. *Salem Register,* 23 March 1835; *Temperance Journal* (April 1834).

31. *Salem Register,* 30 March 1834; *Christian Watchman,* 21 March 1834; speech by Mr. Simmons of Roxbury, *Worcester Palladium,* 25 March 1835.

32. "Petition of Collins Darby and Thirty-nine Others from the Town of Pawtucket for Repeal of the Law Concerning County Commissioners,"

Papers Relating to Laws of the Commonwealth of Massachusetts, 1835, ch. 152, MSA.

33. See, for example, "Petition of Thomas B. Richmond and 144 Other Inhabitants of Dighton Praying That the County Commissioners May be Chosen by the People," Papers Relating to Laws of the Commonwealth of Massachusetts, 1835, ch. 152.

34. *Laws of the Commonwealth of Massachusetts, Passed by the General Court, . . . One Thousand Eight Hundred and Thirty-five* (Boston: Dutton and Wentworth, 1835), ch. 152, sec. 2.

35. *Boston Daily Advertiser*, 11, 13, 15, 19, 22 May 1835; *Worcester Massachusetts Spy*, 20 May 1835; *Worcester Republican*, 20 May 1835; *Hampshire Gazette*, 24 June 1835. I have no information on the county commissioner elections in Franklin and Middlesex counties, but these counties did continue to grant licenses. In Worcester, there was no division on the license question at the election. Licensing in Boston remained in the hands of the board of aldermen, and with the selectmen in the case of Nantucket.

36. "The License Power," *Worcester Massachusetts Spy*, 14 April 1841.

37. "Address of the Temperance Convention," *Salem Register*, 15 March 1838; "An Address before the 'Washington Temperance Society of Worcester,' November 16th, 1846,—by Hon. Abijah Bigelow, of Worcester," *Massachusetts Cataract*, 1 December 1846.

38. See the decisions of the county commissioners, *Boston Recorder*, 1 July 1836, and *Pittsfield Sun*, 27 April 1843.

39. *Laws of the Commonwealth of Massachusetts*, 1837, ch. 242, sec. 2.

40. License Laws, 1 March 1838. Testimony before the committee of the general court, by Moses Grant, Lucius M. Sargent, and John Pierpont, and report of the committee recommending the license bill, 1838, Linus Child, chairman, MS filed with Papers Relating to the Laws of the Commonwealth of Massachusetts, 1838, ch. 157; Suffolk County Temperance Society meeting, speech by Moses Grant, *Boston Evening Mercantile Journal*, 20 February 1838; Massachusetts Temperance Convention resolution on prohibition, and memorial to the legislature, *JATU* 2 (March 1838): 38; resolutions of the Essex County Temperance Convention, *Salem Register*, 12 March 1838.

41. Horace Mann to Mary P. Mann, 28 February 1837, Horace Mann Papers, MHS; editorial, *Christian Watchman*, 30 March 1838; *Boston Evening Mercantile Journal*, 20 February 1838; report of the committee to which was referred the Roxbury petition appealing against the commissioners' no-license decision, *Norfolk Advertiser*, 4 February 1837; report of the committee on the license bill, 1838, Linus Child, chairman, in License Laws, 1 March 1838, MSA.

42. *Twenty-first Annual Report of the Massachusetts Temperance Society*, p. 14.

43. Editorial, *Norfolk Advertiser*, 6 May 1837.

44. *Christian Watchman*, 19 January 1838.

45. *Twenty-first Annual Report of the Massachusetts Temperance Society*, p. 14.

46. *Salem Register*, 7 April 1836; *Norfolk Advertiser*, 6 May 1837.

47. *Laws of the Commonwealth of Massachusetts, Passed by the General Court, . . . One Thousand Eight Hundred and Thirty-eight* (Boston: Dutton and Wentworth, 1838), ch. 157.

48. *Boston Evening Mercantile Journal*, 17 April 1838; *JATU* 2 (March 1838): 38.

49. Reports of meetings of the pro-license forces in Worcester, Middlesex, Essex, and Franklin counties, *Temperance Journal* (August 1839); *An Appeal to the Good Sense of the People of Massachusetts* ([Boston]: n.p., [1838]), pp. 2-3.

50. Herbert Ershkowitz and William G. Shade, "Consensus or Conflict? Political Behavior in the State Legislatures during the Jacksonian Era," *Journal of American History* 58 (December 1971): 608-09, 617-18; Lee Benson, *The Concept of Jacksonian Democracy: New York as a Test Case* (Princeton, N.J.: Princeton University Press, 1961), pp. 198-200; Ronald P. Formisano, *The Birth of Mass Political Parties: Michigan, 1827-1861* (Princeton, N.J.: Princeton University Press, 1971), pp. 116-19.

51. There is no good study of Massachusetts politics in this period. See A. B. Darling, *Political Changes in Massachusetts, 1824-1848: A Study of Liberal Movements in Politics* (New Haven: Yale University Press, 1925).

52. Everett to J. H. Clifford, 24 June 1839, Clifford Papers, MHS. For samples of the varying electoral tactics of local Democrats, see "Democrats of Needham," *Norfolk* (Dedham, Mass.) *Democrat*, 21 September 1839; "Democrats of Tyringham," *Pittsfield Sun*, 7 November 1839; and *Worcester Palladium*, 9 October 1839. Everett correctly appraised Morton's position on prohibition. See his inaugural message to the legislature, *Norfolk Democrat*, 25 January 1840.

53. For Everett's attempts to escape the prohibition issue, see Everett to Edward Brooks, 27 June 1839, vol. 68, p. 293, Everett Papers, MHS. For Whig attempts to renege on prohibition, see *Worcester Massachusetts Spy*, 16, 30 October 1839, and *Northampton Courier*, 7 November 1838.

54. Darling, *Political Changes in Massachusetts*, p. 241.

55. *Norfolk Democrat*, 8 February 1840; *Worcester Palladium*, 15 January 1840; *Temperance Journal* (February 1840).

56. *Report of the American Temperance Union for 1841* (New York: S.

W. Benedict, 1841), p. 22; *Third National Temperance Convention*, p. 31.

57. *JATU* 6 (July 1842): 107; *Worcester Massachusetts Spy*, 5 April 1843; *Boston Post*, 14 May 1847; *Massachusetts Cataract*, 2 May 1850. It must be noted, however, that the victory in Suffolk County was only temporary. The board of aldermen of Boston were preparing to reverse the city's no-license policy early in 1852, before the statewide prohibitory law came into effect, and they actually did issue licenses. See Roger Lane, *Policing the City, Boston, 1822-1885* (Cambridge: Harvard University Press, 1967), pp. 78-79.

58. *JATU* 7 (May 1843): 69; *Worcester County Cataract*, 19 April 1843; *Pittsfield Sun*, 27 April 1843; "The License Power," *Worcester Massachusetts Spy*, 14 April 1841.

59. *Pittsfield Sun*, 27 April 1843.

60. J. E. A. Smith, *The History of Pittsfield (Berkshire County), Massachusetts, from the Year 1800 to the Year 1876* (Springfield, Mass.: C. W. Bryan, 1876), p. 483.

61. Percy Bidwell, "The Agricultural Revolution in New England," *American Historical Review* 26 (July 1921): 683-702.

62. Report of the Berkshire Agricultural Show, speeches by Henry W. Bishop and Reverend John Todd, *Pittsfield Sun*, 12 October 1843; Henry Colman, *An Address Delivered October 2, 1839, at Concord Mass., before the Middlesex Society of Husbandmen and Manufacturers at Their Annual Cattle Show* (Boston: Weeks and Jordan, 1839), p. 12.

63. *Boston Post*, 14 May 1847; *Massachusetts Cataract*, 15 March 1849.

64. "Proceedings of the Worcester County Temperance Convention," *Massachusetts Cataract*, 13 September 1849; "Address to the Electors of Berkshire," *Pittsfield Sun*, 22 February 1844.

65. *Boston Recorder*, 8 October 1846. Henry B. Stanton, 1805-1887, was a lawyer, journalist, and abolitionist. His wife was Elizabeth Cady Stanton, the famous advocate of women's rights.

66. Charles Jewett, *Speeches, Poems, and Miscellaneous Writings on Subjects Connected with Temperance and the Liquor Traffic* (Boston: John P. Jewett, 1849), p. 165.

67. For local prohibition activity in other states during the 1830s and 1840s, see, for Connecticut, *Report of the American Temperance Union for 1846* (New York: S. W. Benedict, 1846), p. 10; for Pennsylvania, Asa Martin, "The Temperance Movement in Pennsylvania Prior to the Civil War," *Pennsylvania Magazine of History and Biography* 49 (July 1925): 216-17; for New York, E. C. Delavan to J. H. Cocke, 10 May 1847, Cocke Papers, UV; and Gerrit Smith, "To the Commissioners of Excise of the Town of Smithfield," June 1841, letterbook, vol. 1, Gerrit Smith Miller Collection; for Rhode Island, *Extracts from the Proceedings and Reports of the Rhode-*

Island State Total Abstinence Society, from Its Organization, Jan. 1841, to January 1846, with the Constitution of the Society, and the License Law of 1846 (Providence: B. T. Albro, 1846), pp. 18, 23; for Wisconsin, *New York Organ*, 5 May 1849; for Vermont, David Ludlum, *Social Ferment in Vermont, 1791-1850* (New York: Columbia University Press, 1939), pp. 81-82; and for Maine, Dow, *Reminiscences*, pp. 269-70, 278-80.

68. Floyd B. Streeter, "History of Prohibition Legislation in Michigan," *Michigan History* 2 (April 1918): 293; Charles E. Canup, "Temperance Movements and Legislation in Indiana," *Indiana Magazine of History* 16 (March 1920): 20-21; Dan C. Clark, "History of Liquor Legislation in Iowa, 1846-1861," *Iowa Journal of History and Politics* 6 (January 1908): 57; *The Cyclopedia of Temperance and Prohibition* (New York: Funk and Wagnalls, 1891), pp. 296, 334; Formisano, *Birth of Mass Political Parties*, p. 119; Alice E. Smith, *The History of Wisconsin*, vol. 1: *From Exploration to Statehood* (Madison: State Historical Society of Wisconsin, 1973), pp. 629-30; Arthur H. Cole, *The Era of the Civil War, 1848-1870* (Springfield: Illinois Centennial Commission, 1919), p. 207.

69. Joseph Schafer, "Prohibition in Early Wisconsin," *Wisconsin Magazine of History* 8 (March 1925): 281; Allan M. Winkler, "Drinking on the American Frontier," *Quarterly Journal of Studies on Alcohol* 29 (June 1968): 414.

70. Winkler, "Drinking on the American Frontier," p. 414.

71. J. D. B. De Bow, *Statistical View of the United States . . . Being a Compendium of the Seventh Census . . .* (Washington, D.C.: A. O. P. Nicholson, 1854), p. 182.

72. There is no good study of the economics of the liquor industry and its connection with farm economics and changes in transportation. However, see Paul Gates, *The Farmer's Age: Agriculture, 1815-1860* (New York: Holt, Rinehart and Winston, 1960), pp. 13, 162; Cyrus Haldeman, *A Few Reasons Why a "Maine Liquor Law" Should Not Be Passed in the State of Pennsylvania . . .* (Lancaster, Pa.: n.p., 1852), pp. 10-12; and David Schob, *Hired Hands and Plowboys: Farm Labor in the Midwest, 1815-60* (Urbana: University of Illinois Press, 1975), p. 100.

73. Lois K. Mathews, *The Expansion of New England: The Spread of New England Settlement and Institutions to the Mississippi River, 1620-1865* (Boston: Houghton Mifflin, 1909), pp. 204, 207-08, 217; Cole, *Era of the Civil War*, pp. 207-10; Francis P. Weisburger, *The Passing of the Frontier, 1825-1850* (Columbus: Ohio State Archeological and Historical Society, 1941), pp. 51, 59-60; Emma Lou Thornborough, *Indiana in the Civil War Era, 1850-1880* (Indianapolis: Indiana Historical Bureau, 1965), p. 540; De Bow, *Statistical View of the United States*, p. 177; Schafer, "Prohibition in Early Wisconsin," p. 281.

10

THE POLITICS OF MAINE LAW PROHIBITION

A new term entered American political debate in the 1850s. When Americans spoke of the Maine Law, they described the stringent, statewide prohibitory law enacted first in Maine and adopted in modified form in twelve other states and territories in the North by 1855. Americans debated the Maine Law with roughly as much emotion as they devoted to the fugitive slave issue. Moreover the hero of prohibition and author of the Maine Law, Neal Dow of Portland, won the fame and notoriety usually accorded to a William Lloyd Garrison.

Dow quickly became the symbolic leader of the prohibition movement, and a more appropriate symbol could not have been found because, like many other temperance reformers, Dow was a successful businessman. He owned a prosperous tannery, promoted railroads, and speculated in real estate in his native Portland. A boundless commercial future awaited the United States, Dow believed, if only the blight of intemperance could be removed from the land. Dow inherited this passion for temperance from Quaker parents, but his prejudices were confirmed by his observations of poverty, crime, and drunkenness in Portland. Frequently he rode about the city in his carriage, pointing out to companions the ravages of intemperance. "Rum did that!" he would exclaim whenever he came across a particularly distressing case of poverty. A prosperous man who had won success through sober conduct, he had little patience with what he called vices of the poor, whose economic condition he automatically ascribed to moral weakness. As befitted such a morally righteous and rigid man, Dow had a stern physical presence. Small in stature and with a grim, determined face, the so-called Napoleon of Temperance was a humorless and unpleasant little man who vigorously pursued his vision of a sober society.[1]

Despite the sudden emergence of Neal Dow and the Maine Law in the 1850s, statewide prohibition was not a dramatic reversal of temperance tactics. Middle-class temperance reformers had endorsed legal action long before 1851, and the no-license campaigns of the 1830s had illustrated the early political appeal of legal action to eradicate the use of liquor. It would be wrong to depict prohibition as a sudden shift in the tactics of temperance agitation, which came in response to the massive immigration which occurred from 1845 to 1855.[2] As a tactic, the Maine Law agitation was a logical development which grew out of the reformers' experience with local prohibition in the northeastern states during the 1830s and 1840s. State prohibition was a pragmatic response to the failures of the no-license and local option campaigns. Each provision of the new prohibitory laws was designed to overcome a specific problem of enforcement which the no-license campaigns had exposed. By 1850, prohibitionists had lost all patience with no-license and local option and were determined to seek new, stricter, and more effective laws against the liquor traffic. To obtain the statewide prohibition they wanted, temperance reformers intensified the political campaigns they had begun in the no-license phase and so ushered in almost a decade of intense political turmoil and cultural conflict over drink.

The Maine Law

The goal of eradicating drink through legal action may seem impractical late in the twentieth century. Yet if the goal of the reformers is accepted, the elaborate and ingenious legal strategies devised in the 1850s were by no means impractical. Charles Jewett, the temperance lecturer and agitator, accurately suggested the character of the

Maine Law and the circumstances surrounding its adoption. The law "did not grow up like a mushroom in a night"; it was "an accretion of provisions suggested by the failures of earlier statutes."[3] Neal Dow carried his prohibitionist sentiments to the point of fanaticism, but he was nonetheless a skilled and practiced organizer. His campaigns for prohibition were, like the man himself, highly methodical. They were based on elaborate organization and careful attention to detail which made all the difference both to the initial success of his campaign and to the character of the Maine Law itself. Dow tirelessly lobbied and petitioned the state legislature; and as president of the Maine Temperance Union, he organized political campaigns to defeat anti-prohibitionists at the polls. He also engineered the support of antislavery Democrats by convincing the legislative representatives of his own party, the Free-Soilers, to vote for the election of the antislavery Democrat, Hannibal Hamlin, to the United States Senate. By exploiting the divisions within the major political parties over the slavery and temperance issues, Dow was able to put together a legislative coalition favorable to the Maine Law. During the summer of 1851, the tough antiliquor law passed the Maine legislature by a vote of eighty-one to forty in the House of Representatives, and by eighteen to nine in the Senate.[4]

The prohibitory laws of the 1850s all adopted certain distinctive provisions which Dow first designed in his Maine Law of 1851. Discussion of these detailed provisions illustrates how the failures of the licensing laws in the 1840s shaped the legal remedies sought by prohibitionists. Prohibitionists proposed to close the many loopholes in the existing laws by sweeping away the old laws and erecting elaborate new institutional restraints on the liquor traffic; thereby they hoped to make enforcement of the law certain and efficient. The major innovations of the Maine Law, derived from experience with the workings of the old laws, concerned perjury and the difficulties of obtaining evidence, inadequate punishments, slow and haphazard prosecution, and the difficulties created by the medical use of liquor.

Evidence was always difficult to come by under the old laws, and therein lay the origins of the first critical, distinguishing mark of the Maine Law: its search and seizure clause. The provision authorized search warrants for the investigation of illegal sales and the seizure and destruction of liquors held contrary to law. By seizing the liquor itself, reformers hoped to escape from two intractable problems of enforcement which had vitiated the no-license campaigns. Under all prior laws, temperance reformers and prosecutors had to establish that a sale had taken place before a conviction could be obtained. The mere possession of liquor in a saloon, with intent to sell, was not sufficient evidence. To obtain conviction, temperance men had to persuade drinkers to testify that a sale took place. But drinkers understandably proved reluctant to do so. In a letter read and endorsed at the Massachusetts State Temperance Convention in 1852, Horace Mann explained the common bond between seller and buyer as yet another degrading and disgusting result of the "diseased" appetite for strong drink. Mann did not recognize the bonds of class and culture which linked seller and common working people together against the moralistic reformers. Instead he raged, like Jesse Goodrich of Worcester, against the "iron grip" of the seller over "the poor infatuated victims of appetite" who perjured themselves daily in the police courts. The incidence of perjury frustrated reformers who longed to convict all illegal sellers. "I have known witnesses," said Mann, "whose faces must have been twenty years in receiving their deep coats of varnish, to swear they did not know how brandy tasted." Under the search and seizure provisions of the Maine Law, Mann expected the problem of perjury to vanish. "A drunken witness is not called into court to equivocate or perjure himself; but the liquid devil is forced to attend bodily, to make confession of all the crimes he was about to commit prefatory to being executed."[5]

The new law dealt with a second serious flaw of the old license laws. Even if the illegal seller of liquor was successfully prosecuted, the fines levied were too small to worry the offender. Since in Maine the fine for first offenders was only one dollar, Neal Dow discovered that many liquor sellers accepted the occasional fine as one of the hazards of the occupation and returned to their illegal selling immediately.[6] Prohibitionists like Dr. Charles Jewett raged against the convicted "rum-seller [who] returns to his place of business, well stocked with maddening poisons," ready for another day's work corrupting the morals of the community.[7] If an offender was unable to pay the fine, he (or she) could sell off his property in liquor in order to avert the house of correction, and, wrote Professor Moses

Stuart of Andover, "some new viceregent of the devil occupies his place."[8] In contrast with the old license laws, the Maine Law drastically increased the cost of being caught: destruction of the stock in hand. Prohibitionists thereby sought to break the cycle of arrest, conviction, light fine, release, and felony.[9]

The search and seizure clauses prompted legal challenges in the courts. The traditional common-law respect for property rights and the American tradition of opposition to unreasonable searches created a spate of legal obstacles to enforcement of the Maine Law. But the Massachusetts State Temperance Convention correctly argued that, under certain circumstances, search and seizure had long been endorsed in state law in the United States.[10] There were several circumstances in which the Revised Statutes of Massachusetts authorized search and seizure. Lotteries, stolen property, and obscene books all provided ample precedent for the search and seizure provisions. The Massachusetts Supreme Court had upheld the search and seizure provision of the lottery law in *Commonwealth* v. *Dana* (1841). Although prohibitionists expected legal challenges to the Maine Law's search and seizure provision, they believed they would win in court.[11]

Similarly the prohibitionists thought they had covered the legal ground in the matter of destruction of property. Again, the destruction of lottery tickets provided the analogy and—they hoped—the precedent. To prohibitionists like Gerrit Smith of Peterboro, New York, liquor selling was as much a public nuisance as the lottery, and the sellers of liquor should thereby forfeit all legitimate property rights in their commodity.[12] The power of a community to destroy a public nuisance had the eminent backing of Supreme Court Justice John McLean in his opinion on the License Cases. Once the legislature defined liquor selling as inimical to the morals of the community, in McLean's legal judgment, the state could destroy the dangerous substance to protect the public health and morals.[13]

Other provisions of the Maine Law were designed to deal realistically with the low conviction rates prevalent under the old license laws. Discretionary trial procedures allowed offenders to escape punishment under the old laws. Liquor cases crowded the dockets of muncipal and county courts in the late 1840s.[14] District attorneys who did not favor prohibition, or who balked at the litigation, often resorted to continuations or entered nolle prosequis. Under the old license laws, offenders in Portland, Maine, were released by sympathetic prosecutors without conviction or punishment. The defendant had only to pledge that he would not again violate the law and that he had already ceased selling liquor. In one such case, which Neal Dow personally observed, the repentent seller went straight from the courtroom back to plying his wares. [15] Such "miscarriages" of justice by district attorneys frustrated reformers throughout New England. In Massachusetts, one of the principal virtues which Jesse Goodrich of the *Massachusetts Cataract* found in the Maine Law was its provision for outflanking the "compromising clemency" of the district attorneys who discontinued cases. [16] Equally galling to Goodrich was the practice of continuing liquor cases indefinitely. The *Cataract* complained that "justice, when applied to rumselling criminals, seems to be both more *tardy*, and more tempered with *mercy* and *forbearance*, than when applied to many and in fact to all other classes of criminals." It pointed out that four hundred liquor cases had accumulated on the Worcester court dockets during 1849, but other cases were "generally pushed through, . . . at the first term of the court in which they are entered." [17]

One of the virtues of Dow's law, from the point of view of prohibitionists, was its procedures for preventing the obstruction of liquor prosecutions. The Massachusetts version of the law stated that "the Court and the prosecuting officer shall not have authority to enter a *nolle prosequi*, or to grant a continuance in any case arising under this Act, either before or after the verdict, except with the concurrence of the Court." [18] To expedite liquor prosecutions, the law provided that liquor cases should take precedence over other litigation before the superior courts, "except in criminal cases in which the parties are actually under arrest awaiting a trial." [19] Prohibitionists hoped thereby to prevent prosecuting officers from pleading crowded dockets as the reason for continuance or nolle prosequi.

Prohibitionists were concerned that punishment for illegal selling be certain and severe. In part, the destruction of liquor constituted a punishment, and prohibitionists designed it as such. [20] Nevertheless the prohibitory laws of the 1850s also stiffened other legal sanctions against the traffic. Small fines, not imprisonment, had faced violators of the old license laws. In Massachusetts, for example, offenders

[257]

could be imprisoned upon the third conviction, but the courts almost never administered such penalties. Incarceration was restricted almost exclusively to small retailers who were too poor to pay the fines levied against them. In contrast, the prohibitory laws of the 1850s sought to make punishment equitable and certain, so that the law would fall equally on small retailers and on the proprietors of what Jesse Goodrich of Worcester called the "fashionable wine saloons, and brandy hotel palaces," which preyed "upon the morals of the community."[21] The Maine Law introduced throughout New England included heavy fines for common sellers and mandatory imprisonment for three to six months upon a third conviction.

Yet another source of dissatisfaction with the working of local prohibition in the 1840s, which shaped the prohibitory laws of the 1850s, was the provision in no-license decisions for the "chemical and medicinal use" of liquor.[22] Temperance men fully conceded the industrial uses of alcohol, but they discounted its medical benefits. Yet the testimony of temperance societies was futile while individual doctors refused to proscribe the medical use of liquor. One tactic used by temperance societies was employment of temperance doctors like Reuben Mussey, Charles Jewett, and Daniel Drake to dispel the persistent belief in the medical uses of liquor. At the same time, prohibitionists insisted that as long as the sale of liquor as a medicine did continue, it must do so only under effective controls.[23] Neither the Maine nor the Massachusetts liquor laws in the 1840s contained any safeguards to ensure that liquor in no-license towns would be bought only for "medicinal or mechanical purposes."[24] Where special licenses were granted for these purposes, licensees often sold liquor as a beverage. Since no legal provision regulated the special licenses, county commissioners and local law enforcement authorities had no means of ascertaining whether sellers had violated the conditions of their liquor permits. The policy of county commissioners, the *Worcester Palladium* correctly predicted, would not stop the sale of liquor as a beverage but merely "cause a portion of the people to make more frequent application for *medical aid*."[25] The inherent difficulties of isolating the medical use were compounded by common licensing practices. In Worcester County, the commissioners normally licensed one physician in each town to dispense liquor, but if the town selectmen refused to recommend a doctor, the commissioners would license an innholder or trader to sell for medicinal purposes. In practice, this provision made the policing of the no-license policy very difficult.[26]

It was vital to the plans of the prohibitionists that these loopholes in the licensing laws be removed.[27] The Maine Law of 1851 (and the Massachusetts law of 1852 copied from it) authorized the appointment by selectmen of "some suitable person or persons" to sell intoxicating liquor for medicinal purposes. Designated agents were to receive a "fixed and definite salary," to remove the temptation to raise earnings by selling more.[28] Yet despite these innovations, the first prohibitory laws did not completely satisfy prohibitionists. The Massachusetts state temperance convention of 1852 urged selectmen to require agents "to keep open books" so that zealous reformers could scrutinize the sales.[29] Within three years, prohibitionists achieved such controls and much more. The prohibitory law introduced in Massachusetts in 1855 forced agents to keep detailed accounts of all purchases, and these records were to be open to the public, as well as to municipal officials. Agents were required to post bonds of six hundred dollars to ensure compliance with the purposes of the act, and penalties of five to twenty dollars were set for false statements of purpose by purchasers of liquor.[30] In Maine, the controls went further, banning innholders from receiving an agent's permit.

On a superficial level, the elaborate arrangements for the sale of liquor by licensed agents resembled the compléx eighteenth-century restraints on the drink trade. Both types of regulation envisaged restricted sale, supervised by local authorities who would license only men of good moral character. The Maine Law differed markedly, however, in its total proscription of liquor as a beverage and in its refusal to rely mainly on the character of the agents appointed. The Maine Law's stiff penalties for abuse of the liquor licenses demonstrated the unwillingness of prohibitionists to trust the agents appointed. Prohibitionists did not eschew institutional restraints on the sale of liquor. Faced with the undeniable fact that many people still believed in the medicinal qualities of liquor, the prohibitionists responded by devising elaborate legal and institutional safeguards to regulate the medicinal use. The licensing of liquor agents for special purposes was, like every other aspect of the Maine Law, a pragmatic response to the many flaws in the old licensing system. [31]

It was not utopianism, then, that brought reformers to accept and launch campaigns for statewide prohibition in the 1850s. The common experience in the northeastern states impressed upon prohibitionists that only new and more effective laws would circumvent the obstacles to enforcement of prohibition. The temperance movement must obtain laws which would end perjury, eliminate the loopholes in the existing laws, and make justice prompt, certain, and severe. To effect such drastic changes, prohibitionists concluded that they must sweep away the existing system of local regulation and introduce statewide prohibition. Only statewide laws would ensure uniformity of enforcement and eliminate the legal loopholes which undermined the effectiveness of local prohibition in New England in the 1840s. Prohibitionists had come fully to accept the need for state power to enforce sobriety on American society.

The Politics of the Maine Law

The prohibitionist victory in Maine in 1851 spurred a new wave of political activity by prohibitionists in every northern and western state. Massachusetts, Minnesota, Rhode Island, and Vermont all adopted Maine Laws during 1852. Michigan followed in 1853 and Connecticut in 1854. Then in 1855 New York, Indiana, Delaware, Iowa, Nebraska, and New Hampshire joined the prohibitionist column. The political appeal of prohibition in the early 1850s was even more extensive than the passage of Maine Laws suggested. Several other states almost went dry during the upsurge of political pressure from temperance groups. A Wisconsin referendum favored prohibition in 1854, but the state legislature could not agree on the details of the measure. The following year, the legislature did pass a Maine Law, but the Democratic governor vetoed it. In the same year, New Jersey's lower house endorsed prohibition but the bill was rejected in the Senate. Ohio and Pennsylvania both narrowly rejected the Maine Law but adopted stringent anti-saloon laws which prevented the sale of liquor in small quantities for consumption in liquor shops. Not a state or territory throughout the North escaped the impact of dry sentiment. The prohibitionists appeared politically triumphant. [32]

Since prohibition necessarily involved the temperance crusade in political action, it is especially important to clarify the relationship between prohibition and the politics of the party system. It is possible that the Maine Law conflict might be explained in terms of partisan rivalries between Whigs and Democrats, since prohibition was clearly more popular among Whigs than among Democrats. [33] Yet even though the prohibitionist drive does seem at times to be nothing more than an agitation within the Whig party, the relationship between party and prohibition was more complex than such a view would allow. Prohibition had significant cross-party support in the early 1850s, and it was precisely this characteristic that made prohibition agitation so disruptive of existing party loyalties.

Contemporary observers often depicted the Democrats as the "whiskey and lager beer" party, as Horace Greeley did in 1854, yet there were significant areas of support for the Maine Law within the party. [34] In Maine, the house vote on the prohibitory liquor bill in 1851 saw forty-two Democrats (63 percent of the total number of Democrats), together with thirty-one Whigs (67 percent of Whigs) and all eight Free-Soilers vote for the bill; moreover, a Democratic governor, John Hubbard, signed the bill into law. Support for the Maine Law cut, as Neal Dow emphasized, directly across existing party lines. The consequences for the Democratic party were severe, for within a year of passage of the Maine Law, the party had split down the middle with pro-liquor Democrats bolting to run a liberal ticket in the 1852 state elections. When the pro-liquor forces gained control of the party the following year, the Maine Law faction then bolted and joined with Free-Soilers, disaffected Whigs, and anti-Nebraska men to form a political coalition that eventually became the Republican party. [35]

That the Maine Law cut across party loyalties to include a sizable number of Democrats is further demonstrated in the Massachusetts case. In 1852 "a coalition of Free-Soilers, Whigs, and a bare majority of Democrats" in the state legislature passed a prohibitory law. Though there were many Democrats disturbed by this dry stand, the wettest gubernatorial candidate in the succeeding state election was the Whig, John H. Clifford, who tried to exploit Irish and Hunker

Democrat opposition to the Maine Law by steadfastly opposing it. 36
Democratic prohibitionist support was not confined to New England. In all the northern and some border states, minorities of Democrats supported the Maine Law. In Maryland, for example, a race for sheriff of Baltimore county in 1855—an election which revolved around enforcement of the liquor laws—saw a drift of at least 10 percent of Democratic votes cast in the gubernatorial contest away from the Democratic nominee for sheriff to the Maine Law candidate. 37 There was a similar drift in the Wisconsin general election of 1853, where at least 10 percent of the Democratic gubernatorial votes went to the Maine Law in a prohibition referendum held simultaneously. 38

These losses or potential losses were, of course, small in comparison with the wet votes which the Democrats could pick up by courting the pro-liquor sentiments of urban immigrants, particularly in such western towns as Milwaukee and Cincinnati and such eastern cities as New York and Philadelphia. 39 Here the Democratic party stood strongly against the Maine Law. Yet elsewhere, in Pennsylvania, for example, the prohibitionists had substantial support among Democrats. When the state temperance convention endorsed during the 1854 state election a slate of candidates favorable to prohibition, eight of the twenty-eight endorsements went to Democratic candidates, while the rest were shared by Whigs and Free-Soilers. 40

Though in many of these cases only a minority of Democrats favored prohibition the numbers were often large enough to cause trouble for the party. The displeasure of temperance Democrats with the anti-Maine Law stand of the Democratic party in both Illinois and Indiana fed the successful fusionist or anti-Nebraska revolts in the state elections of 1854, and the legislators so elected quickly passed Maine Laws in each state in 1855. (In Illinois the law was subject to a referendum, where the prohibitionists went down to a narrow defeat.) Similarly in Iowa, the Whigs had profited in a situation where the two major parties were evenly balanced. The Iowa Whigs challenged the previously ascendant Democracy by running on a Maine Law platform which drew away sufficient Democratic votes to give the Whigs the victory in the gubernatorial race and a majority in the legislature. 41

Despite the opportunistic action of the Iowa Whigs, the most striking aspect of the relationship between prohibition and partisan involvement was the widespread unwillingness of major party leaders—both Whig and Democrat—to introduce into party politics an issue which would be so disruptive of party loyalties. This was why so many legislatures—Illinois, Iowa, Wisconsin, Michigan, and Pennsylvania—either relegated the prohibition issue to a special referendum or made passage of a prohibitory law subject to approval by the people at a referendum divorced from the election of state and local officials. In Ohio, the two major parties denied even the referendum approach, and both refused to endorse the Maine Law at all for fear of losing votes. Yet neither wished to be branded as the pro-liquor party. Thus the Democratic-dominated legislature, with Whig support, balanced rejection of the Maine Law with passage of the Adair Law of 1854, which promoted tighter regulation of the liquor traffic and enforced tougher laws against public intoxication.[42] Even in Maine, the premier prohibition state, Neal Dow reported the reluctance of party newspapers and many party leaders, both Whig and Democratic, to make the Maine Law "a political question."[43] In Ohio and in Maine, the attitudes of the major parties to the prohibition question reflected the values and practices of the "second party system." Politicians sought either to keep distracting and divisive moral issues out of politics altogether or, if they failed, they tried to placate insistent pressure groups by offering them a compromise measure.[44]

The compromising stance of many regular party leaders earned stern condemnation from evangelical and moral reformers. Leading prohibitionists of the Maine Law period often complained, as Horace Mann did, about "the roar and stench of that black and sulphurous lake" of partisan politics.[45] This was also the view of Gerrit Smith, who showed contempt for those who "had become so partyized, as to be far more concerned for their party than for Temperance or Freedom."[46] The same distrust of party entanglements and contempt for the corrupt electoral bargains of Whigs and Democrats can be found among more obscure reformers, such as those who attended the Worcester County Temperance Convention in September 1849 and declared that "as the experience of the past has shown, . . . men elected to the legislature on political grounds, without reference to their temperance character or principles, cannot be relied upon." It was this sentiment, echoed in county conventions across the North, which fueled the revolt against the major parties and underlay the most widely adopted prohibitionist tactic of the 1850s: the allocation of prohibitionist votes to Maine Law candidates irrespective of party. [47]

This rhetorical revulsion against party politics did not however, stop prohibitionists from dabbling in party intrigue to further their own fortunes and those of the Maine Law; and equally important, the distaste for the major political parties and their compromises, which Maine Law men sometimes espoused, did not extend to the Free-Soilers, whose candidates were much more willing than those of the other two parties of the early 1850s to take a strong stand for prohibition. Free-Soilers from Massachusetts, to Ohio, to Wisconsin seem to have been almost uniformly for the Maine Law, and they frequently got the votes of militant prohibitionists, as in Massachusetts in 1852, and in Ohio in 1853 where the Maine Law vote swelled the Free-Soil party to a record total. [48]

Ultimately most prohibitionists would enter the Republican party and thus ironically would learn to make the political compromises they thundered against in the early 1850s. Yet the immediate impact of their growing enthusiasm for the Maine Law was not to consolidate a new party but to disrupt the old ones. A survey of the tangled relations between prohibition and political parties in the early 1850s prompts one obvious conclusion. We cannot find the sources of conflict over prohibition in party rivalry. The impulse lay outside partisan prejudice and disrupted established party structures and relationships.

Nativism and the Maine Law

Party cannot alone explain the Maine Law upsurge of the 1850s, yet it may nevertheless be that temperance served as a vehicle for the expression of nativist tensions. Joseph Gusfield tended to depict the prohibitionist phase of the temperance movement as a response to and a means of controlling and Americanizing German and Irish immigrants. [49] That Know Nothingism did become closely allied with temperance for a time in the mid-1850s is strongly suggested by the rhetoric of temperance reformers. The testimonies in *The Maine Law Illustrated*, a survey of the impact of prohibition by two Canadian reformers, frequently referred to whiskey-drinking Irish as the chief opponents of the Maine Law and obstacles to the triumph of the prohibitionist crusade. [50]

Yet a good deal of evidence suggests that, far from being uniformly in favor of either temperance or prohibition, the nativist secret orders and parties harbored groups which were either indifferent or hostile to temperance. In New York City, membership lists of the Alpha chapter of the Order of United Americans, the antiforeign, anti-Catholic order founded there in 1844, included liquor sellers, grocers, hotel keepers, oyster house proprietors, and restauranteurs, all men with obvious anti-temperance credentials. [51] Nor was the nativist impulse limited to sellers of liquor, for there is evidence that antiforeign prejudices flourished among hard-drinking, native-born workers in the northeastern cities. During the 1840s and 1850s, the Bowery district of New York City harbored several saloon-based, antiforeign gangs such as the Bowery Boys. Moreover the Bowery district, with its liquor shops and gambling and prostitution houses, was also the home of several chapters of the Order of United Americans. Indeed one Bowery chapter, Liberty 5, had as its chief scribe the young William M. Tweed. [52] Though this event occurred long before Tweed's Tammany days, it is suggestive of the links between nativism and lower-class subcultures.

Evidence from Pittsburgh reinforces doubts about the respectability of some nativists. There Joe Barker, a ranting anti-Catholic and anti-temperance agitator, won the mayoral election in 1850 and ran for sheriff in 1852 with the support of propertyless Protestant workingmen. [53] In addition, there are some further indications of hostility toward prohibition among lower-class nativist groups in both Boston and Worcester. In Boston, the Know Nothings of the 1850s won support from artisans who constituted a pro-liquor faction within the party; in Worcester, the social support for the Know Nothings contrasted quite sharply with that for prohibition. [54] A one in ten sample of the members of Council 49 of the American party in Worcester revealed only two prohibitionists out of a total of forty-three names examined, and both of these joined toward the end of the party's short but spectacular career. Whereas the prohibitionists in Worcester appealed most strongly to the wealthy and respectable classes, the American party support was strongest among artisans and young men, often boarders who had come to the city seeking employment. They were either propertyless or very small property holders who had not put down strong roots in the community.[55] These were the same groups which the *Worcester Spy* proclaimed a major source of intemperance in the town; they were the footloose youths and rough workingmen whom the *Spy* identified as patrons of the city's illegal liquor shops and taverns. These groups, although antagonistic toward the city's growing Irish population, apparently did not find prohibition attractive. According to George W. Richardson, the Know Nothing mayor of Worcester in 1854—and a prominent anti-prohibitionist in the 1830s—the voters who had elected him were "tired of talk about rum and talk about niggers."[56]

If nativism included lower-class groups either hostile or indifferent to prohibition, there were also more respectable nativists who fell into the same categories. The American Protestant Association, an anti-Catholic organization founded in Philadelphia in 1842 and committed to the preservation of the "public and domestic institutions" of the United States "from the assaults of Romanism," included only three well-known prohibitionists among its ninety-four founding members: the Reverend John Chambers, a Philadelphia independent Presbyterian, the Reverend Pennell Coombe of Lancaster, Pennsylvania, a Methodist, and Stephen Tyng, at that time a Philadelphia Episcopalian minister.[57] The absence of significant numbers of temperance and prohibitionist leaders from the APA list contrasts sharply with the overlap between temperance organizations and those of interdenominational benevolent institutions and organizations noted elsewhere in this study. The result is to suggest that the anti-Catholic, nativist bodies represented somewhat different constituencies from the temperance societies. We know this to be true, at least in part, for Episcopalians, German Reformed, Old School Presbyterians, and Lutherans were found in the association's ranks. Temperance sentiment within all of these churches was only modest at most, and the Episcopalians and Lutherans gave little or no support to the prohibitionist cause.[58]

The patterns of nativist support suggest that prohibition had a more uniformly middle-class, more respectable following than did nativism. The antiforeign and anti-Catholic impulse drew in lower-class groups hostile to both prohibition and the competition of immigrants for jobs. On the other hand, the American Protestant Association was able to win the support of wealthy Episcopalians who largely ignored the temperance crusade. Despite a few prominent prohibitionists such as the Reverend Stephen Tyng, Episcopalians generally saw both prohibition and teetotalism as unscriptural, as an abrogation of clerical authority, as a denial of individual freedom, and as incompatible with the social custom among the upper classes of drinking wine with dinner. [59]

If nativism won support from many who were either indifferent or downright hostile toward the temperance crusade, many temperance reformers were lukewarm toward nativism, at least before 1850. Temperance literature before the 1850s gave surprisingly little attention to the problem of intemperance among immigrants. When temperance reformers did discuss immigration before 1850, they stressed the same measures advocated for native Americans. In the 1830s, John Marsh had speculated that immigrants would reject prohibitory laws as the work of bigots, and he argued that immigrants had to be "persuaded in kindness" to be temperate. [60] Until 1850, the only distinctive response of the American Temperance Union to the problem of immigrant drinking was to distribute foreign language pamphlets emphasizing the dangers of intemperance facing immigrants. Temperance reformers did not at this time distinguish clearly between solution of the native American and solution of the immigrant drinking problem. The American Temperance Union blamed the "rum dealer who . . . poisoned the immigrant" and deprived him of the opportunity for material advancement which American society presented. [61] The mild attitudes of reformers toward the problem of immigrant drinking reflected both the minor dimensions of the problem before the late 1840s and the reformers' perfectionist belief that American society could assimilate divergent cultures.

By 1850, however, temperance propaganda evidenced a heightened awareness of immigrant drinking and its consequences for the prohibitionist crusade. With the influx of immigrants who pushed up the consumption of liquor, temperance men began to despair of eliminating intemperance from American society. The intemperance of the immigrants could be controlled by stiffer laws and harsher punishments, prohibitionists believed, but it could not be effectively eliminated. Zimri Howe, a prohibitionist from Castleton, Vermont, dismissed the Irish as "a class of people that you can make nothing of." Along with the mounting despair went a deepening contempt for the Irish. They "come here, with all their vicious habits and grovelling tastes uncontrolled," commented the editor of the *Maine Temperance Watchman*, D. B. Beck of Portland, "and they think they can make money at this thing, and they set to work. They have had no previous training in habits of temperance, and they die out before they are reclaimed."[62] John Tappan admitted that the temperance offensive had stalled in the cities because of "the trebling and quadrupling of the foreign populations of the lower classes." Even the ever optimistic John Marsh began to describe states like Pennsylvania and Wisconsin, which had large German populations, as "drenched with Lager Bier" and "ever slow" to adopt habits of temperance.[63]

The heightened hostility toward immigrant drinking drove the Maine Law men into an alliance with the nativist political organizations in the northeastern states, an alliance which proved politically profitable for the prohibitionists, but only in the short term. Before 1854, the Maine Law had been adopted in five states—Maine, Massachusetts, Vermont, Michigan, and Rhode Island—and in the territory of Minnesota.[64] Then during 1854 and 1855, prohibitionists won new victories in eight states and territories. In addition, Maine Law men won new and more stringent prohibitory laws in Maine, Massachusetts, and Michigan. The surge of prohibitory activity, its extension to many new states, and the intensified Maine Laws passed in Maine and Massachusetts were won with nativist appeals and with the help of nativist political support.[65]

Yet though, for example, the American party won the votes of many Massachusetts temperance men in 1854 and 1855, it did so largely because no alternative to the nativists existed. The Whig party was in the process of disintegration; the Free-Soilers were a small minority. For many who voted the nativist ticket, temperance and antislavery were higher priorities; in 1856, many of these antislavery and temperance Whigs and Democrats switched to the newly formed Republican party. The nativist cause in Massachusetts proved to be a highly unstable coalition of disparate groups which had used the American party to assert their own political programs.[66] In Michigan, a similar process occurred, with the American party serving as a way station for certain antislavery and temperance Whigs to enter the Republican ranks. Ronald Formisano notes that some temperance and antislavery men within the American party broke from it in 1855 and formed a Know-Something party. This short-lived organization deprecated the rabid antiforeign and anti-Catholic feelings of the nativists and promised support for prohibitory legislation and a strong stance against slavery. From such groups came an important part of the Republican coalition in Michigan.[67]

In summary, the alliance between nativism and prohibition was essentially a short-term tactical one growing out of the experience of temperance agitation. Though prohibitionists were always potential recruits for the virulent nativism which flourished in the mid-1850s, nativism did not become a central and critical part of the prohibitionist program until immigration emerged as a dangerous obstacle in the way of the triumph of prohibition. The attraction of the American party for prohibitionists in the mid-1850s was its claim to control and virtually to eliminate the menace of the foreign vote, which threatened to deny political victory at the polls to prohibitionists. When the party proved unable to deliver its promise and when the larger issue of slavery threatened the unity of the nativists, many temperance and antislavery men deserted the party for the Republicans. Nativism was thus tied up with the surge in prohibitionist support in the 1850s, but it was not the critical element.[68]

The Social Support for the Maine Law

A unique document on the Maine Law states prepared by two Canadian prohibitionists gives some important insights into the social roots of the prohibition movement. A. Farewell and G. P. Ure toured New England in 1855 on behalf of the Canadian Prohibitory Liquor Law League. Befitting outsiders, their report was somewhat more detailed and detached than those of American prohibitionists writing on the Maine Law. The conclusions of the report were strongly biased in favor of prohibition, but Farewell and Ure did listen to and report contrary testimony. Although the report does not provide much reliable evidence on the success of the Maine Law (many witnesses were constrained to show that the law was especially effective), the witnesses were quite candid about both the opposition to and the support for the Maine Law.

Both the witnesses chosen and the arguments used in favor of the Maine Law suggest that by the 1850s prohibition had become a respectable solution to disruptive social conflicts which were class based in character. Most of the men interviewed were influential opinion leaders in their communities: newspaper publishers, manufacturers, merchants, bankers, churchmen, and politicians. Most spoke strongly in favor of the Maine Law and, more important, did not hide their reasons for supporting prohibition. They cited their fears of high pauper taxes, crime, and the drinking of immigrants and native-born workers. David Hawley, the Hartford, Connecticut, city missionary, cited "distress among the laboring classes" who were "constantly under the influence of liquor." John Wait, a lawyer and banker of Norwich, Connecticut, commented that "many of our working people of Norwich were against it [the Maine Law]." Joseph Low, the mayor of Concord, New Hampshire, found that "our professional men, our men of influence and our wealthy men; our clergy and our judges, are all on the side of temperance." Since the introduction of prohibition in the city, he said, "our pauper accounts have been reduced more than one half within the last two years, and there are no nightly brawls in the city." In Springfield, Massachusetts, Farewell and Ure found manufacturers strongly in favor of the law. Already they practiced prohibition within their factories; now they wanted to extend their power over the working classes beyond the factory yard. Eliphalet Trask, the proprietor of a local foundry and the city mayor, did not expect the Maine Law to have much effect on his own business because "for the last twenty years I have adhered to the principle of keeping no man about me addicted to drink." Yet prohibition's effects upon the city would be, he observed, "very beneficial."[69]

That the split over prohibition was not rural-urban but socioeconomic is shown by detailed evidence for the state of Maine, the original home of the Maine Law. The towns of Portland, Bangor, Bath, and Biddeford, among others, sustained the law both electorally and legally through the actions of their municipal authorities. A petition circulated in Portland in 1853 and favorable to enforcement of the Maine Law was signed by "433 of the most respectable of the citizens, clergymen, merchants, and businessmen generally."[70] While there were significant areas of urban support for the Maine Law among the middle classes, Farewell and Ure also reported that in rural areas the law provoked some equally significant opposition. The rural county of Oxford split evenly over the Maine Law, and the center of anti-prohibitionist activity was the far northern county of Aroostook. This was lumberjack country, and Senator Shepard Cary, himself a former lumberman, took the lead in opposing the prohibitory legislation both in the state legislature and on the electoral stumpings. Yet in Aroostook, as elsewhere, the split over prohibition seemed to be a social one; the lumber merchants generally praised the Maine Law for the order and efficiency it seemed to have enhanced among the hard-drinking lumberjacks.[71]

More precise information on prohibitionist support in Worcester both clarifies and in some ways extends the argument that the Maine Law conflict revealed social cleavages between the middle and lower classes. In 1848, the temperance forces entered city politics in the form of a "temperance party"; they demanded stricter enforcement of the license laws than had been practiced by earlier town administrations or would be forthcoming from their so-called nonpartisan opponents in the municipal elections. The conflict was not over the principle of prohibition, for Worcester had had no-license since 1841, but over the degree of enforcement of the law. In one sense, that the conflict took this form showed how a consensus had begun to replace the conflict within respectable society which had figured so largely in the early days of the Worcester no-license dispute. Now there were virtually no spokesmen for restoration of licensing in Worcester, and merchants, who had at first feared the effects of prohibition on commerce, were now commonly associated with the prohibition cause.

Apart from that change, the profile of Worcester prohibitionists in the temperance party bore strong similarities to the list of 1835. Seventy-four percent of the 39 names published in support of prohibition were associated with the manufacturing sector—including artisans (18 percent of the total list), factory employees (5 percent), and businessmen employing between 5 and 150 employees (49 percent); among these businessmen were some of the most successful and upwardly mobile manufacturers in Worcester. No comparable list of opponents of prohibition is available, though the aldermanic candidates of the nonpartisan ticket included Stephen Salisbury and John W. Lincoln, both members of long-established and wealthy mercantile, professional, and political families in Worcester. It must be emphasized, however, that the division between the two groups on prohibition was not clear-cut, since the prohibitionist *Massachusetts Spy* supported the nonpartisan ticket and refused to concede any "temperance zeal" to its opponents in the municipal elections. [72]

The evidence does not prove that only manufacturers supported prohibition, but it does indicate that the impetus toward a tougher stand on prohibition came from the same groups which had championed the no-license cause in 1835. At the same time there was mounting evidence of the broadening appeal of prohibition among not only manufacturers and their allies, but also all respectable and propertied elements in the community. For a time in the mid-1850s, when the campaign to enforce the Maine Law was at its height, there was virtually no opposition to prohibition from the articulate and respectable elements in Worcester society. Some propertied people may have had their reservations about the Maine Law, but they remained silent. The campaign in Worcester during this period was dominated by the fears of middle-class people that the "dangerous classes"—itinerants and the urban poor—were about to engulf them. Maine Law meetings in 1854 elicited the support of respectable and well-to-do Worcester society, including evangelical clergy, professional men, merchants, lawyers, and the city's manufacturers, as well as some clerks and tradesmen on the margins of the propertied classes. [73] In contrast, opposition to prohibition, much more than in the no-license years, was of a violent and inarticulate kind, and it centered largely among the growing Irish population of the town. Irish liquor sellers resisted arrest under the Maine Law and provoked several incidents bordering on riot, while the Irish made up the bulk of the arrests for drunkenness in the town. [74]

The Maine Law in New England, at least, seems to have been sustained by the more prosperous and respectable classes. The conflict in the community over the liquor laws was not geographic in character, pitting city against country, but rather was social: employers, people in the professions and in commerce, and the evangelical churches (and middle-class women) versus transients, itinerant workers, factory operatives, Irish immigrants, liquor sellers, and their political allies.

If the Maine Law represented the revulsion of the respectable and propertied against immigrant and working-class drinking, we must still inquire why the Maine Law impulse arose at the particular time that it did. From the point of view of committed reformers, the Maine Law was the logical culmination of years of agitation. Yet the peaks of the Maine Law enthusiasm of the mid-1850s came suddenly. It is clear that the upsurge of prohibitionist support was connected with the influx of foreigners in the decade after 1845. The reports of Farewell and Ure documented a good deal of hostile commentary on the subject of Irish immigrants. Yet the witnesses did not attack immigration as such but rather deplored some of the economic and social consequences of the rapid growth, of which Irish and German immigration was an integral part. They stressed crime and especially pauperism, which seemed to accompany economic change. Rather than rest the case for the Maine Law on moral, religious, or ethnic grounds, supporters seemed obsessed with the costs which poverty threatened to impose on their communities. The "political economy of the Maine Law," to quote the title of a popular American Temperance Union tract, was uppermost in the minds of prohibitionists. [75] Intemperance raised poor rates and taxes; prohibition reduced these burdens on the respectable and industrious portions of the community. As Moses L. Church of Burlington, Vermont, pointed out, "When this law is thoroughly carried out our poor taxes will be reduced about a $1000 a year." [76] The Massachusetts State Temperance Convention of 1852 advanced the same claim, stressing that "taxes will be reduced," and "pauperism, crime, and the various forms of misery" would be "greatly lessened." Convention members further emphasized the class character of their appeals when they forecast that the "salutary effects" of prohibitory legislation would be felt most strongly "among the poor and laboring classes." [77]

Neal Dow reemphasized the social and economic fears of prohibitionists when he wrote just after the Maine Law went into effect:

The majority of these drinks were consumed by the working people, and in order to obtain them they were compelled to forego many articles of comfort and necessity to their families. When the temptation to indulge is removed out of their way, they will not take much trouble to obtain strong drink, their habits will be changed, their appetites will no longer torment them, their money will be spent for articles useful to their families, their health and character will be restored, and they will earn more, enjoy more, and save more than they ever did before.

Dow especially emphasized that the city's almshouse had become inadequate to deal with rising poverty. For ten years the citizens had discussed its replacement at a possible cost of $50,000. Now, he claimed, the Maine Law had taken pressure off the institution by reducing pauperism.[78] By compelling sobriety among the poor, Dow believed the Maine Law would alleviate misery at the same time that it relieved the burdens of caring for the poor.

There is no doubt that the problems of poverty and crime were especially severe during the period of intense prohibitionist agitation. While the years from 1845 to 1855 saw generally vigorous economic expansion, growth was frequently interrupted by sharp recessions and seasonal fluctuations in economic activity. The economic downturn of 1854, which occurred at the height of the Maine Law agitation in the North, was the most severe of these periodic fluctuations. Economic growth, which the Maine Law men both praised and promoted, brought to New England and to the North generally factory operatives and itinerant laborers—often Irish immigrants—who worked on the building construction sites, the railroads, the canals, and the other manifestations of what temperance men sincerely believed to constitute economic progress. Farewell and Ure gave an excellent example of the problems which these unskilled and semiskilled workers presented for the respectable, stable populations of American communities undergoing the early stages of industrial change. Samuel Colt, of Colt revolver fame, was erecting an armory in the vicinity of Hartford, Connecticut, during 1854. Since the spring, he "had more than a thousand laborers, Irish and German, constantly employed, . . . but since the 1st December, when the frost became severe, this outside work has stopped, and hundreds of these poor creatures had nothing else to depend on." So testified

David Hawley, the Hartford city missionary. For Hawley, the great virtue of the Maine Law, which was operating in Connecticut, was the assistance it gave to these workers to preserve more of their earnings during their months of employment rather than spend money on liquor. Thus they would not be so dependent on relief in the months when work was hard to get.[79]

This problem of itinerant and irregular work lay at the heart of the prohibition agitation and constituted a critical concern of social workers. Robert Hartley, the agent for the New-York Association for Improving the Condition of the Poor (NYAICP), faced similar problems to those experienced by Hawley but in larger dimensions and with bewildering variety. Three-quarters of the people relieved by the society were foreigners, and three-quarters of these were "common laborers among the men; and washers, house-cleaners, sewers, etc., among the women." Since these people had few skills, they were forced to accept "irregular and precarious" employment and were often in need of public relief. Hartley, who had come to the NYAICP from a similar position as agent of the New-York City Temperance Society, quite understandably found the problem of irregular labor vastly complicated by the "vice" of "intemperance."[80] Though the NYAICP as an organization did not endorse the Maine Law, Hartley was one of its most insistent advocates in New York City.

These temperance reformers were correct in linking the problem of casual labor to the incidence of intemperance. The irregularity of such labor, its heavy physical demands, and often its loneliness encouraged the use of liquor in excessive quantities. This pattern held true in the mining camps of the West, among lumbermen and rural laborers in eighteenth- and early nineteenth-century New England, as well as for the itinerant Irish and German laborers who came to New England in the 1840s and 1850s. Binge drinking and the heavy consumption of alcohol thrived under such conditions regardless of ethnocultural backgrounds, and it is not surprising that men who drank in this way proved troublesome to the police and, in turn, found themselves inmates of the almshouses, asylums, and houses of correction.

Economic progress had greatly increased the complexity and scope of the problems which charity workers faced in the early

1850s. In response, prohibitionists like Hartley and Hawley sought to encourage thrift, industry, and sobriety among the floating populations of the northeastern cities; but unfortunately itinerant laborers were difficult to reach through moral suasion. Samuel Chipman, a temperance editor from Rochester, New York (who earned his reformer's reputation by demonstrating in a celebrated pamphlet what he believed was the connection between intemperance and the cost of poor relief) noted the ineffectiveness of moral suasion among the transient poor. Chipman studied the relationship of intemperance, crime, and correction in fourteen counties in New York State between 1844 and 1847 and concluded that it was "principally from the floating population that recruits are gathered for our jails, and they comprise a class who cannot be reached by local efforts at moral reform." Because these itinerants were not integrated into the local communities, Chipman believed that legal coercion was essential to the success of the temperance crusade.[81] From such logic came the Maine Law.

Evidence from Salisbury, North Carolina, and Cincinnati suggests that this pattern was a national, not merely a northeastern, one. The southern case is particularly important because it involves a region with considerable differences in social structure and in cultural values and because temperance sentiment was especially weak there. A brief consideration of a southern case provides a useful counterpoint to the study of prohibition's antebellum stronghold, the Northeast.[82]

The origins of the no-license agitation in Salisbury, Rowan County, in the heart of North Carolina's Piedmont, bear some striking resemblances to the sequence of events in Worcester, Massachusetts, though on a smaller scale. In April 1855, twenty years after the Worcester, Massachusetts, agitation began, the town of Salisbury voted against liquor licenses. No-license lasted only briefly in Salisbury because, at the instigation of the town's tavern keepers, the legislature repealed in February 1856 the special law allowing the town to refuse licenses. Yet that brief no-license episode illustrates the social forces producing prohibitionist sentiment in the town. According to the pro-temperance newspaper, the *Carolina Watchman*, the supporters of no-license "comprise the large body of respectable members of the community—merchants, mechanics, and professional men. Most of them are old citizens, owning property in the town and raising families here."[83] While this may seem self-serving propaganda, the circumstances in which no-license was adopted suggest the candor of the statement. Between 1852 and 1855, the building of the North Carolina railroad across the Piedmont proceeded apace. It was the "first railroad to traverse the poor, backward Piedmont" and to open western North Carolina "to the markets of the world."[84] Though the respectable citizens of Salisbury welcomed the railroad for the prosperity they expected it to bring, the short-term result was to create new and undesired social conflict. On February 12, 1852, a reader wrote to the editor of the *Carolina Watchman* complaining against the "sabbath so profanely broken" and "the Rail Road hands staggering to and from the grog shops the whole day, and some of them lying flat on their backs in the street, so much intoxicated as to be unable to walk."[85] Not only disorderly conduct but also crime and poverty upset the propertied residents of Salisbury. Petitions to the state legislature from the Salisbury Sons of Temperance calling for a prohibitory liquor law in North Carolina stressed the issue of pauperism. The memorial of 1852 brought the attention of the legislature "to the fact that great numbers of able-bodied citizens of our commonwealth are rendered lazy, idle, improvident, and incapable of labor by the enervating effects of alcohol"; these drinkers thus became "unprofitable consumers" rather than producers, and they imposed "increased exactions upon the hard earnings of the industrial classes."[86]

No comparable lists of opponents and supporters of no-license in Salisbury exist, so it is impossible to test these claims accurately. Yet there is some supporting evidence available in the form of a list of eighty-one Sons of Temperance members in the town, covering the years from 1847 to 1849. Since the Sons of Temperance was the only functioning temperance organization in the town and since it advocated a policy of prohibition in North Carolina, the list may provide some indication of the social support for no-license in the town. Overwhelmingly, the Sons drew its members from the few small manufacturers in the town, tradesmen, shopkeepers, clerks, merchants, doctors, lawyers, and clergymen. The organization included no semiskilled or unskilled workers at all and very few farmers.[87] Though farmers made up over 95 percent of the population of

Rowan County, fewer than 5 percent of the Sons of Temperance were farmers, even though the society made an effort to recruit members not only from the town of Salisbury but also from the surrounding countryside. The reasons for the abysmal performance of reform in the rural areas of Rowan County lie in the character of the farm economy. Rowan County farmers were mostly small-scale yeomen and producers of both corn and corn whiskey.

The support for prohibition seems to have come from the groups that the *Carolina Watchman* had mentioned: the propertied, middle-class townspeople. Despite considerable differences in social structure and culture between North and South, Salisbury prohibitionists articulated fears of crime and pauperism similar to those of their northern counterparts, and no-license drew its support from strikingly similar groups. The similarity arose from the fact that Salisbury was beginning to experience some of the turbulent economic changes which had set off the Worcester agitation twenty years before. The difference was that the manufacturers who so strongly sustained the northern agitation were neither so numerous in the Salisbury case nor possessed of the same degree of political power and social influence. The differing economic structure of the South, especially the absence of a significant manufacturing sector, helps explain the relative weakness of the prohibition movement in Salisbury.

A recent study of Cincinnati, Ohio, indicates that the pattern of support for prohibition in well-to-do and respectable middle-class society may also hold true for the Midwest. Middle-class, mostly native-born Cincinnatians who joined the prohibition movement in droves in the early 1850s feared "the burden of property taxes" caused by an increase in "pauperism and crime." In Pittsburgh, too, the Maine Law agitation against the specter of poverty peaked at a period of unprecedented unemployment and unprecedented demands on city charities during the winter and early spring of 1854.[88]

Prohibition and the Process of Reform

There is one obvious objection to the argument offered so far. If the groundswell of support for the Maine Law lay in middle-class fears of pauperism engendered by rapid economic growth and the influx of German and Irish immigrants, then why did the prohibitionist agitation not surge to greater heights during and after the panic of 1857? The answer must be sought not in the social structure but in the agitational process, in the history of prohibition between 1851 and 1857. Before 1855, it was possible to represent prohibition as a plausible and politically viable solution to the nation's social ills. By 1857, that was no longer possible. Moreover part of the success—an intangible and unquantifiable part—of the Maine Law between 1851 and 1855 lay in the energetic and effective agitation of the prohibitionists. The subsequent history of prohibition just as surely dissipated those energies and eroded those enthusiasms.

What distinguished the prohibitionist crusade of the early 1850s was not merely the groundswell of support for the prohibitionist position but the effectiveness with which prohibitionist agitators got their message across to the legislators. There can be no doubt that the prohibitionists proved much more effective in organizing on a state-wide level than their opponents. The temperance organizations had, by the 1850s, a long tradition of such agitation and much experience in the mechanics of propaganda campaigns. Their tactics included mass demonstrations, the employment of lobbyists at state legislatures, and widespread pamphleteering, but the most widely adopted technique was the use of the petition. Copied from the antislavery crusade, prohibitionists bombarded state legislators with petitions demonstrating the strength of opposition to the liquor traffic. In Massachusetts, a petition signed by 156,000 people was presented to the state legislature in Boston prior to the passage of the Maine Law of 1852; in New York, over 300,000 signatures were collected for a similar petition in 1853; and in Michigan, there were over 70,000 signatures. [89]

Much of the energy for this massive petitioning campaign came from women, and the success with which the prohibitionists tapped the enthusiasm of middle-class women was one key to their organizational superiority. Women both circulated and signed the petitions. Over a third of the 300,000 New York signatures were those of women. That nonvoting women signed many of the petitions did not make them politically ineffective, for temperance women reminded legislators in their petitions that though they did not themselves vote, their husbands did, and their husbands would be heeding the advice of their spouses. In addition to the petitioning activity of these women, the 1850s saw the emergence of articulate minorities of middle-class temperance women, chiefly in the Women's New York Temperance Society where Amelia Bloomer, Elizabeth Cady Stanton, and Susan B. Anthony were prominent. Temperance women actively entered the political hustings, even to the extent of handing out voting tickets at the polls in New York City in 1854.[90]

Backed by the enthusiastic support of middle-class women and by the organizational network of the Sons of Temperance, the American Temperance Union, and the Order of Good Templars, the prohibitionists in the northern states set out to saturate the country with literature favoring their cause. They established Maine Law committees at the town and county levels in the northern states and tapped the evangelical churches for financial support to provide money for touring temperance agents and for lobbyists at state capitals. Most important, they avoided political partisanship. They deliberately refused to form separate Maine Law parties but sought instead to persuade candidates of the existing political parties to pledge themselves in favor of the Maine Law. Traditional party loyalties, already weakened by the slavery issue, took a further battering from the discontented prohibitionists. A nonpartisan strategy was ideally suited to this fluid political situation and paid dividends handsomely in the early 1850s. Although the Whig party in the North harbored more temperance supporters than did the Democracy, legislatures which passed the Maine Law included five with Democratic majorities.[91]

The agitation of prohibitionists did not cease with the passage of prohibitory laws. There remained the difficult task of enforcement. This task would soon create new problems which would sap prohibitionist strength and dissipate the Maine Law's electoral appeal. Yet the initial impact of the Maine Law seems to have satisfied the expectations of most prohibitionists; prohibition was a partial success in its first years of operation. This interpretation flies in the face of popular conceptions about law and morality, and about prohibition laws in particular, a conception which is largely a legacy of the declining years of national prohibition. Yet as John C. Burnham has demonstrated, prohibition legislation was quite effective in cutting drinking during the early 1920s, especially among the working classes.[92] The key question was the willingness of federal and state authorities to pursue the enforcement of the law with vigor. The same was true of the 1850s. Where local and state authorities supported enforcement of prohibition, the results were, at least initially, gratifying to the prohibitionists. This was made clear in the case of Portland, Maine, where Neal Dow, the author of the Maine Law, was mayor. In the year ending June 2, 1851, seventy-four persons were committed to the Portland House of Correction because of intemperance. In January 1852, prohibitionists could proudly announce that since the passage of the Maine Law, no more commitments had been made. "The House of Correction is now empty," Neal Dow proclaimed. The incidence of crime had been so reduced that city officials now used the Portland city watchhouse only to store seized liquors.[93]

The evidence assembled by prohibitionists must be treated with caution. Changes in the number of arrests for drunkenness may have reflected the policies of law enforcement authorities as much as the level of intemperance. But if the statistics of prohibitionists (and their opponents) remain suspect, the available evidence does suggest that at least temporarily the Maine Law did cut the incidence of drunkenness wherever it was enforced. Prohibition increased the difficulty of obtaining liquor and raised the obstacles in the way of illegal selling, though the Maine Law did not prevent determined buyers from finding illicit supplies.[94]

Because the sale of liquor did not immediately cease, the Maine Law might be considered a failure, but this interpretation misrepresents the prohibitionist position. Although Neal Dow and his supporters knew that the law would not immediately eliminate the problem of intemperance, they regarded the restraint imposed upon the liquor traffic and the reduction of drunkenness as evidence of the power of law to remake social customs. As Thomas Scott Williams, a former chief justice of Connecticut, explained in 1855: "The very fact that [liquor] must be sold illegally, if at all, will prevent many a one from going in [to drinking places] who otherwise would." Moreover it was still possible to believe in 1855—as did J. B. Hill, the chairman of the Maine Law committee in the Maine legislature—

that intemperance could be further restricted and perhaps eliminated entirely by gradually closing the loopholes revealed through "the benefit of experience."[95]

The year 1855 represented the pinnacle of achievement for the organized temperance movement in terms of power and influence. To men like John Marsh and Edward C. Delavan, it seemed that the twenty-five years they had each invested in the cold-water cause had been worthwhile. The nation would soon be one sober republic from the Atlantic to the Pacific. In retrospect, the hopes of prohibitionists seem ludicrous, yet in 1855 history seemed to be on their side. They had the tougher laws which experience showed were necessary. In addition, they had growing public support, as the expansion in the number of Maine Law states indicated. With the erosion of old party loyalties in the early 1850s, prohibitionists seemed to be making heartening gains in political influence.

Nonetheless, the optimism of prohibitionists was short-lived. By the late 1850s, the Maine Law forces no longer expected new gains and found themselves fighting desperately to preserve the ground which they had won. After New Hampshire passed a prohibitory law in August 1855, not a single new state adopted prohibition for the next twenty-five years, and most of the states which had embraced prohibition in the early 1850s modified or repealed their Maine Laws in the late 1850s and 1860s. Prohibitionist spokesmen agreed that the Maine Law agitation had slumped badly from the high point of political activity in the 1850-1855 period. In Massachusetts, Charles Jewett pronounced the state's Temperance Alliance disorganized, impoverished, and demoralized. Even John Marsh, the eternally optimistic propagandist for the American Temperance Union, conceded that prohibition had received grave setbacks and loss of support in most states.[96] The Maine Law phase was over, and the decline of prohibition had begun.

Notes

1. Dow's manuscripts, deposited in the Maine Historical Society, provide few clues to the thought and practice of this leading prohibitionist

during the early years of his career. One must consult Dow, *The Reminiscences of Neal Dow: Recollections of Eighty Years* (Portland, Me.: Evening Express Publishing Company, 1898), and Frank L. Byrne, *Prophet of Prohibition: Neal Dow and His Crusade* (Madison: Wisconsin State Historical Society, 1959).

2. Joseph Gusfield, *Symbolic Crusade: Status Politics and the American Temperance Movement* (Urbana: University of Illinois Press, 1963), pp. 69-70; Ronald P. Formisano, *The Birth of Mass Political Parties: Michigan, 1827-1861* (Princeton, N.J.: Princeton University Press, 1971), p. 116.

3. Charles Jewett, *A Forty Years' Fight with the Drink Demon, or a History of the Temperance Reform as I Have Seen It, and of My Labors in Connection Therewith* (New York: National Temperance Society, 1872), p. 310.

4. Ibid.; *Boston Commonwealth*, 29 January 1852; A. Farewell and G. P. Ure, *The Maine Law Illustrated: Being the Result of an Investigation Made in the Maine Law States* (Toronto: Canadian Prohibitory Liquor Law League, 1855), p. 35; Byrne, *Prophet of Prohibition*, pp. 42-46.

5. Speech by Horace Mann, *Massachusetts Anti-Liquor Law; with an Analysis and Exposition* (Boston: State Temperance Committee, 1852), p. 20; *Massachusetts Cataract*, 8 February 1849, 6 February 1851.

6. Dow, *Reminiscences*, p. 283.

7. Jewett, *Forty Years' Fight*, p. 308.

8. *Letters from Professor Stuart, of Andover, . . . on the Maine Liquor Law* (New York: American Temperance Union, 1851), p. 9.

9. *Massachusetts Anti-Liquor Law*, p. 16.

10. Ibid.

11. *Commonwealth* v. *Dana*, 2 Metcalf, 329 (Massachusetts Reports, 1841).

12. Gerrit Smith to E. C. Delavan, 22 August 1855, Smith Family Papers, NYPL; Byrne, *Prophet of Prohibition*, p. 42; resolutions of the Massachusetts State Temperance Convention, *Norfolk* (Dedham, Mass.) *Democrat*, 23 March 1849.

13. Rufus Clark, *Fifty Arguments in Favor of Sustaining and Enforcing the Massachusetts Anti-Liquor Law* (Boston: John P. Jewett, 1853), pp. 6-7. The License Cases, decided by the United States Supreme Court in 1847, upheld the constitutionality of state legislation in Massachusetts, New Hampshire, and Rhode Island to restrict and to prohibit the sale of liquor within the borders of those states. For details, see Carl B. Swisher, *American Constitutional Development*, 2d ed. (Boston: Houghton Mifflin, 1954), p. 200.

14. *Massachusetts Cataract*, 16 August 1849.

15. Dow, *Reminiscences*, p. 282.

16. *Massachusetts Cataract*, 12 June 1851.

17. "To the District Attorneys of Massachusetts," ibid., 6 September 1849. At the October 1848 session of the county criminal court in Worcester, forty-five new liquor indictments were presented, and all were continued by the district attorney. See ibid., 26 October 1848.

18. *Acts and Resolves Passed by the Massachusetts General Court, in the Year 1852* (Boston: Dutton and Wentworth, 1852), ch. 322, sec. 13 (hereafter cited as *Massachusetts Laws*, 1852, ch. 322); *Public Laws of the State of Maine, Passed in the Years 1842 to 1851 Inclusive* . . . (Hallowell, Me.: Masters, Smith, 1852), ch. 211, sec. 10 (hereafter cited as *Maine Laws*, 1851, ch. 211).

19. *Massachusetts Laws*, 1852, ch. 322, sec. 13.

20. *Massachusetts Anti-Liquor Law*, p. 16.

21. *Massachusetts Cataract*, 14 February 1850.

22. See *Boston Commonwealth*, 20 January 1852, and *Boston Post*, 17 January 1852, for discussions of the industrial use of liquor.

23. Massachusetts State Temperance Convention, *Norfolk Democrat*, 23 February 1849.

24. Not until 1850 did the Massachusetts county commissioners obtain any legal authority for their practice of appointing medical dispensers of liquor, but even the law of 1850, which granted such authority for the first time, did not contain any safeguards to prevent licensees from abusing their power. See *Acts and Resolves Passed by the General Court of Massachusetts, in the Year 1850* (Boston: Dutton and Wentworth, 1850), ch. 232, sec. 2.

25. *Worcester Palladium*, 12 April 1843.

26. *Worcester National Aegis*, 5 April 1843; *Massachusetts Cataract*, 3 January 1844, 27 June 1850.

27. Resolution of the Massachusetts State Temperance Convention, *Norfolk Democrat*, 23 February 1849; Daniel Dorchester, *The Liquor Problem in All Ages* (New York: Phillips and Hunt, 1884), p. 292.

28. *Massachusetts Laws*, 1852, ch. 322, secs. 2, 3; *Maine Laws*, 1851, ch. 211, sec. 2.

29. *Massachusetts Anti-Liquor Law*, p. 30.

30. *Acts and Resolves Passed by the General Court of Massachusetts, in the Year 1855* . . . (Boston: William White, 1855), ch. 215, sec. 6; *Acts and Resolves Passed by the Thirty-fourth Legislature of the State of Maine, 1855* (Augusta, Me.: Stevens and Blaine, 1855), ch. 166, sec. 1.

31. Cf. Stanley Elkins, *Slavery: A Problem in American Institutional and Intellectual Life*, 2d ed. (Chicago: University of Chicago Press, 1968).

32. For these political battles, see Dorchester, *Liquor Problem in All*

Ages, p. 296; *Norfolk Democrat*, 23 February 1849; *Massachusetts Cataract*, 10 May, 13 September 1849; Henry S. Clubb, *The Maine Liquor Law: Its Origin, History, and Results* (New York: Fowler and Wells, 1856); and D. Leigh Colvin, *Prohibition in the United States: A History of the Prohibition Party and of the Prohibition Movement* (New York: George H. Doran, 1926), pp. 32-35.

33. Evidence of the much stronger commitment of Whigs to a whole range of reform movements, including temperance, can be found in Herbert Ershkowitz and William G. Shade, "Consensus or Conflict? Political Behavior in the State Legislatures during the Jacksonian Era," *Journal of American History* 58 (December 1971): 608-09, 617-18.

34. *New York Daily Tribune*, 26 April 1854.

35. Dow, *Reminiscences*, p. 338; Byrne, *Prophet of Prohibition*, pp. 46, 54-57.

36. *Boston Commonwealth*, 24 May 1852; Kevin Sweeney, "Rum, Romanism, Representation, and Reform: Coalition Politics in Massachusetts, 1847-1853," *Civil War History* 22 (June 1976): 129.

37. William J. Evitts, *A Matter of Allegiances: Maryland from 1850 to 1861* (Baltimore: Johns Hopkins University Press, 1975), p. 63.

38. Richard Current, *The Civil War Era, 1848-1873* (Madison: State Historical Society of Wisconsin, 1976), p. 216.

39. On New York Democrats and temperance, see W. J. Rorabaugh, "Rising Democratic Spirits: Immigrants, Temperance, and Tammany Hall, 1854-1860," *Civil War History* 22 (June 1976): 138-57; on Philadelphia, John Chambers to William C. Piatt, 28 March 1856, William C. Piatt Papers, DU.

40. *Proceedings of the Pennsylvania State Temperance Convention . . . 1854* (Philadelphia: William F. Geddes, 1854), pp. 31-32.

41. Dan C. Clark, "History of Liquor Legislation in Iowa, 1846-1861," *Iowa Journal of History and Politics* 6 (January 1908): 70. On these political machinations discussed in this and succeeding paragraphs, see Colvin, *Prohibition in the United States*, pp. 32-36, 47, 55-57; Eric Foner, *Free Soil, Free Labor, Free Men: The Ideology of the Republican Party before the Civil War* (New York: Oxford University Press, 1970), pp. 237-42; Charles E. Canup, "Temperance Movements and Legislation in Indiana," *Indiana Magazine of History* 16 (March 1920): 24.

42. Eugene H. Roseboom, *The Civil War Era, 1850-1873* (Columbus: Ohio State Archeological and Historical Society, 1944), p. 225.

43. Dow, *Reminiscences*, p. 353.

44. The literature on the second party system is enormous. A useful starting point is Ronald P. Formisano, "Toward a Reorientation of Jacksonian

Politics: A Review of the Literature, 1959-1975," *Journal of American History* 76 (June 1976): 42-65.

45. Horace Mann, *A Few Thoughts on the Powers and Duties of Women: Two Lectures* (New York: Fowler and Wells, 1859), p. 97. On antiparty attitudes, see Ronald P. Formisano, "Political Character, Antipartyism, and the Second Party System," *American Quarterly* 21 (Winter 1969): 683-709.

46. Gerrit Smith circular, 10 October 1858, Smith Family Papers.

47. *Massachusetts Cataract,* 20 September 1849; Michael Holt, "The Politics of Impatience: The Origins of Know Nothingism," *Journal of American History* 60 (September 1973): 309-31.

48. On Massachusetts, see *Massachusetts Anti-Liquor Law,* pp. 19-21, and Sweeney, "Rum," p. 129; on Wisconsin, Current, *Civil War Era,* p. 216; on Ohio, Roseboom, *Civil War Era,* p. 22.

49. Gusfield, *Symbolic Crusade,* pp. 69-70; Formisano, *Birth of Mass Political Parties,* p. 116.

50. Farewell and Ure, *Maine Law Illustrated,* pp. 14, 69, 70.

51. *Directory: Alpha Chapter, No. 1, O.U.A. August, 1848* (New York: R. C. Root and Anthony, 1848), passim.

52. Alvin Harlow, *Old Bowery Days: The Chronicles of a Famous Street* (New York: D. Appleton, 1931), pp. 299-300; *O.U.A.* [Journal of the Order of United Americans], 18 November 1848.

53. Michael Holt, *Forging a Majority: The Formation of the Republican Party in Pittsburgh, 1848-1860* (New Haven: Yale University Press, 1969), p. 110.

54. Roger Lane, *Policing the City, Boston, 1822-1885* (Cambridge: Harvard University Press, 1967), p. 92.

55. George H. Haynes, "A Chapter from the Local History of Knownothingism," *New England Magazine,* n.s. 15 (September 1896): 88; Worcester (Mass.) Native American Party Records, AAS.

56. Haynes, "Local History of Knownothingism," p. 88; *Worcester Massachusetts Spy,* 26 September 1850, 13 December 1854.

57. *Address of the Board of Managers of the American Protestant Association; with the Constitution of the Association* (Philadelphia: American Protestant Association, 1843), pp. 8-9.

58. Ray Allen Billington, *The Protestant Crusade, 1800-1850: A Study of the Origins of Nativism* (New York: Macmillan, 1938), pp. 178-80, 183-84.

59. There is no good survey of Episcopalian attitudes toward the liquor question. The best starting point is John Henry Hopkins, *The Primitive Church, Compared with the Protestant Episcopal Church of the Present Day* (Burlington, Vt.: Smith and Harrington, 1835), pp. 128-29, 134-35, 139-41. See also *Infidelity and Benevolent Societies: A Discussion between*

the Rev. *William Watson, and the Editor of the Waterbury American* (Waterbury, CT: E. B. Cooke, 1848), pp. 8-9; *New York Organ*, 23 November 1844; *Norfolk Democrat*, 15 April 1842.

60. *JATU* 1 (April 1837): 50.

61. "Circular to Emigrants and Those Desiring to Remove to the United States of America," *Temperance Recorder* 2 (July 1833): 37; *JATU* 2 (September 1838): 129; E. C. Delavan to Gerrit Smith, 5 July 1838, box 10, Gerrit Smith Miller Collection, SU; Smith to Delavan, 9 July 1838, Letterbook, vol. 1, 1827-43, Gerrit Smith Miller Collection.

62. Farewell and Ure, *Maine Law Illustrated*, pp. 83, 49.

63. *Report of the Executive Committee of the American Temperance Union, 1857* (New York: American Temperance Union, 1857), p. 15; John Tappan to John Marsh, 19 August 1857, in *JATU* 21 (October 1857): 146.

64. Colvin, *Prohibition in the United States*, p. 47.

65. See, for example, Farewell and Ure, *Maine Law Illustrated*, pp. 22, 77-78; Byrne, *Prophet of Prohibition*, pp. 56-58.

66. Haynes, "Local History of Knownothingism," pp. 93-94; Haynes, "A Know Nothing Legislature," *Annual Report of the American Historical Association for the Year 1896* (Washington, D.C.: Government Printing Office, 1897), 1: 175-87; Michael F. Holt, "The Antimasonic and Know Nothing Parties," in Arthur M. Schlesinger, Jr., ed., *History of U.S. Political Parties* (New York: Chelsea House Publishers, 1973), 1: 608; Dale Baum, "Know-Nothingism and the Republican Majority in Massachusetts: The Political Realignment of the 1850s," *Journal of American History* 64 (March 1978): 965-66, 985-86.

67. Formisano, *Birth of Mass Political Parties*, pp. 263-64.

68. Holt, "Antimasonic and Know Nothing Parties," pp. 604-08.

69. Farewell and Ure, *Maine Law Illustrated*, pp. 23, 31, 78, 17-18.

70. Ibid., pp. 71-72.

71. Ibid., pp. 58-59; Dow, *Reminiscences*, pp. 335, 338; Byrne, *Prophet of Prohibition*, p. 46.

72. *Worcester Massachusetts Spy*, 12 April 1848; for the temperance party lists, see *Massachusetts Cataract*, 13, 20 April 1848. Names have been traced in the manuscript population schedule and schedule of manufactures (Worcester), Seventh Census, 1850, microfilm, National Archives; city directories; and other biographical and genealogical sources.

73. *Worcester Daily Spy*, 11 March 1854. See also the similar agitation in New Worcester, ibid., 18 March 1854, and *Massachusetts Cataract*, 16 December 1852.

74. *Worcester Daily Spy*, 4, 14 May, 23 August, 13 September, 21 December 1852.

75. Albert Barnes, *The Political Economy of the Maine Law* (New York: American Temperance Union, [1852]).

76. Farewell and Ure, *Maine Law Illustrated*, p. 79.

77. *Massachusetts Anti-Liquor Law*, p. 25.

78. Dow, *Reminiscences*, pp. 372, 406-07.

79. Farewell and Ure, *Maine Law Illustrated*, p. 23.

80. *Ninth Annual Report of the New-York Association for Improving the Condition of the Poor* (New York: By the association, 1852), pp. 26-28.

81. Quoted in *New York Organ*, 9 October 1847.

82. The availability of temperance society records and evidence of no-license agitation determined the choice of the case study, Salisbury, North Carolina.

83. *Salisbury Carolina Watchman*, 22 July 1856.

84. Hugh T. Lefler and Albert R. Newsome, *North Carolina: The History of a Southern State* (Chapel Hill: University of North Carolina Press, 1954), p. 349.

85. *Salisbury Carolina Watchman*, 12 February 1852.

86. MS. in Legislative Papers, 1852, North Carolina Department of Archives and History. See also *Salisbury Carolina Watchman*, 20 January 1853. For a general view of the liquor question in antebellum North Carolina, see Daniel J. Whitener, *Prohibition in North Carolina, 1715-1945* (Chapel Hill: University of North Carolina Press, 1945), p. 42.

87. Sons of Temperance membership list, in minute book, Washington Temperance Society of Salisbury, North Carolina, in Oren Davis Collection, Southern Historical Collection, UNC. For the socioeconomic background, see James S. Brawley, *The Rowan Story, 1753-1953: A Narrative History of Rowan County North Carolina* (Salisbury, N.C.: Rowan Print Co., 1953), pp. 172-73.

88. Jed Dannenbaum, "The Crusader: Samuel Cary and Cincinnati Temperance," *Cincinnati Historical Society Bulletin* 33 (Summer 1975): 137; Erasmus Wilson, ed., *Standard History of Pittsburgh Pennsylvania* (Chicago: H. R. Cornell, 1898), pp. 889, 908.

89. Dorchester, *Liquor Problem in All Ages*, pp. 299-300; Formisano, *Birth of Mass Political Parties*, p. 230.

90. *Lily* 6 (November 1854): 158; Ida Harper, *The Life of Susan B. Anthony* (Indianapolis: Bowen-Merrill Company, 1898-1908), 1:70.

91. Prohibitionists won their prohibitory laws from legislatures of a variety of political complexions, as Colvin demonstrates in *Prohibition in the United States*, p. 47. Legislatures controlled by the Democratic party, which passed the Maine Law, were Maine, Michigan, Minnesota, Rhode Island, and Nebraska. In Massachusetts, a coalition of Free-Soil and Democratic

parties controlled the legislature, and support for the Maine Law did not correspond to party affiliation. Governor George Boutwell, a Democrat, at first vetoed the law but later changed his mind. See *Boston Commonwealth*, 24 May 1852.

92. John C. Burnham, "New Perspectives on the Prohibition 'Experiment' of the 1920's," *Journal of Social History* 2 (Fall 1968): 51-68.

93. *An Appeal to the Public from the Well Authenticated Results of the Maine Law* (New York: American Temperance Union, 1854), p. 6; Neal Dow, "Operation of the Liquor Law in Portland," 15 January 1852, box 2/9, Neal Dow Papers, MeHS; Report of Neal Dow, *Portland* (Me.) *Temperance Watchman*, 4 October 1851.

94. Dow, "Operation of the Liquor Law"; report of Neal Dow, *Portland Temperance Watchman* (Extra), September 1851; Farwell and Ure, *Maine Law Illustrated*, pp. 14, 15, 78, 83; Clubb, *Maine Liquor Law*, p. 255.

95. Farwell and Ure, *Maine Law Illustrated*, pp. 21, 65; see also Dow, *Reminiscences*, p. 389.

96. E. C. Delavan to Gerrit Smith, 14 February 1859, box 11, Gerrit Smith Miller Collection; Gerrit Smith open letter, 10 October 1858, Smith Family Papers; Amasa Walker to T. H. Barker, Secretary of the United Kingdom Alliance, n.d., c. 1859, Amasa Walker Papers, MHS; Jewett, *Forty Years' Fight*, p. 351; *Report of the Executive Committee of the American Temperance Union, 1856* (New York: American Temperance Union, 1856), p. 5.

11

THE DECLINE OF PROHIBITION

Prohibition agitation subsided as quickly as it had risen. To temperance partisans, the fading fortunes of the Maine Law seemed a direct result of legal reverses and political opportunism within the major political parties. What prohibitionists did not fully acknowledge, however, was a social climate increasingly unfavorable to the Maine Law; it was the growing popular opposition to enforcement of prohibition which made possible the successful challenges to the Maine Law in the courts and in the legislatures. Problems of enforcement quickly tarnished the claim that suppression of the liquor traffic would promote social order. Rather, the violence that accompanied enforcement made the law a political liability for aspiring politicians and an embarrassment for many former supporters.

Prohibition and the Courts

Legal challenges to prohibition contributed to the demise of the Maine Law agitation. In several states, the courts obstructed the progress of prohibition by declaring the Maine Law unconstitutional. The Massachusetts Supreme Court, in the case of *Fisher* v. *McGirr* (1854), struck down the search and seizure clause of the state's antiliquor law as a deprivation of property without due process of law. The court cited in support of its ruling the guarantee of property in the state's Declaration of Rights. The judges further condemned the Massachusetts prohibitory law because the provisions for obtaining search warrants encouraged "unreasonable search and seizure" within the meaning of the Declaration of Rights.[1] Another legal setback occurred during the same year when Michigan's supreme court "practically nullified" the state's prohibitory law of 1853; the court split four to four on the constitutionality of the law's referendum provision. Four justices of the court held the law an unconstitutional delegation of legislative power.[2]

The Maine Law would suffer further reverses in Indiana and Minnesota, but the most damaging legal blow to the cause came in New York State during 1856. New York was the most populous of the United States, and the American Temperance Union attached special significance to the adoption of prohibition in New York in 1855. Much to the disappointment of prohibitionists, the victory was brief. In 1856, the state court of appeals declared in the *Wynehamer* v. *People* case that the seizure clause of the New York prohibitory law entailed a denial of the property rights guaranteed in the state constitution.[3] In both New York and Massachusetts, the court decisions stopped prosecutions and weakened the morale of the temperance organizations. Equally damaging was the protracted litigation which preceded the eventual court rulings. Many law enforcement authorities refused to act and juries refused to convict while appeals on the constitutionality of the Maine Law were pending in state courts. The sale of liquor meanwhile continued unmolested.[4]

In considering these legal setbacks, it is important to remember that many of the decisions were highly contentious; the judgments could have gone either way. The split court in Michigan reflected this fact; so too did the discrepancies in the rulings from one state to another. While Massachusetts invalidated aspects of its 1852 law as violations of property rights guaranteed in the state constitution, the Connecticut Supreme Court rejected a similar challenge to the Connecticut law, despite the existence of similar constitutional guarantees. Vermont took advantage of the absence of a specific guarantee of property rights in the state constitution to uphold the prohibition law there; the Indiana court ignored the absence of such specific guarantees in Indiana's constitution and struck down the state's law in *Beebe* v. *State*.[5]

The contentious character of these legal rulings arose from the fact that the judges brought their social values and political convictions with them to the bench. This aspect was seen most clearly in the *Beebe* case, where Samuel Perkins, an anti-Maine Law Democrat elected to the Indiana state bench in 1852, wrote a blatantly Democratic denunciation of the Maine Law drawn from Jacksonian laissez-faire ideology. The opinion, which stressed the absolute property rights inherent in liquor, did not accord with previous rulings of the Supreme Court of the United States in the License Cases or with the subsequent judgments of legal scholars.[6] It is only fair to add that some of the opinions sustaining the Maine Law, notably Justice Henry M. Waite's in Connecticut, were also shaped by prior convictions, though the decision in the Connecticut case was much more congruent with established legal precedents in that state.

On legal grounds, then, the prohibitionists had reason to be upset with some of the adverse rulings and legal obstacles placed in their way. Yet the divided judiciary and adverse legal rulings reflected deep political divisions within the community on the liquor question. Although prohibitionists blamed the courts for their failures, the legal setbacks were secondary to the social and political ones. Central to the failure of prohibition was the widespread public opposition to the Maine Law which developed by 1855. The prohibitionists' loss of public support and confidence stemmed from a variety of sources. Enforcement had proven much more difficult than the framers of the Maine Law had expected. As prohibitionists plugged up loopholes in the prohibitory laws, they found that opposition to the Maine Law increased. The Maine Laws did not, for example, prevent large-scale importation of liquor from out of the state. Individuals could band together in a club and buy liquor in large quantities from interstate suppliers. The law was also powerless to prevent individuals from ordering supplies to be brought to a home by expressmen or common carriers within a particular state. When the prohibitionists attempted to close these loopholes, they found that opposition to the Maine Law increased. Many who were prepared to acquiesce in the law while their own private supplies remained untouched became alienated by the more rigid laws passed in the mid-1850s. [7]

Enforcement and Its Consequences

The critical problem of enforcement centered on the shortcomings of the enforcement authorities themselves. The patterns of enforcement paralleled in some ways those of national prohibition in the 1920s, yet there was one very important difference. In the 1920s professional police forces and a federal bureaucracy had the capability to enforce prohibitory laws with vigor, provided politicians were prepared to give those agencies the requisite funding. [8] But in the 1850s, only the largest cities had police forces, and prohibition had not yet become a federal issue. The police forces which did exist were not fully professional, and because of their structure and composition, they were often far from enthusiastic about the Maine Law. The New York City police force, for example, owed its allegiance to the Democratic administration of Mayor Fernando Wood, an outspoken opponent of the Maine Law. Moreover the police force in New York used a neighborhood recruiting policy which made enforcement difficult, for in the poorest wards of the city where the saloons were concentrated, the police were drawn from the very social classes they were supposed to coerce. [9]

Thus detection and enforcement frequently depended not on public officials or police but on the zeal of prohibitionists who, in effect, had to create private police forces to plug the gaps created by inefficient and unwilling local authorities. This condition was both recognized in and to some extent encouraged by the provisions of the Maine Law, which required three complainants before a search could be initiated by the sheriff, city marshal, or policeman. In addition, one complainant had to swear before a justice of the peace or before a police court that a sale had taken place. Therein lay the origins of the Carson League and the Temperance Watchmen, though neither of these organizations restricted its activities to gathering evidence and making complaints. The Carson League, begun in New York State in the early 1850s, soon spread throughout the Northeast.

Sobering Up

It collected fees from members to establish a fund for the litigation anticipated upon the passage and enforcement of the Maine Law. Like the Temperance Watchmen, the Carson League also used informers to enter bars to obtain evidence of illegal sales of liquor and worked for the election of state and local officials who were pledged to maintain and enforce the Maine Law.[10]

The Carson League was only a temporary expedient, however. Its activities were both wearing and financially taxing. Its vigilance had to be constant if the law were to be effectively enforced. The detailed tasks of enforcement were not considered suitable for women, and they were often distasteful or onerous for the busy middle-class businessmen who swelled the prohibitionist ranks. Informants were difficult to come by, in part because of the stigma attached to informing within artisan and working-class culture, in part because well-known temperance men could not be used, in part because prohibitionists found going inside saloons distasteful. In fact, the Carson League frequently used paid informants, but this practice added to the organization's expenses.

Perhaps more important, the use of what amounted to virtual private police forces engendered enormous hostility. As John Marsh noted, the Carson League turned the prohibition battle into an explicit and naked power struggle between prohibitionists and their opponents. The point of the Maine Law was to interpose state authority on the side of prohibition, to give the prohibitionist cause a legality which could come only if clothed with that state power. Under the actions of the Carson League, law did not seem to be an impartial authority administered in the interests of the whole community; rather it tended to become the plaything of the most extreme prohibitionists. Opposition was, as Marsh explained, more likely to be created than diffused by the use of private police forces. "Such combinations provoke a resistance" which would not be made to regular law enforcement authorities.[11] There is evidence that the activities of the Carson League did indeed provoke retaliation, for there were reported several cases of incendiarism against known members of the Carson League in New York and Massachusetts. Sometimes the retaliation was more open. In Worcester, George Peckham was pelted with rotten eggs for his part in a liquor seizure;

Lewis Thayer, a complainant in a liquor law violation, was knocked unconscious by two men who assaulted him with a brick in front of his home. [12]

Reprisals against Carson League members were only small examples of the widespread violence which accompanied the enforcement of the Maine Law. This violent resistance was extremely important in discrediting prohibition, for Neal Dow had made large claims that his law would eliminate violence and crime from the community. Moderates deserted the law when experience showed that enforcement of it produced more disorder than it eliminated. Much of this social disorder accompanying the Maine Law received little coverage or publicity outside the immediate vicinity. A typical example occurred in Worcester, Massachusetts, when a group of Irish laborers broke into a rail car carrying liquor. They stole a barrel of gin and then set fire to the rest of the cars to conceal the felony. [13] Like the fistfights and street brawls which sometimes accompanied the arrests of drinkers and sellers of liquor, the Worcester incident was one of many small, isolated acts of violence which occurred as a result of the Maine Law.

An outburst of social violence which was much more highly publicized throughout the nation, and much more damaging to the prohibitionist cause, occurred in Portland, Maine, in 1855. While mayor of Portland, Neal Dow was accused by his political and antiprohibitionist opponents of speculating in liquor for personal profit. The *Portland Eastern Argus* alleged that Dow had bought liquor for the city's liquor agency, which dispensed spirits for industrial and medicinal purposes, whereas only the liquor agent was authorized under the law to make such purchases. Dow's opponents, angered by the mayor's rigid enforcement of prohibition, attempted to stir up opposition to his illegal purchase. An angry mob assembled at the liquor agency on the night of June 2, 1855, after the existence of the liquor had become common knowledge. The mob demanded destruction of the liquor and threatened to break into the agency if the demand were not met and Neal Dow arrested for violation of his own law. Dow, who was always quick to look to force in defense of morality, assembled the local Rifle Guards. In the confrontation which followed with the stone-throwing mob, Dow ordered his troops to fire when several rioters broke into the liquor agency. The fracas left one rioter dead and seven wounded.[14]

Dow's opponents, especially Democrats, seized on the issue and denounced him as a murderer and tyrant. They made the "tyranny" of the Maine Law the central issue of the state elections in the fall of 1855 and captured control of the legislature. The controversy surrounding the enforcement of prohibition in Maine also hurt the temperance cause in other states. Dow's action and Maine's 1855 election discredited his claims of broad community support for the Maine Law. Gloating over Dow's embarrassment, the liquor sellers of New York proclaimed that "the sanguinary code inaugurated in Maine, and written in the blood of the people of Portland has excited a horror of prohibition philanthropy." Even the *New York Times*, a paper favoring prohibition, found the event deplorable. Most of the adverse public comment involved the fear that the violence produced by prohibition in Maine could easily erupt in other states. As the *Boston Investigator*, a journal sympathetic to temperance but opposed to prohibition, pointed out:

Portland . . . is comparatively a quiet place; and if its citizens have to be shot down by a fanatical Mayor, to enable him to enforce an absurd law, it is not unreasonable to suppose that in larger and more turbulent cities, where this same law is in operation, the same means must be adopted to execute it thoroughly.[15]

Already in Chicago, Illinois, an anti-prohibition riot in April 1855 had left one dead and several wounded, and the prospect of further violent clashes featured prominently in anti-prohibitionist propaganda during succeeding months.[16]

The Maine Law provoked violence because it hit the liquor traffic harder than any previous law had. The more stringent the law, the more pronounced the resistance became. Liquor sellers responded to the Carson League with the formation of Liquor Leagues to fight prohibition in the courts, to provide legal defense funds and bail money, and to exert political influence by supporting anti-Maine Law candidates in state and local elections. These organizations sprang up in 1855 in such cities as Philadelphia, New York, Boston, and Milwaukee; they presaged the formation of the politically powerful United States Brewers' Congress in 1862.[17]

Immigrants and Prohibition

While the Maine Law provoked unparalleled opposition from native American drinkers, the most pronounced resistance came from new immigrant groups. The Irish and German immigrants who entered the United States in increasing numbers after 1845 presented a far more formidable and intractable challenge to prohibition than that faced by the temperance forces in the no-license campaigns of the 1830s and early 1840s. In the New England states, immigrants, chiefly Irish, constituted the chief problem of intemperance in the 1850s. Four-fifths of the arrests for drunkenness in Boston in the mid-1850s were of foreigners, and in Norfolk County and Worcester, Massachusetts, most detected drunkenness was among the Irish. The witnesses in *The Maine Law Illustrated* reported that this pattern held true not only for rural and small-town Massachusetts but also for Maine, Vermont, and New Hampshire.[18]

It is too simple an explanation to blame the intemperance of Irish or German immigrants on their cultural inheritance alone, on the traditions they brought with them to the New World. Social conditions in the United States acted powerfully to reinforce and shape cultural preferences. Immigrants congregated in walks of life where intemperance was difficult to avoid. Over 95 percent of New York's laboring force was composed of immigrants (almost all the rest were blacks).[19] Indeed laboring was the largest single category of employment for Irish males in New York in 1855, accounting for more than a fifth of that ethnic group's total employment (male and female). In Boston, a city which provided even less occupational diversity for the Irish, the comparable figure was 48 percent. German employment patterns were much more varied, but many German immigrants in New York worked in a variety of outdoor jobs of an unskilled or semiskilled nature: as market gardeners, builders' laborers, cartmen, and boatmen. In the building trades over half of the New York labor force was Irish by 1855, and another quarter was German.[20]

These Irish and German immigrants were thus concentrated in work which often involved exposure to the elements, was physically demanding, dirty and unpleasant, and irregular in duration. All of these conditions encouraged the use of alcohol, but the irregularity of work probably contributed most powerfully. Horace Greeley noted that in New York "hundreds of our carmen, laborers, etc. in our city are annually seduced into habits of intemperance by the necessity of having some place to stay while awaiting business." Though Greeley put a moralistic construction on what he observed, he rightly understood that the taverns and grocers' shops functioned in Manhattan as they did in other large cities: as informal labor exchanges and places of refuge from the elements for casual laborers. [21]

Saloons had more than economic functions for the immigrant; they served as social centers, as places of refuge where countrymen could gather together in fraternal association. [22] This social function was also related to the demographic structure of the immigrant labor force and to the market forces which shaped that labor supply. Like most other populations emigrating to find jobs, immigrant groups in the antebellum period had an excess of young, single, able-bodied males. More than twice as many male as female immigrants between the ages of fifteen and thirty passed through the port of New York between 1820 and 1860. In fact, 64 percent of all immigrant males fell into this age group, compared with a figure of 29 percent for the total white male population of the United States in 1850. [23]

Given the maldistribution of immigrant communities by sex and age, it is hardly surprising that immigrants should seek their social life not at home but among their fellow workers in the taverns. Young, single males, away from the restraints of family and community, sought refuge and entertainment in the drinking culture. Moreover the taverns were doubly important because they provided access to women. William Sanger's quite sophisticated (for 1858) study of prostitution in New York reveals the close connection of saloons, prostitution, and ethnic subcultures in large American cities. Among the prostitutes and the clienteles Sanger studied, immigrants were disproportionately represented. [24]

If the economic and social condition of immigrant groups made them more susceptible to drink than many native-born Americans, it is nevertheless necessary to distinguish between the drinking and the temperance activity of the two major immigrant groups of the period: the Germans and the Irish. The use of whiskey, the high incidence of saloons in poor Irish neighborhoods, and the especially heavy concentration of the Irish in itinerant and irregular labor combined to give the Irish a higher incidence of intemperance than was present among the Germans. Yet the Irish also displayed a much stronger commitment to the elimination of intemperance than the Germans did and were much more likely to form their own temperance societies. The two went together: the severity of the drinking problem among the Irish made them more susceptible to temperance appeals, as the history of the Father Mathew agitation indicated.

Father Mathew was an Irish Capuchin priest who gained a reputation as a temperance reformer of remarkable charisma and influence in his native land during the 1840s. The American Temperance Union reformers invited Mathew to the United States in 1849 to minister the pledge to his countrymen who had emigrated. The societies of Catholic abstainers which started during Mathew's visit showed that temperance agitation was not confined to Protestants; it included a sizable Irish component, for Mathew administered the temperance pledge to a boasted 600,000 of his countrymen in America. Leaving aside the question of the veracity of these figures, it is nevertheless true that several factors vitiated the strength of Irish-Catholic temperance in America in the 1850s. The Father Mathew movement was grounded in Mathew's own charisma, it lacked a strong organizational base, and it was dependent on communities with high numbers of lower-class transients.

More important for consideration of the Maine Law, Irish-Catholic temperance did not favor prohibition, though Mathew himself endorsed it before he died in 1856. Moral suasion was the standard tactic of American bishops and priests who preached in their sermons against "the dreadful sin of drunkenness," as Bishop James Bayley did in Newark, New Jersey, in 1861.[25] The failure of Catholics to support the Maine Law stemmed partly from the theological and moral outlook of the Catholic hierarchy. Catholic bishops did not welcome outside competition for moral influence in the form of secular or Protestant temperance reformers attempting to use the state to impose sobriety on society. Nor could the clergy accept the idea of coercion in prohibition, which seemed from a Catholic point of view to deny free will and moral responsibility for evil. However, Catholics were not alone in entertaining these reservations about secular moral reform and state-imposed morality; upper-class Episcopalians often expressed similar viewpoints. [26]

What really distinguished the Irish was the critical place of the liquor trade within the Irish communities. Saloon keeping, and the liquor-supply business to a lesser extent, provided avenues of mobility for poor Irish immigrants, as John F. Maguire pointed out in his survey of Irish-America in 1868: "Requiring little capital, at least to commence with, the Irish rush into it [saloon keeping]." A rented shop front could serve as a liquor store, and the family could sleep in the back. [27] Prevented by discrimination and economic barriers from entering many professions and businesses, the Irish could hardly have resisted the opportunities offered in the liquor trade. Thus to prohibit the sale of liquor involved not only an attack on Irish cultural preferences for drinking; the Maine Law meant economic ruin to Irish grocers and saloon keepers. In Burlington, Vermont, one of the Irishmen on trial for illegal selling in 1855 defended himself by stating that "as it was 'hard times' if they could make a little money selling rum it was nobody's business."[28] The problem was rendered still more complex by the involvement of many of the most wealthy and prestigious Irish-Americans in the liquor trade. The Friendly Sons of St. Patrick and the Hibernian Society of Philadelphia, an organization which dispensed relief to poor Irish immigrants, included within its ranks distillers, saloon keepers, tavern keepers, grocers, and restauranteurs. Thirty percent of the members who joined between 1840 and 1860 were connected with the liquor traffic. [29] Supporting prohibition meant attacking the Irish community's own success stories, the men who funded its benevolent societies and contributed largely to Catholic charitable and other church-related activities.

The German liquor problem differed in one important respect. Among Germans, the most popular beverage was beer, a much less intoxicating drink than either whiskey or even the older porters and ales, which had been brewed in America since colonial times. [30] Thus the Germans tended to be more temperate than the Irish, and yet they also had less enthusiasm for temperance. In Newark, New Jersey, German drinkers expressed surprise at the fury of the prohibitionists and defended "the temperate use of good spirituous liquors, such as beer and wine." Rather than a source of misery, beer for these German immigrants was "indispensable to our well being." Especially galling to the Germans were the temperance reformers' incursions on the "innocent amusements" of the Germans' "beer and wine saloons" and the reformers' sabbatarian aversion to tippling on Sundays. The Germans did not accept the Puritan New England version of the Sabbath; they dedicated "Sundays not only to pious contemplations, but also to rest, recreations, and amusements."[31] In Wisconsin, Milwaukee's "Lager Bier Halls" remained open each Sunday in defiance of the state liquor laws, and temperance reformers complained not only of the resultant intemperance but also of the riotous behavior and the noise created by the Sunday revelers. In addition, the German drinkers of Wisconsin carried their opposition to prohibition into politics. When the state voted on the Maine Law in an 1853 referendum, Milwaukee Germans arrived at the polls replete with free liquor; because of German votes, Milwaukee went against prohibition.[32]

In addition to offending anti-sabbatarian and anti-Puritan sentiments, prohibition also clashed directly with the economic and social functions of drink in German-American society. Here the German case paralleled the Irish, though the beverage was different. The brewing and sale of lager beer was a major industry and a source of employment for German-Americans, and in addition it formed the basis of a number of German-American fortunes. In Milwaukee, brewing was the most important avenue of advancement "from small scale artisan to manufacturer" among German immigrants; and for employees brewing provided higher wages than those prevailing in many other trades. In addition were the ancillary services, including cooperage, carting, and retailing. By 1860, Germans provided 80 percent of the coopers in Milwaukee and, along with the Irish, they dominated the retail liquor outlets.[33]

Just as there clearly were economic motives for opposing prohibition in German communities, so too did the social functions of alcohol in German immigrant society work against support for prohibition. Liquor played an integral part in German entertainments, with the saloons serving as social centers for male artisans and casual laborers the same way that they did among Irish and native-born communities. But in addition, the Germans brought with them their concept of the "lager bier hall," which often provided Sunday afternoon concerts for the whole family. Because Germans were more likely to come to the United States in family groups than were the Irish, there was a greater demand for such entertainments, and the drinking in the lager beer halls was rather more sedate than that in saloons frequented by lonely German and Irish itinerant laborers and artisans. [34]

The organized temperance agitation made little progress among either Protestant or Catholic Germans. Though there were some 15,000 non-Catholic Germans in New York City as early as the late 1830s—many of them Protestants—217 Germans were enrolled in the German Temperance Society, and only 39 were teetotalers. Temperance societies reported little further headway during the next ten years. Clearly the pietist-liturgical dispute so beloved of historians of antebellum cultural and social history cannot explain such a phenomenon as effectively as an analysis of the structure of immigrant communities. [35]

Though differing in their drinking practices and their responses to the temperance crusade, both German and Irish immigrants were numbered among the opponents of the Maine Law, and through their political opposition at the polls and their defiance of law, they helped to undermine prohibition. Partly as a consequence of the upsurge of immigration in the second half of the 1840s the per-capita consumption of liquor began to rise after several decades of decline. Official figures show that the per-capita consumption of intoxicating liquors had fallen from 5 ½ gallons to just over 4 gallons between 1810 and 1850. Despite the prohibitory legislation of the 1850s, it rose during the decade after 1850 and reached 6 gallons by 1860. Though the official figures show a small increase in the consumption of spirits, much more striking was the rise in the consumption of beer. While fermented and malt liquors accounted for 37 percent of the consumption of intoxicating liquor in 1850, they comprised more than half of the consumption in 1860. [36] The 1850s were boom years for the brewing industry, and it was lager beer, produced by and for Germans, which made the most startling impact on the liquor business.

Yet the aspect of foreign immigration which most alarmed prohibitionists was the influx of foreigners into the selling of liquor, because the Maine Law men were primarily concerned with the elimination of liquor selling as the first step to eliminating intemperance. The *New York Organ*, while making a report on intemperance in New York City in 1850, emphasized "the vast multitude of beerhouses, and other drinking places—kept by foreigners—chiefly Germans and Irish." A report on vice in Newark, New Jersey, stated that four-fifths of the retail liquor trade in that city had fallen into the hands of foreigners, "who, for the most part, consider themselves under no moral restraint in dealing out the poison."[37] Samuel Fenton Cary reported from Cincinnati, Ohio, that there were 1,200 liquor sellers in the city, and over a thousand were Germans.[38] The temperance reformers believed that their campaign to discourage the respectable from the traffic had worked by 1850; however, the ranks of the liquor sellers had been replaced by the hordes of new immigrants.[39]

Immigrants were the most obvious violators of the Maine Law and its staunchest opponents in New England and in certain midwestern states, such as Wisconsin.[40] Yet the conflict over drink never assumed the simple proportions of a native-foreign division. Many native-born Americans joined immigrants in defying the Maine Law, for hard-drinking American gangs and native-born workers in such cities as Philadelphia continued to use liquor in the manner accustomed to preindustrial artisans.[41] That the anti-prohibition forces were not confined simply to the foreign population is clear also from the Worcester evidence. The *Daily Spy* reported the names of illegal sellers, and some were Anglo-Saxons; more important, the *Spy* noted that many of the "denizens" of the city's "bar rooms, billard rooms, and bowling alleys" were young men from rural New England who "come here, strangers, for the purpose of learning trades, or employing their industry in our workshops and stores." The *Spy* pointed to the same sorts of people who flocked to the Know Nothing banner in 1854; and apart from the obvious difference in ethnic background, the native-born drinker had similar characteristics to his foreign counterpart—he was a young, male, mobile workingman. The tavern culture provided social entertainment, an avenue of social intercourse for both immigrant and native-born workers. Once again, the structure of the labor market created a social problem which overtaxed the social institutions of Worcester. [42]

Voting statistics also point to an anti-prohibitionist interest which transcended the native-foreign division. In no state did the foreignborn population exceed 36 percent of the total population. The strong opposition to prohibition in such states as Pennsylvania, Illinois, and Ohio cannot be explained in terms of a foreign-born component which was less than 14 percent of the total population. [43] The case against immigrant domination of the opposition to prohibition is best understood by looking at the premier prohibitionist state, Maine. The anti-Maine Law candidate in the 1852 state election, Anson G. Chandler, polled 22,000 votes in the gubernatorial race. Yet there were only 17,000 foreign-born males in the state, and the foreign born made up only 5.45 percent of the population. Given these figures, it seems highly unlikely that the foreign born accounted for more than one-third of the anti-Maine Law vote. The Maine Law controversy clearly cut across such ethnic lines. [44]

Thus the defeat of the Maine Law cannot be blamed simply on the intemperance of immigrants. Drinking among immigrants was only the most visible element of resistance. To account for the failure of prohibition, we must consider the legal challenges, the resistance of both native-born and immigrant drinkers, the opposition of liquor sellers, and the inherent difficulties which followed from the inadequacy of the agencies of law enforcement. Of these factors, the opposition of native-born drinkers was probably the most crucial; if the prohibitionists had succeeded in turning the entire native-born population against the drinking of immigrant minorities, the Maine Law would have been sustained politically much more than it was. Instead by 1855 the opposition of both immigrant and native-born workers had greatly tarnished the appeal of the Maine Law. Prohibitionists had claimed that they had devised a workable answer to the social problems which accompanied rapid economic change in the 1840s and 1850s. Yet the Maine Law had clearly exacerbated social tensions and provoked widespread resistance, which had quite frequently erupted into violence. The political appeal of prohibition quickly evaporated as a consequence.

The Political Decline of Prohibition

The Republican party's treatment of the Maine Law issue illustrated the waning political power of prohibitionists. Although Free-Soilers and anti-Nebraska men had been strong supporters of the Maine Law before 1855, the fledgling Republican party, which emerged after 1855, tried to avoid prohibition because it had proved so controversial and divisive; it threatened the Republican strategy of building a winning coalition around the single issue of free soil.[45] In a number of states, Republicans refused to back the Maine Law agitation with promises of further legislative support to overcome the legal setbacks in the courts or to plug the loopholes which enforcement of the Maine Law revealed.

The Republican strategy varied from region to region, and from state to state, according to the local political situation. In the Midwest, the desire to woo immigrants away from the Democrats resulted in Republican state legislators' modifying the Maine Law in Iowa and Michigan to allow the sale of beer and wine. The quest of Wisconsin Republicans for German votes resulted in the total repudiation of the Maine Law by the party in that state.[46] In New England, the pattern was more complicated, for the supporters of prohibition there were more powerful both in the party and in the society than in Wisconsin. Under the resulting compromise, the state Republican organizations retained the Maine Law, but local city and county Republican officials did not enforce prohibition where immigrants or other groups opposed to the law threatened political retaliation against the Republican party, "especially in some of the cities where there is a large foreign vote."[47] Henry Dutton, a prohibitionist and ex-governor of Connecticut, reported that the fear of naturalized voters "paralyzed the efforts of many of the staunch friends" of prohibition among the Republicans. "They have acted on the supposition that if it [the Maine Law] was rigidly enforced, it would bring the other party into power."[48]

The political demise of the prohibitionists was seen most clearly not in New England, where they retained some residual power within the Republican coalitions, but in New York. Despite the desperate entreaties of temperance men at the inaugural Republican state convention in 1855, the party majority in New York State refused to adopt a prohibitionist stance. In the following year, the party declined to renominate Myron Clark as the Republican candidate for governor of the state in the fall election. Clark had signed into law the prohibitory measure which the New York Court of Appeals had later declared unconstitutional. The state temperance convention endorsed Clark for governor in 1856, and John Marsh attended the state Republican convention to lobby for Maine Law candidates. But Republican party managers repudiated Clark and resisted the attempts of prohibitionists to insert a Maine Law plank in the party platform. The committee on resolutions at the Republican convention declared that "the sole issue with the people is the nonextension of slavery."[49] As Marsh recalled, "The slavery question was now the great question before the nation. Temperance men, for humanity's sake, must yield to that. Thousands of men, we were told, there were in the State, who would vote for an anti-slavery Governor, who would not vote for prohibition."[50]

Even though prohibitionists like Marsh were bitter about the Republican party strategy, they could do little to reverse the Republicans' refusal to support the Maine Law. Marsh threatened the Republicans with loss of prohibitionist support if the party continued to ignore the law; but no viable alternative to the party existed. A separate prohibitionist party could have been formed, but when Gerrit Smith ran for governor in 1858 as a prohibitionist and radical abolitionist, he drew only 6,000 votes away from the Republicans. Thereafter the prohibitionist threat of bolting with a hundred thousand votes became an empty and ludicrous boast. By 1858, the Maine Law had been reduced to political impotence in New York State.[51]

Because the Republican party played down the prohibition issue after 1855, there has arisen the myth, encouraged by John Marsh and by later prohibitionist historians such as D. Leigh Colvin, that the Republican party had betrayed the prohibitionist cause in the interests of antislavery.[52] Certainly it is true that much of the popular electoral enthusiasm which prohibition had mustered in the North was now directed against the South. Given the Free-Soil sympathies of most prohibitionists and the growing sectional crisis after 1856, this transfer of reform enthusiasms from an antidrink to an anti-southern crusade is not surprising.

One important point must, however, be made. Prohibition was not swept aside by the larger issue of slavery. The demise of prohibition in New York as elsewhere after 1855 revealed the loss of public support for the extreme prohibitionist stance. The Republicans could ignore the threats of prohibitionist leaders like Marsh only because of declining public confidence that the Maine Law offered a panacea for America's social ills. After 1855, even some former partisans of the Maine Law no longer had confidence in the law as a viable solution to the problem of intemperance. The famed temperance lecturer, John B. Gough, reported that the Maine Law was "a dead letter everywhere" and claimed that "more liquor was sold than ever I knew before in Massachusetts, and in other states it is almost as bad."[53] While never repudiating the principle of prohibition entirely, Gough, Delavan, and other former Maine Law supporters urged renewed emphasis on moral suasion campaigns.

Although the Maine Law crusade had clearly disintegrated by the time Gough announced its demise in 1857, prohibition and temperance activity did not abruptly cease. Temperance societies continued to press for the enforcement of existing prohibitory laws and licensing laws restricting the supply of liquor. Prohibitionists in New York, for example, turned from the Maine Law to the issue of enforcing Sunday closing laws in New York City in 1859.[54] More important still was the movement of prohibitionists into agitation for changes to the institutional structures within which prohibitionists had to operate. Temperance reformers who had participated in the Maine Law agitation learned an important lesson from their failures in enforcing prohibitory laws. After the mid-1850s, their energies turned toward cleaning up city politics, rationalizing city administrations, and curbing ethnic influences in politics.[55]

Though these impulses have been well documented for postbellum reform, what is less widely known is the extent to which the drives to rationalize and reform the structure of urban government had its origins in the turbulent social conflicts of the Maine Law era. The dynamics of agitation can best be demonstrated by looking at the case of police reform. We have already seen that enforcement of the Maine Law suffered at the hands of law enforcement authorities, which were at times both uncooperative and inefficient. Only a few of the biggest cities had the rudiments of a professional police force, and the city administrations in these areas proved hostile to the Maine Law. The result was to spur prohibitionists to seek changes in the state laws governing police administration. In New York, the state Republican party took control of the New York City police force away from the Democratic city administration and placed it under state control in Albany. The poor performance of the Democratic administration in enforcing the Maine Law was one of several factors prompting upstate Republicans to make this change. Thereafter the new metropolitan police force began to enforce the Sunday closing law in a vigorous campaign, which led to violent clashes between the police and mobs of Germans and Irish.[56] There was a similar trend to state control in a number of other states between the late 1850s and the 1870s; cities affected included Jersey City, Cleveland, and Detroit. In Massachusetts, prohibitionist forces succeeded in getting a state constabulary established in 1865, and this new police force under state control made 1866 and 1867 "the high point of the attempt to enforce prohibition in Massachusetts."[57]

The increasing concern of prohibitionists with structural and institutional change was also demonstrated in the moves underway in the latter part of the 1850s to professionalize firefighting services in the larger cities. The old volunteer companies were a source of much intemperance (and political corruption). Intemperance characterized firefighting in part because of the nature of the work, partly because of the character of the firefighters themselves. Hard-drinking lower-class youths, both immigrant and native born, dominated most of the fire companies of the 1840s and 1850s, and they turned firefighting into a participant sport, which involved the free use of alcohol and pitched battles between rival companies. Thus antebellum firefighting was enormously inefficient, and both moralists and insurance companies condemned the volunteer system. Moses Grant, the Boston temperance reformer, had received only abuse from the volunteers when he attempted to pass out cakes and coffee at Boston blazes in the 1840s. Such actions, however, won the hearty support of insurance companies, which lost millions of dollars on account of the inefficiency of firefighting. Thus arose the strong impulse to professionalize the service in such cities as Cincinnati, Ohio, New York City, and Lynn, Massachusetts.[58]

Because these changes proceeded beyond the Civil War, it is not necessary to pursue further the growing commitment to clean and efficient government. It is simply necessary to observe the origins of this more institutional and structural approach to reform in the pre-Civil War period. Indeed the Maine Law marked the beginnings of this search. While the prohibitory laws of the 1850s marked the climax of the highly moralistic and perfectionist aspirations of antebellum temperance reformers, the Maine Law also revealed a growing appreciation that vice could not be eliminated through simple moral or legalistic solutions. Intricate institutional arrangements would be necessary if intemperance were to be removed. There was a trend for Maine Law men to emphasize the immediately restrictive aspects of the prohibitory system rather than the ultimate anticipated redemption of the land from the misery of intemperance. The Maine Law in fact marked the shift of the antebellum mind from what John Higham has called a spirit of "boundlessness" to one of "consolidation." The search for more effective Maine Laws, with ever more intricate legal and institutional restrictions on the trade, and the growing involvement of temperance and like-minded reformers in police administration and other aspects of the reform of city governments, reveal the emergence of this new cast of mind among the men and women who had launched the campaigns for prohibition in the 1840s. It was not so much that temperance reform had ceased to be of political and social significance. Rather many prohibitionists assumed that more complex institutional restraints and a more professional approach to enforcement would have to accompany another drive toward state and ultimately national prohibition.

Notes

1. *Fisher* v. *McGirr*, 1 Gray 2, 38 (Mass. Reports, 1854); Frederick R. Johnson and Ruth R. Kessler, "The Liquor License System—Its Origins and

Constitutional Development," pt. 2, *New York University Law Quarterly Review* 15 (April 1938): 380-81.

2. Floyd B. Streeter, "History of Prohibition Legislation in Michigan," *Michigan History* 2 (April 1918): 296-97. The split decision sent the case back to the Wayne County Circuit Court for disposition, where Justice Douglas had only to affirm his original ruling in favor of the unconstitutionality of the prohibitory law.

3. Johnson and Kessler, "Liquor License System," p. 381; *Report of the Executive Committee of the American Temperance Union, 1856* (New York: American Temperance Union, 1856), pp. 5, 19-26; John Marsh, *Temperance Recollections* (New York: Charles Scribner, 1866), pp. 291-92.

4. "Minutes of Temperance Committee," Massachusetts State Committee, B. W. Williams, Secretary, *JATU* 21 (September 1857): 141.

5. *State v. Brennan's Liquors*, 25 Conn. Reports (1856), 278-89; *Lincoln v. Smith and others*, 27 Vermont Reports, 328; *Beebe v. State*, 6 Indiana Reports (1856), 510-56; Johnson and Kessler, "Liquor License System," pp. 384-85.

6. Emma Lou Thornborough, *Indiana in the Civil War Era, 1850-1880* (Indianapolis: Indiana Historical Bureau, 1965), p. 69; *Beebe v. State*, 510-18; Lawrence M. Friedman, *A History of American Law* (New York: Simon and Schuster, 1973), p. 314.

7. A. Farewell and G. P. Ure, *The Maine Law Illustrated: Being the Result of an Investigation Made in the Maine Law States* (Toronto: Canadian Prohibitory Liquor Law League, 1855), pp. 28, 32, 60, 65, 83; editorial, *New York Times*, 2 May 1855; Roger Lane, *Policing the City, Boston, 1822-1885* (Cambridge: Harvard University Press, 1967), p. 89; Theodore D. Bacon, *Leonard Bacon: A Statesman in the Church* (New Haven: Yale University Press, 1931), p. 505; Henry Dutton to J. B. Gough, 27 June 1857, *JATU* 21 (September 1857): 142.

8. John C. Burnham, "New Perspectives on the Prohibition 'Experiment' of the 1920's," *Journal of Social History* 2 (Fall 1968): 51-68.

9. Wilbur R. Willer, *Cops and Bobbies: Police Authority in New York and London, 1830-1870* (Chicago: University of Chicago Press, 1977), p. 30.

10. The Carson League was named for its founder, Thomas L. Carson of Syracuse, New York. See Ernest H. Cherrington, *The Evolution of Prohibition in the United States of America* (Westerville, Ohio: American Issue Press, 1920), p. 148; Henry S. Clubb, *The Maine Liquor Law: Its Origin, History, and Results* (New York: Fowler and Wells, 1856), p. 255; George F. Clark, *History of the Temperance Reform in Massachusetts* (Boston: Clark and Carruth, 1888), pp. 83-85; *The Carson League Unveiled . . .* (New

York: n.p., 1855); *Portland* (Me.) *Temperance Watchman*, 9, 16 April 1853; *Massachusetts Cataract*, 8, 22 July 1852; John Fitzgibbon, "King Alcohol: His Rise, Reign and Fall in Michigan," *Michigan History* 2 (October 1918): 749.

11. *JATU* 21 (September 1857): 137-38. There is an excellent summary of the mode of operation of the Carson League, and further evidence of the hostility it raised, in Clubb, *Maine Liquor Law*, p. 251.

12. *New York Times*, 30 January 1855; *Worcester Massachusetts Spy*, 14 August, 13 September 1852.

13. *Massachusetts Cataract*, 23 September 1852.

14. Frank L. Byrne, *Prophet of Prohibition: Neal Dow and His Crusade* (Madison: Wisconsin State Historical Society, 1959), pp. 61-67, fully describes the incident. See also Neal Dow, *The Reminiscences of Neal Dow: Recollections of Eighty Years* (Portland, Me.: Evening Express Publishing Company, 1898), pp. 531-35.

15. *Report of the Executive Committee of the American Temperance Union, 1856*, p. 7; E. C. Delavan to J. H. Cocke, 12 October 1855, Cocke Papers, UV; *New York Daily Tribune*, 31 October 1855; *New York Times*, 5 June 1855; *Boston Investigator*, 13 June 1855.

16. *New York Times*, 26 April 1855; *Standard Encyclopedia of the Alcohol Problem* (Westerville, Ohio: American Issue Publishing Company, 1925-1930), 2:570.

17. D. Leigh Colvin, *Prohibition in the United States: A History of the Prohibition Party and of the Prohibition Movement* (New York: George H. Doran, 1926), pp. 55-56, 62; *New York Daily Tribune*, 1, 3 November 1855; Thomas C. Cochran, *The Pabst Brewing Company: The History of an American Business* (New York: New York University Press, 1949), p. 39; editorial, *New York Times*, 2 May 1855.

18. Lane, *Policing the City*, pp. 111-13; *Massachusetts Cataract*, 23 September 1852; report of the Worcester City Marshall, 30 September 1852, *Massachusetts Cataract*, 28 October 1852; *Worcester Daily Spy*, 18 June, 10 July 1850; *Norfolk* (Dedham, Mass.) *Democrat*, 13 February 1858; Farewell and Ure, *Maine Law Illustrated*, pp. 11-84; Oscar Handlin, *Boston's Immigrants: A Study in Acculturation*, 2d ed. (Cambridge: Harvard University Press, 1959), pp. 123, 198-200.

19. Robert Ernst, *Immigrant Life in New York City, 1825-1863* (New York: King's Crown Press, 1949), p. 216.

20. Oscar Handlin, *Boston's Immigrants*, p. 240; Phillip Taylor, *The Distant Magnet: European Emigration to the U.S.A.* (New York: Harper and Row, 1971), p. 174; Ernst, *Immigrant Life in New York City*, p. 69. In New York, only 7 percent of all immigrants (men and women) were in white-

collar (professional or clerical) occupations; 14 percent were laborers and 22 percent servants and laundresses.

21. Horace Greeley, *New York Daily Tribune*, 11 February 1842.

22. *New York Workingman's Advocate*, 14 September 1844.

23. J. B. D. De Bow, *Statistical View of the United States, . . . Being a Compendium of the Seventh Census . . .* (Washington, D.C.: A. O. P. Nicholson, 1854), p. 57; see also Frederich Kapp, *Immigration, and the Commissioners of Emigration of the State of New York* (New York: Nation Press, 1870), p. 228.

24. William Sanger, *The History of Prostitution . . .* (New York: Harper, 1858), pp. 460, 558-65; *Letters of the Rev. John Chambers . . .* (Philadelphia: Henry B. Ashmead, 1856), p. 25.

25. Bishop Bayley, in Joseph M. Flynn, *The Catholic Church in New Jersey* (New York: Publisher's Printing Company, 1904), pp. 283-84. There is no adequate history of the Father Mathew movement or of subsequent Catholic temperance organizations. However, see Joan Bland, *Hibernian Crusade: The Story of the Catholic Total Abstinence Union of America* (Washington, D.C.: Catholic University of America Press, 1951), and John F. Maguire, *Father Mathew: A Biography* (London: Longmans, Green, 1865).

26. *Truth Teller*, 24 January 1857, quoted in W. J. Rorabaugh, "Rising Democratic Spirits: Immigrants, Temperance, and Tammany Hall, 1854-1860," *Civil War History* 22 (June 1976): 148.

27. John F. Maguire, *The Irish in America* (London: Longmans, Green, 1868), p. 286; Dennis Clark, *The Irish in Philadelphia: Ten Generations of Urban Experience* (Philadelphia: Temple University Press, 1973), p. 115.

28. Farewell and Ure, *Maine Law Illustrated*, p. 79.

29. John F. Campbell, *History of the Friendly Sons of St. Patrick and of the Hibernian Society for the Relief of Emigrants from Ireland* (Philadelphia: Hibernian Society, 1892).

30. See *People* v. *Maurer*, *New York Times*, 18, 21 May 1858; see also Frederick W. Salem, *Beer: Its History and Its Economic Value as a National Beverage* (Hartford, CT: F. W. Salem, 1880), pp. 74-83, 178-84; Stanley Baron, *Brewed in America: A History of Beer and Ale in the United States* (Boston: Little, Brown, 1962).

31. *The German Petition to the Common Council of the City of Newark; Demanding the Virtual Repeal of Those Laws which Forbid Sabbath Tippling and Sabbath Desecration: with the Reply of the Common Council, and an Introduction* (Newark, N.J.: Daily Mercury Office, 1853), pp. 5-6.

32. Joseph Schafer, "Prohibition in Early Wisconsin," *Wisconsin Magazine of History* 8 (March 1925): 295; Frank L. Byrne, "Maine Law Versus Lager Beer: A Dilemma of Wisconsin's Young Republican Party," *Wiscon-*

sin Magazine of History 42 (Winter 1958): 115-19; Streeter, "History of Prohibition Legislation in Michigan," pp. 297-98, notes similar German opposition to prohibition in Michigan.

33. Baron, *Brewed in America*, p. 211; Kathleen Neils Conzen, *Immigrant Milwaukee, 1836-1860: Accommodation and Community in a Frontier City* (Cambridge: Harvard University Press, 1976), pp. 105, 109. The 1850s also saw the establishment of a major brewing industry in Cincinnati with the introduction of lager beer by German brewers. See William L. Downard, *The Cincinnati Brewing Industry: A Social and Economic History* (Athens: Ohio University Press, 1973), pp. 15-20.

34. *New York Organ*, 14 December 1850; Conzen, *Immigrant Milwaukee*, pp. 157-58.

35. *Eighth Annual Report of the New-York City Temperance Society . . .* (New York: D. Fanshaw, 1837), pp. 25, 45-46; *Thirteenth Annual Report of the New-York City Temperance Society*, in minutes of the New-York City Temperance Society, 27 May 1842, p. 274, NYPL; *JATU* 12 (April 1848): 57, and 13 (August 1849): 116; Paul Kleppner, *The Cross of Culture: A Social Analysis of Midwestern Politics, 1850-1900* (New York: Free Press, 1969), pp. 69-91; Ronald P. Formisano, *The Birth of Mass Political Parties: Michigan, 1827-1861* (Princeton, N.J.: Princeton University Press, 1971), pp. 182-85; Richard Jensen, *The Winning of the Midwest: Social and Political Conflict, 1888-1896* (Chicago: University of Chicago Press, 1971), pp. 68-69.

36. *The Seventh Census: Report of the Superintendent of the Census, for December 1, 1852; to Which Is Appended the Report for December 1, 1851* (Washington, D.C.: Robert Armstrong, 1853), p. 75; Daniel Dorchester, *The Liquor Problem in All Ages* (New York: Phillips and Hunt, 1884), p. 315; Joseph C. G. Kennedy, *Preliminary Report on the Eighth Census, 1860* (Washington, D.C.: Government Printing Office, 1862), pp. 178-79.

37. *New York Organ*, 14, 21 December 1850; Farewell and Ure, *Maine Law Illustrated*, pp. 14, 49.

38. *New York Organ*, 26 January 1850. For similar statistics concerning Philadelphia in a later period, see Dorchester, *Liquor Problem in All Ages*, p. 401; and for Boston, see Handlin, *Boston's Immigrants*, p. 123.

39. Farewell and Ure, *Maine Law Illustrated*, pp. 14, 49, 83; *New York Organ*, 7 June 1851; J. Henry Clark, *The Present Position and Claims of the Temperance Enterprise* (New York: Baker and Scribner, 1847), pp. 8, 14.

40. Schafer, "Prohibition in Early Wisconsin," pp. 290-99.

41. See Bruce Laurie, " 'Nothing on Compulsion': Life Styles of Philadelphia Artisans, 1820-1850," *Labor History* 15 (Summer 1974): 364.

42. *Worcester Daily Spy*, 26 September 1850.

43. De Bow, *Statistical View of the United States*, p. 61.

44. Dow, *Reminiscences*, pp. 434-35, 442.

45. On the Republican strategy of building a successful coalition around the free soil issue, see Eric Foner, *Free Soil, Free Labor, Free Men: The Ideology of the Republican Party before the Civil War* (New York: Oxford University Press, 1970), pp. 241-42.

46. Jensen, *Winning of the Midwest*, p. 91; Foner, *Free Soil, Free Labor, Free Men*, pp. 241-42; Fitzgibbon, "King Alcohol," pp. 748-49; Byrne, "Maine Law Versus Lager Beer," pp. 115-19.

47. Henry Dutton to John B. Gough, 27 June 1857, *JATU* 21 (September 1857): 142; L. D. Sawyer (prosecuting attorney for Carroll County, New Hampshire) to John B. Gough, 4 June 1857, *JATU* 21 (September 1857): 142; Charles Jewett, *A Forty Years' Fight with the Drink Demon, or a History of the Temperance Reform as I Have Seen It, and of My Labors in Connection Therewith* (New York: National Temperance Society, 1872), p. 299.

48. Dutton to Gough, 27 June 1857, *JATU* 21 (September 1857): 142.

49. *New York Times*, 28 September 1855; *New York Daily Tribune*, 19 September 1856.

50. Marsh, *Temperance Recollections*, p. 297; *JATU* 20 (August 1856): 138, and (November 1856): 168; *New York Daily Tribune*, 18, 19 September 1856.

51. E. C. Delavan to Gerrit Smith, 14 February 1859, box 11, Gerrit Smith Miller Collection, SU; Gerrit Smith open letter, 10 October 1858, Smith Family Papers, NYPL; *New York Daily Tribune*, 4 October 1858.

52. Colvin, *Prohibition in the United States*, pp. 46-47.

53. Gough's letter on the Maine Law, 27 March 1857, *JATU* 21 (September 1857): 140; E. C. Delavan to Gerrit Smith, 14 February 1859, box 11, Gerrit Smith Miller Collection; *New York Congregationalist* and *New York Independent*, quoted in *JATU* 21 (October 1857): 152, and 22 (February 1858): 17.

54. *The Sunday Liquor Traffic* (New York: John A. Gray, 1859), pp. 2-5.

55. See, for example, Samuel P. Hays, "The Politics of Reform in Municipal Government in the Progressive Era," *Pacific Northwest Quarterly* 55 (October 1964): 157-69; Robert H. Wiebe, *The Search for Order, 1877-1920* (New York: Hill and Wang, 1967).

56. James F. Richardson, *The New York Police: Colonial Times to 1901* (New York: Oxford University Press, 1970), pp. 92-93, 98, 108-20.

57. Robert M. Fogelson, *Big-City Police* (Cambridge: Harvard University Press, 1977), p. 14; Lane, *Policing the City*, pp. 136-38.

58. *Norfolk Democrat*, 21 April 1843; *History of Cincinnati, Ohio, with Illustrations and Biographical Sketches* (Cleveland: L. A. Williams, 1881),

p. 387; Lowell M. Limpus, *History of the New York Fire Department* (New York: E. P. Dutton, 1940), pp. 187, 241; Alan Dawley, *Class and Community: The Industrial Revolution in Lynn* (Cambridge: Harvard University Press, 1976), pp. 111-12. See also Richard B. Calhoun, "New York City Fire Department Reorganization, 1865-1870: A Civil War Legacy," *New-York Historical Society Quarterly* 60 (January-April 1976): 7-34; and Bruce Laurie, "Fire Companies and Gangs in Southwark: The 1840s," in Allen F. Davis and Mark H. Haller, eds., *The Peoples of Philadelphia: A History of Ethnic Groups and Lower-Class Life, 1790-1940* (Philadelphia: Temple University Press, 1973), pp. 71-88.

CONCLUSION

The collapse of the Maine Law agitation brought to an end a decade of political and cultural turmoil over the drink question. After
1860, the number of Maine Law states rapidly declined, and by
the late 1870s only Vermont, Maine, and New Hampshire remained
dry. Not until the early twentieth century did prohibition regain its
antebellum importance. When prohibitionist sentiment did revive as
a national force, the center of agitation had shifted from the Northeast to the South and West.

The fall in liquor consumption which marked the first forty years
of temperance agitation did not survive the 1850s. Much to the
dismay of temperance reformers, liquor consumption rose steadily
after the Civil War. The only encouragement which reformers could
find in the changing patterns of liquor consumption was the relative
unpopularity of spirit drinking. Hard liquor did not regain the pre-
eminent place in the affections of American drinkers which it had
held in 1810. A survey taken in 1890 showed that the per-capita consumption of distilled spirits was less than one-quarter of the figure
recorded in 1810. In contrast, the consumption of beer rose more
than twelve times over the same period.[1]

The decline in the consumption of spirits was not necessarily the
result of temperance agitation. Rising prices for spirits relative to

beer and the scarcity of spirits as per capita production fell affected the drinking of hard liquor adversely from the 1850s through the end of the century. These changes in the production and price of spirits had their origins in the transformation of agriculture before the Civil War. The price for spirits relative to the price for cereals fell between 1810 and 1860, thus making it more profitable for farmers to send their grain to wider markets rather than distill it. Behind this trend in prices lay the beginnings of urbanization. Though the level of urbanization was much lower than it would later become (just under 20 percent in 1860), the period from 1840 to 1860 produced the fastest spurt of urban growth in the nation's history. Then, especially after the Civil War, came the opening up of European grain markets, though these took up to 30 percent of the Midwest's exportable surplus even in the 1850s. From these emerging urban and overseas markets came the increased demand for grain and meat which farmers, particularly in the Midwest, began to exploit. At the same time, the transportation revolution from the 1820s to the 1860s, with the building first of canals and then railroads, enabled farmers to send more of their abundant supplies of grain to market in their original form. This change can be observed not only in the declining per-capita production of liquor but also in the declining numbers of farm-based distilleries from the 1820s to the 1850s, which in the case of Pennsylvania and New York were decimated over that period.[2]

Although teetotalism and prohibition reached a low ebb in the immediate postwar period, the temperance movement had profoundly influenced American values. Reform helped to popularize the idea of self-improvement and strengthened the bourgeois ethic of frugality, sobriety, and industry in American society. Until the 1830s, Americans saw no necessary link between temperance, respectability, and self-improvement; as a result of temperance agitation, middle-class culture and all who aspired to middle-class status would be deeply influenced by the temperance ethic for decades to come.

In politics as in popular culture, the influence of temperance reformers did not evaporate with the collapse of the Maine Law. Although prohibition had failed as a statewide movement, it nevertheless retained strong support at the local level after the Civil War and continued as a powerful force in local politics. Richard Jensen makes clear that in the Midwest, many Protestant, native-born Americans supported prohibition throughout the second half of the nineteenth century.[3] Local option provisions, which replaced prohibition in many American states, allowed the maintenance of prohibition at the local level wherever popular sentiment favored it. Some rural localities in New England, for example, remained as dry after the Civil War as they had been at the height of the Maine Law agitation.[4] The persistence of prohibition on the local level suggests that there was much more continuity in prohibitionist activity between the 1850s and the postwar decades than a survey of state legislation would indicate.

The social base of this residual prohibitionist sentiment lay among similar groups to those which had shaped the antebellum crusades. The same entrepreneurial groups so important in the inception of temperance agitation could be found supporting prohibition in subsequent campaigns. Of nearly 7,000 employers who answered a Department of Labor inquiry concerning liquor in 1897, more than three-quarters expressed concern over the drinking habits of their employees. As John C. Burnham points out, many American businessmen during the Progressive era believed that "a sober, temperate worker was a more productive, a more stable, and a happier worker."[5] Allied with these industrial entrepreneurs were the small-town and urban middle-class people, particularly professionals, small businessmen, and women, all of whom displayed an increasing concern with intemperance among the working classes.

Another vital (and related) legacy of antebellum temperance was the continuing identification of the mainstream evangelical denominations—the Baptists, Methodists, Presbyterians, and Congregationalists—with temperance. From this residual base of evangelical support the later movements for state and national constitutional prohibition drew their leadership and financial backing. The Women's Christian Temperance Union, founded in Ohio in 1874, owed its inception to the evangelical fervor of midwestern Protestant women; the Anti-Saloon League, founded in 1893 as a pressure group for prohibition, was closely linked with the evangelical churches in its leadership and support. From the Anti-Saloon League came the renewed and successful drive for national prohibition in the second decade of the twentieth century.

Yet perhaps the greatest legacy of antebellum prohibition was not the persistence of evangelical support but the survival of the conviction that legal action could quash drinking. As prohibitionists perceived it, the Maine Law had come close to triumph. Only inadequate law enforcement and the betrayal of the cause by the Republican party had cheated them of their just victory.[6] Despite the political and legal reverses which the Maine Law suffered after 1855, Americans would have to wait more than seventy years before the prohibitionist movement had run its full course.

Since the demise of national prohibition in 1933, the temperance movement has receded into the memory of Americans as an irrational and bigoted attempt to impose a dubious morality on society. If historians have taken the temperance cause seriously at all, they have found in it a deeply conservative response to the social disorder of Jacksonian society. While it is true that the social problems of Jacksonian America gravely disturbed temperance men and women, they were not conservatives or reactionaries. The goals of teetotalism and prohibition were novel solutions to nineteenth-century social problems. The sponsors of these goals were in fact seeking a radical change in both law and custom, and they were prepared to disrupt the social order to achieve their ends. These reformers were not the status-conscious conservatives of so much historical writing.[7] They did not seek to restore the power of a Federalist-Congregationalist elite. The conservative impulse dominated only the abortive attempt to organize a temperance movement in Massachusetts during the second decade of the nineteenth century. The temperance reformers of the 1820s and 1830s were not fearful of the future. They were excited by the economic progress and vast potential of the United States. Because the nation's character was still being forged, temperance reformers believed that they had a unique opportunity to shape the future. By vigorous efforts, they could create a sober society, which would serve as an example to the world of the virtues of republican government.

Although the crusade for sobriety in the 1820s was sponsored by deeply religious men who found in temperance a satisfying outlet for their moral fervor, these evangelical reformers were not anxious defenders of a religious status quo. Success in religious endeavors rather than failure prompted the reform campaigns of the 1820s. The success of religious revivalism in the early nineteenth century spurred the creation of moral reform societies dedicated to abstinence and provided organizational techniques, which were expected to reap harvests of converts for temperance, just as itinerant preachers had done for the evangelical churches.

If the initial impetus to temperance reform came from religious men, the temperance crusade from its earliest days was concerned above all with the solution of social problems made more urgent by the pace and direction of change. The temperance movement was deeply bound up with the economic transformation of the antebellum Northeast and received its strongest support in the 1830s from the very men who were promoting both industrialization and the commercialization of agriculture. The temperance crusades of the 1820s and 1830s were shaped and directed by an alliance of evangelicals, middle-class, upwardly mobile entrepreneurs, and professionals, all of whom hoped to perpetuate material and moral progress both for themselves and for American society through total abstinence. Their diagnosis of social ills was deeply influenced by their own experience and social backgrounds. Their own formula for success was individual restraint so they prescribed large doses of frugality, industry, and sobriety for society at large. While it was shortsighted for these reformers to attribute almost every social ill to the moral weakness of individuals, reformers lived in a world which increasingly placed responsibility for success on the individual and explained failure in terms of moral defects. The call for sobriety was a logical and plausible answer to the social problems which agitated antebellum temperance reformers.

The history of temperance reform is in large part the story of the attempts of these groups to convert the American republic to their vision of sobriety. Given the extent of drinking in 1810 and the economic and social interests tied up with the liquor business, it is perhaps not remarkable that the temperance crusade was only partially successful. Americans did as a whole drink less in 1860 than they had in 1810, millions of Americans had signed the pledge, and the prohibitionists had won a wide variety of legal successes in the 1840s and early 1850s.

Yet a number of groups remained opposed to the temperance

movement entirely, while still others advocated moral suasion but would not support the Maine Law. The South remained largely unconverted; as the case of Salisbury, North Carolina, suggests, a social structure very different from the North, the lucrative trade in corn whiskey in southern farming communities, and the absence of the urban, industrial middle class, which supplied the backbone of northern temperance support, all served to stymie the temperance crusade in the South.

Next to southern opposition, the most visible opponents of the temperance crusade were the German and Irish immigrants who came to the United States in increasing numbers after 1845. The demographic and occupational structure of the immigrant populations served to retard the temperance cause among these groups. By the 1850s, the opposition of immigrants began to frustrate prohibitionists so profoundly that the Maine Law crusade became closely allied with the nativist movement in a bid for political power and social control; yet the prohibition issue cut across the native-foreign division to the extent that many native-born working-class people opposed the Maine Law. Prohibition divided the community along lines of property and class. The fact was that the new immigrant groups mostly filled the lowest occupational strata; they were disproportionately represented in unskilled and semiskilled jobs, and people who had such jobs, whether they were immigrants or native-born workers, tended to drink on the job and frequent taverns in their spare time for reasons related to the character of their employment and their social situation. In addition, the increasing importance of immigrants in the liquor business—a reflection in part of the declining status of the trade brought about by two decades of temperance agitation among the respectable native-born classes—created additional resistance among immigrant groups to prohibition.

The undeniable fact that many Americans failed to support the Maine Law and ultimately voted prohibition off the statute books in most of the northern states during and after the Civil War does not mean that these same people were uniformly hostile to temperance. Even among the Irish, the Father Mathew societies in the early 1850s had demonstrated the broad appeal of temperance as a moral reform, though it was not until after the Civil War that Irish-Catholic temperance emerged as a major, organized force through the formation of a National Union of Catholic Total Abstinence Societies in Baltimore in 1872. Yet though Irish Catholics displayed considerable concern over the incidence of intemperance in their own communities, their movement remained quite distinct from mainstream, evangelical temperance, and, more important, few Catholics supported prohibition, particularly in the decades before the Civil War.[8]

Similarly within the native-born artisan classes were many who accepted the temperance ethic of self-discipline through sobriety but were either indifferent or hostile to prohibition. Though the middle-class temperance movement did find allies within artisan temperance, it did so mainly among those who embraced middle-class values and aspired to self-improvement. The 1840s saw the failure of mainstream temperance to build a stable and effective alliance with working-class temperance. In response to middle-class efforts to control the Washingtonians and to turn the attention of the reformed men away from moral suasion to coercion, the Washingtonian temperance movement shattered into numerous competing societies, which reflected not merely personal rivalries and tactical disputes but fundamental contests about the meaning and direction of temperance reform.

In the short run, the failure of temperance regulars to convert so many groups to the banner of prohibition did not matter. Clearly by the 1840s the prohibitionists had superior organizational skills to those of the liquor interests, considerable financial resources, and very vocal support. They included in their ranks men of influence and prestige, and they were able in addition to exploit the energies of middle-class women, who by the 1850s increasingly dominated the petitioning drives of the temperance societies. The fact that these articulate and well-organized reformers did not command solid majority support among voting males did not deter them; local successes encouraged larger, statewide action, and experience with the failure of the license laws pointed toward stringent statewide prohibition as the ultimate and logical solution. The degree of success which prohibitionists achieved before 1850 was a tribute to the importance of the process of agitation and an example of the power which well-organized groups could exert in a liberal-democratic political system. By 1850, prohibitionists had the organizations and the coherent solution with which to exploit social tensions produced by industrialization and immigration. From this conjunction of circumstances came the Maine Law alliance of property and respectability against the paupers and criminals of the lower classes.

Winning prohibition was much easier than maintaining it. Many who would not normally vote until their right to drink had been successfully challenged came to the polls in droves to vote against prohibition (and they resisted in many other ways). Though prohibitionists expected to retain broad popular support long enough to reshape community morality, prohibition's popular appeal quickly evaporated after 1855. Like all other panaceas, the Maine Law was bound to deliver less than it promised, but in addition, the cultural and political conflict created served to undermine the claims of prohibition as a solution to social chaos. The newly formed Republican party, anxious to build a national coalition around the free-soil issue, shunned the prohibitionist cause. Disillusioned, and drained of financial support by the long battles to pass and enforce the Maine Law, the prohibitionists retreated. By 1860 their dream of a sober republic achieved through legal action was in ruins. Nonetheless the impact of antebellum temperance on American politics and society would continue to be felt for generations.

Notes

1. Figures for 1885-1889 indicate that per-capita consumption of spirits was 1.05 gallons compared with 4.5 gallons in 1810. In contrast, consumption of fermented liquors jumped from one to 12.5 gallons. *The Cyclopedia of Temperance and Prohibition* (New York: Funk and Wagnalls, 1891), p. 129; Joseph Rowntree, *The Temperance Problem and Social Reform*, 7th ed. (London: Hodder and Staughton, 1900), p. 609.

2. Based on Dorothy S. Brady, "Price Deflators for Final Product Estimates," in *Output, Employment, and Productivity in the United States after 1800*, Studies in Income and Wealth, vol. 30 (New York: National Bureau of Economic Research, 1966), p. 106; George Rogers Taylor, "The National Economy Before and After the Civil War," in David T. Gilchrist and W. David Lewis, eds., *Economic Change in the Civil War Era* (Greenville, Del.:

Eleutherian Mills-Hagley Foundation, 1965), pp. 2, 8, 11-13; Cyrus Haldeman, *A Few Reasons Why a "Maine Liquor Law" Should Not Be Passed in the State of Pennsylvania* . . . (Lancaster, Pa.: n.p., 1852), pp. 10-12. On changes in communications, see George Rogers Taylor, *The Transportation Revolution, 1815-1860* (New York: Holt, Rinehart and Winston, 1951).

3. Richard Jensen, *The Winning of the Midwest: Social and Political Conflict, 1888-1896* (Chicago: University of Chicago Press, 1971), pp. 89-121; Paul Kleppner, *The Cross of Culture: A Social Analysis of Midwestern Politics, 1850-1900* (New York: Free Press, 1969), p. 112.

4. Rowntree, *Temperance Problem and Social Reform*, pp. 226, 253.

5. John Koren, *Economic Aspects of the Liquor Problem* (Boston: Houghton Mifflin, 1899), pp. 37-38; John C. Burnham, "New Perspectives on the Prohibition 'Experiment' of the 1920's," *Journal of Social History* 2 (Fall 1968): 53-54. See also Norman H. Clark, *The Dry Years: Prohibition and Social Change in Washington* (Seattle: University of Washington Press, 1965), pp. 74, 121-22; James H. Timberlake, *Prohibition and the Progressive Movement, 1900-1920* (Cambridge: Harvard University Press, 1963); and Herbert Gutman, "Work, Culture, and Society in Industrializing America, 1815-1919," *American Historical Review* 78 (June 1973): 583.

6. D. Leigh Colvin, *Prohibition in the United States: A History of the Prohibition Party and of the Prohibition Movement* (New York: George H. Doran, 1926), pp. 46-47.

7. Cf. Clifford S. Griffin, *Their Brothers' Keepers: Moral Stewardship in the United States, 1800-1865* (New Brunswick, N.J.: Rutgers University Press, 1960), and Joseph Gusfield, *Symbolic Crusade: Status Politics and the American Temperance Movement* (Urbana: University of Illinois Press, 1963), pp. 39-44. For another reform movement, see David Donald, "Toward a Reconsideration of Abolitionists," in his *Lincoln Reconsidered: Essays on the Civil War Era* (New York: Alfred A. Knopf, 1956), pp. 19-36.

8. Joan Bland, *Hibernian Crusade: The Story of the Catholic Total Abstinence Union of America* (Washington, D.C.: Catholic University of America Press, 1951), chaps. 1, 2, and John F. Maguire, *Father Mathew: A Biography* (London: Longmans, Green, 1865).

APPENDIX

The following lists of names were used in compiling quantitative data presented in chapter 4.

Worcester Pro-license Sample (1835-38)

Drawn from the *Worcester National Aegis*, 3 October 1838, and the *Worcester Paladium*, 8 April 1835.

Alvan Allen
Edward Babbett
T. W. Bancroft
William Barker
E. L. Barnard
Lewis Barnard
Lewis Bigelow
Charles Blair
Francis Blake
Oliver H. Blood
David Bonney
Ebenezer H. Bowen

George Bowen
Moses T. Breck
Josiah Brittain
Silas T. Brooks
Luther Burnett
Simeon Burt
Benj. Butman
Charles T. Chamberlain
Lysander C. Clark
William C. Clark
William Coe
Edward Conant

Otis Corbett
Isaac S. Davis
Merrill Davis
E. F. Dixie
Levi A. Dowley
Nathan Elder
Elisha Flagg
Maturin L. Fisher
Gordon Gould
James Green
John Green
John Hammond
Jubal Harrington
Daniel Heywood
Edwin Howe
Aaron Howes
William Jennison
George Jones
Timothy Keith
John Kendall
Daniel W. Lincoln
John W. Lincoln
Joseph Lovell
Asa Mathews
Francis T. Merrick
Pliny Merrick
Ephraim Mower

Caleb Newton
Guy S. Newton
Rejoice Newton
Charles Paine
Henry Paine
Ivers Phillips
M. D. Phillips
Leonard M. Poole
John Pratt
Joseph Pratt
William Pratt
Orrin Rawson
George T. Rice
George Richardson
Henry Rogers
J. B. Smith
Nathan Tead
Reuben Totman
Horatio Tower
George A. Trumbull
Joshua B. Tyler
Artemas Ward 2nd
Samuel Ward
William R. Weston
Isreal Whitney
Calvin Willard
James Worthington

Worcester No-License Sample (1835)

Drawn from the *Worcester Massachusetts Spy*, 8 April 1835.

Willington Aldrich
Jonas B. Allen
Silas Barber
Ira Barton
William Bickford
Abijah Bigelow

Walter Bigelow, Jr.
John Bixby
Elijah Brigham
Nathaniel Brooks
Thomas Chamberlain
George Chandler

Benj. N. Childs
Benj. K. Conant
George T. S. Curtis
Samuel Davis
Edward Earle
Benj. Flagg
Enoch Flagg
William F. Flagg
William B. Fox
Joshua Freeman
Paul Goodale
Benj. Goodard II
Daniel Harrington
Oliver Harrington
Samuel Harrington, Jr.
Jonas Hartshorn
Nathan Heard
Charles Hersey
Pliny Holbrook
Southwarth A. Howland
Abiel Jacques
George Johnson
John P. Kettell
John Moore

Jonathan Nelson
Nathan Nickerson
John Park
William W. Patch
Josiah G. Perry
Samuel Perry
Benj. Read
Eben. Read
Clement O. Read
Darius Rice
Sewell Rice
Thomas H. Rice
Benj. F. Smith
Francis Thaxter
Benj. F. Thomas
Marchant Tobey
David Wadsworth
Emory Washburn
Ichabod Washburn
James White
Jonas White
Jonathan A. White
Luther White
Martin Wilder

NOTE ON SOURCES

Since the chapter notes list full citations and extensive bibliographical information, this source guide concentrates on directing readers to the major areas of source materials.

Manuscript collections proved generally disappointing for the study of antebellum temperance. Many were rich in political history but very thin on social matters. Nevertheless some were useful, particularly for organizational and tactical questions. Especially valuable for these issues was the Gerrit Smith Miller Collection, George Arents Research Library, Syracuse University; included were many letters from Edward C. Delavan, John Marsh, Justin Edwards, and Gerrit Smith's own letterbooks. Equally important were the John Hartwell Cocke Papers, Alderman Library, University of Virginia; these center on the southern temperance movement, but because Cocke served for seven years as president of the American Temperance Union, there is extensive correspondence with northern temperance leaders. In the Simeon Gratz Autograph Collection at the Historical Society of Pennsylvania, the section on churchmen and clergymen included important letters from Justin Edwards on the organization and tactics of the American Temperance Society. At the Maine Historical Society, the Neal Dow Papers proved to be quite disappointing. What little material there was on the antebellum period revealed only the methodical and dull character of this important prohibitionist. The Massachusetts Historical Society's collections include many with references to the temperance movement. Most useful were the Horace Mann Papers and the Edward Everett Papers (both were enlightening on the connections between temperance and Massachusetts politics in the 1830s); the John Collins Warren Papers, on the medical profession and temperance; and the minute book of the Massachusetts Society for the Suppression of Intemperance, covering the period from 1813 to the 1920s. The Massachusetts State Archives contains Papers Relating to Laws of the Commonwealth of Massachusetts. Here I found petitions on the subjects of temperance and prohibition, draft bills, and reports of legislative committees on liquor legislation. The collection was especially useful for Massachusetts politics and temperance in the 1830s. At the New York Public Library, the Smith Family Papers include more letters of Gerrit Smith; and, on New York City's temperance movement, the minutes of the New-York City Temperance Society were indispensable, especially for the society's early opposition to teetotalism and its relations with the Washingtonians. The John B. Gough Papers at the American Antiquarian Society revealed the essential banality of Gough's mind.

Pamphlets

Much more helpful than manuscript sources were the collections of pamphlets, especially those held at the American Antiquarian Society, Worcester, Massachusetts; the Boston Public Library; the Widener and Houghton libraries of Harvard University; the Presbyterian Historical Society, Philadelphia; the Library of Congress; Duke University; and the New York Public Library, which houses the James Black Collection, the most important collection of published materials on temperance and prohibition.

Newspapers and Periodicals

Temperance newspapers abound, but very few maintained themselves for long periods of time. Only in exceptional cases could I find long runs. The *Journal of Humanity* (1829-1833), published at Andover, Massachusetts, expressed the policies of the American Temperance Society. The *Temperance Journal* (1834-1842), published in Boston, served for most of its existence as the organ of the Massachusetts Temperance Society and for a short while (from 1838 to 1842) as the organ of the Massachusetts Temperance Union. The *Journal of the American Temperance Union*, edited by John Marsh, ran from 1837 to 1865 and provided the most comprehensive official picture of the temperance crusade. There is a complete run at the New York Public Library. The *Temperance Recorder* (Albany, N.Y.), 1832-1836, echoed the views of Edward C. Delavan and the executive of the New York State Temperance Society. Other viewpoints within the temperance movement can be found in the *Genius of Temperance*, (1825-1833), a radical teetotal sheet edited by William Goodell and published in New York.

Among the Washingtonian papers, the most revealing were: the *New York Crystal Fount*, edited by James Aikman, 1842-1843, succeeded by the *Crystal Fount and Rechabite Recorder*, 1843-1847; the *New York Pearl*, 1846-1847; and the *Columbia* (Hudson, N.Y.) *Washingtonian*. For the Sons of Temperance, the almost complete file of the *New York Organ*, 1844-1851, at the New York Public Library, is indispensable. Also very helpful for radical and working-class temperance was the *Lynn* (Mass.) *Pioneer*, later the *Lynn Pioneer and Herald of Freedom*, 1845-1849. Essential for the Washingtonian movement in Worcester was the *Worcester County Cataract*, later the *Massachusetts Cataract*, 1843-1853.

Of the general papers, I used Horace Greeley's *New York Daily Tribune* extensively, along with the *New York Times* for the 1850s and the *Norfolk* (Dedham, Mass.) *Democrat*, a pro-temperance paper with much material on the Washingtonians, Democrats and temperance, and Free-Soil and temperance.

For the Worcester case study, the key newspaper sources are: the *Massachusetts Spy* (pro-temperance wing of the Whig party); the *Aegis* and *Palladium* (anti-temperance and pro-license Whigs); and the *Worcester Republican* (Democrats).

Among the religious papers I consulted, the following were the most helpful: *New York Evangelist* (New School Presbyterian), *New York Observer* (Old School Presbyterian), *Boston Recorder* (Orthodox Congregationalist); *Boston Christian Watchman* (Baptist); *New York Christian Advocate* and *Boston Zion's Herald* (Methodist).

Church Minutes

Also essential for the connections between religion and temperance were the published minutes of the General Conference of the Methodist Church, the minutes of the General Assembly of the Presbyterian Church, and the minutes of the Congregational Associations. For the Baptists, the absence of general conferences entailed reliance on histories of the Baptist church.

Temperance Reports

Indispensable were the reports of the *American Temperance Society*, the fourth to ninth reports being published as *Permanent Temperance Documents of the American Temperance Society* (Boston, 1835). *The Reports of the American Temperance Union* were equally valuable for the years 1837-1851; see also the *Reports of the Executive Committee of the American Temperance Union* for the 1850s in the New York Public Library. Sons of Temperance proceedings were voluminous and ubiquitous for the various local, state, and national divisions. See especially *Journals of the Proceedings of the National Division of the Sons of Temperance*. Also extensively used were the reports of the various state temperance societies, particularly the New York State Temperance Society, the Massachusetts Temperance Society, the Pennsylvania Society for Discouraging the Use of Ardent Spirits, the New-York City Temperance Society, and the Maine Temperance Society.

Biographical Data

There is a wealth of information in *Standard Encyclopedia of the Alcohol Problem*, 6 vols. (Westerville, Ohio, 1925-1930); in *The Cyclopedia of Temperance and Prohibition* (New York, 1891); and in the standard biographical sources, especially *Appleton's Cyclopedia of American Biography; National Cyclopedia of American Biography; Dictionary of American Biography; New England Historical and Geneological Register;* and *Who Was Who in America, Historical Volume, 1607-1896.* For religious temperance leaders, very useful is William B. Sprague, *Annals of the American Pulpit,* 9 vols. (New York, 1857-1869). For the Worcester case study, and for Rowan County, North Carolina, and New York temperance, much use has been made of the manuscript population schedules for the Seventh Census, 1850 (microfilm, National Archives) and city directories.

INDEX

Adams, John, 24
Adulteration of liquor, 136-37, 152 n.5
Agents, traveling, and American Temperance Society, 65-66
Agitation, process of: in temperance reform generally, 10, 322-23; in teetotalism, 136-40 passim, 151; in local prohibition, 226-45 passim; and Maine Law, 253, 278-82. *See also* Organizations
Aikman, James H., 192-93, 203
Albany, New York, 114, 141, 144
Alexander, James, 147, 149
Allen, Alvan, 95
Allen, Virginia, 192-93
American Bible Society, 68
American Board of Commissioners for Foreign Missions, 59, 62, 66, 68
American party, 215, 265, 266, 268, 269. *See also* Know Nothingism
American Protestant Association, 266-67
American Republican party, 215
American Revolution, and drinking, 25, 40
American Society for the Promotion of Temperance. *See* American Temperance Society
American Temperance Society: foundation of, 6, 8, 12, 54-55, 61; aims of, 55, 77-79; divides evangelical churches, 55-58; evangelical leadership of, 58-62; original membership of, 62-63; tactics and organization of, 63-67; local carriers of reform for, 68-69; perceptions of drink problem in, 69-70; concepts of deviancy in, 71; and moderate drinking, 72-73, 77, 78; and Christian traffickers, 73-74, 77, 78; and failure of Massachusetts Society for the Suppression of Intemperance, 74; and moral suasion, 74-75; and use of organizations, 75-76; and drunkards, 76; growth of, 87-88; and medical evidence, 89; supports legislative temperance societies, 91; organized power of, feared by local elites, 106-07; in western New York, 114; and teetotalism, 136, 138, 140, 150; and local prohibition, 226-27
American Temperance Union: estab-

Index

Cleveland, Ohio, 308
Clifford, John H., 261
Cobb, Sylvanus, 233
Cobden, Richard, 4
Cocke, John H., 127, 193
Cold water pledge. *See* Teetotalism
Collier, William, 171
Colt, Samuel, 274
Columbian Temperance Society (New York City), 194
Colvin, D. Leigh, 306
Commonwealth v. Dana, 256
Communion issue, 145-47
Concord, New Hampshire, 270
Congregational church: social position of, and temperance, 36-37; and American Temperance Society, 56-57, 63, 87; and communion issue, 146-47; attacks Washingtonians, 199; and temperance after Civil War, 318. *See also* Free Congregational Church
Connecticut: election treating in, 18; laws against tippling, 23; Congregational clergy, 37; temperance in, 113; local prohibition in, 243; Maine Law in, 260, 275, 291-92, 305
Connecticut Society for the Promotion of Good Morals, 37
Connecticut Temperance Society, 113
Conservatives, interpretation of reformers as, criticized, 6, 78, 125-26, 128, 319. *See also* Anti-traditionalism; Displaced elite
Coombe, Pennell, 266
County commissioners. *See* Liquor regulation
Courts, and prohibition, 256, 283 n.13, 290-92
Covert, Isaac, 178, 194-95
Crosby, Nathan, 240
Cross, Whitney R., 114
Crystal Fount (New York), 178, 203
Cult of true womanhood, 181-82
Cultural factors, and drinking, 275, 297, 302, 303-04. *See also* Immigration

Daggett, David, 229
Dane, Nathan, 45
Davis, Isaac, 109

Davis, Margaret L., 181
Dedham, Massachusetts, 236
Delavan, Edward C., 88-89; on lower-class drinking, 106-07; and Sewall's plates, 117 n.14; on technological change, 128; and teetotalism, 139-40, 144; and communion issue, 146; and ultraism, 147-48; and upper-class drinking, 150; and Maine Law, 282, 307
Delaware, 260
Delirium tremens, 90
Democratic party: in Worcester, 109; in Massachusetts generally, 109-10, 122-23 n.85, 235, 237-38, 240; and Maine Law, 254, 261-63, 280, 292, 296, 305, 308
Denominational tensions, in temperance reform, 57, 199, 210
Depression of 1837-43: and temperance funds, 150; and Washingtonians, 168, 174
Detroit, Michigan, 308
Deviancy, and drink, 15 n.8. *See also* American Temperance Society
Disestablishment of Congregationalism, and temperance crusade, 37
Displaced elite, theory of temperanceism, and temperance crusade, 37
Displaced elite, theory of temperance reform examined, 33-34, 40-41. *See also* Anti-traditionalism; Conservatives
Distilling, 14 n.5, 19-20, 25-26, 244, 316-17. *See also* Liquor consumption; Spirits; Whiskey
Dodge, Ossian E., 178-79, 217
Dorchester, Massachusetts, 92, 233
Dow, Neal, 130; character of, 252-53; frames Maine Law pragmatically, 254, 255, 257; on party politics, 261; admits class basis of prohibition agitation, 273-74; and enforcement of Maine Law, 281, 295-96
Drake, Daniel, 258
Dramshops. *See* Retail shops
Drinking. *See* Drunkards; Drunkenness; Liquor consumption
Drunkards: and American Temperance Society, 71, 76; and adoption of teetotalism, 138-39; and Wash-

immigrants and, 297, 299-305 passim; decline of, 282, 304-09, 316, 323; lessons for future reformers, 309, 319; opposition to, summarized, 321. *See also* Dow, Neal; Maine; Prohibitionists

Maine Law Illustrated, The, 265, 297

Maine Temperance Society, 55, 56, 57, 149

Males, and drinking, 181, 189 n.78, 298, 303-04. *See also* Women

Mann, Cyrus, 72

Mann, Horace, 129, 236, 255, 263

Manufacturers, and origins of temperance, 8; in Worcester, 96-98, 101, 108, 111; in United States generally, 106-08, 127; in Connecticut, 113; in New York City, 114; in Philadelphia, 115; and teetotalism, 140; and Washingtonians, in Worcester, 205-06; and prohibition issue in New England, 270-72; weakness of in South, and prohibition, 278. *See also* Employers; Entrepreneurs; Industrial revolution; Work

Marine Temperance Society (New York City), 165-66

Marsh, John, 65; writes *Putnam and the Wolf*, 70, 84 n.47; and moderate drinking, 72-73; and teetotalism, 139; secretary of American Temperance Union, 144-45; career of, 156 n.33; comments on Washingtonian temperance, 163; attacks Washingtonians, 196, 198, 199, 201-02; notes improvement in Washingtonian meetings, 204-05; and Sons of Temperance, 213-15; and no-license, 229; hails fifteen-gallon law, 237; and return to local prohibition, 239; and immigration, 267, 268; pinnacle of success of, 282; and Carson League, 294; lobbies New York Republicans, 306; declining power of, 307

Martha Washingtonian societies. *See* Women

Maryland, 18, 262

Masonry, fears of, and Sons of Temperance, 212-14

Massachusetts: origins of temperance

in, 12; colonial liquor laws in, 21-23; emergence of first temperance societies in, 33-35; Congregational clergy in, 37-38; Federalism in, 38-40; attempts to enforce colonial liquor regulations in, 41-44, 47; no-license in, 92; Democrats and temperance in, 109-10, 237-38; social support for temperance societies in, 113; teetotalism in, 144; local prohibition in, 227-43; Maine Law in, 261-62, 264, 268, 279; American party in, 268-69; decline of prohibition movement in, 282; Supreme Court on Maine Law, 290-91; immigrant drinking in, 297; nonenforcement of Maine Law in, 307; conservative character of first temperance reformers in, 319. *See also* Massachusetts Society for the Suppression of Intemperance; individual towns

Massachusetts Cataract (Worcester), 257

Massachusetts Society for the Suppression of Intemperance: established, 6, 8, 33, 37; social and economic origins of, 34-40; conservative nature of, 40-47 passim; decline of, 44-48; compared with American Temperance Society, 54-55, 58-59, 65-67, 74, 78. *See also* Massachusetts Temperance Society

Massachusetts State Temperance Convention (1852), 256, 259, 273

Massachusetts Temperance Society, 107, 149-50

Massachusetts Temperance Union, 192, 237

Massachusetts Young Men's Temperance Convention (1834), 141, 143

Mather, Cotton, 19

Mather, Increase, 16, 24

Mathew, Theobald, 299. *See also* Catholics; Irish

Mechanics. *See* Artisans; Manufacturers

Mechanics and Workingmen's Temperance Society (Philadelphia), 115, 140

Mechanics' institutes, 102, 130

About the Author

Ian R. Tyrrell is a lecturer in the School of History at the University of South Wales in Sydney, Australia. His articles on American and Australian social history have appeared in scholarly journals and collections.